US Military Aircraft

Recognition Guide

D1513763

Jane's Recognition Guides

Aircraft
Airline
Guns
Special Forces
Tank
Warship
Vintage Aircraft
Train

US Military Aircraft
Aircraft
Recognition Guide

Tony Holmes

Collins

First published in 2007 by **Collins**

HarperCollins Publishers
77-85 Fulham Palace Road
Hammersmith
London w6 8jb
UK
www.collins.co.uk

HarperCollins Publishers Inc
10 East 53rd Street
New York
NY 10022
USA
www.harpercollins.com

www.janes.com

ISBN 978-0-00-722900-0
ISBN-10 0-00-722900-3

Layout: Susie Bell
Editorial: Louise Stanley, Constance Novis

Printed and bound by
Printing Express, Hong Kong

Contents

A–Z of Aircraft

Introduction

This particular volume fills what I perceive to be a gap in world aviation literature. It attempts to concisely chronicle the development and operational history of every single American-built aircraft that has seen service in significant numbers with the US military since 1909. Surprisingly, given the diversity of types—many of them very famous—to wear the "stars and bars" on their fuselage and wings, no single volume has exclusively detailed American combat aircraft types ranging from the Wright Flyer through to the Lockheed Martin F-35 Joint Strike Fighter for almost 20 years.

Since the late 1980s, the US military has drastically downsized after playing its part in winning the Cold War. The US Air Force has amalgamated Strategic and Tactical Air Commands into Air Combat Command, retiring more than 1000 fighters and bombers in the process. Stalwarts such as the B-52, B-1B, F-15, F-16, F-117, KC-135, KC-10, C-130, and C-5 still soldier on, however, joined recently by newer, more capable aircraft such as the C-17 and F-22, as well as unmanned aerial vehicles including the Predator and Global Hawk.

The US Navy has also felt the effects of the post-Cold War peace dividend, with its frontline force of carrier air wings being chopped from 15 to ten during the early 1990s. And august combat aircraft types such as the A-7 Corsair II, A-6 Intruder, and, most recently, the F-14 Tomcat have all been replaced on carrier decks by a seemingly endless number of F/A-18 Hornets and Super Hornets. Unlike the Navy, the Marine Corps has experienced a less dramatic downsizing, and it continues to operate "old favorites" such as the CH-46, CH-53, AH-1W, and AV-8B (and, of course, more Hornets!), with the long-awaited MV-22 Osprey in the wings.

Since the late 1980s, the US Army has also experienced change in respect to its rotary-winged force, the UH-60 Black Hawk family assuming many of the roles previously undertaken by the UH-1 Iroquois of Vietnam fame. The AH-64 Apache has also completely replaced another Vietnam veteran in the form of the AH-1 HueyCobra. At opposite ends of the size spectrum, the CH-47 Chinook and the OH-58 Kiowa still soldier on in updated form, however. Both types, along with the UH-60 and AH-64, have seen widespread service in Iraq and Afghanistan as part of the ongoing war on terror.

But this book is not exclusively about modern aircraft. Three-quarters of the 350 entries feature aircraft that saw service prior to 1980. The interwar section is a particular favorite of mine, because it lists some rather esoteric types that nevertheless attained production status and served with the Army Air Corps and/or the Navy and Marine Corps. Aircraft such as the Berliner Joyce OJ-2 observation biplane and the Northrop A-17A attack monoplane feature in this section alongside more famous machines such as the Boeing F4B/P-12 and Grumman F2F/F3F biplane fighters. It is amazing to think that 85 different airplane types entered frontline service with the US armed forces between 1919 and 1941, yet few of these survived to make their mark in World War II.

As is always the case when producing a book of this size (it contains more than 100,000 words and 500+ photographs), this volume would have been much poorer in terms of its illustrated content had it not been for the massive contribution made by the following individuals—Jan Jacobs and Doug Siegfried of the Tailhook Association, Jamie Hunter, Phil Jarrett, Peter March, Michael O'Leary, and Thomas Withington.

Finally, I would like to thank my editor, Louise Stanley, at HarperCollins who, like her predecessors, has had to cope with the delayed delivery of my latest book!

Tony Holmes
Sevenoaks, Kent
June 2006

This volume is dedicated to my wife Katy,
and my two sons Thomas and William

1909–1919

Aeromarine 39-A/B

two-seat, single-engined biplane/seaplane trainer

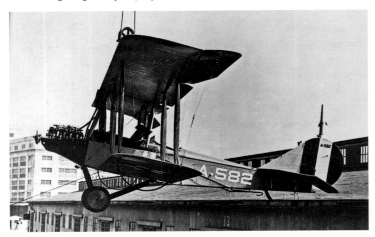

The Aeromarine Plane and Motor Company of Keyport, New Jersey, received an order for 50 Model 39-A and 150 39-B trainers from the Navy in 1917, which was the largest single airplane purchase it had made up to that time. The Aeromarine aircraft could be equipped with either wheels or floats, the latter version featuring a single main pontoon and small wingtip floats. The principal difference between the 39-A and the 39-B centered on their powerplants, with the former being fitted with the 100-hp Hall-Scott A-7A and the latter a Curtiss OXX-6, which also produced 100 hp. A number of 39-Bs survived World War I, and two participated in the Navy's early aircraft carrier landing trials on a dummy deck at Langley Field, Virginia, in 1921. These aircraft were fitted with the forerunner of the modern tailhook. The trials culminated, on October 26, 1922, with the first landing of a 39-B on the deck of the Navy's first carrier, USS *Langley*.

SPECIFICATION (39-B):

ACCOMMODATION:
Two pilots in tandem

DIMENSIONS:
LENGTH: 30 ft 4.5 in (9.28 m)
WINGSPAN: 47 ft 0 in (14.32 m)
HEIGHT: 12 ft 0 in (3.65 m)

WEIGHTS:
EMPTY: 1939 lb (879 kg)
MAX T/O: 2505 lb (1136 kg)

PERFORMANCE:
MAX SPEED: 73 mph (117 kmh)
RANGE: 273 miles (437 km)
POWERPLANT: Curtiss OXX-6
OUTPUT: 100 hp (75 kW)

FIRST FLIGHT DATE:
Late 1916

FEATURES:
Biplane wing layout, with upper-wing of greater span; exposed engine cylinder heads and exhaust forward of cockpit; center pontoon and wingtip floats (seaplane variant only)

Aeromarine 40F

two-seat, single-engined flying-boat trainer

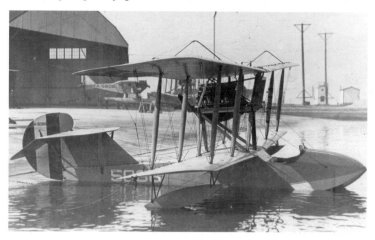

By the final year of World War I, the Navy's fleet of Curtiss F and improved MF flying boats were beginning to show their age. Both were based on a 1912 design, and although only used as trainers for larger Curtiss types, the Navy felt that something more modern was needed to supplement them in the tuitional role. It chose a "pusher" design from Aeromarine to fulfill its requirements, despite this firm having never built such a machine before. Looking remarkably like the Curtiss flying boats it was meant to replace, the Aeromarine 40F was powered by the same 100-hp Curtiss OXX-6 engine as fitted to the F and MF. The pilot and student sat side-by-side in a single open cockpit forward of the biplane wings within the 40F's wooden hull. Following successful flight testing, the Navy ordered no fewer than 200 examples, but the Armistice of November 1918 resulted in most of these being canceled prior to construction. Just 50 reached the Navy, and they saw limited use into the early 1920s.

SPECIFICATION:

ACCOMMODATION:
Two pilots seated side-by-side

DIMENSIONS:
LENGTH: 28 ft 11 in (8.56 m)
WINGSPAN: 48 ft 6 in (14.81 m)
HEIGHT: 11 ft 7in (3.56 m)

WEIGHTS:
EMPTY: 2061 lb (628 kg)
MAX T/O: 2592 lb (790 kg)

PERFORMANCE:
MAX SPEED: 71 mph (114 kmh)
RANGE: endurance of 4.5 hours
POWERPLANT: Curtiss OXX-6
OUTPUT: 100 hp (75 kW)

FIRST FLIGHT DATE:
Mid-1918

FEATURES:
Biplane wing layout, with upper-wing of greater span; pusher configuration; exposed engine immediately behind pilot; laminated wood-veneer flying-boat hull; side-by-side open cockpit

Boeing Model c/c-1F

two-seat, single-engined seaplane trainer

In early 1917, fledgling aircraft manufacturer Boeing submitted its c-5 and c-6 machines (only the sixth and seventh aircraft it had ever built) to the Navy for evaluation as potential primary seaplane trainers. Following the success of these tests, Boeing received an order for 50 production aircraft, which established the company as a major manufacturer. Called the Model c both by Boeing and the Navy, the aircraft was remarkable for its unusually high degree of wing stagger and dihedral. Although all 50 had been delivered by late 1917, none saw service with training schools because of the poor performance of the aircraft's Hall-Scott A-7A engine, which regularly burst into flames in flight. Many Model cs were sold off as surplus postwar, still in their original Boeing packing crates. Once the shortcomings of the A-7A had become clear, the Navy ordered an additional Model c powered by a Curtiss oxx-6. This machine, built only once, was designated the c-1F because it had only one main float instead of two as fitted to the standard Model c.

SPECIFICATION (MODEL C):

ACCOMMODATION:
Two pilots in tandem

DIMENSIONS:
LENGTH: 27 ft 0 in (8.22 m)
WINGSPAN: 43 ft 10 in (13.13 m)
HEIGHT: 12 ft 7 in (3.87 m)

WEIGHTS:
EMPTY: 1898 lb (861 kg)
MAX T/O: 2395 lb (1086 kg)

PERFORMANCE:
MAX SPEED: 72.7 mph (116 kmh)
RANGE: 200 miles (320 km)
POWERPLANT: Hall-Scott A-7A
OUTPUT: 100 hp (75 kW)

FIRST FLIGHT DATE:
Early 1917

FEATURES:
Two-bay biplane wing layout, with significant stagger and dihedral; exposed engine cylinder heads and radiators forward of cockpit; twin pontoons

Curtiss Pushers

two-seat, single-engined biplane/seaplane trainer

The handful of early pusher-type biplanes built by pioneer aircraft manufacturer Curtiss for the Army and Navy had no firm designations, hence they are usually grouped together as "Pushers." The Navy's very first airplane was a Curtiss Pusher seaplane designated the A-1, while its tripod landing gear equivalent for the Army (its second airplane) was designated the Model D. These aircraft were derived from the basic Curtiss Pusher that had been in production since 1909. Glenn Curtiss had successfully developed the world's first seaplane from this design in early 1911, which led directly to the Navy's purchase of the A-1 in July of that year. The landplane-configured A-2 soon followed, and the Navy eventually received more than two dozen pushers up to World War I. These were known as AH for "Airplane, Hydro," and ranged in designation from the AH-8 to the AH-11. The Army's single Model D was followed by three Model ES, which featured multipanel wings for easy transportation on horse-drawn wagons.

SPECIFICATION (A-1):

ACCOMMODATION:
Two pilots seated side-by-side

DIMENSIONS:
LENGTH: 28 ft 7.2 in (8.75 m)
WINGSPAN: 37 ft 0 in (11.27 m)
HEIGHT: 8 ft 10 in (2.46 m)

WEIGHTS:
EMPTY: 925 lb (420 kg)
MAX T/O: 1575 lb (714 kg)

PERFORMANCE:
MAX SPEED: 60 mph (96 kmh)
RANGE: 273 miles (437 km)
POWERPLANT: Curtiss V-8
OUTPUT: 75 hp (56 kW)

FIRST FLIGHT DATE:
July 1, 1911

FEATURES:
Equal-span biplane wing layout; pusher configuration; exposed engine immediately behind pilot; tripod landing gear or center pontoon and wingtip floats (seaplane variant only); fore- and aft-mounted elevators

Curtiss F-Boat

two-seat, single-engined flying-boat trainer

Developed from the Curtiss Pusher, the F-Boat designation covers a handful of flying boats built initially as c- and then AB- models, followed eventually by the definitive F-Boats. The latter boasted a hull built up of laminated veneer strips that were then shaped and glued up in a jig prior to being married to the wooden hull frame. Wing shape varied throughout the long production life of the F-Boat, which ran from 1912 (with the c-1) through to 1918 F-models). The c-models became ABS in 1914, the letter A designating Curtiss as the Navy's first aircraft manufacturer and the B identifying it as a flying boat. Heavily involved in early Navy aeronautical development between 1912 and 1915, c/ABS participated in the first catapult trials ashore and at sea. Several ABS also became the first US military aircraft to conduct operations against another country when they looked for Mexican mines off Vera Cruz in April 1914. At least 144 of the definitive F-Boat trainers were eventually built for the Navy.

SPECIFICATION (F-BOAT):

ACCOMMODATION:
Two pilots seated side-by-side

DIMENSIONS:
LENGTH: 27 ft 9.75 in (8.52 m)
WINGSPAN: 45 ft 1.40 in (13.75 m)
HEIGHT: 11 ft 2.75 in (3.43 m)

WEIGHTS:
EMPTY: 1860 lb (844 kg)
MAX T/O: 2460 lb (1116 kg)

PERFORMANCE:
MAX SPEED: 69 mph (110 kmh)
RANGE: endurance of 5.5 hours
POWERPLANT: Curtiss OXX
OUTPUT: 100 hp (75 kW)

FIRST FLIGHT DATE:
Late 1912 (C-1)

FEATURES:
Biplane wing layout, with upper-wing of greater span; pusher configuration; exposed engine immediately behind pilot; laminated wood-veneer flying-boat hull; side-by-side open cockpit

Curtiss N-9

two-seat, single-engined seaplane trainer

Developed privately by Curtiss as a dedicated seaplane variant of the JN-4B, the N-9 was soon acquired by the Navy as its standard primary and advanced seaplane trainer. In order to cope with the extra weight associated with a central float and stabilizing tip floats, Curtiss fitted a larger engine and increased the aircraft's wingspan by ten feet. The N-9 entered service in 1916, and 560 were built for the Navy and 14 for the Army—the latter conducted seaplane operations at the time. Although an ideal trainer, the basic N-9 proved underpowered when it came to teaching aircrew bombing and gunnery techniques. As a solution to this problem, Curtiss replaced the aircraft's 100-hp OXX-6 with a license-built 150-hp Hispano-Suiza Model A engine. The new aircraft was designated the N-9H, and 50 were constructed postwar through the assembly of airframes comprised in the main of surplus spare parts left over after the completion of N-9 production in 1918. The N-9/9H remained in Navy service until 1926.

SPECIFICATION (N-9):

ACCOMMODATION:
Two pilots in tandem

DIMENSIONS:
LENGTH: 32 ft 7.25 in (9.97 m)
WINGSPAN: 53 ft 4 in (16.27 m)
HEIGHT: 10 ft 8.50 in (3.30 m)

WEIGHTS:
EMPTY: 1860 lb (844 kg)
MAX T/O: 2390 lb (1084 kg)

PERFORMANCE:
MAX SPEED: 65 mph (104 kmh)
RANGE: 179 miles (286 km)
POWERPLANT: Curtiss OXX-6
OUTPUT: 90 hp (67 kW)

FIRST FLIGHT DATE:
Late 1915

FEATURES:
Three-bay biplane wing layout, with upper-wing of greater span; exposed engine cylinder heads and exhaust forward of cockpit; center pontoon and wingtip floats; upper-wing "skid plates"

Curtiss JN-4 Jenny

two-seat, single-engined biplane trainer

America's most successful training aircraft of World War I, the Curtiss JN-4 was an improved version of the JN-3, which had itself been developed through the combination of the best structural features of the preceding J- and N-models. Only the second tractor-engined design put into production by Curtiss, the J had been designed in England in 1913 by B. Douglas Thomas of Avro—the N was essentially the same aircraft, but with repositioned ailerons between the wings in true early Curtiss fashion. A handful of J/N-models reached the Army in 1914, after which the two types were combined to form the JN series in 1915. Its model designation soon saw the aircraft unofficially called the "Jenny," and this appellation stuck for the rest of its long career.

Large-scale procurement by the Army commenced in 1916 when an order for 94 JN-4s was placed. These were destined for use both as trainers and as observation platforms along the Mexican border during Gen Pershing's pursuit of the bandit Pancho Villa. Some 261 were also acquired by the Royal Flying Corps as trainers prior to the Americans entering the war, the aircraft's docile handling qualities and robust Curtiss OX-5 engine securing it a sound reputation in the instructional role. The US commitment to the war in Europe in April 1917 resulted in Jenny orders totaling 6000+ examples by the time production ended soon after Armistice Day.

Having been the most widely used trainer in both the US Army and Royal Canadian Air Force in World War I, the Jenny became the most influential type in the postwar development of aviation in North America when hundreds of surplus machines were sold cheaply to private buyers. Helping to establish civil aviation across this vast continent, the Jenny became the favorite mount of the 1920s Barnstormers, who enjoyed great popularity during the decade. JN-4/6s remained in service with both the Army and Navy well into the 1920s, with the last examples being retired from National Guard service as late as September 1927.

SPECIFICATION (JN-4D):

ACCOMMODATION:
Two pilots in tandem

DIMENSIONS:
LENGTH: 27 ft 4 in (8.34 m)
WINGSPAN: 43 ft 7 in (13.31 m)
HEIGHT: 9 ft 11 in (2.77 m)

WEIGHTS:
EMPTY: 1580 lb (717 kg)
MAX T/O: 2130 lb (966 kg)

PERFORMANCE:
MAX SPEED: 75 mph (120 kmh)
RANGE: 250 miles (400 km)
POWERPLANT: Curtiss OX-5
OUTPUT: 90 hp (67 kW)

FIRST FLIGHT DATE:
Early 1916

FEATURES:
Biplane wing layout, with upper-wing of greater span; exposed engine cylinder heads and exhaust forward of cockpit; tail skid

Curtiss R Series

two-seat, single-engined observation/scout/trainer/seaplane

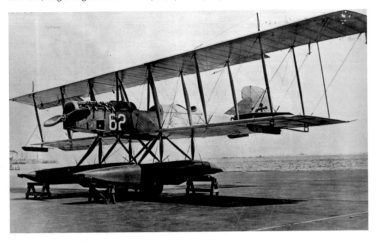

Used by both the US Army and Navy, as well as the Royal Naval Air Service, the R Series (R-3, R-6, and R-9 for the Navy and R-2, R-4, R-6, and R-9 for the Army) were basically enlarged J- and N-models built between 1915 and 1918. Using several different wingspans depending on whether the aircraft was configured with an undercarriage (short span) for land use or floats (long span) as a seaplane, these machines performed a variety of roles. Navy R-6s became the first US-built aircraft to serve overseas with US armed forces in World War I when a squadron was based at Ponta Delgada, in the Azores, to undertake antisubmarine patrols starting in January 1918. Army R-4s were also employed on aerial patrols of the Mexican border, before being relegated to training and general hack duties. Postwar, modified R-6Ls became the Navy's first torpedo carriers, while the Army converted six Liberty-engined R-4Ls into R-4LM mailplanes. More than 160 R-Series aircraft were built in total.

SPECIFICATION (R-6L):

ACCOMMODATION:
Pilot and observer sat in tandem

DIMENSIONS:
LENGTH: 33 ft 5 in (10.21 m)
WINGSPAN: 57 ft 1.25 in (17.41 m)
HEIGHT: 14 ft 2 in (4.32 m)

WEIGHTS:
EMPTY: 3325 lb (1508 kg)
MAX T/O: 4500 lb (2041 kg)

PERFORMANCE:
MAX SPEED: 100 mph (160 kmh)
RANGE: 565 miles (904 km)
POWERPLANT: Liberty 12A
OUTPUT: 400 hp (298 kW)

FIRST FLIGHT DATE:
Late 1915

ARMAMENT:
One light torpedo (R-6L only)

FEATURES:
Biplane wing layout, with upper-wing of greater span; exposed engine cylinder heads and exhaust forward of cockpit; twin pontoon floats on seaplane variant

Curtiss H-12/16

four-seat, twin-engined biplane patrol/bomber flying boat

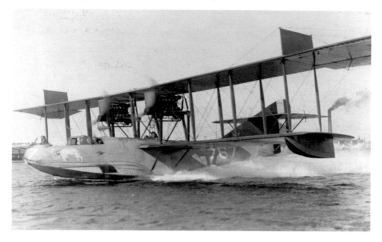

Developed from the daring *America* flying boat commissioned by businessman Rodman Wanamaker in 1914 expressly for transatlantic flight, the first H-12 was ordered by the Navy in 1916 after it had monitored the Royal Naval Air Service's experiences with Model H aircraft derived from the revolutionary civilian machine. Some 20 H-12s were built prior to the development of the improved H-16 in early 1917. This variant had more powerful Liberty engines (as did the re-engined H-12L) in place of the original Curtiss V-X-X power-plants. With Curtiss busy building other wartime models, the Navy was forced to undertake H-16 production at the newly opened Naval Aircraft Factory (NAF). The first example was completed on March 27, 1918. The final version of the H-16 developed by Curtiss had its engines turned around to drive pusher propellers in an effort to squeeze better performance out of the long-lived design. This aircraft also featured slight wing sweep. The Navy built 150 H-16s and Curtiss 20 H-12s and 104 H-16s, and these remained in service until 1928.

SPECIFICATION (H-16):

ACCOMMODATION:
Two pilots, navigator/nose gunner, flight engineer

DIMENSIONS:
LENGTH: 46 ft 1.5 in (14.06 m)
WINGSPAN: 95 ft 0.75 in (28.97 m)
HEIGHT: 17 ft 8.60 in (5.44 m)

WEIGHTS:
EMPTY: 7400 lb (3357 kg)
MAX T/O: 10,900 lb (4944 kg)

PERFORMANCE:
MAX SPEED: 95 mph (152 kmh)
RANGE: 378 miles (604.80 km)
POWERPLANT: two Liberty 12s
OUTPUT: 800 hp (596 kW)

FIRST FLIGHT DATE:
Early 1917

ARMAMENT:
Three Lewis 0.30-in machine guns on pivoted mount for observer/gunner in bow and rear hull cockpits; bomb load of 920 lb (417 kg) on underwing racks

FEATURES:
Biplane wing layout; laminated wood veneer flying-boat hull; open side-by-side cockpit; two tractor/pusher engines between the wings; wingtip sponsons; upper-wing "skid plates"

Curtiss HS Series

two/three-seat, single-engined biplane patrol flying boat

This aircraft was essentially a scaled-down version of the twin-engined H Series. In fact, the HS in its designation stood for H, Single engine. Initially powered by a Curtiss V-X-X engine, the prototype HS-1 was used as the test bed for the first flight of the all-new Liberty 12 on October 21, 1917. The Navy ordered 664 Liberty-powered HS-1LS from Curtiss, which was way beyond the company's production capacity, so five other manufacturers also built the aircraft under license. Once in service, it was discovered that the HS-1L's 180-lb depth-bomb was ineffective against submarines. In order to carry 230-lb bombs, the aircraft's wingspan had to be increased by 12 ft to improve lift, and the resulting variant was designated the HS-2L. In May 1918, eight HS-1LS became the first American-built aircraft issued to US forces in France, and by war's end 182 had been shipped across the Atlantic. Postwar, five improved flying boats with revised hull lines were built as HS-3S. The HS-2L remained the Navy's standard single-engine patrol and training flying boat until 1926.

SPECIFICATION (HS-2L):

ACCOMMODATION:
Two pilots, navigator/nose gunner

DIMENSIONS:
LENGTH: 39 ft 0 in (11.88 m)
WINGSPAN: 74 ft 0.50 in (22.57 m)
HEIGHT: 14 ft 7.25 in (4.48 m)

WEIGHTS:
EMPTY: 4300 lb (1950 kg)
MAX T/O: 6432 lb (2918 kg)

PERFORMANCE:
MAX SPEED: 83 mph (132 kmh)
RANGE: 517 miles (827 km)
POWERPLANT: one Liberty 12
OUTPUT: 350 hp (261 kW)

FIRST FLIGHT DATE:
Early 1917 (HS-1)

ARMAMENT:
One/two Lewis 0.30-in machine guns on pivoted mount for observer/gunner in bow; depth-bomb load of 460 lb (208 kg)

FEATURES:
Biplane wing layout; laminated wood-veneer flying-boat hull; open side-by-side cockpit; one pusher engine between the wings; wingtip sponsons; upper-wing "skid plates"

Curtiss MF

two-seat, single-engined biplane flying-boat trainer

Curtiss built the MF (Modified F) in 1918 to replace venerable F-Boats that had been in service with the Navy since late 1912. Despite the new aircraft's designation, the MF shared very little in common with its predecessor other than its pusher configuration and wooden hull. Using design techniques developed for the highly successful H series, the MF featured a flat-sided hull and sponsons for improved forward buoyancy. Just 22 of the 53 examples initially ordered by the Navy had been delivered by war's end, with the remainder being canceled. However, a further 80 were eventually built by the NAF. Deemed surplus to requirements in the early 1920s, a number of MFS were sold to the Cox-Klemm company of Long Island, which modified the flying boats for civilian use in the sportsman-pilot market that existed prior to the onset of the Great Depression. Curtiss also developed a civilian version of the MF soon after the war, which it called the Seagull. This proved to be a commercial failure, however.

SPECIFICATION:

ACCOMMODATION:
Two pilots, seated side-by-side

DIMENSIONS:
LENGTH: 28 ft 10 in (8.56 m)
WINGSPAN: 49 ft 9 in (15.20 m)
HEIGHT: 11 ft 7 in (3.56 m)

WEIGHTS:
EMPTY: 1850 lb (839 kg)
MAX T/O: 2488 lb (1129 kg)

PERFORMANCE:
MAX SPEED: 72 mph (115 kmh)
RANGE: 345 miles (552 km)
POWERPLANT: one Curtiss OXX
OUTPUT: 100 hp (75 kW)

FIRST FLIGHT DATE:
Early 1918

FEATURES:
Biplane wing layout; laminated wood-veneer flying-boat hull; open side-by-side cockpit; one pusher engine between the wings; wingtip sponsons; upper-wing "skid plates"

Curtiss F-5L

four-seat, twin-engined biplane patrol flying boat

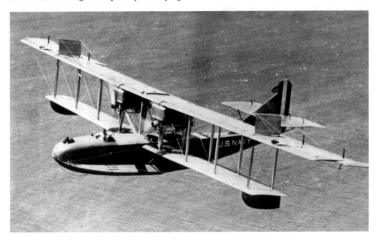

The F-5L of 1918 was an improved British version of Curtiss's H-12/16 flying boat, which had been modified by the Royal Naval Air Station at Felixstowe in 1915-16 as the F-2/3/5. The latter were powered by British engines and had improved hull designs for better performance in rough water when heavily loaded. In late 1917 the US Navy chose to adapt the F-5 for its own use, fitting Liberty engines (hence the L in the F-5L designation). Some 227 were duly built by Curtiss (60), Canadian Aeroplanes Ltd. (30), and the NAF (137), with the final two NAF machines being completed as improved F-6Ls. Aside from its powerplants, the F-5L differed from the H-16 in its use of ailerons and parallel leading and trailing edges, instead of the latter's distinctively tapered trailing edges. Postwar, surviving F-5Ls were also fitted with much larger vertical tails, which had initially been developed for the F-6L. The F-5L, along with the near-identical H-16, served as the Navy's standard patrol flying boat until the late 1920s.

SPECIFICATION:

ACCOMMODATION:
Two pilots, navigator/nose gunner, flight engineer

DIMENSIONS:
LENGTH: 49 ft 3.75 in (15.04 m)
WINGSPAN: 103 ft 9.25 in (31.67 m)
HEIGHT: 18 ft 9.25 in (5.76 m)

WEIGHTS:
EMPTY: 8720 lb (3955 kg)
MAX T/O: 13,600 lb (6169 kg)

PERFORMANCE:
MAX SPEED: 90 mph (144 kmh)
RANGE: 830 miles (1328 km)
POWERPLANT: two Liberty 12AS
OUTPUT: 800 hp (597 kW)

FIRST FLIGHT DATE:
Early 1918

ARMAMENT:
Six/eight Lewis 0.30-in machine guns on pivoted mount for observer/gunner in bow and rear hull cockpits; bomb load of 920 lb (417 kg)

FEATURES:
Biplane wing layout; laminated wood-veneer flying-boat hull; open side-by-side cockpit; two tractor/pusher engines between the wings; wingtip sponsons; upper-wing "skid plates"; parallel leading/trailing wing edges

Curtiss/Eberhart SE 5a/E

single-seat, single-engined biplane fighter/advanced trainer

When the United States entered World War I in April 1917, it had no homegrown military aircraft in service that were deemed to be suitable for combat in Europe. A decision was quickly made to build modern British and French fighters and bombers in American factories, rather than spend time designing comparable types. One of the aircraft chosen for manufacture was the Royal Aircraft Factory SE 5a, which was among the best fighting scouts on the Western Front in the last 18 months of the war. Curtiss was contracted to build 1000 SE 5as for US service, but only one had been constructed before the Armistice saw the remainder canceled. A further 57 British-built airframes were assembled in America immediately postwar, and these served as the Army's frontline pursuit force until indigenous designs became available in the early 1920s. In 1922-23, the Eberhart Aeroplane & Motor Company rebuilt 50 aircraft with 180-hp Wright-Hispano E engines and plywood-covered fuselages as SE-5E advanced trainers, and these gave valuable service for several more years.

SPECIFICATION (SE-5E):

ACCOMMODATION:
One pilot

DIMENSIONS:
LENGTH: 20 ft 10 in (6.12 m)
WINGSPAN: 26 ft 9 in (8.19 m)
HEIGHT: 9 ft 6 in (2.92 m)

WEIGHTS:
EMPTY: 1400 lb (635 kg)
MAX T/O: 2060 lb (934 kg)

PERFORMANCE:
MAX SPEED: 122 mph (195 kmh)
RANGE: endurance of 2.25 hours
POWERPLANT: Wright-Hispano E
OUTPUT: 180 hp (134 kW)

FIRST FLIGHT DATE:
January 12, 1917

ARMAMENT:
One fixed Vickers 0.303-in machine gun on port fuselage side and one Lewis 0.303-in machine gun on Foster mount on upper-wing; bomb load of 100 lb (44 kg) on fuselage racks

FEATURES:
Equal-span biplane wing layout; inline engine; exposed exhaust manifold; plywood-covered head fairing behind cockpit

de Havilland (Airco) DH-4/4B "Liberty Plane"

two-seat, single-engined biplane bomber/utility aircraft

Like the SE 5a, the de Havilland (Airco) DH-4 was chosen in 1917 by the US government's Bolling Commission for rapid production in American factories so that the aircraft could be supplied to Army Aviation units that were due in France by year-end. Dubbed the "Liberty Plane" in the spirit of the day by the Americans, the DH-4 had originally been built by de Havilland in response to a British Air Ministry request issued in early 1916. The DH-4 was unique in having a wide separation between the pilot and observer, this layout being adopted to give the pilot the best possible field of view and the observer the best field of fire. Such an arrangement made it difficult for the crew to communicate, and the gasoline tank fitted in the space was judged to be a safety hazard by the Americans.

British-built examples started reaching the Western Front in March 1917, and improved US-built DH-4s, fitted with the vastly superior 400-hp Liberty engine, went into mass production later that year. No fewer than 4846 American DH-4s were eventually built in three large plants in Ohio and New Jersey. Although the aircraft was obsolescent by the time it was issued to American Expeditionary Force units in France starting in August 1918, DH-4s nevertheless equipped some 13 Aero squadrons on the Western Front in the final weeks of the war.

The many combat deficiencies plaguing the DH-4 eventually saw the aircraft extensively redesigned as the DH-4B, although the latter type was developed too late to see service in World War I. Only 612 DH-4s were shipped back to the US postwar, and many of these were rebuilt as DH-4Bs in a program that kept the struggling American aircraft industry alive in the early 1920s. Seeing considerable service with the Army as general utility aircraft, the last DH-4M-2P (a variant built by Boeing) was finally retired in 1932.

SPECIFICATION (DH-4B):

ACCOMMODATION:
Pilot and gunner/observer in tandem

DIMENSIONS:
LENGTH: 29 ft 11 in (8.87 m)
WINGSPAN: 42 ft 5 in (12.95 m)
HEIGHT: 9 ft 8 in (2.98 m)

WEIGHTS:
EMPTY: 2939 lb (1333 kg)
MAX T/O: 4595 lb (2084 kg)

PERFORMANCE:
MAX SPEED: 118 mph (188 kmh)
RANGE: endurance of 3.25 hours
POWERPLANT: Liberty 12A
OUTPUT: 416 hp (310 kW)

FIRST FLIGHT DATE:
October 29, 1917 (US-assembled DH-4)

ARMAMENT:
Two fixed Marlin 0.30-in machine guns forward of cockpit and twin manually aimed Lewis 0.303-in machine guns for gunner/observer on Scarff ring; bomb load of 460 lb (209 kg) on fuselage and wing racks

FEATURES:
Biplane wing layout; pilot and gunner/observer sat some distance apart; inline engine; rectangular radiator; exposed exhaust stubs

Engineering Division XB-1

two-seat, single-engined fighter

Yet another aircraft type recommended for US production by the Bolling Commission in 1917, the XB-1 was a less successful version of Bristol's F 2B Fighter, which had made its mark in combat with the British starting in 1917. Curtiss received contracts in late 1917 to build 2000 F 2BS, and these were to be powered by the 400-hp Liberty 12 engine instead of the 200-hp Hispano-Suiza initially fitted by Bristol. Some re-engineering was required in order accommodate the larger American engine, and the resulting design was designated the 0-1. Just 26 aircraft had been built when production was halted in the spring of 1918 following flight trials that showed the 0-1 to be overpowered and unsafe. The aircraft was then extensively reworked by the US Army Engineering Division at McCook Field, in Dayton, Ohio. A 300-hp Wright H was married to an entirely new plywood fuselage, and the resulting aircraft, designated the XB-1A, made its first flight on July 3, 1919. Forty examples were subsequently built in 1920-21 at McCook Field.

SPECIFICATION:

ACCOMMODATION:
Pilot and gunner in tandem

DIMENSIONS:
LENGTH: 25 ft 6 in (7.80 m)
WINGSPAN: 39 ft 4.50 in (12.02 m)
HEIGHT: 9 ft 9.50 in (3.03 m)

WEIGHTS:
EMPTY: 2201 lb (998 kg)
MAX T/O: 3679 lb (1669 kg)

PERFORMANCE:
MAX SPEED: 122 mph (195 kmh)
RANGE: endurance of 3.80 hours
POWERPLANT: Wright H
OUTPUT: 300 hp (224 kW)

FIRST FLIGHT DATE:
July 3, 1919

ARMAMENT:
Two fixed Browning 0.30-in machine guns forward of cockpit and twin manually aimed Browning 0.30-in machine guns for gunner on Scarff ring

FEATURES:
Biplane wing layout of equal span; pilot and gunner sat virtually back-to-back; inline engine; oval radiator; exposed exhaust stubs; tail skid

LWF Model v

two-seat, single-engined biplane trainer/observation aircraft

The LWF (Lowe, Willard, and Fowler) Engineering Company formed in College Point, Long Island, in 1915. Its small team of aeronautical engineers were soon engaged by the Army and Navy in the development of trainers, combat types, seaplanes, and flying boats. The most successful of several designs put forward was the Model v two-seat observation and training aircraft. A total of 23 were acquired by the Army in 1916, followed by a further 112 in 1917-18. This production run was made up of four variants, designated the v, v-1, v-2, and v-3. The principal difference between these types centered on the powerplants used, the v being equipped with a 135-hp Thomas, the v-1 a 140-hp Sturtevant, the v-2 a 165-hp Hall-Scott and the v-3 a 200-hp Sturtevant. The final variant proved its durability in late 1917 when an example flew 1184 miles from Rantoul, Illinois, to San Antonio, Texas, in nine hours and 15 minutes. The aircraft, carrying a pilot and an Army officer, stopped for fuel twice.

SPECIFICATION:

ACCOMMODATION:
Two pilots in tandem

DIMENSIONS:
LENGTH: 25 ft 4 in (7.74 m)
WINGSPAN: 39 ft 8 in (12.13 m)
HEIGHT: 9 ft 6 in (2.89 m)

WEIGHTS:
EMPTY: 1725 lb (782 kg)
MAX T/O: 2630 lb (1193 kg)

PERFORMANCE:
MAX SPEED: 110 mph (176 kmh)
RANGE: 620 miles (992 km)
POWERPLANT: Sturtevant Type 5A-4
OUTPUT: 200 hp (149 kW)

FIRST FLIGHT DATE:
Early 1916

FEATURES:
Biplane wing layout, with upper-wing of greater span; cowled, watercooled vee-engine; tail skid

Martin Models T/TT and S

two-seat, single-engined trainer/observation seaplane

One of the longest-lived names in American aviation, Martin achieved its first sale to the US military when 17 T and TT trainers were acquired by the Army between 1914 and 1916. These were destined for the Army Aviation School in San Diego, which was struggling to keep its elderly and obsolete Curtiss Pushers airworthy. Having purchased engineless Martin airframes, the Army had them fitted with 90-hp Curtiss OX-2s removed from the now-grounded Pushers. The Model TT of 1915 featured improved streamlining, a larger wing and a more powerful 125-hp Hall-Scott or 135-hp Sturtevant engine, as well as the OX-2. The Model S seaplane, which was a direct development of the Model TT, followed in 1916. This aircraft was fitted with a Hall-Scott engine, and had ailerons built into the upper-wings, rather than between the wings as with the Model T/TT. Fourteen were acquired by the Army in 1915-16, with an additional two airframes being purchased by the Navy. The Model T/TTs were eventually replaced by Curtiss JN-4s.

SPECIFICATION
(MODEL TT):

ACCOMMODATION:
Pilot and observer in tandem

DIMENSIONS:
LENGTH: 26 ft 3.50 in (8.03 m)
WINGSPAN: 38 ft 8 in (11.82 m)
HEIGHT: 9 ft 4 in (2.86 m)

WEIGHTS:
EMPTY: 1320 lb (599 kg)
MAX T/O: 1720 lb (780 kg)

PERFORMANCE:
MAX SPEED: 96 mph (153 kmh)
RANGE: 350 miles (560 km)
POWERPLANT: Curtiss OX-2
OUTPUT: 90 hp (67 kW)

FIRST FLIGHT DATE:
Early 1915

FEATURES:
Biplane wing layout; cowled engine; wheeled skid (Model T/TT) forward of undercarriage; central pontoon float and wingtip floats (Model S); ailerons between wings (Model T/TT)

Martin MB-1/MBT/MT

four/five-seat, twin-engined biplane bomber/reconnaissance/torpedo carrier

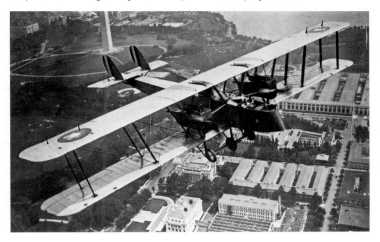

In late 1916 American aviation pioneer Glenn L. Martin resigned from the Wright-Martin company, which he had helped form earlier that year, and established a new firm in Cleveland, Ohio. By the end of 1917 he had been asked by the Army to design a new bomber that had a better performance than the British Handley Page O/400 (eight Liberty-engined examples of which were assembled by Standard in the USA). A contract for ten Glenn Martin Bombers was signed, and the first MB-1 flew on August 17, 1918. Powered by two Liberty engines, the aircraft had good performance but only a modest bomb load due to its relatively small size when compared to the O-400. Some 22 MB-1s were delivered to the Army in 1918-19, and these performed long-range observation and bombing missions. The Navy bought two MB-1s in 1920, which it designated MBTs (Martin Bomber-Torpedoes). A further eight improved MTs (Martin Torpedoes) were later purchased, these utilizing the larger wings of the Army's MB-2 variant (see interwar section).

SPECIFICATION
(MODEL MB):

ACCOMMODATION:
Pilot, copilot, engineer, and two gunners

DIMENSIONS:
LENGTH: 44 ft 10 in (13.67 m)
WINGSPAN: 71 ft 5 in (21.77 m)
HEIGHT: 14 ft 7 in (4.45 m)

WEIGHTS:
EMPTY: 6702 lb (3040 kg)
MAX T/O: 10,225 lb (4638 kg)

PERFORMANCE:
MAX SPEED: 105 mph (169 kmh)
RANGE: 390 miles (630 km)
POWERPLANT: two Liberty 12AS
OUTPUT: 800 hp (597 kW)

FIRST FLIGHT DATE:
August 17, 1918

ARMAMENT:
Two flexible Marlin 0.30-in machine guns in nose, two in rear dorsal cockpit, and one in rear ventral hatch; maximum bomb load of 1040 lb (472 kg) under wings and fuselage

FEATURES:
Equal-span biplane wing layout; engines mounted between wings; four-wheeled undercarriage; open cockpit; gunner in extreme nose

Navy/Curtiss NC

six-seat, four-engined biplane long-range patrol flying boat

Famed for being the first aircraft to complete a crossing of the Atlantic (in stages), the Navy/Curtiss flying boat was developed in response to Germany's successful U-Boat campaign of 1917. The aircraft had to be able to fly across the Atlantic, because there was no space available for flying boats to be shipped to the UK. Such a machine needed an endurance of 15-20 hours, which meant that it would have to be large, multi-engined, and rugged enough to endure forced landings at sea. Curtiss was alone among US manufacturers in having experience of building such aircraft, and it produced a 28,000-lb biplane based on the Navy's hull design. Designated the NC for Navy and Curtiss (each of the NCs had their own number, NC-2, NC-4), the first example was completed too late to see action in World War I. Nevertheless, three NC flying boats set off across the Atlantic on a proving flight in May 1919, but only NC-4 made it to the UK. Six more NC flying boats were built postwar, and these remained in service into the late 1920s.

SPECIFICATION:

ACCOMMODATION:
Two pilots, navigator/nose gunner, radio operator, and two flight engineers

DIMENSIONS:
LENGTH: 68 ft 3 in (20.80 m)
WINGSPAN: 126 ft 0 in (38.40 m)
HEIGHT: 24 ft 6 in (7.49 m)

WEIGHTS:
EMPTY: 15,874 lb (7200 kg)
MAX T/O: 26,386 lb (11,968 kg)

PERFORMANCE:
MAX SPEED: 85 mph (136 kmh)
RANGE: 1470 miles (2352 km)
POWERPLANT: three Liberty 12AS
OUTPUT: 800 hp (597 kW)

FIRST FLIGHT DATE:
October 4, 1918

ARMAMENT:
Single Browning 0.30-in machine guns on pivoted mount for observer/gunner in bow and rear hull cockpits

FEATURES:
Biplane wing layout; laminated wood-veneer flying-boat hull; three tractor engines between the wings; wingtip sponsons

Orenco/Curtiss D

single-seat, single-engined biplane fighter

In the final months of World War I, the Ordnance Engineering Corporation of Baldwin, Long Island, designed a single-seat fighter of sufficient promise that the recently formed US Army Air Service (USAAS) selected it for limited production. Called the Orenco D, the aircraft was of all-wooden construction with plywood fuselage skinning. The first of four prototypes was delivered to the USAAS in January 1919, and by the time testing had been completed Ordnance Engineering had gone out of business after failing to secure any other sales in a market awash with surplus World War I aircraft. Undeterred, the USAAS requested that other US manufacturers tender for the production of 50 Orenco Ds, and the contract was awarded to Curtiss. Minor modifications to the original design were introduced by Curtiss, including a slightly larger upper-wing. Armed with two 0.30-in Browning machine guns (light bombs could also be carried between the undercarriage struts), 50 Orenco Ds were delivered during 1920-21. They proved unsuccessful in service, however, and were soon retired.

SPECIFICATION:

ACCOMMODATION:
One pilot

DIMENSIONS:
LENGTH: 21 ft 6 in (6.54 m)
WINGSPAN: 33 ft 0 in (10.06 m)
HEIGHT: 8 ft 3.50 in (2.54 m)

WEIGHTS:
EMPTY: 1907 lb (865 kg)
MAX T/O: 2820 lb (1279 kg)

PERFORMANCE:
MAX SPEED: 139 mph (224 kmh)
RANGE: 342 miles (550 km)
POWERPLANT: Wright Model H
OUTPUT: 300 hp (224 kW)

FIRST FLIGHT DATE:
January 1919

ARMAMENT:
Two fixed Browning 0.30-in machine guns forward of cockpit

FEATURES:
Biplane wing layout; closely cowled v-8 engine; tail skid; small headrest on upper fuselage decking

Sloan/Standard H-2/3

two-seat, single-engined trainer/reconnaissance biplane

Typical of the handful of tractor-engined biplanes that were built in small numbers for the Army immediately prior to America's entry into World War I, the H-2 of 1916 was designed by ex-Martin engineer Charles Healey Day for the Sloan Aircraft Company—the latter was owned by John A. Sloan, son-in-law of Thomas Edison. Powered by a ubiquitous Hall-Scott A-5 engine, the modest H-2 biplane differed from its contemporaries in having a ten-degree sweepback of its equal-span wings. The design garnered an initial order of three airframes from the Army for employment as reconnaissance platforms—the aircraft's stock in trade with the US military prewar. The improved H-3 enjoyed more success some months later when the Army acquired nine examples for use as trainers. When the Sloan Aircraft Company was absorbed by the Standard Aero Corporation in late 1916, the surviving H-2/3s still in service with the Army became known as Standards. All had been replaced by JN-4 Jennies by 1917.

SPECIFICATION (H-3):

ACCOMMODATION:
Two pilots in tandem

DIMENSIONS:
LENGTH: 27 ft 0 in (8.22 m)
WINGSPAN: 40 ft 1 in (12.22 m)
HEIGHT: 9 ft 9 in (3.01 m)

WEIGHTS:
EMPTY: 2100 lb (953 kg)
MAX T/O: 2700 lb (1225 kg)

PERFORMANCE:
MAX SPEED: 84 mph (134 kmh)
RANGE: 270 miles (432 km)
POWERPLANT: Hall-Scott A-5
OUTPUT: 125 hp (93 kW)

FIRST FLIGHT DATE:
Early 1916

FEATURES:
Equal-span biplane wing layout, with modest sweepback; exposed engine cylinder heads and exhaust forward of cockpit; tail skid

Standard J/R Series

two-seat, single-engined biplane trainer

Standard produced three J Series models between 1916 and 1918, and these were all essentially improved versions of the Sloan H series. Again designed by Charles Healey Day, the first variant built was the SJ, which was ordered in quantity by the Army to share the role of primary trainer with the JN-4 Jenny. Both aircraft looked remarkably similar, although the SJ had the distinctive Sloan swept-back wings. The re-engined JR Pursuit was introduced in early 1917, but only six were acquired by the Army for use as advanced trainers. Nevertheless, several features of the JR were incorporated into the SJ, and the resulting aircraft was bought in significant numbers by the Army as the J-1. The latter machine never proved as reliable in service as the Jenny, however, with the trainer's Hall-Scott A-7 engine proving prone to in-flight fires. Standard revised the J-1 in 1918, with the resulting JR-1B being powered by a Wright-Hispano engine and featuring equal-span wings and new tail surfaces. The Army bought just six examples.

SPECIFICATION (SJ):

ACCOMMODATION:
Two pilots in tandem

DIMENSIONS:
LENGTH: 26 ft 7 in (8.13 m)
WINGSPAN: 43 ft 10 in (13.13 m)
HEIGHT: 10 ft 10 in (3.07 m)

WEIGHTS:
EMPTY: 1557 lb (706 kg)
MAX T/O: 2070 lb (939 kg)

PERFORMANCE:
MAX SPEED: 85 mph (136 kmh)
RANGE: 290 miles (464 km)
POWERPLANT: Hall-Scott A-7A
OUTPUT: 100 hp (75 kW)

FIRST FLIGHT DATE:
Late 1916

FEATURES:
Biplane wing layout, with modest sweepback; exposed engine cylinder heads and exhaust forward of cockpit; narrow vertical radiator on top of fuselage ahead of upper-wing; auxiliary wheel ahead of main wheels; tail skid

Wright Flyers

two-seat, single-engined biplane/seaplane observation/trainer

Having made history by flying the world's first powered aircraft in December 1903, the Wright brothers wrote to the US War Department in early 1905 offering to supply the Army with airplanes that could be used for scouting and observation. It took until February 1908 for the Wrights to convince the US government to purchase a single two-seat Model A Flyer, which was assembled at Fort Myer, Washington, D.C. Orville Wright flew a series of demonstration flights from the Fort's parade ground in August and September 1908, occasionally with passengers.

On September 17, the aircraft was fitted with slighter larger propellers, and in the subsequent flight these were fouled by a diagonal wire that vibrated excessively when the Model A reached a certain speed. Passenger Lt. Thomas B. Selfridge was killed in the resulting crash and Wright injured. The Model A was duly rebuilt and accepted for Army service in 1909—this aircraft remains on display in the Smithsonian Institution today. Wright also sold the improved Models B and C to the Army, these variants differing from the Model A in having their elevators moved aft from forward of the wings. Wheeled landing gear also supplemented the skids of the original Flyer.

The Model Bs were used as trainers, with the instructor and student pilot sharing certain controls because the latter were not fully duplicated. This arrangement changed with the seven C-models supplied to the Army in 1911, as these had full dual controls. The Navy also bought three Model C-H seaplanes in 1912, these aircraft being similar to the Army's Model B, but with the addition of two pontoon floats. Boasting modest performance, the Navy Wright Flyers could only just take off from smooth water.

SPECIFICATION (MODEL A):

ACCOMMODATION:
One pilot and one passenger seated side-by-side

DIMENSIONS:
LENGTH: 29 ft 0 in (8.84 m)
WINGSPAN: 41 ft 0 in (12.50 m)
HEIGHT: 9 ft 7 in (2.90 m)

WEIGHTS:
EMPTY: 710 lb (322 kg)
MAX T/O: 1050 lb (476 kg)

PERFORMANCE:
MAX SPEED: 44 mph (71 kmh)
RANGE: 80 miles (129 km)
POWERPLANT: Wright four-cylinder
OUTPUT: 21 hp (16 kW)

FIRST FLIGHT DATE:
Summer 1908

FEATURES:
Equal-span biplane wing layout; two chain-driven propellers in pusher configuration; exposed engine immediately behind pilot; landing skids; fore- and aft-mounted elevators

Standard E-1/M-Defense

single-seat, single-engined biplane fighter/advanced trainer

The Charles H. Day-designed E-1/M-Defense was Standard's only fighter project to actually reach series production. Built specifically as a lightweight target defense interceptor, six M-Defense aircraft were ordered by the Aviation Section of the Army Signal Corps in late 1917. The first two were delivered in January 1918, and although the design proved to be easy to fly and highly maneuverable, its overall performance was considered inadequate for frontline service in its intended role. The remaining four M-Defense fighters were duly canceled, and the aircraft instead modified to perform the advanced trainer role. Redesignated the E-1, some 168 airframes were delivered to the Army powered by Gnome 100-hp or 80-hp Le Rhône rotary engines. Postwar, several E-1s were modified by Sperry into pilotless, radio-controlled, aerial torpedoes, these machines featuring lengthened fuselages and various radio equipment. The modified aircraft were redesignated Sperry Messenger Aerial Torpedoes.

SPECIFICATION:

ACCOMMODATION:
One pilot

DIMENSIONS:
LENGTH: 18 ft 10 in (5.74 m)
WINGSPAN: 24 ft 0 in (7.31 m)
HEIGHT: 8 ft 1 in (2.46 m)

WEIGHTS:
EMPTY: 800 lb (363 kg)
MAX T/O: 1150 lb (522 kg)

PERFORMANCE:
MAX SPEED: 97 mph (155 kmh)
RANGE: endurance of 1.8 hours
POWERPLANT: Le Rhône 9C
OUTPUT: 80 hp (60 kW)

FIRST FLIGHT DATE:
January 1919

FEATURES:
Equal-span biplane wing layout; closely cowled rotary engine; tail skid; small headrest on upper fuselage decking

Thomas-Morse SH-4

two-seat, single-engined biplane trainer and observation seaplane

Acquired prior to America's entry into World War I in 1917, the SH-4 was the first type to be bought by the Navy from a manufacturer with experience selling its aircraft to military customers. When trading as the Thomas Aeroplane Company, the Thomas-Morse Aircraft Corporation had sold several of its biplane designs to the Royal Naval Air Service (RNAS) in 1915-16. The SH-4 trainer and observation seaplane was based on the Thomas T 2, designed by Englishman B. D. Thomas, who was not related to the company owners. With the RNAS having acquired 24 T 2s, the US Navy contracted the company in 1916 to produce 14 similar aircraft with a longer wingspan, centerline/wingtip pontoon floats, and a more powerful 100-hp Thomas engine. By the time production started in January 1917, Thomas, founded in Hammondsport, New York, in November 1909, needed a larger plant and more capital, so the English-born Thomas brothers merged with the Morse Chain Company to form the Thomas-Morse Aircraft Corporation.

SPECIFICATION:

ACCOMMODATION:
Pilot and observer in tandem

DIMENSIONS:
LENGTH: 29 ft 9 in (9.11 m)
WINGSPAN: 44 ft 0 in (13.41 m)
HEIGHT: 10 ft 8 in (3.29 m)

WEIGHTS:
EMPTY: 2300 lb (1043 kg)
MAX T/O: 2800 lb (1270 kg)

PERFORMANCE:
MAX SPEED: 83 mph (133 kmh)
RANGE: 260 miles (416 km)
POWERPLANT: Thomas
OUTPUT: 100 hp (75 kW)

FIRST FLIGHT DATE:
Late 1916

FEATURES:
Equal-span biplane wing layout; closely cowled inline engine; central pontoon float and wingtip floats

Thomas-Morse s-4

single-seat, single-engined biplane fighter trainer

The Thomas-Morse Aircraft Corporation formed in January 1917 when the English-born Thomas brothers went into partnership with the American-based Morse Chain Company. Their chief designer was B. D. Thomas (no relation), who had previously worked for Curtiss on the JN-4 Jenny. His first offering for his new employer was also a trainer in the form of the single-seat s-4, this diminutive machine being ordered by the US Signal Corps as an advanced trainer to the tune of 100 examples. Designated the s-4B, the aircraft was powered by the Gnome Monosoupape rotary, although the engine proved to be unreliable due to its propensity for oil leaks. In fact, the Gnome was so bad that the follow-on batch of 400 s-4cs, ordered in January 1918, utilized the less powerful, but infinitely more durable, Le Rhône 9c. Used exclusively in America, the "Tommy," as it was dubbed in service, also saw limited service with the Navy (14 examples) as a trainer. Postwar, many surplus s-4s found employment as air racers or in Hollywood movie work.

SPECIFICATION (s-4c):

ACCOMMODATION:
One pilot

DIMENSIONS:
LENGTH: 19 ft 10 in (5.82 m)
WINGSPAN: 26 ft 6 in (8.01 m)
HEIGHT: 8 ft 1 in (2.73 m)

WEIGHTS:
EMPTY: 940 lb (426 kg)
MAX T/O: 1330 lb (603 kg)

PERFORMANCE:
MAX SPEED: 97 mph (155 kmh)
RANGE: endurance of 2 hours
POWERPLANT: Le Rhône 9c
OUTPUT: 80 hp (60 kW)

FIRST FLIGHT DATE:
June 1917

ARMAMENT:
Occasionally one fixed Marlin 0.30-in machine gun forward of cockpit

FEATURES:
Equal-span biplane wing layout; closely cowled radial engine; tail skid

Interwar

Atlantic c/ta/ra Series

ten-seat, three-engined parasol monoplane transport

Formed in late 1923, the Atlantic Aircraft Corporation was established expressly to manufacture Fokker aircraft in the United States, because the Dutch-owned parent company feared that Anthony Fokker's allegiance to the German war effort in World War I would adversely affect sales in North America. Fokker's outstanding f viia/3m caught the eye of the Army Air Corps following the 1925 Ford Reliability Tour, and it ordered three c-2s, followed by eight c-2as—six c-7s, based on the Fokker f 10, were also acquired in 1929. The Navy had followed the Army's lead in 1926, purchasing three f viia/3ms, which it designated ta-1s. Like the c-2s, these differed from civilian Fokker trimotors in having wider fuselages and Wright j-5 engines. Entering service with the Marine Corps in Nicaragua in 1927-28, the ta-1s soon became ra-1s when the Navy decided that its t-for-Transport designation clashed with the letters used for its torpedo aircraft. A handful of longer-winged ta-2s (subsequently ra-2s) were also acquired, and like the ra-1s, they were later re-engined with j-6s.

SPECIFICATION
(MODEL TA-1):

ACCOMMODATION:
Pilot, copilot, and eight passengers

DIMENSIONS:
LENGTH: 49 ft 1 in (14.96 m)
WINGSPAN: 63 ft 4.50 in (19.33 m)
HEIGHT: 13 ft 4 in (4.08 m)

WEIGHTS:
EMPTY: 5400 lb (2449 kg)
MAX T/O: 9000 lb (4082 kg)

PERFORMANCE:
MAX SPEED: 116 mph (186 kmh)
RANGE: 460 miles (736 km)
POWERPLANT: three Wright J-5s
OUTPUT: 660 hp (492 kW)

FIRST FLIGHT DATE:
Late 1926

FEATURES:
Single parasol wing layout; three uncowled radial engines, two mounted under the wings and the third on the nose; fixed undercarriage; enclosed cockpit

Berliner Joyce OJ-2

two-seat, single-engined biplane observation scout

In 1929, the Navy's Bureau of Aeronautics issued a request seeking a lightweight aircraft for use from the fleet's *Omaha*-class cruisers, which were limited to machines of just 5450 lb on their catapults. On June 28, 1929, prototypes were ordered from Berliner Joyce (XOJ-1) and Keystone (XOK-1), with the stipulation that the aircraft be powered by air-cooled radials in the 400-hp range. Following flight testing, the Navy ordered the Berliner Joyce design into production as the OJ-2, and 39 were built in 1933. Powered by a 400-hp Pratt & Whitney R-985-A Wasp Junior radial engine, and armed with two 0.30-in machine guns, the versatile OJ-2 could be fitted with floats for operations from cruisers and landing gear for aircraft carrier or shore-based flight. The OJ-2s were assigned to VS-5B and VS-6B, which embarked two-aircraft detachments aboard the cruisers until 1935. After that, most surviving OJ-2s were assigned to shore-based units, and the Navy Reserve, where they were utilized as hacks until the late 1930s.

SPECIFICATION:

ACCOMMODATION:
Pilot and observer/gunner

DIMENSIONS:
LENGTH: 25 ft 8 in (7.86 m)
WINGSPAN: 33 ft 8 in (10.30 m)
HEIGHT: 11 ft 2 in (3.41 m)

WEIGHTS:
EMPTY: 2520 lb (1143 kg)
MAX T/O: 3629 lb (1646 kg)

PERFORMANCE:
MAX SPEED: 151 mph (242 kmh)
RANGE: 510 miles (816 km)
POWERPLANT: Pratt & Whitney
R-985-A Wasp Junior
OUTPUT: 400 hp (298 kW)

FIRST FLIGHT DATE:
Early 1931

ARMAMENT:
One Browning 0.30-in machine gun mounted on upper wing and one on flexible mounting for observer/gunner

FEATURES:
Biplane wing layout; cowled radial engine; fixed undercarriage or pontoon floats; open cockpit

Boeing PW-9

single-seat, single-engined biplane fighter

The manufacturer of a handful of successful fighter designs in the interwar years, Boeing secured a contract to build 200 Thomas-Morse MB-3A fighters in 1921. Realizing that it could create a better aircraft, Boeing designed the Model 15, which featured a fabric-covered welded steel-tube fuselage and wooden wings. The Army evaluated the new aircraft and ordered 30, designated the PW-9 (pursuit water-cooled design 9). The first of these was delivered to squadrons in Hawaii and the Philippines in October 1925, and follow-on batches of 25 PW-9As (with duplicated flying and landing wires for safety), 40 PW-9Cs (with larger wheels, and cockpit and landing gear changes), and 16 PW-9Ds would also be placed with Boeing. The latter version, ordered in August 1927, was eight percent heavier than the original PW-9, and featured a balanced rudder, wheel brakes, and a revised cowl and radiator profile. Once in service, the PW-9 was rated the leading home-produced fighter of the mid-1920s, combining a good performance with excellent maneuverability.

SPECIFICATION (PW-9D):

ACCOMMODATION:
One pilot

DIMENSIONS:
LENGTH: 23 ft 5 in (7.14 m)
WINGSPAN: 32 ft 0 in (9.75 m)
HEIGHT: 8 ft 2 in (2.49 m)

WEIGHTS:
EMPTY: 2328 lb (1056 kg)
MAX T/O: 3234 lb (1467 kg)

PERFORMANCE:
MAX SPEED: 155 mph (249 kmh)
RANGE: 390 miles (628 km)
POWERPLANT: Curtiss D-12D Vee
OUTPUT: 435 hp (324 kW)

FIRST FLIGHT DATE:
April 29, 1923 (Model 15)

ARMAMENT:
Two fixed Browning 0.30-in machine guns (or one Browning 0.50-in machine gun) in upper fuselage cowling; bomb load of 244 lb (111 kg) could be carried under fuselage on racks

FEATURES:
Sesquiplane wing layout; closely cowled vee-engine; tail skid; deep radiator chin below engine

Boeing FB Series

single-seat, single-engined biplane fighter

Following on from its successful sale of PW-9s to the Army, Boeing also managed to secure an order for its Model 15 from the Navy, which signed up for 16 in early 1925. These aircraft were virtually duplicates of the Army's original PW-9, with the first ten being delivered between December 1 and 22, 1925. Designated FB-1s, these aircraft were supplied to Marine Corps units VF-1M, -2M, and -3M. Nine of these aircraft were later assigned to the Expeditionary Force in China in 1927-28, where they were operated by VF-10M (VF-3M redesignated). The FB-1 was not equipped for carrier operations, unlike its FB-5 successor. Featuring a strengthened fuselage and cross-axle undercarriage, as well as a more powerful Packard engine, 27 FB-5s were delivered to the Navy on January 21, 1927. Initially equipping VF-1B and VF-6B aboard USS Langley, FB-5s also served with VF-3B, embarked in USS Lexington. The type was restricted to land-based use from 1929 after the Navy decided to standardize on radial air-cooled engines for shipboard aircraft.

SPECIFICATION (FB-1):

ACCOMMODATION:
One pilot

DIMENSIONS:
LENGTH: 23 ft 5 in (7.14 m)
WINGSPAN: 32 ft 0 in (9.75 m)
HEIGHT: 8 ft 2 in (2.49 m)

WEIGHTS:
EMPTY: 1936 lb (878 kg)
MAX T/O: 2835 lb (1286 kg)

PERFORMANCE:
MAX SPEED: 159 mph (254 kmh)
RANGE: 390 miles (628 km)
POWERPLANT: Curtiss D-12D Vee
OUTPUT: 435 hp (324 kW)

FIRST FLIGHT DATE:
April 29, 1923 (Model 15)

ARMAMENT:
Two fixed Browning 0.30-in machine guns (or one Browning 0.30-in and one Browning 0.50-in machine gun) in upper fuselage cowling; bomb load of 244 lb (111 kg) could be carried under fuselage on racks

FEATURES:
Sesquiplane wing layout; closely cowled vee-engine; tail skid; deep radiator chin below engine

Boeing F2B/F3B

single-seat, single-engined biplane fighter

The development of the 425-hp Wasp engine by Pratt & Whitney in 1926 saw the Navy decide to opt for radial powerplants for all of its shipboard aircraft from then on due to their ease of maintenance and better reliability. Boeing quickly designed the Model 69 fighter to make use of the Wasp, this machine retaining many features of the FB series. Following successful testing of the prototype, the Navy ordered 32 F2B-1s in March 1927. The first of these was delivered on January 30, 1928, aircraft being assigned to VF-1B and VB-2B (a bomber unit, despite the F2B-1 being a fighter) aboard USS *Saratoga*. The follow-on F3B-1 entered Navy service in August 1928, this machine having a revised wing and tail layout (the latter featuring semi-monocoque all-metal construction for the first time) and a strengthened undercarriage. A total of 74 F3B-1s were acquired, with VF-2B (*Langley*), VB-2B (*Saratoga*), VF-3B (*Lexington*), and VB-1B (*Lexington*), receiving examples by the end of 1928. Most had been retired from frontline use by 1932.

SPECIFICATION (F3B-1):

ACCOMMODATION:
One pilot

DIMENSIONS:
LENGTH: 24 ft 10 in (7.56 m)
WINGSPAN: 33 ft 0 in (10.06 m)
HEIGHT: 9 ft 2 in (2.79 m)

WEIGHTS:
EMPTY: 2179 lb (988 kg)
MAX T/O: 2945 lb (1336 kg)

PERFORMANCE:
MAX SPEED: 157 mph (253 kmh)
RANGE: 340 miles (544 km)
POWERPLANT: Pratt & Whitney R-1340 Wasp
OUTPUT: 425 hp (317 kW)

FIRST FLIGHT DATE:
March 2, 1927

ARMAMENT:
One fixed Browning 0.30-in machine gun and one Browning 0.50-in machine gun in upper fuselage

FEATURES:
Biplane wing layout; uncowled radial engine; arrestor hook; tail skid; N-shaped bracing struts

Boeing NB

two-seat, single-engined primary and gunnery biplane trainer

Having succeeded in becoming the Navy's principal source for fighters in the early 1920s, Boeing made a concerted effort to corner the primary trainer market with its Model 21. Designated the VNB-1 by the Navy, the prototype proved too docile to adequately teach pupils how to cope with advanced biplane fighters in the frontline. Once Boeing modified the airframe so that it could be spun (a prerequisite for any primary trainer), the Navy placed an order for 42 NB-1s. Deliveries began on December 5, 1924, with the first machines being powered by Lawrance J series 200-hp engines. A second batch of 30 followed, fitted with Navy surplus 180-hp Wright-Hispano E-4s. Designated NB-2s, some were operated as seaplanes with a single pontoon float and wingtip stabilizers. The aircraft was used both for pilot and gunnery training, with the rear cockpit boasting a Scarff ring for a single 0.30-in machine gun. Some 32 NBs were based at NAS Pensacola with VN-1D8 and VN-4D8, and the aircraft was also by the Marine Corps.

SPECIFICATION (NB-1):

ACCOMMODATION:
Two pilots, or pilot and observer/gunner

DIMENSIONS:
LENGTH: 28 ft 9 in (8.80 m)
WINGSPAN: 36 ft 10 in (11 m)
HEIGHT: 11 ft 8 in (3.59 m)

WEIGHTS:
EMPTY: 2136 lb (969 kg)
MAX T/O: 2837 lb (1287 kg)

PERFORMANCE:
MAX SPEED: 99 mph (159 kmh)
RANGE: 300 miles (480 km)
POWERPLANT: Lawrance J-1
OUTPUT: 200 hp (149 kW)

FIRST FLIGHT DATE:
Early 1924

ARMAMENT:
One flexible Browning 0.30-in machine gun in Scarff ring in rear cockpit

FEATURES:
Equal-span biplane wing layout; uncowled engine; tail skid, or single float in seaplane configuration; N-shaped bracing struts

Boeing F4B/P-12

single-seat, single-engined biplane fighter

Built as the private-venture Model 83/89 by Boeing in 1928, these diminutive machines were the natural successors to the company's F2B/F3B naval fighters. The new design's big advantage rested in its smaller and lighter airframe, which combined with Pratt & Whitney's latest specification Wasp radial to produce an aircraft that was 32 mph faster than the Boeing fighters then in service. After testing two prototypes, the Navy ordered 27 F4B-1s, followed in 1931 by 46 F4B-2s, fitted with engine cowls, Frise ailerons, a tailwheel, and a supercharged engine, 21 F4B-3s with a entirely new light-alloy monocoque fuselage, and finally 92 F4B-4s with a wider undercarriage. The F4B-1s entered fleet service between June and August 1929, with VB-1B (later redesignated VF-5B) and VF-2B taking them to sea in their respective carriers (*Lexington* and *Langley*).

Subsequent variants entered Navy and Marine Corps service up to February 1933, and examples of the F4B-4 remained on carrier decks until 1937, when they were replaced by faster Grumman biplanes. Relegated to shore stations, where they flew utility tasks, some 34 were still on Navy charge when Pearl Harbor was attacked in December 1941. In a rare display of service unity, the Army also ordered the Model 83/89, which it duly designated the P-12. The Army Air Corps' purchases started in June 1929 with 90 P-12Bs (the largest single Army order for fighters since 1921), and was followed by 96 P-12Cs, 35 P-12Ds, 110 P-12Es, and finally, 25 P-12Fs in 1933. These machines, which differed only in minor detail from their Navy brethren, remained in frontline service until replaced by Boeing's P-26A "Peashooter" in 1934-35. Used throughout the 1930s firstly as frontline fighters and then in the advanced training role, the last F4BS/P-12S were phased out of service in 1940-41. Of those machines that were deemed surplus to requirements by the Army Air Corps, 23 assorted P-12S were acquired by the Navy (and redesignated F4B-4AS) in 1940 for use as radio-controlled target drones.

SPECIFICATION (P-12E):

ACCOMMODATION:
One pilot

DIMENSIONS:
LENGTH: 20 ft 3 in (6.17 m)
WINGSPAN: 30 ft 0 in (9.14 m)
HEIGHT: 9 ft 0 in (2.74 m)

WEIGHTS:
EMPTY: 1999 lb (907 kg)
MAX T/O: 2690 lb (1220 kg)

PERFORMANCE:
MAX SPEED: 189 mph (304 kmh)
RANGE: 540 miles (869 km)
POWERPLANT: Pratt & Whitney R-1340-17 Wasp
OUTPUT: 550 hp (410 kW)

FIRST FLIGHT DATE:
September 29, 1930

ARMAMENT:
Two fixed Browning 0.30-in machine guns in upper fuselage

FEATURES:
Biplane wing layout; radial engine; arrestor hook (Navy variants only); tail skid (early Army variants); tailwheel (all Navy variants, and P-12E/F); N-shaped bracing struts; "turtleback" headrest (F4B-3/4 and P-12E/F)

Boeing P-26

single-seat, single-engined monoplane fighter

Yet another private-venture fighter produced by Boeing in the early 1930s, the iconic P-26 started life as the Model 248 in September 1931. Featuring an advanced monoplane layout and all-metal construction, the first of three prototypes was flown on March 20, 1932 with the designation XP-936. This was changed to XP-26 when the aircraft was purchased by the USAAC, the latter placing a record order for 111 examples of the improved Model 266 (P-26A in frontline service). The first production aircraft took to the skies on January 10, 1934, and by June 30 all 111 had been delivered.

A further 25 aircraft were delivered as P-26B/Cs, these featuring modified powerplants and armament. Twelve export P-26s were also constructed as the Model 281, eleven of these going to China, and the twelfth machine being sent to Spain for evaluation. Dubbed the "Peashooter" in frontline service because of its tubular gunsight mounted above the forward fuselage, P-26s were supplied to 17 USAAC squadrons in Michigan, California, and Louisiana, as well as overseas in Hawaii and the Panama Canal Zone. Capable of 227 mph in level flight and an initial climb rate of 2300 ft per minute, the highly maneuverable P-26 thoroughly outclassed the P-12 that it was bought to replace. Unlike the Boeing biplane, the "Peashooter" could be a handful to fly if not treated with respect. Indeed, its landing speed of 82.5 mph made the P-26 difficult to handle until the Army developed landing flaps.

A design that bridged the gap between biplane fighters of the 1920s and early 1930s and the monoplane pursuit types that would dominate the skies in

World War II, the P-26 was replaced by the Seversky P-35 and Curtiss P-36 in 1938-39. Relegated to service with units in Panama and the Philippines by 1940, a small number of "Peashooters" flown by Army Air Corps and Philippine Air Force pilots attempted to defend Manila and Bataan from Japanese aerial attacks in 1941-42. They were decimated by attacking Mitsubishi A6M Zero-sen fighters, however.

SPECIFICATION:

ACCOMMODATION:
Pilot

DIMENSIONS:
LENGTH: 23 ft 10 in (7.26 m)
WINGSPAN: 27 ft 11.50 in (8.52 m)
HEIGHT: 10 ft 5 in (3.17 m)

WEIGHTS:
EMPTY: 2196 lb (996 kg)
MAX T/O: 3015 lb (1368 kg)

PERFORMANCE:
MAX SPEED: 234 mph (377 kmh)
RANGE: 560 miles (901 km)
POWERPLANT: Pratt & Whitney R-1340-27 Wasp
OUTPUT: 600 hp (447 kW)

FIRST FLIGHT DATE:
March 20, 1932

ARMAMENT:
Two fixed Browning 0.50-in machine guns (or one Browning 0.30-in and one Browning 0.50-in machine gun) in fuselage near wing roots; maximum bomb load of 200 lb (90 kg) on underfuselage bomb rack

FEATURES:
Monoplane wing layout; Townend radial engine; spatted fixed undercarriage; prominent headrest

Boeing/Stearman PT/NS Kaydet

single-engined biplane trainer

Built as a private venture by the Stearman Aircraft Company (bought by Boeing in 1934) utilizing the firm's Model C as a base, the X70, as it was designated by the manufacturer, was submitted as a contender for the USAAC's primary trainer requirement of 1934. It was rather ironic, therefore, that the first service to show interest in the design was the Navy, who ordered 61 (designated NS-1s) in early 1935—these were to be powered by surplus Wright J-5s , which the Navy had a considerable stock of. Following a prolonged evaluation of the X70, the USAAC finally bought an initial batch of 26 airframes (designated PT-13s) in 1936. This small quantity reflected the paucity of the funding then available to the Army Air Corps, but this changed with the outbreak of World War II—3519 PT-17s were built in 1940 alone. By then production had centered on the improved Model 75 of 1936, which featured a 215-hp Lycoming engine. In 1940 the 220-hp Continental engine was adopted, and the PT-13 became the PT-17 (N2S-1 in Navy service). Production of this version for the Army alone totaled 2942 airframes, with a further 2702 being supplied to the Navy.

Full interchangeability between Army and Navy aircraft was finally achieved in 1942 with the advent of the PT-13D/N2S-5 (Model E-75), which featured a Lycoming R-680-17 radial and overall silver finish in place of the Navy's traditional trainer yellow. A total of 1768 E-75s were built in 1942-43, of which 1430 were issued to the Navy. "North of the border," the 300 Canadian machines supplied as Lend-Lease PT-27s were given the appellation "Kaydet," and this name is now universally applied to all Model 75s. After just four months of active service with the Royal Canadian Air Force, the PT-27s were traded back the US for Fairchild Cornells because of the unsuitability of their open cockpits for winter training. By the time production finally ceased in early 1945, more than 10,300 Kaydets had been built, making it America's most-produced biplane.

SPECIFICATION (N2S-5/PT-13D):

ACCOMMODATION:
Two pilots in tandem

DIMENSIONS:
LENGTH: 25 ft 0.25 in (7.63 m)
WINGSPAN: 32 ft 2 in (9.80 m)
HEIGHT: 9 ft 2 in (2.79 m)

WEIGHTS:
EMPTY: 1936 lb (878 kg)
MAX T/O: 2717 lb (1232 kg)

PERFORMANCE:
MAX SPEED: 124 mph (200 kmh)
RANGE: 505 miles (813 km)
POWERPLANT: Continental R-670-4 or Lycoming R-680-17
OUTPUT: 220 hp (164 kW)

FIRST FLIGHT DATE:
December 1933 (Stearman x70)

FEATURES:
Biplane wing layout; uncowled radial engine; N-shaped bracing struts

Boeing B-9

five-seat, twin-engined monoplane bomber

Yet another Boeing private venture project, the B-9 was built by the Seattle-based manufacturer when it realized that the Army had no all-metal stressed-skin monoplane bomber planned for service introduction in the near future. Having gained experience of such techniques with the revolutionary Model 200 Monomail, Boeing commenced work on the Curtiss-engined Model 214 and the Pratt & Whitney-powered Model 215 in 1930. Boasting a bomb load of 2260 lb, they were armed with four 0.50-in machine guns and had a retractable undercarriage. The Army bought both aircraft, designating them the Y1B-9 (Model 214) and YB-9 (Model 215). In August 1931, Boeing received an additional order for five B-9 service test machines, all of which were fitted with Pratt & Whitney Hornet engines—this powerplant had proven superior to the Curtiss V-1570. Capable of speeds of up to 188 mph, and with a range of 450 miles, these aircraft were the first of more than 18,000 bombers that would be built by Boeing over the next three decades.

SPECIFICATION:

ACCOMMODATION:
Pilot, bombardier/navigator, radio operator, and two gunners

DIMENSIONS:
LENGTH: 51 ft 9 in (17.77 m)
WINGSPAN: 76 ft 10 in (23.42 m)
HEIGHT: 12 ft 0 in (3.66 m)

WEIGHTS:
EMPTY: 8941 lb (4056 kg)
MAX T/O: 14,320 lb (6496 kg)

PERFORMANCE:
MAX SPEED: 188 mph (303 kmh)
RANGE: 1240 miles (1984 km)
POWERPLANT: two Pratt & Whitney R-1860-11 Hornets
OUTPUT: 1200 hp (895 kW)

FIRST FLIGHT DATE:
April 13, 1931

ARMAMENT:
Four Browning 0.50-in machine guns on flexible mounts in nose/rear dorsal hatch, or single Browning 0.30-in machine guns in similar positions (B-9); maximum bomb load of 2260 lb (1025 kg) in bomb bay and underwing racks

FEATURES:
Monoplane wing layout; retractable undercarriage

Brewster SBA/SBN

two-seat, single-engined monoplane scout-bomber/trainer

Brewster commenced aircraft manufacture in the early 1930s and initially concentrated on building seaplane floats, tail units, and wings under subcontract to other manufacturers. In 1934 the company decided to produce its own aircraft, starting with a design for a monoplane two-seat scout-bomber to serve aboard the new carriers USS *Enterprise* and *Yorktown*. On April 15, 1936, the prototype Brewster XSBA-1 completed its maiden flight. The midwing monoplane of all-metal construction featured an internal bomb bay, trailing-edge flaps, and a hydraulically rectractable undercarriage. Initially powered by a 750-hp Wright Cyclone, this was soon deemed to be inadequate, so a 950-hp version was installed. The Navy ordered 30 SBAS, which were ultimately constructed as SBN-1s by the NAF facility in Philadelphia because Brewster lacked the infrastructure to build such aircraft. This severely delayed production, and the first SBN-1 was not delivered to VB-3 until November 1940. Obsolescent by then, the aircraft were used primarily for training purposes.

SPECIFICATION:

ACCOMMODATION:
Pilot and gunner

DIMENSIONS:
LENGTH: 27 ft 8 in (8.43 m)
WINGSPAN: 39 ft 0 in (11.89 m)
HEIGHT: 8 ft 7 in (2.64 m)

WEIGHTS:
EMPTY: 4400 lb (1996 kg)
MAX T/O: 6759 lb (3066 kg)

PERFORMANCE:
MAX SPEED: 254 mph (406 kmh)
RANGE: 1015 miles (1633 km)
POWERPLANT: Wright XR-1820-22 Cyclone
OUTPUT: 950 hp (708 kW)

FIRST FLIGHT DATE:
April 15, 1936 (XSBA-1)

ARMAMENT:
One flexible Browning 0.30-in machine gun in rear cockpit; maximum bomb load of 500 lb (227 kg) in bomb bay

FEATURES:
Mid-fuselage-mounted monoplane wing layout; rectractable landing gear; close-cowled radial engine; aerial mast on port side forward of enclosed cockpit

Brewster F2A Buffalo

single-seat, single-engined monoplane fighter

In 1936 the Navy issued a requirement for a new generation of carrier-based fighter. It stated that the aircraft had to be a monoplane fitted with wing flaps, a retractable undercarriage, an enclosed cockpit, and arrestor gear. The winning design would replace biplane fighters then in widespread service with the fleet. The Navy ordered prototypes from Grumman, Seversky, and Brewster, and the latter manufacturer's XF2A-1 was declared the winner in June 1938. A contract for 54 F2A-1s was signed, and the first examples were delivered to VF-3 in June 1939. A further 43 improved F2A-2s were ordered by the Navy in early 1939, these machines featuring a more powerful engine, redesigned rudder, and an electric propeller. This variant entered service in September 1940, and four months later the Navy acquired 108 F2A-3s. This aircraft boasted extra armor protection for the pilot and self-sealing fuel tanks. The weight affected the fighter's performance, and only VF-2, VF-3, and VS-201 saw extended sea service. F2As served as advanced trainers on the East Coast until 1944.

SPECIFICATION (F2A-3):

ACCOMMODATION:
Pilot

DIMENSIONS:
LENGTH: 26 ft 4 in (8.03 m)
WINGSPAN: 35 ft 0 in (10.67 m)
HEIGHT: 12 ft 1 in (3.68 m)

WEIGHTS:
EMPTY: 4732 lb (2146 kg)
MAX T/O: 7159 lb (3247 kg)

PERFORMANCE:
MAX SPEED: 321 mph (516 kmh)
RANGE: 965 miles (1553 km)
POWERPLANT: Wright R-1820-40
OUTPUT: 1200 hp (895 kW)

FIRST FLIGHT DATE:
December 1937

ARMAMENT:
Four fixed Browning 0.50-in machine guns, two in the nose and one in each wing; maximum bomb load of 200 lb (90 kg) on underwing racks

FEATURES:
Mid-fuselage-mounted monoplane wing layout; rectractable landing gear; close-cowled radial engine; enclosed cockpit

Consolidated PT/NY

single-engined biplane primary trainer

Consolidated began its association with the US military with the PT/NY trainer series, which had started life in 1922 as the Dayton-Wright TW-3. Ordered by the Army as a Jenny replacement, TW-3 production had just started when Dayton-Wright was closed down by owner General Motors. The TW-3 contract was acquired by the newly formed Consolidated Aircraft Corporation, and its PT-1s (221 built) were effectively refined TW-3s with tandem rather than side-by-side seating. The Navy also bought 76 aircraft, which it designated the NY-1. These featured a more powerful Wright J-4 engine and larger fin/rudder for use in seaplane configuration. The next variants to enter Army service were the PT-3 (130 built) and PT-3A (120 built), which mated the fuselage of the PT-1 with a Wright J-5 radial. The National Guard received 29 O-17s at this time, which were effectively armed PT-3s. The Navy's NY-2 also utilized the J-5 engine, and bigger wings—186 were bought. The final Navy variant was the Wright R-760-engined NY-3, and these were not retired until 1939.

SPECIFICATION (PT-3A):

ACCOMMODATION:
Two pilots in tandem

DIMENSIONS:
LENGTH: 28 ft 1 in (8.56 m)
WINGSPAN: 34 ft 6 in (10.54 m)
HEIGHT: 9 ft 0 in (2.74 m)

WEIGHTS:
EMPTY: 1785 lb (810 kg)
MAX T/O: 2481 lb (1125 kg)

PERFORMANCE:
MAX SPEED: 102 mph (163 kmh)
RANGE: 300 miles (480 km)
POWERPLANT: Wright R-790-8
OUTPUT: 220 hp (164 kW)

FIRST FLIGHT DATE:
Late 1923 (PT-1)

ARMAMENT:
One flexible Browning 0.30-in machine gun mounted on Scarff ring for observer/gunner (O-17 only)

FEATURES:
Equal-span biplane wing layout; inline (PT-1 only) or cowled radial engine; fixed undercarriage or single pontoon float (NY-2 only); open cockpit

Consolidated P-30/PB-2A

two-seat, single-engined monoplane fighter

The only two-seat monoplane fighter to attain operational status with the Army Air Corps between the wars, the PB-2A traced its lineage back to Lockheed's speedy Altair racer. A military version, designated the XP-900, was acquired by the Army as the YP-24 in 1931, with further prototypes ordered. However, these remained unbuilt when Lockheed went bankrupt in 1932. The aircraft's chief designer, Robert Wood, duly joined Consolidated, and the company produced the Y1P-25 for the Army in 1932. Four more examples followed, powered by the turbo-supercharged Curtiss V-1570. Designated the P-30, these were tested in mid-1934 and a contract for 50 P-30AS issued. Featuring the all-important turbo-supercharged V-1570 engine, these aircraft were the Army's fastest machines for the first three years of their service. Redesignated PB-2AS (PB standing for Pursuit Biplace) shortly after their delivery in 1935, the aircraft flew with the 1st Pursuit Group for several years before being replaced by the P-36. The last examples were withdrawn in 1941.

SPECIFICATION:

ACCOMMODATION:
Pilot and gunner

DIMENSIONS:
LENGTH: 30 ft 0 in (9.14 m)
WINGSPAN: 43 ft 11 in (13.38 m)
HEIGHT: 8 ft 3 in (2.51 m)

WEIGHTS:
EMPTY: 4306 lb (1953 kg)
MAX T/O: 5643 lb (2560 kg)

PERFORMANCE:
MAX SPEED: 274 mph (441 kmh)
RANGE: 508 miles (820 km)
POWERPLANT: Curtiss Conqueror V-1570-61
OUTPUT: 700 hp (533 kW)

FIRST FLIGHT DATE:
Mid-1934 (P-30)

ARMAMENT:
Two fixed Browning 0.30-in machine guns above engine and one on flexible mounting in rear cockpit

FEATURES:
Monoplane wing layout; rectractable landing gear; close-cowled inline engine, with turbo-supercharger on left side; enclosed cockpits; three-bladed propeller

Consolidated P2Y

five-seat, twin-engined sesquiplane patrol flying boat

Consolidated's first flying boat was effectively a bridge between the biplane designs that had dominated Navy squadrons since before World War I and the monoplane machines that would serve in great numbers from the mid-1930s through to the 1960s. The P2Y was a sesquiplane that featured a parasol wing and a smaller wing mounted at the top of the hull. Based on the XPY-1 drawn up by the Bureau of Aeronautics in the late 1920s and built by Consolidated, the P2Y-1 went into production in July 1931. A total of 23 were built, and they entered service in mid-1933 with VP-5F and VP-10F. An additional 23 examples of the improved P2Y-3 were ordered in December of that year, this variant having its engines installed on the wing leading edge rather than below it as with the P2Y-1. At least 21 P2Y-1s were also upgraded to P2Y-3 configuration in 1936. The aircraft saw service with a dozen squadrons both at home and abroad until finally retired in 1941.

SPECIFICATION (P2Y-3):

ACCOMMODATION:
Pilot and copilot, flight engineer/gunner, navigator/gunner, and observer/gunner

DIMENSIONS:
LENGTH: 61 ft 9 in (18.86 m)
WINGSPAN: 100 ft 0 in (30.48 m)
HEIGHT: 19 ft 1 in (5.82 m)

WEIGHTS:
EMPTY: 12,769 lb (5792 kg)
MAX T/O: 25,266 lb (11,460 kg)

PERFORMANCE:
MAX SPEED: 139 mph (222 kmh)
RANGE: 1180 miles (1888 km)
POWERPLANT: two Wright R-1820-90S
OUTPUT: 1500 hp (1119 kW)

FIRST FLIGHT DATE:
April 1932

ARMAMENT:
One Browning 0.30-in machine gun on flexible mount in the bow and two in dorsal gun hatches behind wings; maximum bomb load of 2000 lb (907 kg)

FEATURES:
Sesquiplane wing layout; cowled radial engines; boat-shaped hull; twin fins; enclosed cockpit

Curtiss CS (Martin SC)

three-seat, single-engined biplane seaplane torpedo-bomber

Curtiss's first torpedo-bomber, the CS was typical of the handful of types that performed this mission for the Navy in the 1920s. A large three-seater, powered by a Wright inline engine, it carried a torpedo under the fuselage. The CS also had the ability to swap its pontoon floats for a wheeled undercarriage. Flown in prototype form in 1923, the CS-1 was of conventional layout, bar its upper wing, which was shorter in span than the lower wing. Six CS-1s were delivered to the Navy, followed by two CS-2s, which featured an uprated engine, more fuel, and an optional third float. Delivered in April 1924 to VT-1, these aircraft proved so successful that the Navy issued a production contract for additional airframes. Glenn Martin underbid Curtiss, and it duly delivered 35 aircraft (designated SC-1s) in early 1925 to VT-1, VT-2, and VS-1. An additional four re-engined SC-2s followed (a number of SC-1s were also fitted with bigger Wright T-3s), and the aircraft served the Navy until it was retired in 1928.

SPECIFICATION:

ACCOMMODATION:
Pilot, observer, and gunner

DIMENSIONS:
LENGTH: 37 ft 9 in (11.54 m)
WINGSPAN: 56 ft 7 in (17.28 m)
HEIGHT: 14 ft 8 in (4.51 m)

WEIGHTS:
EMPTY: 5007 lb (2271 kg)
MAX T/O: 8422 lb (3820 kg)

PERFORMANCE:
MAX SPEED: 103 mph (165 kmh)
RANGE: 1018 miles (1629 km)
POWERPLANT: Wright T-3
OUTPUT: 585 hp (436 kW)

FIRST FLIGHT DATE:
Late 1923

ARMAMENT:
One Browning 0.30-in machine gun flexibly mounted for gunner; one 1618 lb (734 kg) torpedo, externally carried

FEATURES:
Biplane wing layout, with upper wing shorter than lower wing; cowled inline engine; fixed undercarriage or twin pontoon floats; open cockpit

Curtiss PW-8

single-seat, single-engined biplane fighter

Developed from the successful Curtiss R-6 racing aircraft, which dominated competition in the US in 1922, the Model 33 was a fighter that featured the former's untapered wood/fabric wings, welded steel-tube fuselage, cowled Curtiss D-12 engine, and flush radiators on the upper-wing surfaces. Impressed by the aircraft's 171 mph top speed, the Army ordered three examples in April 1923. These were given the designation XPW-8, and after minor modifications to the aircraft's landing gear and cowling, and the fitting of strut-connected ailerons and unbalanced elevators, the Army Air Service contracted Curtiss to build an additional 25 PW-8 airframes (PW standing for Pursuit, Water-cooled). The second production aircraft gave a clear demonstration of the fighter's capabilities when, on June 23, 1924, 1Lt. Russell Maughan used it to complete the first coast-to-coast crossing of the USA between dawn and dusk. Most production aircraft were delivered to the elite 1st Pursuit Group, which regularly entered them into racing events such as the Mitchell Trophy in 1924-25.

SPECIFICATION:

ACCOMMODATION:
One pilot

DIMENSIONS:
LENGTH: 23 ft 1 in (7.04 m)
WINGSPAN: 32 ft 0 in (9.75 m)
HEIGHT: 8 ft 10 in (2.70 m)

WEIGHTS:
EMPTY: 2191 lb (994 kg)
MAX T/O: 3155 lb (1431 kg)

PERFORMANCE:
MAX SPEED: 171 mph (275 kmh)
RANGE: 440 miles (710 km)
POWERPLANT: Curtiss D-12 Vee
OUTPUT: 435 hp (324 kW)

FIRST FLIGHT DATE:
May 1923

ARMAMENT:
Two fixed Marlin 0.30-in machine guns in upper fuselage cowling

FEATURES:
Equal-span biplane wing layout; closely cowled vee-engine; tail skid; headrest; N-shaped bracing struts

Curtiss B-2 Condor

four-seat, twin-engined biplane heavy bomber

Gaining vital experience building 50 NBS-1 heavy bombers derived from the Martin MB-2, Curtiss improved this design with the creation of the NBS-4 in 1924. The new variant featured a fuselage made up of welded-steel tubing and distinctive gunners' cockpits in the aft section of both engine nacelles. Powered by two Curtiss Conqueror V-12s, a single prototype was ordered by the Army as the XB-2 in 1926, and this flew for the first time in July 1927. Following service testing, a further 12 B-2 Condors were acquired, and these entered service with 11th Bomb Squadron in 1929. Curtiss also modified the Condor into a transport, this version —designated the T-32 by the manufacturer— featuring a much larger fuselage with an enclosed cockpit, single fin, radial engines, and retractable main wheels. The Army purchased two, which were give the YC-30 designation, and the Navy also acquired a pair in 1934. Designated R4C-1s, they were operated by Marine Corps squadron VJ-7M and attached to the US Antarctic expedition in 1940-41.

SPECIFICATION (B-2):

ACCOMMODATION:
Pilot and three gunners

DIMENSIONS:
LENGTH: 47 ft 4.50 in (13.70 m)
WINGSPAN: 90 ft 0 in (27.43 m)
HEIGHT: 16 ft 4 in (4.98 m)

WEIGHTS:
EMPTY: 9300 lb (4218 kg)
MAX T/O: 16,591 lb (7526 kg)

PERFORMANCE:
MAX SPEED: 132 mph (212 kmh)
RANGE: 805 miles (1295 km)
POWERPLANT: two Curtiss
GV-1750-7 Conquerors
OUTPUT: 1260 hp (940 kW)

FIRST FLIGHT DATE:
July 1927

ARMAMENT:
Six Browning/Lewis 0.30-in
machine guns in pairs on flexible
mounts in the nose and rear of
engine nacelles; maximum bomb
load of 2508 lb (1138 kg)

FEATURES:
Equal-span biplane wing layout;
two uncowled radial engines
between wings; fixed undercarriage; open cockpit and
gunners' positions

Curtiss F6C Hawk

single-seat, single-engined biplane fighter

Just as Boeing succeeded in selling versions of its biplane fighters to the Navy, so too did rival manufacturer Curtiss. The breakthrough came in March 1925 when the Navy ordered nine F6C-1 Hawks, which were effectively navalized versions of the USAAS's P-1 Hawk. The primary difference between the two aircraft was that the F6C-1 could be fitted with Macchi floats for waterborne operations. Two F6C-1s were delivered with arrestor hooks and strengthened landing gear for carrier deck trials with VF-2, which proved successful. Some 35 carrier-capable F6C-3s were ordered in 1927, followed by a further 31 Pratt & Whitney R-1340-powered F6C-4s after the Navy chose to standardize on air-cooled radials for its aircraft. Although lighter and more maneuverable than the Curtiss-powered F6C-3s, the F6C-4s were deemed obsolete by the time production examples reached the fleet—they cruised just once with VF-2B aboard USS Langley in 1929-30. Following their replacement by the F4B, a number of F6Cs were used as advanced trainers.

SPECIFICATION (F6C-4):

ACCOMMODATION:
Pilot

DIMENSIONS:
LENGTH: 22 ft 6 in (6.86 m)
WINGSPAN: 31 ft 6 in (9.60 m)
HEIGHT: 10 ft 11 in (3.33 m)

WEIGHTS:
EMPTY: 1980 lb (898 kg)
MAX T/O: 2785 lb (1263 kg)

PERFORMANCE:
MAX SPEED: 155 mph (249 kmh)
RANGE: 361 miles (581 km)
POWERPLANT: Pratt & Whitney R-1340
OUTPUT: 410 hp (306 kW)

FIRST FLIGHT DATE:
Early 1925

ARMAMENT:
Two fixed Browning 0.30-in machine guns on upper fuselage; maximum bomb load of 232 lb (105 kg) on underwing racks

FEATURES:
Tapered biplane wing layout; closely cowled vee-engine; radial engine (F6C-4); arrestor hook; N-shaped bracing struts; deep chin-mounted radiator

Curtiss P-1 to P-6E Hawk

single-seat, single-engined biplane fighter

All bearing the Hawk appellation, this family of Curtiss machines came to represent all American biplane fighters of the interwar period. The original P-1 of 1925 was effectively a refined PW-8 fitted with tapered wings, and the USAAS ordered 15 for the 1st Pursuit Group. The P-1A (25 built) soon followed, this variant featuring a longer fuselage, while the P-1B (23 built) of 1926 was fitted with a more powerful Curtiss V-1150-3 engine, a bigger radiator, and larger tires. In 1929, 33 near-identical P-1Cs were also built, followed by 71 P-1D/ES, which were originally delivered to the Army in 1927 as Wright-engined AT-5/5A advanced trainers. With their Wright radials replaced by Curtiss V-1150-3s producing twice the horsepower, the Hawks were ushered into frontline service.

In 1928, Curtiss married the proven Hawk airframe with its new 600-hp V-1570 engine, and the resulting YP-6 was ordered to the tune of 18 airframes by the Army. Later fitted with turbochargers and redesignated P-6DS, these machines proved heavy and unreliable in service. The P-6E, by contrast, was a great success, the final production machine in the long-lived Hawk series being created when Curtiss combined the V-1570 engine, cowling, three-bladed propeller, and main undercarriage of its XP-22 fighter prototype with the airframe of the YP-20 in the fall of 1931. The end result was designated the XP-6E, and the USAAC ordered it into limited production. Like previous Curtiss fighter designs, only a small number of P-6Es were built—46 were delivered between December 1931 and late 1932. Differing from previous Hawks by having a single-strut undercarriage with spats, a tailwheel, and a redesigned tail section, most P-6ES were issued to either the 1st PG at Selfridge Field, in Michigan, or the 8th PG at Langley Field, Virginia.

The P-6E was a contemporary of Boeing's P-12 in USAAC service, and the two types were the principal American biplane fighters in the inter-war years. A handful of P-6ES remained in service as communication "hacks" with frontline pursuit groups until 1938, when they were retired.

SPECIFICATION (P-6E):

ACCOMMODATION:
Pilot

DIMENSIONS:
LENGTH: 23 ft 2 in (7.06 m)
WINGSPAN: 31 ft 6 in (9.60 m)
HEIGHT: 8 ft 10 in (2.69 m)

WEIGHTS:
EMPTY: 2699 lb (1224 kg)
MAX T/O: 3392 lb (1539 kg)

PERFORMANCE:
MAX SPEED: 197 mph (317 kmh)
RANGE: 570 miles (917 km)
POWERPLANT: Curtiss V-1570-23
OUTPUT: 600 hp (447 kW)

FIRST FLIGHT DATE:
May 1925 (P-1)

ARMAMENT:
Two fixed Browning 0.30-in machine guns on sides of nose

FEATURES:
Biplane wing layout; tail skid or tailwheel (P-6E only); headrest; N-shaped bracing struts; removable wheel spats (P-6E only)

Curtiss F7C Seahawk

single-seat, single-engined biplane fighter

Yet another member of the Hawk family, the F7C was the first Curtiss fighter to be built from the outset for shipboard use, rather than as a "navalized" derivative of a land-based aircraft. The fighter was designed around the Pratt & Whitney R-1340 Wasp engine, which had become the Navy's powerplant of choice in the mid-1920s when it switched from inlines to radials because the latter were easier to maintain at sea. Differing from its F6C-4 predecessor in respect to its wing planform (only the upper wing was tapered), rudder shape, and fuselage outline, the prototype XF7C-1 flew for the first time on February 28, 1927. As part of its flight trials, the aircraft was fitted with a single central float and outriggers. Just 17 F7C-1s were subsequently ordered, these being accepted by the Navy between December 1928 and January 1929. Frontline machines differed from the prototype in having tripod main undercarriage members rather than the cross-axle type. The F7C-1 would exclusively equip the Marine Corps' VF-5M in frontline service.

SPECIFICATION:

ACCOMMODATION:
Pilot

DIMENSIONS:
LENGTH: 22 ft 2 in (6.75 m)
WINGSPAN: 32 ft 8 in (9.96 m)
HEIGHT: 10 ft 4 in (3.15 m)

WEIGHTS:
EMPTY: 2038 lb (924 kg)
MAX T/O: 2782 lb (1262 kg)

PERFORMANCE:
MAX SPEED: 151 mph (243 kmh)
RANGE: 330 miles (531 km)
POWERPLANT: Pratt & Whitney
R-1340B Wasp
OUTPUT: 450 hp (336 kW)

FIRST FLIGHT DATE:
February 28, 1927

ARMAMENT:
Two fixed Browning 0.30-in
machine guns on upper fuselage

FEATURES:
Biplane wing layout (upper wing
tapered); exposed radial engine;
arrestor hook; N-shaped bracing
struts; tail skid

Curtiss F9C Sparrowhawk

single-seat, single-engined biplane fighter

Only eight F9C Sparrowhawks were built for the Navy, the aircraft being designed to meet a lightweight shipboard fighter requirement. The latter called for the production of a very small aircraft, yet despite being just 20 ft long and with a wingspan of only 25 ft, the XF9C-1 proved too large for the Navy! However, these modest dimensions meant that the Sparrowhawk was small enough to pass through the hangar door built into the dirigibles USS *Akron* and *Macon*. These airships were constructed with hangar space for four airplanes apiece, which were launched and retrieved by means of a trapeze. The aircraft would hang from the trapeze by a skyhook fitted to the upper wing. Curtiss also raised the aircraft's top wing by four inches and fitted a more powerful Wright radial. Six F9C-2s were ordered in October 1931, and the first hook-on to *Akron* was made on June 29, 1932. No Sparrowhawks were lost when *Akron* crashed in 1933, but four were destroyed with the loss of *Macon* two years later.

SPECIFICATION:

ACCOMMODATION:
Pilot

DIMENSIONS:
LENGTH: 20 ft 7 in (6.27 m)
WINGSPAN: 25 ft 5 in (7.75 m)
HEIGHT: 10 ft 11.50 in (3.34 m)

WEIGHTS:
EMPTY: 2089 lb (947 kg)
MAX T/O: 2770 lb (1256 kg)

PERFORMANCE:
MAX SPEED: 176 mph (284 kmh)
RANGE: 350 miles (563 km)
POWERPLANT: Wright R-975-E3
OUTPUT: 438 hp (327 kW)

FIRST FLIGHT DATE:
February 12, 1931

ARMAMENT:
Two fixed Browning 0.30-in machine guns on upper fuselage

FEATURES:
Biplane wing layout, with upper wing gull-shaped; N-shaped bracing struts; spatted undercarriage; close-cowled radial engine; skyhook assembly above upper wing

Curtiss F11C/BFC/BF2C Goshawk

single-seat, single-engined biplane fighter-bomber

Originally ordered in April 1932 as a carrier-based biplane interceptor, the F11 became a multirole fighter-bomber when the Navy specified that it had to be able to dive-bomb targets too—ordnance was to be carried either on a special fuselage-mounted crutch or on underwing racks. Following flight trials of the XF11C-2, the Navy ordered 28 in October 1932, and deliveries were completed by May of the following year. Only VF-1B was issued with F11C-2s, and its aircraft became BFC-2s in March 1934 when the Navy created its fighter-bomber category. Although the unit was renumbered twice, it kept these aircraft until February 1938. A follow-on order for 27 F11C-3s was placed in February 1934, this variant featuring a retractable undercarriage and R-1820-04 Wright Cyclone engine. Redesignated the BF2C-1 the following month, the aircraft was issued exclusively to VF-5B from October 1934. These machines saw limited service, as they suffered from near-incurable sympathetic metal-wing vibration caused by the engine running at cruising rpm.

SPECIFICATION (BFC-2):

ACCOMMODATION:
Pilot

DIMENSIONS:
LENGTH: 25 ft 0 in (7.62 m)
WINGSPAN: 31 ft 6 in (9.60 m)
HEIGHT: 10 ft 7.25 in (3.23 m)

WEIGHTS:
EMPTY: 3037 lb (1378 kg)
MAX T/O: 4120 lb (1869 kg)

PERFORMANCE:
MAX SPEED: 205 mph (330 kmh)
RANGE: 560 miles (901 km)
POWERPLANT: Wright R-1820-78 Cyclone
OUTPUT: 785 hp (585 kW)

FIRST FLIGHT DATE:
Early 1932

ARMAMENT:
Two fixed Browning 0.30-in machine guns on upper fuselage; racks under lower wings for 448 lb (204 kg) of bombs, or a single 500 lb (227 kg) bomb on centreline crutch

FEATURES:
Biplane, staggered wing layout; N-shaped bracing struts; retractable undercarriage (BF2C only); close-cowled radial engine; arrestor hook

Curtiss F8C/O2C Helldiver

two-seat, single-engined biplane observation/scout aircraft

Although only operated in small number, Curtiss's Falcon saw extensive service with the Marine Corps in the fighter, dive-bomber, and observation roles in Nicaragua and China. Sensing a requirement for a machine that bombed as well as the Falcon in horizontal flight, but could also be just as accurate as a dive-bomber, Curtiss developed a new aircraft based on the OC that was capable of carrying a 500-lb bomb under its fuselage or two 116-lb bombs under the wings. In order to make the new type durable enough for dive-bombing, its upper wing was shortened and the fuselage strengthened. Given the popular name Helldiver, the aircraft was ordered by the Navy in 1929 as the F8C-4 and issued primarily to VF-1B aboard *Saratoga*. After subsequent service with the Marine Corps, the Helldivers were passed onto the Reserve in late 1931. An additional batch of 63 F8C-5s was acquired that same year for observation duties, and these served as O2C-1s with the Marine Corps until transferred to the Reserve in 1934.

SPECIFICATION:

ACCOMMODATION:
Pilot and observer/gunner

DIMENSIONS:
LENGTH: 25 ft 8 in (7.86 m)
WINGSPAN: 32 ft 0 in (9.75 m)
HEIGHT: 10 ft 3 in (3.13 m)

WEIGHTS:
EMPTY: 2520 lb (1143 kg)
MAX T/O: 4020 lb (1823 kg)

PERFORMANCE:
MAX SPEED: 146 mph (234 kmh)
RANGE: 720 miles (1152 km)
POWERPLANT: Pratt & Whitney R-1340-4
OUTPUT: 450 hp (336 kW)

FIRST FLIGHT DATE:
1929

ARMAMENT:
Two fixed Marlin 0.30-in machine guns mounted in upper wings and one on flexible mounting for gunner; maximum bomb load of 500 lb (91 kg), either one 500-lb bomb centrally slung or two 116-lb bombs under each wing

FEATURES:
Equal-span biplane wing layout, with sweepback on upper plane; radial engine; fixed under-carriage; open cockpit

Curtiss O-1/O-11/A-3 and F8C/OC Falcon

two-seat, single-engined biplane observation/scout/attack aircraft

For six years following the end of World War I, the Army relied on the ubiquitous DH-4B/M to perform observation and light bombing roles. Having wrung the life out of these veteran machines, the Army decided in 1924 that it needed an all-new type to fill these roles. Two separate trials were arranged at McCook Field so that a new observation type could be selected, with the first competition involving Liberty-engined aircraft. Curtiss's XO-1 lost out to the Douglas OX-2, so the company fitted a Packard 1A-1500 engine in place of the Liberty for the second competition and carried the day.

The Packard powerplant failed to reach service expectations, however, and the first ten O-1 Falcons ordered by the Army in 1925 were fitted with Curtiss V-1150s instead. A handful of production batches would follow over the next seven years, all of which were powered by Curtiss engines bar the Liberty-engined O-1A and O-11—66 of the latter were built in 1927-28. All Falcons

featured wooden wings, with sweepback on the upper plane, and a fuselage truss of aluminum tubing and steel-tie bracing, covered in fabric. Major Curtiss-powered production variants for the Army included the O-1B (27 built) of 1927, the O-1E (37) of 1929, the O-1G (30) of 1930, and the O-39 (10) of 1932.

The Army's A-3 attack aircraft of 1927 was effectively an O-1B with extra 0.30-in weapons fitted in the lower wings and a twin Lewis mounting on a Scarff ring for the gunner. Curtiss delivered 76 in 1927-28 and 78 A-3BS, based on the O-1E, in 1930. The Navy also chose the Falcon for service from land bases with the Marine Corps, selecting the O-11 airframe to be paired with a Pratt & Whitney Wasp radial engine. Ordered as the F8C-1, four were delivered in 1927 and immediately redesignated OC-1S once in service. An additional 21 OC-2S were delivered to VO-8M and VO-10M the following year, these aircraft being used for strafing, dive-bombing, air evacuation, and observation in Nicaragua and China.

SPECIFICATION (A-3B):

ACCOMMODATION:
Pilot and observer/gunner

DIMENSIONS:
LENGTH: 27 ft 2 in (8.28 m)
WINGSPAN: 38 ft 0 in (11.58 m)
HEIGHT: 10 ft 6 in (3.20 m)

WEIGHTS:
EMPTY: 2875 lb (1304 kg)
MAX T/O: 4476 lb (2030 kg)

PERFORMANCE:
MAX SPEED: 139 mph (224 kmh)
RANGE: 628 miles (1010 km)
POWERPLANT: Curtiss V-1150-5
OUTPUT: 435 hp (324 kW)

FIRST FLIGHT DATE:
Late 1925 (O-1)

ARMAMENT:
Two fixed Browning 0.30-in machine guns mounted above nose and two on flexible mounting for observer/gunner for O series, and two additional guns in lower wings for A series; maximum bomb load of 200 lb (91 kg)

FEATURES:
Biplane wing layout, with sweepback on upper plane; cowled inline engine, except for O-11 and Navy Falcons, powered by radials; fixed undercarriage; open cockpit

Curtiss SBC Helldiver

two-seat, single-engined biplane scout-bomber

Having the distinction of being the very last combat biplane built in America, the SBC Helldiver actually began life as the XF12C-1 parasol-wing fighter. A two-seat design with retractable gear, it flew for the first time in 1933, powered by a Wright Whirlwind radial. Its role was soon changed to scouting by the Navy in December 1933, and then scout-bombing the following month. By then designated the XSBC-1, the aircraft suffered a structural failure of the wing during dive-bombing trials in September 1934. Curtiss built a new prototype with a more conventional biplane layout, powered by Pratt & Whitney's Wasp 825-hp engine, in 1935, and the Navy ordered 83 SBC-3 production examples in August of the following year. Armed with two forward-firing and one flexible 0.30-in machine guns and a single 500-lb bomb beneath its fuselage for dive-bombing attacks, the 237-mph Helldiver entered service with VS-5 aboard USS *Yorktown* in July 1937. VS-3 (*Saratoga*) and VS-6 (*Enterprise*) had also received SBC-3s by year-end. The last aircraft in this order was used as a prototype for the improved SBC-4, which featured the more powerful 950-hp Wright R-1820-22 engine. Now capable of carrying a 1000-lb bomb, the revised Helldiver was quickly ordered into production by the Navy in January 1938 to the tune of 164 airframes. The first of these reached the fleet in March 1939, and in early 1940 50 examples were diverted by the Navy to France, which had ordered 90 Helldivers soon after Europe had been plunged into war in September 1939. The Navy's shortfall was soon made good by delivering 50 from the French order, these aircraft differing from standard examples in having self-sealing fuel tanks. When Japan bombed Pearl Harbor on December 7, 1941, the Navy still had 69 SBC-3s and 117 SBC-4s on strength, with VB-8 and VS-8 operating the latter type from the deck of USS *Hornet*. Marine Corps unit VMO-151 was also equipped with SBC-4s, but all Helldivers were soon relegated to training duties.

SPECIFICATION (SBC-4):

ACCOMMODATION:
Pilot and observer/gunner

DIMENSIONS:
LENGTH: 28 ft 4 in (8.64 m)
WINGSPAN: 34 ft 0 in (10.36 m)
HEIGHT: 12 ft 7 in (3.84 m)

WEIGHTS:
EMPTY: 4841 lb (2196 kg)
MAX T/O: 7632 lb (3462 kg)

PERFORMANCE:
MAX SPEED: 237 mph (381 kmh)
RANGE: 590 miles (950 km)
POWERPLANT: Wright R-1820-34 Cyclone 9
OUTPUT: 950 hp (708 kW)

FIRST FLIGHT DATE:
December 9, 1935 (XSBC-2)

ARMAMENT:
One fixed Browning 0.30-in machine gun mounted in upper fuselage and one on flexible mounting for gunner; maximum bomb load of 1000 lb (454 kg) centrally slung

FEATURES:
Biplane wing layout, with sweepback on upper plane; close-cowled radial engine; retractable undercarriage; enclosed cockpit

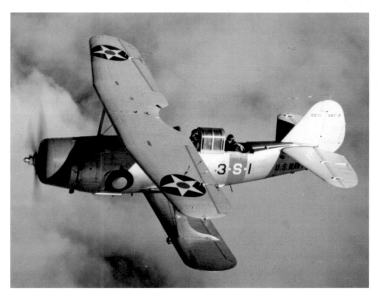

Curtiss SOC Seagull

two-seat, single-engined biplane scout/observation sea/landplane

The SOC Seagull was the last of the Curtiss biplanes to see operational service with the Navy, examples sailing aboard battleships and cruisers for a full decade from 1935 to 1945. Beating rival designs from Douglas (XO2D-1) and Vought (XO5U-1) in a 1933 competition to find the Navy's new scouting/observation aircraft that would operate from its capital ships, the XO3C-1 became the SOC-1 when ordered into production in 1934.

This designation change came about when the scouting and observation roles were combined that year—observation types had previously deployed on battleships and scouts on cruisers. The initial prototype had an amphibious landing gear, with twin wheels incorporated into the central main float, but this was deleted on production aircraft. The latter was simply a seaplane, with optional nonretractable tailwheel-type landing gear that had to be fitted instead of the floats. The initial production run of 135 aircraft began reaching the frontline in November 1935, and VS-5B, VS-6B, VS-9S, VS-10S, VS-11S, and VS-12S would all receive SOC-1S.

Forty land-based SOC-2S then followed, after which 83 SOC-3S were delivered with interchangeable alighting gear. The final version to reach the fleet was the SON-1, which was the SOC-3 equivalent built by the NAF as per Navy regulations that stipulated that ten percent of its Service aircraft had to be constructed "in house." Some 64 were delivered up to the spring of 1938, after which no further Seagulls would be built. By then Curtiss had commenced work on its monoplane replacement, the SO3C. This aircraft proved less than successful in the frontline, however, and the SOCs remained in service until late 1945—its SO3C replacements, meanwhile, had been retired early in 1944. Seeing action across the globe in World War II, a number of Seagulls fitted with fixed undercarriages were also equipped with arrestor gear in 1942 for carrier operations. These aircraft were redesignated SOC-2/3AS. Surviving Seagulls were quickly retired after the war, thus ending an era of US naval aviation, for no aircraft replaced them aboard battleships and cruisers.

SPECIFICATION
(SOC-1 SEAPLANE):

ACCOMMODATION:
Pilot and observer/gunner

DIMENSIONS:
LENGTH: 26 ft 6 in (8.08 m)
WINGSPAN: 36 ft 0 in (10.97 m)
HEIGHT: 14 ft 9 in (4.50 m)

WEIGHTS:
EMPTY: 3788 lb (1718 kg)
MAX T/O: 5437 lb (2466 kg)

PERFORMANCE:
MAX SPEED: 165 mph (266 kmh)
RANGE: 675 miles (1086 km)
POWERPLANT: Pratt & Whitney
R-1340-80 Wasp
OUTPUT: 600 hp (447 kW)

FIRST FLIGHT DATE:
April 1934

ARMAMENT:
One fixed Browning 0.30-in machine gun in lower wing and one on flexible mounting for observer/gunner; maximum bomb load of 650 lb (295 kg) on external wing racks

FEATURES:
Equal-span biplane wing layout; cowled radial engine; fixed undercarriage or central pontoon float and wingtip floats; enclosed cockpit

Curtiss N2C Fledgling

two-seat, single-engined biplane primary trainer

Despite its anachronistic appearance, the humble XN2C-1 Fledgling was actually the winner of a 1928 competition staged by the Navy to find a new primary trainer. Looking barely removed from Curtiss's JN-4 Jenny, the aircraft featured numerous struts and wires despite the trend at the time to reduce such things. The aircraft was developed in parallel with commercial versions destined for use at numerous Curtiss-Wright Flying Services schools spread across the US. The XN2C differed from its civilian brethren in the fitment of military-specified equipment and the use of a 220-hp Wright J-5 Whirlwind radial instead a 165- to 185-hp Curtiss Challenger. Evaluated as both a land and seaplane, the XN2C-1 prototype saw off rival designs from Keystone (XNK-1) and Boeing (XN2B-1) to win the competition. Curtiss was duly awarded a contract to build 31 aircraft, followed by a second batch of 20 machines. The latter aircraft were designated N2C-2s, as they were powered by 240-hp Wright R-760-94s. Most Fledglings spent their entire careers assigned to Reserve training squadrons.

SPECIFICATION (N2C-2):

ACCOMMODATION:
Two pilots in tandem

DIMENSIONS:
LENGTH: 27 ft 4.25 in (8.35 m)
WINGSPAN: 39 ft 5 in (12.03 m)
HEIGHT: 10 ft 8.50 in (3.30 m)

WEIGHTS:
EMPTY: 2138 lb (970 kg)
MAX T/O: 2860 lb (1297 kg)

PERFORMANCE:
MAX SPEED: 116 mph (186 kmh)
RANGE: 384 miles (614 km)
POWERPLANT: Wright R-760-94
OUTPUT: 240 hp (179 kW)

FIRST FLIGHT DATE:
Early 1928

FEATURES:
Equal-span biplane wing layout; uncowled radial engine; fixed undercarriage; open cockpit

Curtiss A-8/10/12 Shrike

two-seat, single-engined monoplane attack aircraft

The XA-8 Shrike was devised by Curtiss in 1930 in response to an Army request for an all-metal low-wing attack monoplane. The prototype first flew the following year, and having seen off the rival XA-7 from General Aviation/Fokker, the XA-8 was ordered into limited production in the form of five service test YA-8s and eight YIA-8s. The aircraft featured a then new smooth skin semi-monocoque fuselage with conventional two-spar wings, the latter fitted with optional racks for up to ten bombs. The YA/YIA-8s, powered by inline Conqueror engines, commenced service testing in July 1932 with the 3rd Attack Group. By then the unique YA-10, powered by a Pratt & Whitney Hornet radial, had flown, and this engine was subsequently adopted for the 46 A-12s built in 1933-34. This variant also saw the rear gunner's position moved forward from mid-fuselage to just behind the cockpit. The first A-12s reached the 3rd Attack Group in December 1933, and they remained in service until 1942—all surviving A-8s had been retired in 1938.

SPECIFICATION (A-12):

ACCOMMODATION:
Pilot and gunner

DIMENSIONS:
LENGTH: 32 ft 3 in (9.84 m)
WINGSPAN: 44 ft 0 in (13.41 m)
HEIGHT: 9 ft 4 in (2.86 m)

WEIGHTS:
EMPTY: 3898 lb (1768 kg)
MAX T/O: 5900 lb (2676 kg)

PERFORMANCE:
MAX SPEED: 175 mph (280 kmh)
RANGE: endurance of 3.5 hours
POWERPLANT: Wright R-1820-37
OUTPUT: 690 hp (515 kW)

FIRST FLIGHT DATE:
1931

ARMAMENT:
Four Browning 0.30-in machine guns in the undercarriage fairings, and one on flexible mounting for gunner; maximum bomb load of 400 lb (181 kg) on external wing racks

FEATURES:
Monoplane wing layout; fixed, spatted undercarriage; single cowled radial engine (A-12); guns in undercarriage fairings positions; open cockpit

Curtiss O-52 Owl

two-seat, single-engined parasol heavy observation aircraft

Built by Curtiss in response to an Army requirement for a two-seat observation aircraft, the Owl was a very capable machine with good low-speed maneuverability and landing characteristics. Designated the Model 85 by the company, the all-metal design relied on full-span automatic leading-edge slots working in conjunction with wide-span trailing-edge flaps to achieve low-speed agility. Ordered into production in 1939, a total of 203 O-52 Owls were built for the Army from 1940 onward, although none actually saw frontline service—19 of these machines were eventually passed on to the Soviet Union. Following the US entry into World War II, the Army Air Force determined that the O-52 did not possess sufficient performance for combat operations overseas, resulting in the Owls being relegated to flying courier duties within America. A small number also flew short-range submarine patrols over the Gulf of Mexico and Atlantic and Pacific Oceans soon after war was declared. By late 1942 virtually all O-52s had been retired.

SPECIFICATION:

ACCOMMODATION:
Pilot and observer in tandem

DIMENSIONS:
LENGTH: 26 ft 4 in (8.03 m)
WINGSPAN: 40 ft 9.50 in (12.43 m)
HEIGHT: 9 ft 3.25 in (2.83 m)

WEIGHTS:
EMPTY: 4231 lb (1919 kg)
MAX T/O: 5364 lb (2433 kg)

PERFORMANCE:
MAX SPEED: 220 mph (354 kmh)
RANGE: 700 miles (1127 km)
POWERPLANT: Pratt & Whitney R-1340-51 Wasp
OUTPUT: 600 hp (447 kW)

ARMAMENT:
One fixed Browning 0.30-in machine gun on upper fuselage and one on flexible mounting for gunner

FIRST FLIGHT DATE:
1938

FEATURES:
Parasol wing; retractable undercarriage; close-cowled radial engine; tailwheel

Curtiss-Wright SNC

two-seat, single-engined monoplane advanced trainer

This rather obscure aircraft was ordered by the Navy in 1940 to fulfill the scout trainer role, its layout being based on the Curtiss CW-21 fighter of 1938. Unlike the latter machine, the SNC had a tandem cockpit arrangement and an engine of far less power—a 420-hp Wright Whirlwind in place of the 1000-hp Cyclone from the same manufacturer—as befitted its training role. Unofficially named the "Falcon," the SNC was fully equipped to undertake instrument flying, high-altitude training, air gunnery, and bomb delivery. An initial contract for 150 aircraft was placed with Curtiss in November 1940, followed by subsequent orders for 150 and five the following year. With the delivery of the 305th SNC in late 1941, the production line was terminated. The SNC was soon replaced by navalized versions of the ubiquitous T-6 Texan, known as the NJ/SNJ in Navy service.

SPECIFICATION:

ACCOMMODATION:
Two pilots in tandem

DIMENSIONS:
LENGTH: 26 ft 6 in (8.08 m)
WINGSPAN: 35 ft 0 in (10.67 m)
HEIGHT: 7 ft 6 in (2.29 m)

WEIGHTS:
EMPTY: 2610 lb (1184 kg)
MAX T/O: 3626 lb (1645 kg)

PERFORMANCE:
MAX SPEED: 201 mph (323 kmh)
RANGE: 515 miles (829 km)
POWERPLANT: Wright R-975-E3 Whirlwind 9
OUTPUT: 420 hp (313 kW)

FIRST FLIGHT DATE:
1939

FEATURES:
Monoplane wing; retractable undercarriage; close-cowled radial engine; tailwheel; tapered rear fuselage

Curtiss P-36

single-seat, single-engined monoplane fighter

Forerunner of the famous "Hawk" series of fighters produced in great numbers by Curtiss during World War II, the privately financed Model 75 was the losing design in a competition fly-off held by the USAAC for a new monoplane fighter in mid-1935. Beaten by the Seversky P-35, the Curtiss prototype was overhauled by the company primarily through the fitment of a more powerful Twin Wasp engine. Featuring smooth stressed-skin construction, a multispar wing, sliding cockpit canopy, variable-pitch Hamilton Standard propeller, hydraulic split flaps, and main gear legs that retracted backward into the wing, the Model 75, paired with the 900-hp Wright R-1670 radial engine, was a "hot ship" at the time. Designated the Y1P-36 by the Army, just three were initially ordered for evaluation in August 1936. However, these proved so outstanding during flight testing that Curtiss received the biggest peacetime pursuit contract ever (worth just over $4 million) in July 1937 when 210 P-36As were ordered.

The first of these aircraft began to reach pursuit squadrons in April 1938, and by early 1939 all 210 had been delivered. The final 31 P-36s had been completed as C-models, which had an additional 0.30-in gun in each wing and were powered by the 1200-hp Pratt & Whitey R-1830-7 engine. The P-36s suffered various teething problems during their first two years in service, resulting in no fewer than 81 major and minor modifications being incorporated into the airframe by Curtiss. This meant that P-36s did not deploy overseas until February 1941, when a single squadron was posted to Alaska and two to Hawaii. Although being largely obsolete by the time America was plunged into World War II in December 1941, a small number of Army Hawks saw early combat during the Pearl Harbor raid and the Japanese invasion of the Aleutians.

Most had been relegated to training roles by 1942, surviving P-36s serving with units churning out fighter pilots destined to fly more modern piston-engined combat types such as the P-38, P-40, and P-47 in the China-Burma-India theater, the Pacific, and Europe.

SPECIFICATION (P-36C):

ACCOMMODATION:
Pilot

DIMENSIONS:
LENGTH: 28 ft 6 in (8.69 m)
WINGSPAN: 37 ft 3.50 in (11.37 m)
HEIGHT: 12 ft 2 in (3.71 m)

WEIGHTS:
EMPTY: 4620 lb (2096 kg)
MAX T/O: 6150 lb (2790 kg)

PERFORMANCE:
MAX SPEED: 311 mph (500 kmh)
RANGE: 825 miles (1328 km)
POWERPLANT: Pratt & Whitney R-1830-7
OUTPUT: 1200 hp (895 kW)

FIRST FLIGHT DATE:
May 15, 1935 (Model 75) and February 1937 (Y1P-36)

ARMAMENT:
One Browning 0.30-in and one 0.50-in machine gun above cowling, with two additional 0.30-in machine guns in wings

FEATURES:
Monoplane wing; retractable undercarriage; close-cowled radial engine; enclosed cockpit; three-bladed propeller

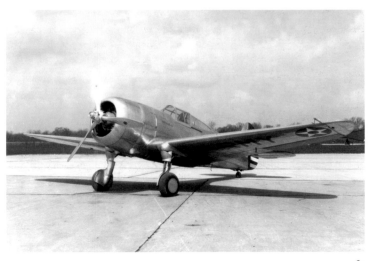

Douglas DT

two-seat, single-engined biplane land/seaplane torpedo-bomber

The first military aircraft built by Douglas, the DT-1 was strongly influenced in its layout by the company's Cloudster. Designed by Donald W. Douglas, who had recently set up his own company following a spell as Glenn L. Martin's chief engineer, the DT-1 emerged in 1921 as a large single-seat biplane powered by a Liberty engine. Featuring folding wings and an interchangeable wheel/float chassis, the aircraft could carry a single 1835-lb torpedo beneath its forward fuselage. Three were ordered by the Navy, but only one was delivered as a DT-1. The remaining two were redesignated as DT-2s, featuring a second cockpit for an observer. Aside from 36 aircraft constructed by Douglas between 1922 and 1924, six more DT-2s were built by the NAF and 20 by LWF. Although designed primarily as a torpedo-bomber, the DT-2 proved suited to scouting (three were fitted with extra fuel tanks in a deeper fuselage by Dayton-Wright), observation, and aerial gunnery training, as well as experimental flying. The last DT-2s were retired in 1926.

SPECIFICATION
(SEAPLANE):

ACCOMMODATION:
Pilot and observer

DIMENSIONS:
LENGTH: 37 ft 8 in (11.52 m)
WINGSPAN: 50 ft 0 in (15.24 m)
HEIGHT: 15 ft 1 in (4.60 m)

WEIGHTS:
EMPTY: 4528 lb (2054 kg)
MAX T/O: 7293 lb (3308 kg)

PERFORMANCE:
MAX SPEED: 99 mph (158 kmh)
RANGE: 274 miles (438 km)
POWERPLANT: Liberty 12
OUTPUT: 400 hp (298 kW)

FIRST FLIGHT DATE:
November 1921

ARMAMENT:
One 1835-lb (832-kg) torpedo,
externally carried

FEATURES:
Equal-span biplane wing layout;
close-cowled inline engine; fixed
undercarriage or twin pontoon
floats; open cockpit

Douglas T2D/P2D

three-seat, twin-engined biplane land/seaplane torpedo-bomber

Designed by the Bureau of Aeronautics in 1925 in an effort to provide the Navy with an aircraft that outperformed existing torpedo-bombers, the prototype XTN-1 was built by the NAF in Philadelphia. Powered by two Wright R-1750s, the biplane could operate on either wheels or floats. A production contract for three T2D-1s (as the type was designated) was awarded to Douglas in early 1927, and these were delivered to VT-2 in May of that same year. Soon sent to sea aboard *Langley*, the T2D-1 became the first twin-engined aircraft to operate from a carrier deck. Nine more T2D-1s were ordered from Douglas in the wake of these sea trials, but criticism by the Army that the Navy was operating land-based bombers saw these delivered in seaplane configuration. A further 18 were ordered in June 1930, and these were redesignated as P2D-1 patrol aircraft so as to avoid further political wrangling with the Army. Near identical to the older T2D-1s, these machines flew with VP-3 in the Panama Canal Zone until 1937.

SPECIFICATION (SEAPLANE):

ACCOMMODATION:
Pilot and two gunners

DIMENSIONS:
LENGTH: 44 ft 11.50 in (13.70 m)
WINGSPAN: 57 ft 0 in (17.37 m)
HEIGHT: 14 ft 7.75 in (4.45 m)

WEIGHTS:
EMPTY: 6011 lb (2727 kg)
MAX T/O: 10,890 lb (4940 kg)

PERFORMANCE:
MAX SPEED: 124 mph (200 kmh)
RANGE: 422 miles (680 km)
POWERPLANT: two Wright R-1750 Cyclones
OUTPUT: 1050 hp (783 kW)

FIRST FLIGHT DATE:
January 27, 1927

ARMAMENT:
One Marlin 0.30-in machine gun on flexible mount in bow and one in rear cockpit; one 1618-lb (734-kg) torpedo, externally carried, or equivalent bomb load

FEATURES:
Equal-span biplane wing layout; two uncowled radial engines between wings; fixed under-carriage or twin pontoon floats; open cockpit and gunners' positions

Douglas B-7/O-35

four-seat, twin-engined gull-winged monoplane bomber/observation aircraft

Among the numerous small-run bombers and observation aircraft bought by the Army in the 1920s and early 1930s, perhaps the most distinctive was the Douglas B-7/O-35. Designed in 1929, two prototypes (XO-35 and XO-36) were ordered the following year—these differed only in the type of engine gearing that they used. More advanced than any of their rivals at the time, these aircraft featured all-metal stressed skinning and retractable main gear legs. Their gull-wing layout was also unique, and this gave the Douglas design excellent maneuverability for an aircraft of its size. The Army ordered seven Y1B-7s and Y1O-35s in 1932, and after being evaluated, they remained in frontline service —designated B-7s and O-35s, respectively—with the 31st Bomb Squadron. Featuring smooth rather than the corrugated skinning seen on the XO-35/36, these machines were otherwise unchanged. Intensively flown, four were lost in bad weather crashes in 1934 during the four months that the Army carried the mail across the USA. Popular with their crews, the last O-35 was retired in 1939.

SPECIFICATION:

ACCOMMODATION:
Two pilots, navigator/gunner, and bombardier/gunner

DIMENSIONS:
LENGTH: 46 ft 7 in (14.20 m)
WINGSPAN: 65 ft 3 in (19.89 m)
HEIGHT: 11 ft 7 in (3.54 m)

WEIGHTS:
EMPTY: 5519 lb (2503 kg)
MAX T/O: 11,177 lb (5070 kg)

PERFORMANCE:
MAX SPEED: 182 mph (293 kmh)
RANGE: 411 miles (660 km)
POWERPLANT: two Curtiss V-1570-53 Conquerors
OUTPUT: 1350 hp (1007 kW)

FIRST FLIGHT DATE:
March 1931

ARMAMENT:
Two Marlin/Lewis 0.30-in machine guns on flexible mounts in the nose and aft of the wing; maximum bomb load of 1200 lb (544 kg) on external fuselage racks

FEATURES:
Monoplane gull wing; retractable undercarriage; twin inline engines; open cockpit

Douglas C-21/26/OA/RD

seven-seat, twin-engined high-wing observation/transportation amphibian

In 1930 Douglas introduced the twin-engined Dolphin amphibian into the civilian marketplace, and this immediately provoked interest from both the Navy and Army. Boasting a cantilever wing and all-metal hull, the first Dolphins to enter military service were acquired by the US Coast Guard (USCG). Designated the RD, three examples were delivered in 1931. The Navy received three RD-2s and six RD-3s in 1933, these differing from the USCG aircraft in powerplants only. A further ten RD-4s were bought by the USCG in 1934, and these performed numerous search-and-rescue missions from several Coast Guard Air Stations up until they were impressed into Navy service in December 1941 and tasked to fly security patrols along the American coastline. Prewar, Navy RDs had been used as VIP transports. The Army also operated 14 Dolphins, which were designated C-21s and C-26s depending on their seating capacity and engines. Initially used as transports in 1932-33, they were converted to observation-amphibians in 1934 and redesignated OA-3/4s.

SPECIFICATION (RD-2):

ACCOMMODATION:
Pilot and seven passengers

DIMENSIONS:
LENGTH: 45 ft 2 in (13.77 m)
WINGSPAN: 60 ft 0 in (18.28 m)
HEIGHT: 15 ft 2 in (24.32 m)

WEIGHTS:
EMPTY: 6337 lb (2874 kg)
MAX T/O: 9387 lb (4258 kg)

PERFORMANCE:
MAX SPEED: 153 mph (245 kmh)
RANGE: 770 miles (1232 km)
POWERPLANT: two Pratt & Whitney R-1340-96s
OUTPUT: 900 hp (671 kW)

FIRST FLIGHT DATE:
1930

FEATURES:
Single high wing; radial engines; boat hull and wingtip floats; enclosed cockpit

Douglas O-2/25/32A/38/BT

two-seat, single-engined biplane observation/basic trainer aircraft

Developed from Douglas's DT torpedo bomber, the O-series biplanes proved to be one of the longest-lived designs to see Army service in the interwar years. The family lineage started in early 1924 with the XO-2 prototypes, which participated in an Army competition aimed at finding a new observation type. The aircraft was designed to accommodate either a Liberty engine or a Packard 1A-1500, and the Army selected the former for production. A total of 75 O-2s were ordered, although only 46 were delivered as such. The remainder were built as night-equipped O-2As (18) and dual-control O-2Bs (6), with five other airframes being Packard-powered. The O-2H introduced a larger airframe in 1926, as well as more fuel, heavily staggered wings, and a new tail unit. The Army bought 143, followed by 60 similar dual-control O-2Ks (40 of which became BT-1 trainers).

The XO-25A introduced the Curtiss V-1570 Conqueror to the O-2H airframe, and the Army acquired 29 from Douglas as the O-25A. The Prestone glycol-

cooled Conqueror fitted to the 30 O-25CS delivered in the late 1920s saw the aircraft's nose contours revised yet again. Further engine changes were made with the O-32A, which paired an O-2K airframe with a 450-hp Pratt & Whitney R-1340-3 Wasp radial. Some 30 were delivered to the Army as BT-2/2AS for use as basic trainers, followed by 146 BT-2BS and 20 BT-2CS. The last of the Douglas observation biplanes were grouped together in the O-38 series of 1932-34, these aircraft being similar to the O-29/32 except for their 525-hp Pratt & Whitney R-1690-3 Hornet engines.

A total of 46 were initially built, followed by 63 improved O-38BS. The O-38E/F, 45 of which were handed over to the Army in 1934, featured a deeper and more streamlined fuselage, full engine cowling, an enclosed cockpit, single strut landing gear, and new tail surfaces. Significantly different from all previous O-series aircraft, they were the last to be replaced in the frontline in the late 1930s, after which they served with the National Guard though to 1942.

SPECIFICATION (O-2):

ACCOMMODATION:
Pilot and observer

DIMENSIONS:
LENGTH: 29 ft 6 in (8.99 m)
WINGSPAN: 39 ft 8 in (12.09 m)
HEIGHT: 10 ft 10 in (3.07 m)

WEIGHTS:
EMPTY: 3100 lb (1406 kg)
MAX T/O: 4706 lb (2135 kg)

PERFORMANCE:
MAX SPEED: 126 mph (203 kmh)
RANGE: 300 miles (480 km)
POWERPLANT: Liberty 12A
OUTPUT: 420 hp (313 kW)

FIRST FLIGHT DATE:
Early 1924 (XO-2)

ARMAMENT:
One fixed Browning 0.30/0.50-in machine gun mounted above nose and two on flexible mounting for observer/gunner; maximum bomb load of 400 lb (182 kg)

FEATURES:
Biplane wing layout; inline (O-2/O-25) or radial engine (O-32A/O-38); fixed undercarriage; open cockpit (all bar O-38E/F)

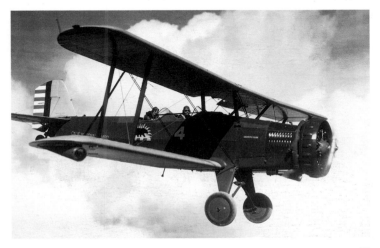

Douglas O-31/43/46

two-seat, single-engined gull/high-winged monoplane observation aircraft

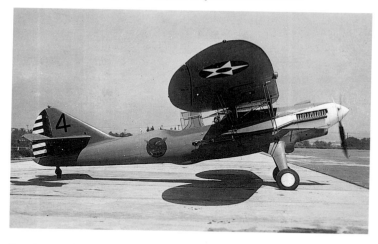

Douglas was the major supplier of observation aircraft to the Army in the 1920s and 1930s, and its first all-metal monoplane in this category was the XO-31 of 1930. Powered by a Curtiss V-1570 V-12 engine, this aircraft featured a unique gull-wing arrangement, with cabane struts, a corrugated-skin fuselage, and an open cockpit aft of the wing for the pilot and observer. Five service test YO-31As that followed in 1930 had smooth skinning, elliptical wings, wheel spats, and enclosed cockpits. The aircraft, in Y1O-43 form, was further refined with parasol wings and cantilever landing gear, and a production run of 24 O-43As followed. The last of these was fitted with a Pratt & Whitney Twin Wasp radial and designated the XO-46. It served as the prototype for the definitive O-46A, which featured a new canopy that was faired into the tail, wing struts in place of wire bracing, and no cabane. Ninety were built in 1936-37, and the 2nd Observation Squadron was still flying them in the Philippines in December 1941.

SPECIFICATION (O-46A):

ACCOMMODATION:
Pilot and observer in tandem

DIMENSIONS:
LENGTH: 34 ft 6.75 in (10.53 m)
WINGSPAN: 45 ft 9 in (13.94 m)
HEIGHT: 10 ft 8 in (3.25 m)

WEIGHTS:
EMPTY: 4776 lb (2166 kg)
MAX T/O: 6639 lb (3011 kg)

PERFORMANCE:
MAX SPEED: 200 mph (322 kmh)
RANGE: 435 miles (700 km)
POWERPLANT: Pratt & Whitney
R-1535-7 Twin Wasp Junior
OUTPUT: 725 hp (541 kW)

FIRST FLIGHT DATE:
Early 1930 (XO-31)

ARMAMENT:
One fixed Marlin (later Browning)
0.30-in machine gun in right
wing and one on flexible
mounting for observer

FEATURES:
Elliptical high wing; fixed
undercarriage; close-cowled
radial engine (O-46A); tailwheel

Douglas R2D/C-32/33/39

18-seat, twin-engined monoplane transportation aircraft

The forerunner of the hugely successful DC-3, the DC-1/2 family of aircraft, along with Boeing's Model 247, revolutionized air transportation in North America in the mid- to late 1930s. Featuring all-metal construction, retractable undercarriages, and seats for 15/16 passengers, these airliners also caught the eye of the US armed forces. However, budgets were tight and orders were slow in coming. In fact, the first military examples of the DC-2 to enter service were just five R2D-1/2s that were delivered to the Navy in 1934. The Army Air Corps acquired its first DC-2s two years later when it bought a single XC-32, two YC-34s, and 18 C-33s—the latter had enlarged vertical tail surfaces and a cargo door. The C-39 was the next variant to be ordered in quantity, 39 of this version, which featured numerous DC-3 components, reaching the Army's Transport Groups in 1939. Once America had entered the war, a further 24 civil DC-2s were also impressed into service as C-32As. The aircraft served primarily in the Pacific in 1941-43.

SPECIFICATION (C-39):

ACCOMMODATION:
Pilot, copilot, and 16 passengers

DIMENSIONS:
LENGTH: 61 ft 6 in (18.75 m)
WINGSPAN: 85 ft 0 in (25.91 m)
HEIGHT: 19 ft 7 in (6 m)

WEIGHTS:
EMPTY: 14,729 lb (6681 kg)
MAX T/O: 21,000 lb (9525 kg)

FIRST FLIGHT DATE:
July 1, 1933 (DC-1)

PERFORMANCE:
MAX SPEED: 210 mph (338 kmh)
RANGE: 900 miles (1448 km)
POWERPLANT: two Wright R-1820-55s
OUTPUT: 1950 hp (1454 kW)

FEATURES:
Monoplane wing; two closely cowled radial engines; retractable undercarriage; large vertical tail surface; flat-sided fuselage

Douglas TBD Devastator

three-seat, single-engined monoplane torpedo-bomber

Built to operate from the Navy's three aircraft carriers *Ranger*, *Yorktown*, and *Enterprise*, which were built in the 1930s, the TBD Devastator would be the world's first operational monoplane torpedo-bomber. The Navy had initiated development of a new torpedo-bomber with the placing of orders for two prototypes from Douglas and the Great Lakes Company. The former would build a cantilever monoplane which was designated the XTBD-1, while the latter would opt for a biplane configuration with its XTBG-1. The Douglas design featured a semi-retractable undercarriage, powered wing-fold actuation, and a large canopy over the pilot, radio operator, and gunner. The prototype made its first flight on April 15, 1935, and during subsequent trials by the Navy, its all-round performance was vastly superior to the XTBG-1.

On February 3, 1936, Douglas signed a contract to build 129 TBD-1s, which at the time was the Navy's largest ever order for aircraft in peacetime. Production aircraft differed only slightly from the prototype, the former being fitted with an uprated Pratt & Whitney R-1830-64 radial engine, a modified cowling, and a taller canopy over the pilot's cockpit covering a crash pylon. The first TBD-1s were issued to VT-3 in October 1937, and during the next 12 months VT-2, VT-5, and VT-6 all commenced operations with the aircraft. All four units were fully operational with the TBD-1 when Pearl Harbor was bombed, and they subsequently saw action in the Pacific in early 1942 during strikes on Japanese targets in the Marshall and Gilbert Islands, and in the Battle of Coral Sea. Dropping both torpedoes and conventional bombs, TBDs from *Lexington* (VT-2),

Enterprise (VT-6), and *Yorktown* (VT-5) enjoyed success. However, on June 4, during the Battle of Midway, three TBD units sent to strike the Japanese carrier force were decimated by defending A6M Zero-sen fighters. Some 45 Devastators had been committed to the battle, and by the time it ended with the sinking of *Yorktown* on June 7, only three TBDS remained. A handful of Devastators lingered on with training units until retired in 1944.

SPECIFICATION:

ACCOMMODATION:
Pilot, torpedo officer/navigator, and gunner

DIMENSIONS:
LENGTH: 35 ft 6 in (10.82 m)
WINGSPAN: 50 ft 0 in (15.24 m)
HEIGHT: 15 ft 1 in (4.60 m)

WEIGHTS:
EMPTY: 7195 lb (3264 kg)
MAX T/O: 10,194 lb (4622 kg)

PERFORMANCE:
MAX SPEED: 206 mph (332 kmh)
RANGE: 435 miles (700 km)
POWERPLANT: Pratt & Whitney R-1830-64 Twin Wasp
OUTPUT: 850 hp (634 kW)

FIRST FLIGHT DATE:
April 15, 1935

ARMAMENT:
One Browning 0.30-in machine gun in right side of nose, and one Browning 0.50-in on flexible mounting for gunner; one 1000-lb (454-kg) torpedo recessed into belly, and up to 500 lb (227 kg) of bombs on external wing racks

FEATURES:
Monoplane wing layout; semi-retractable undercarriage; close-cowled radial engine; extensive cockpit glazing

Douglas B-18 Bolo

six-seat, twin-engined monoplane bomber/transportation/antisubmarine aircraft

A military adaption of Douglas's successful DC-2 commercial transport, the B-18 (designated the DB-1 by its manufacturer) was the winner of the 1934 multi-engined bomber competition staged by the Army to find a replacement for its Martin B-10. The new machine had to be able to carry a ton of bombs over 2000 miles at a speed in excess of 200 mph. Drawing heavily on its experience with the DC-2, the DB-1 boasted the wings of the civilian airliner combined with a deeper and fatter fuselage that contained a bomb bay. Although outclassed by the Boeing Model 299 (later redesignated the B-17) in the competition fly-off, the DB-1 was substantially cheaper. The crash of the prototype Model 299 in October 1935 sealed the order in Douglas's favor, and 132 B-18s were built in 1937-38. A further 217 improved B-18As were also delivered between April 1938 and January 1940. Obsolete as a bomber by 1940, a number of B-18s were destroyed in the attacks on Pearl Harbor and the Philippines in December 1941.

SPECIFICATION:

ACCOMMODATION:
Two pilots, navigator/bombardier, and three gunners

DIMENSIONS:
LENGTH: 56 ft 8 in (17.31 m)
WINGSPAN: 89 ft 6 in (27.30 m)
HEIGHT: 15 ft 2 in (4.63 m)

WEIGHTS:
EMPTY: 15,719 lb (7130 kg)
MAX T/O: 27,087 lb (12,286 kg)

PERFORMANCE:
MAX SPEED: 217 mph (347 kmh)
RANGE: 1150 miles (1840 km)
POWERPLANT: two Wright R-1820-45s
OUTPUT: 1860 hp (1387 kW)

FIRST FLIGHT DATE:
April 1935

ARMAMENT:
Three Browning 0.30-in machine guns on flexible mounts in the nose, dorsal, and ventral positions; maximum bomb load of 4400 lb (1995 kg) carried in bomb bay

FEATURES:
Monoplane wing layout; retractable undercarriage; twin radial engines; nose turret

Douglas B-23 Dragon

six-seat, twin-engined monoplane bomber/transportation/antisubmarine aircraft

The B-23 Dragon was essentially a reworked and improved B-18. Produced as a result of the success of the multi-engined B-17, which had been built at the same time as the B-18, the Dragon boasted a new, more aerodynamic fuselage, greater wingspan and taller vertical tail unit—it was also the first US bomber built with a tail gunner's position. All of these modifications were meant to make the B-23 a better performer, and when married to the greater power of the twin Wright R-2600s, Douglas felt sure that they had an aircraft to rival the Flying Fortress. However, flight trials soon revealed less than inspiring performance figures, particularly in respect to bomb load and range in light of combat information reaching America from Europe. The B-23 was quickly passed over in favor of newer medium bombers under development, and only 38 were delivered. These machines saw limited service as coastal patrol aircraft along the Pacific seaboard, while 12 were later converted into utility transports (designated UC-67s).

SPECIFICATION:

ACCOMMODATION:
Pilot, navigator, bombardier, radio operator, camera operator, and tail gunner

DIMENSIONS:
LENGTH: 58 ft 4 in (17.78 m)
WINGSPAN: 92 ft 0 in (28.04 m)
HEIGHT: 18 ft 6 in (5.64 m)

WEIGHTS:
EMPTY: 19,059 lb (8645 kg)
MAX T/O: 30,475 lb (13,823 kg)

PERFORMANCE:
MAX SPEED: 282 mph (454 kmh)
RANGE: 1455 miles (2342 km)
POWERPLANT: two Wright R-2600-3 Cyclones
OUTPUT: 3200 hp (2366 kW)

FIRST FLIGHT DATE:
July 27, 1939

ARMAMENT:
Three Browning 0.30-in machine guns on flexible mounts in nose/dorsal/aft fuselage positions, one hand-held Browning 0.50-in machine gun in tail; maximum bomb load of 4000 lb (1814 kg) in bomb bay

FEATURES:
Monoplane wing layout; retractable undercarriage; twin radial engines; nose and tail guns

Douglas R3D

24-seat, twin-engined monoplane transportation aircraft

Derived from the legendary DB-7 bomber, the R3D was the military version of the little-known DC-5 airliner. Douglas had hoped to produce the latter alongside the DC-3, the newer design featuring the improved aerodynamics and tricycle landing gear that equipped the DB-7. The aircraft had a short-span, high-mounted wing, which, in combination with its tricycle undercarriage, made the R3D easy to load and unload because of its level fuselage—entry was gained either from the left front or rear at just above ground level. First flown in February 1939, the DC-5 proved to be a failure as a commercial airliner because of the outbreak of war in Europe seven months later. Only 12 were built, and three of these were supplied to the Navy as R3D-1s and four to the Marine Corps as R3D-2s. The latter were used as paratrooper trainers, being fitted with a large sliding cargo door. The USAAF also impressed three ex-KLM DC-5s into service with the Allied Directorate of Air Transport in Australia in 1942-43, designating them C-110s.

SPECIFICATION:

ACCOMMODATION:
Pilot, copilot, and 22 passengers

DIMENSIONS:
LENGTH: 62 ft 2 in (18.95 m)
WINGSPAN: 78 ft 0 in (23.77 m)
HEIGHT: 19 ft 10 in (6.05 m)

WEIGHTS:
EMPTY: 13,674 lb (6202 kg)
MAX T/O: 20,000 lb (9072 kg)

PERFORMANCE:
MAX SPEED: 221 mph (356 kmh)
RANGE: 1600 miles (2575 km)
POWERPLANT: two Wright GR-1820-F62S
OUTPUT: 1700 hp (1268 kW)

FIRST FLIGHT DATE:
February 20, 1939 (DC-5)

FEATURES:
High-mounted monoplane wing; two closely cowled radial engines; retractable tricycle undercarriage; large vertical tail surface

Engineering Division/Sperry Messenger M-1/MAT

single-seat, single-engined communications biplane

Having the distinction of being the smallest aircraft ever used by the Army, the all-wood Engineering Division Messenger was designed in 1920 by Alfred Verville at McCook Field following a request by Gen. William Mitchell. The latter wanted an aircraft that could serve as an "aerial despatch motorcycle," landing in small clearings near the frontline so as to deliver and collect messages issued by field commanders. The Sperry Aircraft Company of Farmingdale, New York, duly received the contract to manufacture 42 Messengers, including the prototype. Never actually employed in the role for which they were designed, the Messengers were used for experimental and research work instead due to their structural simplicity and low cost of purchase ($4000 per aircraft). Of the first 12 built, eight were completed as radio-controlled aerial torpedoes, while others tested wings with differing airfoils. Lawrence Sperry also produced a version that could hook itself to an airship in flight, and successful trials were conducted in late 1924. That same year all Messengers were redesignated M-1/1AS.

SPECIFICATION:

ACCOMMODATION:
Pilot

DIMENSIONS:
LENGTH: 17 ft 9 in (5.10 m)
WINGSPAN: 20 ft 0 in (6.10 m)
HEIGHT: 6 ft 9 in (2 m)

WEIGHTS:
EMPTY: 623 lb (283 kg)
MAX T/O: 862 lb (390 kg)

PERFORMANCE:
MAX SPEED: 97 mph (155 kmh)
RANGE: unknown
POWERPLANT: Lawrance L-4
OUTPUT: 60 hp (45 kW)

FIRST FLIGHT DATE:
Late 1920

FEATURES:
Equal-span biplane wing layout;
engine cylinder heads visible
through nose fairing; fixed
undercarriage; open cockpit;
N-shaped bracing struts

Fairchild PT-19/23/26 Cornell

two-seat, single-engined monoplane primary trainer

Procured by the USAAC in order to better prepare trainee pilots destined to fly monoplane aircraft in the frontline, the Fairchild PT-19 started life as the private-venture M-62. Evaluated in 1939 when the Army was searching for a primary trainer with a higher wing loading and more critical low-speed handling characteristics, the diminutive trainer was ordered into series production in 1940 and entered service as the PT-19 Cornell later that same year.

The aircraft's construction was typical of its type during this period, with a cantilever monoplane wing fitted low on the fuselage. While the former was made of wood, with plywood skinning, the latter was comprised of welded-steel tubing mainly covered in fabric. The tail section was all-wood, however, except for the metal-frame fabric-covered rudder and elevator. Aside from the fitment of an all-weather canopy for Canadian versions, the Cornell's fuselage and wing layout would remain unchanged throughout its production life. The same could not be said for its powerplant. A total of 270 PT-19s had been built (by Aeronca and St. Louis Aircraft Corporation, as well as Fairchild) by the time the re-engined PT-19A came on line in 1941.

A further 3700 had entered Army service when, in 1942, production was seriously affected by a shortage of Ranger inline engines. With engineless airframes backing up at three assembly lines in the Midwest, a solution to the problem was needed quickly, so Fairchild simply fitted an uncowled Continental R-670 radial to a standard PT-19A and produced the PT-23. The "new" aircraft proved to be so successful that a further 6000 were delivered before production finally ceased in 1944. Blind-flying variants of both the PT-19A and PT-23 were included within these production numbers, the aircraft (PT-19B and PT-23A) featuring full blind-flying instrumentation and a hood to cover the pupil's front cockpit during training flights. North of the border, the Canadians found the Fairchild design ideal for the Commonwealth Air Training Scheme, Fleet building substantial quantities of the PT-23 (Cornell I—93 examples) and PT-26A/B (Cornell II—1057 examples) under license.

SPECIFICATION (PT-19):

ACCOMMODATION:
Two pilots in tandem

DIMENSIONS:
LENGTH: 27 ft 8.50 in (8.45 m)
WINGSPAN: 36 ft 0 in (10.97 m)
HEIGHT: 7 ft 7.50 in (2.32 m)

WEIGHTS:
EMPTY: 2022 lb (917 kg)
MAX T/O: 2736 lb (1241 kg)

PERFORMANCE:
MAX SPEED: 122 mph (196 kmh)
RANGE: 400 miles (644 km)
POWERPLANT: Ranger L-440-C5
OUTPUT: 200 hp (149 kW)

FIRST FLIGHT DATE:
March 1939

FEATURES:
Monoplane wing layout; fixed undercarriage; close-cowled inline (PT-19) or exposed radial (PT-23) engine; tandem open cockpits

Ford JR/RR/C Series

17-seat, three-engined high-wing monoplane transport

A civil aviation icon of the late 1920s, the Ford Tri-Motor also found favor in far smaller numbers with both the Army and Navy. The culmination of three years work undertaken by designer Bill Stout with his series of all-metal cantilevered monoplanes, the prototype Tri-Motor was destroyed in a blaze at his factory on January 17, 1926. The Ford Motor Company immediately erected a new factory and commenced work on a replacement aircraft, known as the 4-AT. Subsequent flight testing proved the aircraft's ability, and production examples began reaching airlines both in the USA and overseas in late 1926. The largest all-metal aircraft built in America up to that time, the Tri-Motor was viewed with envious eyes by the cash-strapped military. The Navy would eventually buy just nine examples and the Army 13 between 1927 and 1931. Navy aircraft were initially designated JR-1/2/3s, depending on their wing and engine fits, although they all became RR-2/3/4s in 1930. The Army's Tri-Motors were variously designated C-3/4/9s, again according to their engines and wingspan.

SPECIFICATION (MODEL JR-3):

ACCOMMODATION:
Pilot, copilot, and 15 passengers

DIMENSIONS:
LENGTH: 50 ft 3 in (15.33 m)
WINGSPAN: 77 ft 10 in (23.50 m)
HEIGHT: 13 ft 6 in (4.14 m)

WEIGHTS:
EMPTY: 8149 lb (3696 kg)
MAX T/O: 13,499 lb (6123 kg)

PERFORMANCE:
MAX SPEED: 135 mph (216 kmh)
RANGE: 505 miles (808 km)
POWERPLANT: three Pratt & Whitney R-1340-88s
OUTPUT: 1350 hp (1007 kW)

FIRST FLIGHT DATE:
June 11, 1926 (4-AT)

FEATURES:
Single parasol-wing layout; three ringed radial engines, two mounted under the wings and the third on the nose; fixed undercarriage; corrugated-metal skinning

Great Lakes BG-1

two-seat, single-engined biplane dive-bomber

One of the less successful US manufacturers of military aircraft between the wars, the Great Lakes Aircraft Corporation succeeded in securing just one order from the Navy during the eight years of its existence from 1928 to 1936. The aircraft that finally made it onto carrier decks in late 1934 was the BG-1 dive-bomber, which was developed by the company using the experience it had gleaned from license-production of the Martin T4M torpedo-bomber in the late 1920s. Great Lakes designed and built the prototype XBG-1 in the ex-Martin factory in Cleveland, Ohio, the aircraft subsequently beating off the rival Consolidated XB2Y-1 to win a Navy dive-bomber contract in November 1933. Capable of carrying a 1000-lb bomb beneath its fuselage, 60 BG-1s were built in 1934-35. The only carrier-based squadron to receive aircraft was VB-3B aboard USS *Ranger*, this unit operating 19 BG-1s between late 1934 and mid-1938. Marine Corps squadrons VB-4M and VB-6M also flew the aircraft until they were relegated to training tasks in 1940.

SPECIFICATION:

ACCOMMODATION:
Pilot and observer/gunner

DIMENSIONS:
LENGTH: 28 ft 9 in (8.80 m)
WINGSPAN: 36 ft 0 in (10.97 m)
HEIGHT: 11 ft 0 in (3.35 m)

WEIGHTS:
EMPTY: 3903 lb (1770 kg)
MAX T/O: 6347 lb (2879 kg)

PERFORMANCE:
MAX SPEED: 188 mph (301 kmh)
RANGE: 539 miles (878 km)
POWERPLANT: Pratt & Whitney R-1535-82
OUTPUT: 750 hp (559 kW)

FIRST FLIGHT DATE:
Mid-1933

ARMAMENT:
One Browning 0.30-in machine gun mounted on upper fuselage and one on flexible mounting for observer/gunner; bomb load up to 1000 lb (454 kg) on centerline rack

FEATURES:
Tapered biplane wing layout; cowled radial engine; fixed undercarriage; enclosed cockpit

Grumman FF/SF

two-seat, single-engined biplane fighter/scout

Grumman's long-standing relationship with the Navy effectively started in 1930 when it was tasked with designing and manufacturing floats incorporating retracting land wheels. Building on this humble beginning, the company signed a contract with the Navy in April 1931 to construct a prototype two-seat fighter. Designated the XFF-1, this machine boasted a number of important firsts —the first fighter designed around Wright's powerful R-1820 Cyclone engine, the first Navy fighter built entirely of light alloy, and the first to feature a retractable undercarriage. The prototype topped 200 mph in testing, making it faster than any single-seat fighter then in service. The Navy ordered 27 FF-1 fighters and 33 SF-1 scouts in 1933, and in June of that same year the first FF-1s reached VF-5B, which was assigned to the *Lexington* air group. The SF-1s also served with this air group, equipping VS-3B from March 1934. All had been passed on to Reserve units by late 1936, with whom many of the FF-1s were fitted with dual controls and redesignated FF-2s.

SPECIFICATION:

ACCOMMODATION:
Pilot and observer/gunner

DIMENSIONS:
LENGTH: 24 ft 6 in (7.47 m)
WINGSPAN: 34 ft 6 in (10.51 m)
HEIGHT: 11 ft 1 in (3.40 m)

WEIGHTS:
EMPTY: 3300 lb (1500 kg)
MAX T/O: 4828 lb (2190 kg)

PERFORMANCE:
MAX SPEED: 207 mph (333 kmh)
RANGE: 920 miles (1480 km)
POWERPLANT: Wright R-1820-78 Cyclone
OUTPUT: 750 hp (559 kW)

FIRST FLIGHT DATE:
December 1931

ARMAMENT:
One fixed Browning 0.30-in machine gun on upper fuselage and two on flexible mounting for observer/gunner

FEATURES:
Biplane wing layout; radial engine; arrestor hook; N-shaped bracing struts; deep-bellied fuselage housing retractable undercarriage

Grumman JRF Goose

seven-seat, twin-engined high-wing utility amphibian

Initially built as a private venture for the civil market of the late 1930s, the G-21 Goose evoked immediate interest within the US military, with the Navy ordering one for evaluation in 1938. Designated the XJ3F-1, the prototype was subsequently followed by an order for 20 JRF-1AS in 1939. The first examples were employed as general transports, target tugs, and photographic platforms by both the Navy and Marine Corps. The next batch of ten, designated JRF-4S, could carry bombs or depth charges, and these were followed by variants for the Coast Guard and USAAC (where they were designated OA-9/-13s). The build-up to war in 1941 resulted in Grumman introducing the improved JRF-5, of which 184 examples were eventually built. At least 56 of these were supplied to the RAF as Goose I/IAS in 1943, and they performed navigational training, air-sea rescue, and general ferrying duties. After the war the surviving JRFs were sold into civilian hands, and many were re-engined with turbine powerplants to increase their longevity.

SPECIFICATION:

ACCOMMODATION:
Crew of two and up to five passengers

DIMENSIONS:
LENGTH: 38 ft 6 in (11.73 m)
WINGSPAN: 49 ft 0 in (14.94 m)
HEIGHT: 16 ft 2 in (4.93 m)

WEIGHTS:
EMPTY: 5425 lb (2461 kg)
MAX T/O: 8000 lb (3629 kg)

PERFORMANCE:
MAX SPEED: 201 mph (323 kmh)
RANGE: 640 miles (1030 km)
POWERPLANT: two Pratt & Whitney R-985-AN-6 Wasp Juniors
OUTPUT: 900 hp (670 kW)

FIRST FLIGHT DATE:
June 1937

ARMAMENT:
Two 250-lb (113 kg) bombs or depth charges on underwing racks

FEATURES:
High monoplane wing layout; cowled radial engine; floatplane hull, into which main wheels retract

Grumman JF/J2F Duck

three-seat, single-engined biplane utility amphibian

The first amphibian designed by legendary naval manufacturer Grumman, the Duck was heavily influenced by the company's premier production aircraft, the FF-1. Grumman also borrowed ideas from the Navy's then current amphibian, the Loening OL-9, as well as drawing on its own experience of building amphibian floats. The end result was the XJF-1, which the Navy evaluated as a "paper project" in 1932 and then funded for construction. First flown in April 1933, the aircraft performed without fault and the Navy ordered an initial production run of 27 JF-1s. The first of these was delivered in late 1934, and they soon began to replace the OL-9 in frontline service. The Grumman amphibian's rate of climb, maximum speed, and service ceiling were all vastly superior to its Loening predecessor, and the JF-1 proved popular in the general utility and observation roles. By 1936 examples had also started to reach VJ Squadron too, where they replaced elderly patrol and torpedo types.

Following production of small numbers of JF-2s and -3s, Grumman began manufacturing the J2F-1 in 1937. This aircraft was little changed from previous models, and 111 were built up to 1941 in four production batches. Among these were nine J2F-2As fitted with bomb racks for service with Marine Corps squadron VMS-3 on Neutrality Patrols from St. Thomas, in the Virgin Islands. The outbreak of war in Europe signaled an urgent expansion of the Navy, and with this came an order for 144 J2F-5s in 1940, along with official confirmation of the name Duck, which was already in widespread use in the fleet. The new variant featured a 950-hp Wright R-1820-50 radial engine and a long-chord cowling, which further boosted the aircraft's performance.

These were the last Ducks built by Grumman, but in the wake of the Pearl Harbor attack a further 330 J2F-6s were constructed by the Columbia Aircraft Corporation. The aircraft saw service both in Europe and the Pacific throughout World War II, flying antisubmarine and coastal patrols, air-sea-rescue missions, reconnaissance flights, target towing, and casualty evacuation.

SPECIFICATION (J2F-6):

ACCOMMODATION:
Pilot, observer/gunner, and radio operator

DIMENSIONS:
LENGTH: 34 ft 0 in (10.36 m)
WINGSPAN: 39 ft 0 in (11.89 m)
HEIGHT: 15 ft 1 in (4.60 m)

WEIGHTS:
EMPTY: 5445 lb (2470 kg)
MAX T/O: 7700 lb (3493 kg)

PERFORMANCE:
MAX SPEED: 188 mph (303 kmh)
RANGE: 780 miles (1255 km)
POWERPLANT: Wright R-1820-54 Cyclone
OUTPUT: 1050 hp (783 kW)

FIRST FLIGHT DATE:
April 24, 1933 (XJF-1)

ARMAMENT:
One Browning 0.30-in machine gun on flexible mounting for observer; two 100-lb (45-kg) bombs or 325-lb (147-kg) depth bombs on underwing racks

FEATURES:
Equal-span biplane wing layout; cowled radial engine; single main float, into which main wheels retract; wingtip floats

Grumman F2F/F3F

single-seat, single-engined biplane fighter

Buoyed by the success of its FF-1, Grumman took the logical step of designing a single-seat fighter along the same lines—metal-skinned fuselage, fabric-covered metal wings, big radial engine (in this case a Pratt & Whitney Twin Wasp Junior), and a retractable undercarriage. The design for the aircraft, designated the G-8 by Grumman, was submitted to the Navy in June 1932, and in November it received a contract to build a solitary XF2F-1 prototype.

First flown in October of the following year, the aircraft found favor with the Navy and 54 were ordered. Production aircraft featured a slightly bigger wing and cockpit, and the first examples were delivered to VF-2B (*Lexington*) and VF-3B (*Ranger*) in early 1935. Prior to F2F-1 production commencing in 1934, Grumman had begun work on the improved XF3F-1, which had wings of even greater span and a longer fuselage in an effort to improve the fighter's skittish handling and stability when operating at sea from carriers.

Some 54 F3F-1s were acquired in 1936 and issued to VF-5B (*Ranger*) and VF-6B (*Saratoga*), followed by 81 Wright R-1820-22 Cyclone-powered F3F-2s in 1938 for VF-6 (*Enterprise*) and Marine Corps units VMF-1 and VMF-2. A further 27 F3F-3s ordered by the Navy on June 21, 1938 were the last biplane fighters to be built for any of the US armed services, these aircraft serving with VF-5 (*Yorktown*) for little more than a year.

By 1941 none of the Grumman biplane fighters remained in fleet service, although 23 F2Fs and 117 F3Fs were being regularly flown at Naval Air Stations across America as advanced trainers and general hacks. During the fighter's brief time in the frontline, the Grumman design had proven itself both rugged and highly maneuverable, and many of the Navy's most influential fighter leaders of World War II (Butch O'Hare and Jimmy Thach, to name but two) "cut their teeth" operationally with the F3F in the years leading up to 1941.

SPECIFICATION (F3F-2):

ACCOMMODATION:
Pilot

DIMENSIONS:
LENGTH: 23 ft 2 in (7.07 m)
WINGSPAN: 32 ft 0 in (9.75 m)
HEIGHT: 9 ft 4 in (2.84 m)

WEIGHTS:
EMPTY: 3258 lb (1478 kg)
MAX T/O: 4502 lb (2042 kg)

PERFORMANCE:
MAX SPEED: 264 mph (425 kmh)
RANGE: 825 miles (1328 km)
POWERPLANT: Wright R-1820-22 Cyclone
OUTPUT: 850 hp (634 kW)

FIRST FLIGHT DATE:
October 18, 1933 (XF2F-1)

ARMAMENT:
One Browning 0.30-in and one 0.50-in machine gun forward of cockpit; single 116-lb (53-kg) bombs on racks under each wing

FEATURES:
Biplane wing layout; radial engine; arrestor hook; N-shaped bracing struts; deep-bellied fuselage housing retractable undercarriage

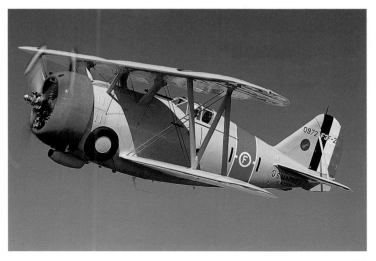

Hall PH

six-seat, twin-engined biplane patrol/search-and-rescue flying boat

The last biplane flying boats to see service with the Navy, the Hall PH series was closely modeled on the NAF PN family of the 1920s. The Hall Aluminum Company had been formed in 1927 to develop the prototype of a new flying boat based on the hull design of the highly successful Felixstowe F series. The XPH-1 was duly ordered by the Navy in December 1927, this machine utilizing the PN-11's hull shape and wing, but with a larger fin and rudder and Wright GR-1750 engines. Following flight testing, Hall received a contract in June 1930 to build nine PH-1s, the first of which appeared in October of the following year. A number of improvements had by then been incorporated, including a change of powerplant (now two Wright R-1820-86s) and an enclosure for the cockpit. The Coast Guard received seven PH-2s for air-sea-rescue work in 1936, followed by a further seven PH-3s three years later. The latter machines, now armed, also flew antisubmarine patrols from late 1941 until they were retired.

SPECIFICATION (PH-3):

ACCOMMODATION:
Pilot and copilot, flight engineer, navigator, and two gunners

DIMENSIONS:
LENGTH: 51 ft 0 in (15.54 m)
WINGSPAN: 72 ft 10 in (22.20 m)
HEIGHT: 19 ft 10 in (6.05 m)

WEIGHTS:
EMPTY: 9614 lb (4361 kg)
MAX T/O: 17,679 lb (8019 kg)

PERFORMANCE:
MAX SPEED: 159 mph (256 kmh)
RANGE: 1937 miles (3117 km)
POWERPLANT: two Wright R-1820-F51 Cyclones
OUTPUT: 1500 hp (1119 kW)

FIRST FLIGHT DATE:
December 1929

ARMAMENT:
Two Lewis 0.30-in machine guns on flexible mount in the bow and two in dorsal gun hatches behind wings; maximum depth charge load of 1000 lb (454 kg)

FEATURES:
Biplane wing layout; cowled radial engines; boat-shaped hull; wingtip floats; large single fin; enclosed cockpit

Howard UC-70 and GH/NH Nightingale

four/five-seat, single-engined high-wing utility aircraft

Designed by Ben Howard of the Howard Aircraft Corporation, the GH-1 started life as the DGA-15 for the civilian market. DGA stood for Darn Good Airplane, and Howard had perfected his trade through a series of limited-run, high-performance, cabin monoplanes stretching back to 1923. His DGA-6, called *Mister Mulligan*, proved so advanced that it won all three major American air races in 1934. The Howard Aircraft Corporation was set up in 1937 to build on the success of the DGA-6, and in 1941, 34 DGA-15s were ordered by the Navy as GH-1 general utility aircraft. The first examples entered service just as America was plunged into war, and additional orders for 131 GH-2s and 115 GH-3s followed—many of these machines were converted into Nightingale air ambulances. The final pro-duction variant for the Navy was the NH-1, 205 of which were used as instrument trainers until war's end. Although never ordering aircraft directly from Howard, the USAAF commandeered 20 DGA-15s in 1941, designated them UC-70s and deployed them as light transportation/communications types.

SPECIFICATION (GH-1):

ACCOMMODATION:
Pilot, copilot, and two/three passengers

DIMENSIONS:
LENGTH: 25 ft 8 in (7.86 m)
WINGSPAN: 38 ft 0 in (11.58 m)
HEIGHT: 8 ft 5 in (2.57 m)

WEIGHTS:
EMPTY: 2700 lb (1225 kg)
MAX T/O: 4350 lb (1973 kg)

PERFORMANCE:
MAX SPEED: 201 mph (323 kmh)
RANGE: 1260 miles (2028 km)
POWERPLANT: Pratt & Whitney R-985 Wasp Junior
OUTPUT: 450 hp (336 kW)

FIRST FLIGHT DATE:
Mid-1941

FEATURES:
High wing; cowled radial engine; fixed undercarriage; cabin-style cockpit; two-bladed propeller

Keystone Light Bomber Series

five-seat, twin-engined biplane heavy bomber

Keystone's Light Bomber Series began life being built by Huff-Daland in 1923 as the LB-1 Pegasus, which was a single-engined machine that carried bombs in its fuselage. Nine service test aircraft were built, but these were found to be underpowered. The twin-engined XLB-3 was ordered in its place, and by the time it was delivered, the company had been reorganized as Keystone. The bomber entered production as the LB-5 Pirate, ten of which were built in 1926, followed by 25 LB-5As, which had twin tails rather than a single tailfin. The bomber's tapered wing was replaced by a straight-chord version with the arrival of the LB-6 Panther in 1927. This version was in turn re-engined as the LB-7 in 1928-29, and 18 were delivered to the Army.

LB-6/7s were used by the 2nd BG, which was the sole US-based bomb group up to 1928, and the Hawaii-based 5th Composite Group. Minor rebuilds of the LB design, featuring different engines and modified twin and single-fin layouts, covered the LB-8 to -14 designations that saw the aircraft built into the early 1930s. The major production variants were the LB-10/13/14 series, 73 of which were constructed up to 1932. Following the USAAC's overhaul of its designation system in 1930, when the separate designation categories for light (LB) and heavy (HB) bombers were scrapped and a new single bomber (B) category introduced, 63 LB-10As entered service as B-3As. By now the tried and tested single fin and rudder layout had been firmly adopted by the Army, although it kept upgrading to more powerful versions of Wright's Cyclone or Pratt & Whitney's Hornet engine throughout the later years of the bomber's long production life. The final versions to enter service were the B-4A (25 built), B-5A (27 re-engined B-3AS), and B-6A (32 completed in 1932). The sheer number of Keystone bombers built allowed the Army to form additional bomb groups in 1928 in the form of the US-based 7th and 19th BGs, as well as units in Hawaii, the Philippines, and the Panama Canal Zone.

SPECIFICATION (B-3A):

ACCOMMODATION:
Pilot/copilot, bombardier, and front and rear gunners

DIMENSIONS:
LENGTH: 48 ft 10 in (14.89 m)
WINGSPAN: 74 ft 8 in (22.76 m)
HEIGHT: 15 ft 9 in (4.80 m)

WEIGHTS:
EMPTY: 7705 lb (3495 kg)
MAX T/O: 12,952 lb (5875 kg)

PERFORMANCE:
MAX SPEED: 114 mph (182 kmh)
RANGE: 855 miles (1368 km)
POWERPLANT: two Pratt & Whitney Hornet R-1690-3s
OUTPUT: 1050 hp (783 kW)

FIRST FLIGHT DATE:
Late 1923 (XLB-1)

ARMAMENT:
Single Lewis 0.30-in machine gun on flexible mount in the nose and in upper and lower mid-fuselage positions; maximum bomb load of 2500 lb (1134 kg) in bomb bay

FEATURES:
Equal-span biplane wing layout (early versions had tapered wings); two uncowled radial engines between wings; fixed undercarriage; open cockpit and gunners' positions

Loening OA/OL

two-seat, single-engined biplane utility amphibian

The Loening Aeronautical Engineering Company built a series of unique designs during its 11-year life between 1917 and 1928. Of these, the most successful was the OA/OL amphibian, which featured a large single float faired into the fuselage of the aircraft. The latter also housed the retractable undercarriage. This arrangement was made possible through the introduction of the inverted Liberty engine in 1923, which raised the propeller high enough for the float to be attached directly to the fuselage, rather than on separate struts. The Army became the type's launch customer, ordering ten COA-1s and fifteen OA-1s (with a revised tail) in 1924-25. The Navy acquired five identical OL-2s in 1925, followed by four OL-3s and six Packard-engined OL-4s. The final Army variants were nine OA-1Bs, ten OA-1Cs, and eight OA-2s, the latter powered by Wright V-1460 engines. The Packard powerplant featured in the Navy's 28 OL-6s, after which Loening switched to the Pratt & Whitney Wasp radial for its 20 OL-8s, 20 OL-8As (with carrier arrestor gear), and 26 OL-9s.

SPECIFICATION (OA-1):

ACCOMMODATION:
Pilot and observer/gunner

DIMENSIONS:
LENGTH: 34 ft 7 in (10.40 m)
WINGSPAN: 45 ft 0 in (13.72 m)
HEIGHT: 12 ft 9 in (3.89 m)

WEIGHTS:
EMPTY: 3440 lb (1560 kg)
MAX T/O: 5010 lb (2273 kg)

PERFORMANCE:
MAX SPEED: 119 mph (192 kmh)
RANGE: 600 miles (960 km)
POWERPLANT: Liberty V-1650-1
OUTPUT: 400 hp (298 kW)

FIRST FLIGHT DATE:
1923 (XCOA-1)

ARMAMENT:
One fixed Marlin 0.30-in machine gun in upper fuselage and one/two Lewis 0.30-in machine guns on flexible mounting for observer

FEATURES:
Equal-span biplane wing layout; cowled inline engine or exposed radial engine; single main float, into which main wheels retract; wingtip floats; angular fin/rudder

Martin MB-2/NBS-1

four-seat, twin-engined biplane night bomber

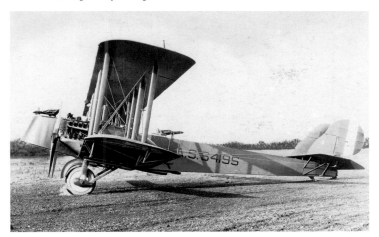

A direct development of Martin's hugely impressive MB-1 of 1918, the MB-2 was effectively the same aircraft, but with an increased wingspan, shorter fuselage, simplified landing gear, and internal bomb bay. Bought by the Army as a night bomber only, the MB-2 sacrificed the speed, range, and maneuverability of the MB-1 for a heavier bomb load. Twenty were ordered in 1920, with the aircraft's designation changing to NBS-1 (night bomber short-range) by the time it reached squadron service. Although a follow-on order for 100 machines was canceled, the NBS-1 was built under license by Curtiss (25), LWF (35), and Aeromarine (25). The Aeromarine aircraft were all shipped to Army units overseas in Hawaii, the Panama Canal Zone, and the Philippines. Never to drop bombs in anger, the NBS-1 nevertheless earned lasting fame as the aircraft used by maverick Gen. Billy Mitchell to sink the ex-German battleship *Ostfriesland* in the controversial bombing exercises of July 1921. The unit involved was the 2nd BG, which flew the NBS-1 until replaced by Keystone bombers in 1927.

SPECIFICATION:

ACCOMMODATION:
Pilot, copilot, and two gunners

DIMENSIONS:
LENGTH: 42 ft 8 in (13 m)
WINGSPAN: 74 ft 2 in (22.61 m)
HEIGHT: 14 ft 8 in (4.47 m)

WEIGHTS:
EMPTY: 7269 lb (3297 kg)
MAX T/O: 12,064 lb (5472 kg)

PERFORMANCE:
MAX SPEED: 99 mph (159 kmh)
RANGE: 558 miles (900 km)
POWERPLANT: two Liberty 12AS
OUTPUT: 840 hp (626 kW)

FIRST FLIGHT DATE:
1920

ARMAMENT:
Two flexible Marlin 0.30-in machine guns in nose, two in rear dorsal cockpit, and one in rear ventral hatch; maximum bomb load of 3000 lb (1361 kg) in bomb bay and on underwing racks

FEATURES:
Equal-span biplane wing layout; engines mounted above lower wings; two-wheeled under-carriage; open cockpit; gunner in extreme nose; twin-tail layout

Martin T3M/T4M

three-seat, single-engined biplane land/seaplane torpedo-bomber scout

Having built Curtiss's CS/SC-1s under license in the early 1920s, Martin was well placed to offer the Navy a replacement torpedo-bomber scout when required in 1925. A total of 24 T3M-1s were duly bought, the aircraft being able to operate on wheels or floats. With this initial design, the pilot and bombardier sat side-by-side, but by the time examples arrived in the fleet, Martin was already building the improved T3M-2, which featured a more conventional tandem seating arrangement. Some 100 of these were delivered, and they were initially issued to VT-1s on *Lexington* and VT-2B on *Langley*. Shore-based floatplane units also received T3M-2s as the aircraft became standard equipment for all torpedo squadrons. The Navy changed its preference from inline to radial engines in 1927, and Martin moved with the times by building 102 Pratt & Whitney Hornet-engined T4M-1s in 1928-29. The final variants delivered to the Navy were constructed by Great Lakes as the TG-1 (18) and TG-2 (32) in 1930, and these remained in fleet service until 1937.

SPECIFICATION (T4M-1):

ACCOMMODATION:
Pilot, bombardier, and gunner

DIMENSIONS:
LENGTH: 35 ft 7 in (10.84 m)
WINGSPAN: 53 ft 0 in (16.15 m)
HEIGHT: 14 ft 9 in (4.50 m)

WEIGHTS:
EMPTY: 3931 lb (1783 kg)
MAX T/O: 8071 lb (3661 kg)

PERFORMANCE:
MAX SPEED: 114 mph (183 kmh)
RANGE: 363 miles (585 km)
POWERPLANT: Pratt & Whitney
Hornet R-1690-24
OUTPUT: 525 hp (391 kW)

FIRST FLIGHT DATE:
1925 (T3M-1)

ARMAMENT:
One flexible Browning 0.30-in machine gun in rear cockpit; one 1835-lb (832-kg) torpedo, externally carried

FEATURES:
Equal-span biplane wing layout (T3M-2/T4M); close-cowled inline engine (T3M-1/2) or uncowled radial (T4M-1/TG-1/2); fixed undercarriage or twin pontoon floats; open cockpits

Martin BM

two-seat, single-engined biplane dive/torpedo-bomber

The employment of dive-bombing techniques by Navy and Marine Corps fighter-bomber units in the 1920s led to the Bureau of Aeronautics issuing a specification for a special-purpose dive-bomber in 1928. One of the main design criteria for this aircraft was that it had to possess the ability to pull out of a terminal velocity dive with its 1000-lb bomb still attached. Both the NAF and Martin submitted designs, and the latter company's XT5M-1 prototype secured a production order for 12 aircraft in April 1931. Designated the BM-1 in fleet service, the first of these was delivered five months after the order was placed. Also capable of performing as a torpedo-bomber, the first BM-1s were issued to VT-1S aboard *Lexington*. An additional 16 BM-2s were ordered in October 1931, these aircraft being virtually identical to the earlier production batch. Finally, four more BM-1s were acquired in 1932. BM-1/2s equipped VB-1B (formerly VT-1S) and VB-3B, aboard *Langley*, until 1937, when they were relegated to shore duty and finally scrapped in 1940.

SPECIFICATION:

ACCOMMODATION:
Pilot and gunner

DIMENSIONS:
LENGTH: 28 ft 9 in (8.80 m)
WINGSPAN: 41 ft 0 in (12.49 m)
HEIGHT: 12 ft 4 in (3.77 m)

WEIGHTS:
EMPTY: 3662 lb (1661 kg)
MAX T/O: 6218 lb (2820 kg)

PERFORMANCE:
MAX SPEED: 146 mph (234 kmh)
RANGE: 413 miles (661 km)
POWERPLANT: Pratt & Whitney
R-1690-44
OUTPUT: 625 hp (466 kW)

FIRST FLIGHT DATE:
1930

ARMAMENT:
One fixed Browning 0.30-in machine gun in nose and one flexibly mounted in rear cockpit; one 1000-lb (454-kg) bomb or one 1835-lb (832-kg) torpedo externally carried

FEATURES:
Biplane wing layout, with upper wing slightly swept; uncowled radial engine; fixed under-carriage; open cockpits; arrestor hook

Martin P2M/P3M

five-seat, twin-engined high-wing monoplane patrol flying boat

Martin's knowledge of flying-boat production initially came from constructing aircraft designed by other manufacturers such as the NAF and Curtiss. It built no fewer than 45 NAF PN series machines in 1930-31, followed by the prototype Curtiss XPY-1. The latter was itself a modified NAF design, which became the Navy's first monoplane flying boat. Following testing, a modified machine was ordered as the P2M-2, this aircraft featuring two, rather than three, Wright radial engines in nacelles on the leading edge of the large monoplane wing. The Navy awarded Martin with a contract to build nine aircraft in this twin-engined configuration as P3M-1s in June 1929, and the first of these appeared in February 1931. The remaining eight machines were fitted with Pratt & Whitney R-1690-32 Hornet radial engines, and they entered service with the designation P3M-2. These aircraft also featured an enclosure over the pilots' cockpit. P3M-1/2s served briefly with VP-10s in 1931-32, but they met with little operational success and were relegated to training and utility duties until scrapped in the late 1930s.

SPECIFICATION (P3M-2):

ACCOMMODATION:
Pilot and copilot, flight engineer/gunner, navigator/gunner, and observer/gunner

DIMENSIONS:
LENGTH: 61 ft 9 in (18.86 m)
WINGSPAN: 100 ft 0 in (30.48 m)
HEIGHT: 16 ft 8 in (5.12 m)

WEIGHTS:
EMPTY: 10,032 lb (4550 kg)
MAX T/O: 17,977 lb (8154 kg)

PERFORMANCE:
MAX SPEED: 115 mph (184 kmh)
RANGE: 1010 miles (1616 km)
POWERPLANT: two Pratt & Whitney R-1690-32s
OUTPUT: 1050 hp (783 kW)

FIRST FLIGHT DATE:
Early 1929 (XPY-1)

ARMAMENT:
Two Browning 0.30-in machine guns on flexible mount in the bow and two in dorsal hatch behind wings

FEATURES:
High-wing layout; radial engines; boat-shaped hull; twin fins; enclosed cockpit on P3M-2 only

Martin B-10/12/14

four-seat, twin-engined monoplane bomber

The first all-metal monoplane bomber to enter full-scale production for the Army Air Corps, the B-10/12/14 family of aircraft were revolutionary in many ways. Derived from the Model 123, which featured such advances as cantilever monoplane wings, flaps, stressed-skin construction, advanced engine cowls, retractable landing gear, an internal bomb bay with power-driven doors, and variable-pitch propellers, the B-10 was much faster than the USAAC's pursuit fighters of the day. Some 152 B-10B/12/14s were built, the first of which arrived at Wright Field in July 1935. Production deliveries to Langley Field began in December of that year, and were completed by August 1936. The B-10B served with the 2nd BG at Langley, the 9th BG at Mitchell Field, the 19th BG at March Field (alongside the similar YB-10), the 6th BG in the Panama Canal Zone and the 28th BG in the Philippines, while the increased-range B-12A performed coastal patrols. The Martin bombers remained in frontline service until replaced by B-17s and B-18s in the late 1930s, after which they performed secondary roles.

SPECIFICATION (B-12B):

ACCOMMODATION:
Pilot, radio operator, and two gunners

DIMENSIONS:
LENGTH: 44 ft 9 in (13.68 m)
WINGSPAN: 70 ft 7 in (21.54 m)
HEIGHT: 15 ft 5 in (4.72 m)

WEIGHTS:
EMPTY: 9681 lb (4391 kg)
MAX T/O: 16,400 lb (7439 kg)

PERFORMANCE:
MAX SPEED: 213 mph (341 kmh)
RANGE: 1240 miles (1984 km)
POWERPLANT: two Wright R-1820-33S
OUTPUT: 1550 hp (1156 kW)

FIRST FLIGHT DATE:
June 1934 (YB-10)

ARMAMENT:
Three Browning 0.30-in machine guns on flexible mounts in the nose, rear cockpit, and rear ventral-hatch positions; maximum bomb load of 1000 lb (454 kg) carried in bomb bay

FEATURES:
Monoplane wing layout; retractable undercarriage; twin radial engines; nose turret; bomb bay

Naval Aircraft Factory TS

single-seat, single-engined biplane fighter sea/landplane

The NAF TS-1 was the very first American airplane to be designed from the outset for carrier-borne operations. Although created by the Bureau of Aeronautics, 34 of the 39 built were constructed by Curtiss under contract—the remaining five were completed by the NAF. Built entirely of wood, with fabric covering, the aircraft was unusual in having its fuselage placed midway between the wings. As with most naval aircraft of the period, the TS-1's wheels could be quickly replaced with floats if required—the seaplane variant had to be craned into the water for takeoff when embarked with the fleet. The prototype TS-1 made its maiden flight in May 1922, just two months after the Navy's first carrier, USS *Langley*, had been commissioned. Curtiss-built fighters went to sea with the vessel six months later, serving with VF-1. This unit also flew float-equipped TS-1s from battleships in 1925-26, following in the footsteps of VO-1, which had first operated the floatplane variant from destroyers, cruisers, and battleships in 1922.

SPECIFICATION:

ACCOMMODATION:
One pilot

DIMENSIONS:
LENGTH: 22 ft 1 in (6.73 m)
WINGSPAN: 25 ft 0 in (7.62 m)
HEIGHT: 9 ft 7 in (2.90 m)

WEIGHTS:
EMPTY: 1240 lb (562 kg)
MAX T/O: 2133 lb (967 kg)

PERFORMANCE:
MAX SPEED: 123 mph (198 kmh)
RANGE: 482 miles (775 km)
POWERPLANT: Wright (Lawrance) J-4
OUTPUT: 200 hp (149 kW)

FIRST FLIGHT DATE:
May 1922

ARMAMENT:
One fixed Marlin 0.30-in machine gun in upper fuselage

FEATURES:
Equal-span biplane wing layout; exposed radial engine; fuselage suspended between wings; N-shaped bracing struts

Naval Aircraft Factory PN

four-seat, twin-engined biplane patrol flying boat

The long-lived PN Series of flying boats were essentially improved versions of the F-5/6L flying boats that had served the Navy so well in World War I. Featuring metal-framed wings with a deeper section profile, the first to appear was the PN-7 in 1922, followed closely by the metal-hulled and re-engined PN-8. Further revisions were included in the PN-9 and -10, of which five were built in total. At this point the Navy switched almost exclusively to radial engines for its aircraft, and following a succession of record flights in 1928, the Wright Cyclone-powered PN-12 was ordered into production. With the NAF unable to handle large orders, PN-12 production was split between Douglas (25 PD-1s), Martin (30 PM-1s and 25 twin-tailed PM-2s), and Keystone (18 twin-tailed PK-1s). Aside from their twin-tails, the PM-2/PK-1s used Hornet radials and featured a redesigned hull that eliminated the sponsons. The aircraft also had an enclosed cockpit. PN series flying boats saw widespread service on both the Pacific and Atlantic coasts, and overseas, until the late 1930s.

SPECIFICATION (PM-1):

ACCOMMODATION:
Pilot and copilot, navigator, and two gunners

DIMENSIONS:
LENGTH: 49 ft 2 in (14.95 m)
WINGSPAN: 72 ft 10 in (22.20 m)
HEIGHT: 16 ft 9 in (5.10 m)

WEIGHTS:
EMPTY: 7669 lb (3479 kg)
MAX T/O: 14,122 lb (6406 kg)

PERFORMANCE:
MAX SPEED: 114 mph (183 kmh)
RANGE: 1937 miles (3117 km)
POWERPLANT: two Wright R-1820-D Cyclones
OUTPUT: 1150 hp (858 kW)

FIRST FLIGHT DATE:
1922 (PN-7)

ARMAMENT:
Two Lewis 0.30-in machine guns on flexible mount in the bow and two in dorsal gun hatches behind wings; maximum depth charge load of 1000 lb (454 kg)

FEATURES:
Biplane wing layout; both cowled inline and exposed radial engines; boat-shaped hull; sponsons on early PNs; wingtip floats; large single fin or twin fins

Naval Aircraft Factory N3N

two-seat, single-engined biplane land/seaplane trainer

Having designed and manufactured aircraft uniquely tailored to its needs throughout the interwar years, the final NAF design to be mass-produced was the N3N primary trainer. Built to replace the Consolidated NY-2S and -3S of the 1920s, the prototype XN3N-1 flew for the first time in August 1935, and following successful trials in both land- and seaplane configurations, an order for 179 production N3N-1s was placed. Although similar in layout to Consolidated's PT/NY and the new Stearman NS, the N3N featured more rugged bolted steel-tube fuselage construction. The first examples were powered by the Wright J-5 radial, although this obsolescent engine was eventually replaced by the R-760 Whirlwind from the same source. The engine swap resulted in a designation change to N3N-3, and a further 816 trainers were procured from 1938 onward. The N3N remained in the primary training role until 1945, after which a handful of seaplane-configured N3N-3s serving with the Naval Academy became the last biplanes to be retired from US military service in 1961.

SPECIFICATION (N3N-3):

ACCOMMODATION:
Two pilots in tandem

DIMENSIONS:
LENGTH: 25 ft 6 in (7.77 m)
WINGSPAN: 34 ft 0 in (10.36 m)
HEIGHT: 10 ft 10 in (3.30 m)

WEIGHTS:
EMPTY: 2090 lb (948 kg)
MAX T/O: 2792 lb (1266 kg)

PERFORMANCE:
MAX SPEED: 126 mph (203 kmh)
RANGE: 470 miles (756 km)
POWERPLANT: Wright R-760-2 Whirlwind
OUTPUT: 235 hp (175 kw)

FIRST FLIGHT DATE:
August 1935

FEATURES:
Biplane wing layout; cowled (N3N-1) and uncowled (N3N-3) radial engine; N-shaped bracing struts; floats for seaplane variant

North American BT-9/14 and NJ-1

two-seat, single-engined monoplane trainer

The BT-9 was the USAAC version of North American Aviation's (NAA) private-venture NA-16 basic trainer. Flown in prototype form in April 1935, the NA-16 revealed performance figures near equal to the Army Air Corps' frontline combat aircraft of the time. Ordered into production as the BT-9, the USAAC took delivery of its first example in April 1936. On the strength of this initial order, NAA moved into an all-new factory in Inglewood, California. A total of 226 BT-9s were built in three different variants (A-, B-, and C-models), while the Navy received 40 NJ-1s, fitted with a 600-hp Pratt & Whitney R-1340 Wasp radial. NAA then produced the BT-14, which had its fabric fuselage covering replaced with lightweight metal sheeting, a revised fin/rudder shape, and refined wing planform. The aircraft also featured a 450-hp Wright R-985 engine. Some 251 were produced for the USAAC, and export orders for the trainer were received from several nations. All BT-9/14s were eventually replaced by the improved Texan from 1941.

SPECIFICATION (BT-9B):

ACCOMMODATION:
Two pilots in tandem

DIMENSIONS:
LENGTH: 27 ft 7 in (8.39 m)
WINGSPAN: 42 ft 0 in (12.80 m)
HEIGHT: 13 ft 7 in (4.13 m)

WEIGHTS:
EMPTY: 3314 lb (1500 kg)
MAX T/O: 4471 lb (2030 kg)

PERFORMANCE:
MAX SPEED: 170 mph (274 kmh)
RANGE: 882 miles (1420 km)
POWERPLANT: Wright R-975-7
OUTPUT: 400 hp (298 kW)

FIRST FLIGHT DATE:
April 1935

FEATURES:
Monoplane wing; fixed undercarriage; close-cowled radial engine; tailwheel

North American NA-50/-68 and P-64

single-seat, single-engined monoplane fighter

A low-cost fighter derived from the NA-16 trainer, the NA-50 was aimed at smaller air forces, which had neither the cash nor the technical expertise to operate the latest monoplane fighters emerging from Europe and the USA. NAA designers reduced the NA-16's seating to one, made the undercarriage retractable, fitted a more powerful Wright R-1820 engine, and armed the fighter with two 0.30-in machine guns. Only seven NA-50s were built, following an order from Peru in January 1938. Used in combat against Ecuador in 1941, the last examples were retired 20 years later. The NA-68 was very similar to the NA-50 (the former had a longer chord cowling, redesigned wingtips and tail surfaces, and two underwing-mounted 20-mm cannon, as well as the 0.30-in guns), the Royal Siam (Thai) Air Force ordering six in 1939 for delivery in 1941. However, Siam was invaded by Japan before it received the fighters, and they were used by the USAAC (with the designation P-64) in the advanced fighter-trainer role instead.

SPECIFICATION (NA-68):

ACCOMMODATION:
Pilot

DIMENSIONS:
LENGTH: 27 ft 0 in (8.23 m)
WINGSPAN: 37 ft 3 in (11.35 m)
HEIGHT: 9 ft 0 in (2.74 m)

WEIGHTS:
EMPTY: 4660 lb (2114 kg)
MAX T/O: 5990 lb (2717 kg)

PERFORMANCE:
MAX SPEED: 270 mph (435 kmh)
RANGE: 630 miles (1014 km)
POWERPLANT: Wright R-1820-77
Cyclone 9
OUTPUT: 870 hp (649 kW)

FIRST FLIGHT DATE:
Early 1939

ARMAMENT:
Two 20-mm cannon in underwing pods and two fixed Browning 0.30-in machine guns in the wings

FEATURES:
Monoplane wing; retractable undercarriage; close-cowled radial engine; tailwheel

North American O-47

three-seat, single-engined monoplane observation aircraft

The O-47 was developed by General Aviation (the precursor to North American Aviation) in response to an Army specification for an observation aircraft. The aircraft broke the mold for this type of machine, for unlike its predecessors, it was a low-wing monoplane with an enclosed cockpit, rather than an open-cockpit parasol/biplane design. The XO-47 prototype was evaluated in late 1935 by the Army, and the aircraft was praised for the field of view it afforded the observer, who had a glazed under-fuselage station immediately beneath the cockpit. NAA received contracts in 1937 for 173 O-47As, these machines being powered by 975-hp Cyclones. An additional 74 O-47Bs, fitted with 1060-hp R-1820-57 engines, were also built. Exercises in 1941 demonstrated shortcomings in the O-47, with commercially available light airplanes proving more capable of operating with troops, while fighters and twin-engined bombers performed reconnaissance and photographic duties. Thus, in World War II, O-47s were restricted to flying coastal and antisubmarine patrols, and towing target tugs.

SPECIFICATION (O-47A):

ACCOMMODATION:
Pilot, observer, and gunner

DIMENSIONS:
LENGTH: 33 ft 7 in (10.24 m)
WINGSPAN: 46 ft 4 in (14.12 m)
HEIGHT: 12 ft 2 in (3.71 m)

WEIGHTS:
EMPTY: 5980 lb (2712 kg)
MAX T/O: 7636 lb (3463 kg)

PERFORMANCE:
MAX SPEED: 221 mph (355 kmh)
RANGE: 750 miles (1207 km)
POWERPLANT: Wright R-1820-49 Cyclone
OUTPUT: 975 hp (727 kW)

FIRST FLIGHT DATE:
June 1935

ARMAMENT:
One fixed Browning 0.30-in machine gun in starboard wing and one Browning 0.30-in machine gun on flexible mount in rear cockpit

FEATURES:
Monoplane wing; retractable undercarriage; close-cowled radial engine; deep center fuselage, fixed tailwheel

Northrop A-17/A-33

two-seat, single-engined monoplane attack aircraft

Developed from the Gamma transport as a private-venture light attack aircraft, the Northrop Gamma 2C was acquired for evaluation by the USAAC in June 1934. Designated the YA-13, the aircraft was re-engined and redesignated the XA-16 soon afterward. Northrop was issued with a contract to build 110 A-17s in 1935, and the first production aircraft were delivered to the USAAC in December of that year. That same month Northrop was awarded a second contract for the improved A-17A. The new version had a retractable undercarriage and was powered by the 825-hp Pratt & Whitney R-1535-13 engine. A total of 129 were built, although 93 of these saw only 18 months of service with the USAAC before being returned to Douglas (which had acquired 49 percent of the Northrop A-17 stock in 1937) for sale to the UK and France. Douglas also developed the Model 8A for export, and 34 were ordered by Peru in 1941. However, 31 were commandeered by the Army in 1942 and impressed into service as A-33s.

SPECIFICATION (A-17A):

ACCOMMODATION:
Pilot and gunner

DIMENSIONS:
LENGTH: 31 ft 8 in (9.65 m)
WINGSPAN: 47 ft 9 in (14.55 m)
HEIGHT: 12 ft 0 in (3.66 m)

WEIGHTS:
EMPTY: 5106 lb (2316 kg)
MAX T/O: 7543 lb (3421 kg)

PERFORMANCE:
MAX SPEED: 220 mph (354 kmh)
RANGE: 730 miles (1175 km)
POWERPLANT: Pratt & Whitney R-1535-13 Twin Wasp Junior
OUTPUT: 825 hp (615 kW)

FIRST FLIGHT DATE:
Fall 1934

ARMAMENT:
Four fixed Browning 0.30-in machine guns in the wings and one Browning 0.30-in machine gun on flexible mount in rear cockpit; maximum bomb load of 900 lb (408 kg) internally or 650 lb (295 kg) on underwing racks

FEATURES:
Monoplane wing; fixed undercarriage (A-17) and retractable undercarriage (A-17A); close-cowled radial engine

Northrop BT

two-seat, single-engined monoplane scout/dive-bomber

Loosely based on the Army's A-17, the BT was a dedicated dive-bomber and scout that was offered to the Navy in prototype form as the XBT-1 following it first flight in August 1935. Unlike the A-17, this aircraft had a semi-retractable undercarriage and split trailing-edge flaps—the latter were crucial for carrier-based aircraft, which required delicate handling at slow speeds around the ship when making their landing approach. Following minor refinements to the XBT-1, the Navy ordered 54 examples as the BT-1. Deliveries commenced to VB-5 in April 1938, followed by VB-6, and finally, VB-3. The aircraft remained in fleet service until 1941, after which survivors were consolidated within VJ-3 and used as trainers and utility "hacks." The final examples were retired in 1943. Northrop also offered the Navy a replacement XBT-2, with fully retractable gear, a Wright radial, and revised canopy and tail, but by the time the aircraft was ready for flight-testing in June 1940 Northrop had become a division of Douglas, and the XBT-2 was redesignated the SBD Dauntless.

SPECIFICATION:

ACCOMMODATION:
Pilot and observer/gunner

DIMENSIONS:
LENGTH: 31 ft 8 in (9.65 m)
WINGSPAN: 41 ft 6 in (12.67 m)
HEIGHT: 9 ft 11 in (2.77 m)

WEIGHTS:
EMPTY: 4606 lb (2089 kg)
MAX T/O: 7197 lb (3264 kg)

PERFORMANCE:
MAX SPEED: 222 mph (355 kmh)
RANGE: 1150 miles (1840 km)
POWERPLANT: Pratt & Whitney R-1535-94
OUTPUT: 825 hp (615 kW)

FIRST FLIGHT DATE:
August 1935

ARMAMENT:
One fixed Browning 0.30-in machine gun in fuselage forward of the cockpit and one Browning 0.30-in machine gun on flexible mount in rear cockpit; one 1000-lb (454-kg) bomb on underfuselage rack

FEATURES:
Monoplane wing; semi-retractable undercarriage; close-cowled radial engine; fixed tailwheel; arrestor hook

Republic P-43 Lancer

single-seat, single-engined monoplane fighter

The first fighter to emerge from the newly formed Republic Aviation Corporation, the P-43 Lancer relied heavily on the Seversky P-35 for its overall layout due to the fact that both fighters had been created by Alexander Kartveli and his engineering team. The primary features that distinguished the P-43 from the smaller P-35 were its turbosupercharged Pratt & Whitney Twin Wasp R-1830-35 engine and large oval cowling, an inward retracting undercarriage housed in a wing that had dihedral from the roots, a revised canopy, and extra wing guns. The Army acquired 13 YP-43s in 1940, and after a thorough examination of these machines, committed to 54 P-43s, 80 P-43As (with the more powerful R-1830-49 engine), and 143 P-43A-1s, which had bigger wing guns and bomb racks. Although capable of speeds up to 356 mph, and with a service ceiling of 38,000 ft, the P-43 had already been rendered obsolete due to fighter development in Europe by the time it entered service in May 1941. Most Lancers, therefore, served as advanced fighter trainers.

SPECIFICATION (P-43A-1):

ACCOMMODATION:
Pilot

DIMENSIONS:
LENGTH: 28 ft 6 in (8.69 m)
WINGSPAN: 36 ft 0 in (10.97 m)
HEIGHT: 14 ft 0 in (4.27 m)

WEIGHTS:
EMPTY: 5996 lb (2720 kg)
MAX T/O: 8480 lb (3847 kg)

PERFORMANCE:
MAX SPEED: 356 mph (573 kmh)
RANGE: 650 miles (1050 km)
POWERPLANT: Pratt & Whitney
R-1830-57 Twin Wasp
OUTPUT: 1200 hp (895 kW)

FIRST FLIGHT DATE:
Mid-1940

ARMAMENT:
Two fixed Browning 0.50-in machine guns in forward fuselage and two fixed 0.50-in machine guns in wings; provision for up to 320 lb (145 kg) of bombs under wings/fuselage

FEATURES:
Elliptical monoplane wing; retractable undercarriage; deep oval cowling surrounding radial engine

Republic (Seversky) AT-12 Guardsman

two-seat, single-engined monoplane advanced trainer

Built as a two-seat development of the USAAC's P-35 fighter of 1937, the privately funded "Convoy Fighter" was designated the 2PA by its manufacturer. Like the single-seater, this aircraft had two 0.30-in or 0.50-in machine guns fitted in the wings, plus a flexibly mounted 0.30-in weapon in the rear cockpit. Two 2PAS were sold to the Soviet Union in 1938, together with a manufacturing license. Some 52 examples were ordered by Sweden the following year, while 20 were also clandestinely bought by the Imperial Japanese Navy for use over China. However, the 2PA's lack of maneuverability and poor rate of climb saw it swiftly relegated from the role of escort fighter to reconnaissance mount over central China. The 2PA eventually joined the ranks of the USAAC in late 1941, when all bar two of the 52 aircraft ordered by Sweden were hastily requisitioned by the Army Air Corps and pressed into service following events in the Pacific. Given the designation AT-12, these aircraft saw limited flying as advanced trainers and general communications hacks.

SPECIFICATION:

ACCOMMODATION:
Pilot and instructor/gunner in tandem

DIMENSIONS:
LENGTH: 26 ft 11 in (8.20 m)
WINGSPAN: 36 ft 0 in (10.97 m)
HEIGHT: 9 ft 9.50 in (2.99 m)

WEIGHTS:
EMPTY: 4581 lb (2078 kg)
MAX T/O: 7658 lb (3474 kg)

PERFORMANCE:
MAX SPEED: 316 mph (508 kmh)
RANGE: 1150 miles (1850 km)
POWERPLANT: Pratt & Whitney R-1830-53C Twin Wasp
OUTPUT: 1100 hp (821 kW)

FIRST FLIGHT DATE:
Late 1937

ARMAMENT:
Two fixed Browning 0.30-in or 0.50-in machine guns in wings, plus a flexibly mounted Browning 0.30-in machine gun in the rear cockpit; provision for up to 350 lb (158 kg) of bombs under wings/fuselage

FEATURES:
Monoplane wing; retractable undercarriage; close-cowled inline engine

Ryan PT-16/20/21/22 and NR-1 Recruit

two-seat, single-engined monoplane trainer

The USAAC's first monoplane primary trainer, the PT traced its ancestry back to Ryan's S-T two-seater design of 1933-34. Highly successful in its civil form, the Ryan garnered military interest in 1939 when the Army began looking for a new primary trainer. A solitary example of the S-T-A was acquired (redesignated the XPT-16), and it was thoroughly tested. A further 15 were purchased to allow a wider evaluation to be completed, and in 1940 an order for 30 was received. After taking delivery of these machines, the USAAC decided that the more powerful Kinner radial would endure the rigors of training better than the Menasco inline engine, and the 100 PT-21s ordered in 1941 were delivered with the radial powerplant. The PT-21 was so successful that Ryan received an order for 1023, which were designated PT-22 Recruits. The Navy also ordered 125 (designated NR-1s), and these were virtually identical to the PT-22. Operated primarily by civilian-run flying training schools, the last PTs were retired toward the end of World War II.

SPECIFICATION (PT-22):

ACCOMMODATION:
Two pilots in tandem

DIMENSIONS:
LENGTH: 22 ft 5 in (6.83 m)
WINGSPAN: 30 ft 1 in (9.17 m)
HEIGHT: 6 ft 10 in (2.08 m)

WEIGHTS:
EMPTY: 1313 lb (596 kg)
MAX T/O: 1860 lb (844 kg)

PERFORMANCE:
MAX SPEED: 131 mph (211 kmh)
RANGE: 352 miles (566 km)
POWERPLANT: Kinner R-540-1
OUTPUT: 160 hp (119 kW)

FIRST FLIGHT DATE:
February 3, 1939

FEATURES:
Monoplane wing; fixed spatted main undercarriage; close-cowled inline (PT-16/20) or exposed radial (PT-21/22) engine; tailwheel

Seversky P-35A

single-seat, single-engined monoplane fighter

The P-35 was the first fighter produced by Seversky (later Republic) of Farmingdale, Long Island. The work of chief designer Alexander Kartveli, the P-35 was the USAAC's first single-seat all-metal fighter with both a retractable undercarriage and an enclosed cockpit. The P-35 started life as the SEV-1XP, which was one of several machines built by Seversky and flown as prototypes and race aircraft. The P-35 beat the Curtiss Hawk Model 75 for the June 16, 1936 Army contract for 77 fighters, the first of which was delivered to Wright Field for testing. Sweden also placed an order for 120 P-35s, designated EP-106s by Seversky (and J9s by the Swedes), although only 60 had been delivered when the US Government enforced an embargo in October 1940. The remaining aircraft were impressed into USAAC ranks as P-35As. By late 1941 around 50 ex-Swedish Seversky fighters remained in service with the 24th PG in the Philippines, and these were destroyed attempting to stave off the Japanese invasion launched on December 7 that year.

SPECIFICATION:

ACCOMMODATION:
Pilot

DIMENSIONS:
LENGTH: 26 ft 10 in (8.18 m)
WINGSPAN: 36 ft 0 in (10.97 m)
HEIGHT: 9 ft 9 in (2.97 m)

WEIGHTS:
EMPTY: 4575 lb (2075 kg)
MAX T/O: 6723 lb (3050 kg)

PERFORMANCE:
MAX SPEED: 310 mph (499 kmh)
RANGE: 950 miles (1529 km)
POWERPLANT: Pratt & Whitney R-1830-45 Twin Wasp
OUTPUT: 1050 hp (783 kW)

FIRST FLIGHT DATE:
April 1935 (SEV-2XP)

ARMAMENT:
Two fixed Browning 0.30-in in forward fuselage and two fixed 0.50-in Browning machine guns in wings; provision for up to 350 lb (158 kg) of bombs under wings/fuselage

FEATURES:
Monoplane wing; retractable undercarriage; close-cowled inline engine

Sikorsky PS/RS/C-6

eight-seat, twin-engined sesquiplane utility amphibian

Sikorsky's S-series amphibians enjoyed significant sales success in the civilian marketplace, and in 1927 the Navy confirmed its interest in the twin boom sesquiplane flying boat when it bought a single S-38, which it redesignated the XPS-1. Evaluated as a potential patrol aircraft, with a gunner seated in the bow, the XPS-1 proved unsuited to this role and was relegated to utility use instead. The Navy persevered with the design nevertheless, acquiring two improved XPS-2s in October 1928 and issuing them to utility squadron VJ-1B. An additional seven, designated PS-3s, were delivered between 1929 and 1932. In 1930 the Navy gave up trying to use the amphibian as a patrol aircraft and issued them with the utility designations RS-1/2/3. Serving with both Navy and Marine Corps units at home and overseas, all RS amphibians had been withdrawn by 1934. Four S-38s were subsequently acquired from Pan American in 1942 and redesignated R4/5s. The Army also acquired ten S-38As in 1930, which it designated C-6As, and used them for transportation and target-towing duties until 1933.

SPECIFICATION (RS-3):

ACCOMMODATION:
Pilot and copilot, flight engineer, navigator, and four passengers

DIMENSIONS:
LENGTH: 40 ft 3 in (12.28 m)
WINGSPAN: 71 ft 8 in (21.88 m)
HEIGHT: 13 ft 10 in (3.99 m)

WEIGHTS:
EMPTY: 6740 lb (3057 kg)
MAX T/O: 10,323 lb (4683 kg)

PERFORMANCE:
MAX SPEED: 124 mph (198 kmh)
RANGE: 594 miles (950 km)
POWERPLANT: two Pratt & Whitney R-1340CS
OUTPUT: 900 hp (671 kW)

FIRST FLIGHT DATE:
1927 (XPS-1)

ARMAMENT:
One Browning 0.30-in machine gun on flexible mount in the bow and one in dorsal gun hatch behind wings

FEATURES:
Sesquiplane wing layout; radial engines; boat-shaped hull; twin boom/tail layout; enclosed cockpit

Sikorsky JRS-1/OA-8

19-seat, twin-engined high-wing monoplane/utility transportation flying boat

Another Sikorsky civilian type acquired by both the Navy and the Army, the JRS-1/OA-8 was a militarized version of the S-43 that was used by a number of American airlines from 1935 until the outbreak of World War II. The Navy initially procured seven in 1937 as JRS-1s for use as utility transports, with an order for ten more being issued in 1938-39. Although similar to the S-43, the JRS-1 was powered by the militarized R-1690-52 version of the Pratt & Whitney Hornet radial engine. The Army also bought five Y1OA-8s at this time, which were fitted out for use by its Military Transport Service. Although typically configured with seating for 15 passengers, the OA-8's cabin could be quickly cleared for cargo only. Eight of the Navy's JRS-1s served with San Diego-based VJ-1, while single examples were also assigned to the Marine Corps' VMJ-1 and VMJ-2 for employment in a variety of roles. Although only small in number, the Sikorsky amphibians were worked hard throughout World War II.

SPECIFICATION:

ACCOMMODATION:
Pilot and copilot, flight engineer, navigator, and 15 passengers

DIMENSIONS:
LENGTH: 51 ft 2 in (15.60 m)
WINGSPAN: 86 ft 0 in (26.21 m)
HEIGHT: 17 ft 8 in (5.38 m)

WEIGHTS:
EMPTY: 12,750 lb (5783 kg)
MAX T/O: 19,096 lb (8662 kg)

PERFORMANCE:
MAX SPEED: 190 mph (306 kmh)
RANGE: 775 miles (1247 km)
POWERPLANT: two Pratt & Whitney R-1690-52s
OUTPUT: 1500 hp (1119 kW)

FIRST FLIGHT DATE:
1937 (JRS-1)

FEATURES:
High-wing layout; radial engines; boat-shaped hull; undercarriage housed in hull; large single fin; enclosed cockpit

Spartan NP

two-seat, single-engined biplane primary trainer

Operated exclusively by the Navy as a primary trainer, the modest NP-1 was effectively a modernized version of the Tulsa, Oklahoma, based Mid-Continent Aircraft Company's C-3 family of three-seater trainers produced from 1927 onward for flight training schools and sportsmen fliers. The company had been reorganized as Spartan Aircraft in 1928, and formed its own school of aeronautics that same year. Having built a series of civilian-trainer types during the 1930s, Spartan was awarded a contract by the Navy in July 1940 to build 201 NP-1s that were to be issued to the newly formed Naval Reserve flight training schools that had just been opened at Naval Reserve Air Bases Atlanta, Dallas, and New Orleans. Featuring a fabric-covered welded chrome moly steel tubing fuselage and laminated spruce spar/truss wings with a Clark Y airfoil section and aluminum leading edges, the NP-1 was powered by a 220-hp Lycoming R-680-B4C radial engine. Used by the Navy throughout World War II, the NP-2's most famous student was President George Bush Snr.

SPECIFICATION:

ACCOMMODATION:
Two pilots in tandem

DIMENSIONS:
LENGTH: 24 ft 3 in (7.40 m)
WINGSPAN: 33 ft 9 in (10.33 m)
HEIGHT: 10 ft 3 in (3.13 m)

WEIGHTS:
EMPTY: 2220 lb (1007 kg)
MAX T/O: 3006 lb (1310 kg)

PERFORMANCE:
MAX SPEED: 108 mph (173 kmh)
RANGE: 450 miles (720 km)
POWERPLANT: Lycoming R-680-8
OUTPUT: 220 hp (164 kw)

FIRST FLIGHT DATE:
Early 1940

FEATURES:
Biplane wing layout; uncowled radial engine; fixed undercarriage and castoring tailwheel

Thomas-Morse MB-3

single-seat, single-engined biplane fighter

Having built s-4 series advanced fighter trainers for the Army in 1917-18, Thomas-Morse was asked to produce the first American-designed fighter in the spring of 1918. This aircraft, designated the MB-3, had to be better than the SPADs, the superb French scouts, then in frontline use. Despite the first prototype not flying until February 1919, the Army showed faith in the design by acquiring 50 MB-3s. In 1920, an order for 200 MB-3As was placed with Boeing under the competitive bidding system which was then in place. Although very similar to the MB-3, the Boeing version had a modified cooling system and a four-bladed propeller. One of the first units to receive the MB-3/3A was the 94th Pursuit Squadron at Selfridge Field, while others were shipped to squadrons overseas. When replaced by newer Boeing and Curtiss fighters in the mid-1920s, the MB-3/3As were sent to Kelly Field, Texas, to serve as MB-3M trainers, until finally being retired in 1928.

SPECIFICATION:

ACCOMMODATION:
One pilot

DIMENSIONS:
LENGTH: 20 ft 0 in (6.10 m)
WINGSPAN: 26 ft 0 in (7.92 m)
HEIGHT: 7 ft 8 in (2.34 m)

WEIGHTS:
EMPTY: 1716 lb (778 kg)
MAX T/O: 2539 lb (1152 kg)

PERFORMANCE:
MAX SPEED: 141 mph (227 kmh)
RANGE: 270 miles (435 km)
POWERPLANT: Wright-Hispano H-3
OUTPUT: 300 hp (224 kW)

FIRST FLIGHT DATE:
February 21, 1919

ARMAMENT:
One fixed Marlin 0.30-in machine gun and one fixed Browning 0.50-in machine gun in upper fuselage cowling

FEATURES:
Biplane wing layout; closely cowled vee-engine; tail skid; headrest

Thomas-Morse O-19

two-seat, single-engined biplane observation aircraft

After years of trying to tempt the Army into buying its all-metal construction biplane types when most machines then in service were made of steel tubing covered in fabric, Thomas-Morse finally succeeded in securing an order for its O-19 observation biplane in 1928. The Wasp-powered machine was loosely based on the Douglas O-2, six of which had been built by Thomas-Morse as XO/O-6s using its characteristic corrugated sheet-metal fuselage construction under contract to the Army. After testing four prototypes fitted with a variety of radial and inline engines, the Army contracted the company to construct 70 O-19Bs, which featured a new cockpit layout and gun mounting. The follow-on O-19C (71 built) had further refinements, as well as a Townend drag ring around the engine. The final version to attain series production was the O-19E (30 built), which had a slightly larger wing and a more powerful R-1340-15 version of the Wasp fitted as standard. The O-19 remained in frontline service into the mid-1930s, after which surviving examples were supplied to the National Guard.

SPECIFICATION (O-19B):

ACCOMMODATION:
Pilot and observer/gunner

DIMENSIONS:
LENGTH: 28 ft 4 in (8.65 m)
WINGSPAN: 39 ft 9 in (12.16 m)
HEIGHT: 10 ft 6 in (3.20 m)

WEIGHTS:
EMPTY: 2722 lb (1235 kg)
MAX T/O: 3800 lb (1724 kg)

PERFORMANCE:
MAX SPEED: 137 mph (221 kmh)
RANGE: 580 miles (928 km)
POWERPLANT: Pratt & Whitney R-1340-7
OUTPUT: 450 hp (336 kW)

FIRST FLIGHT DATE:
Late 1925 (O-1)

ARMAMENT:
One fixed Browning 0.30-in machine gun mounted in fuselage and one on flexible mounting for observer/gunner

FEATURES:
Biplane wing layout; radial engine; fixed undercarriage; open cockpit; corrugated metal fuselage

Vought VE-7/9

single/two-seat, single-engined biplane fighter/trainer/observation seaplane

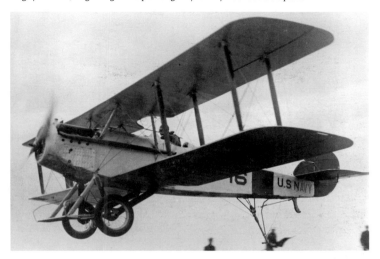

The first Vought aircraft to attain production status, the VE-7 was designed in 1917 specifically as an advanced trainer. Powered by a license-built Hispano-Suiza Model A engine, the aircraft was soon ordered in quantity by the Army. However, just 14 had been built by war's end, after which the Army chose to re-engine surplus JN-4s instead in an effort to save money. In October 1919 the Navy stepped in and ordered a version of the VE-7 powered by the larger Wright-Hispano E. A total of 129 were duly built (69 by the NAF), many of which emerged as VE-7G two-seat and VE-7S single-seat fighters. The latter were subsequently flown by pioneer shipboard fighter unit VF-2 from *Langley* in the early 1920s. Others were built as VE-7H trainers, while the unarmed observation seaplane variant served as the standard catapult-launched observation and scouting aircraft from battleships and cruisers. The VE-9 was identical to the VE-7 except for minor details and its improved E-3 engine, the Navy buying 21 and the Army 23.

SPECIFICATION (VE-7S):

ACCOMMODATION:
Pilot, or pilot and observer (VE-7G)

DIMENSIONS:
LENGTH: 24 ft 5 in (7.44 m)
WINGSPAN: 34 ft 1 in (10.40 m)
HEIGHT: 8 ft 7 in (2.62 m)

WEIGHTS:
EMPTY: 1505 lb (683 kg)
MAX T/O: 2100 lb (953 kg)

PERFORMANCE:
MAX SPEED: 117 mph (188 kmh)
RANGE: 290 miles (467 km)
POWERPLANT: Wright-Hispano E-2
OUTPUT: 180 hp (134 kW)

FIRST FLIGHT DATE:
February 1918

ARMAMENT:
Two fixed Browning 0.30-in machine guns in upper fuselage cowling and one flexibly mounted in rear cockpit (VE-7G only)

FEATURES:
Biplane wing layout; closely cowled vee-engine; tail skid; headrest; wheels or floats

Vought UO/FU

single/two-seat, single-engined biplane observation/fighter land/seaplane

Essentially an improved VE-7/9, the UO-1 was built in large numbers in the early 1920s. Initially designed for the fighter role then filled by the VE-7S, by the time the first prototype had flown, better-performing aircraft were in the pipeline, so the Vought machine was reclassified as an unarmed observation type. Aside from its Wright radial engine and all-new tailplane, the UO differed from the VE by having a more streamlined fuselage and larger forward cockpit. Float-equipped UO-1S started replacing VES in the fleet in 1922-23, with those machines that were specially reinforced for catapult launching being designated UO-1VS. Other UO-1S were fitted with arrestor hooks for carrier operations. Following production of 141 UO-1S, the Navy ordered 20 near-identical FU-1 single-seat seaplane fighters in 1926. The last World War I-style wood-and-wire to be ordered by the US military, the FU-1S were assigned to VF-2B and operated from 12 battleships in the fighter role between October 1927 and June 1928. All UO-2S and FU-1S had been retired by 1932.

SPECIFICATION (UO-1):

ACCOMMODATION:
Pilot, or pilot and observer

DIMENSIONS:
LENGTH: 28 ft 4.25 in (8.65 m)
WINGSPAN: 34 ft 4 in (10.46 m)
HEIGHT: 8 ft 9 in (2.71 m)

WEIGHTS:
EMPTY: 1494 lb (678 kg)
MAX T/O: 2305 lb (1046 kg)

PERFORMANCE:
MAX SPEED: 124 mph (198 kmh)
RANGE: 398 miles (637 km)
POWERPLANT: Wright J-3
OUTPUT: 200 hp (149 kW)

FIRST FLIGHT DATE:
1922

ARMAMENT:
Two fixed Browning 0.30-in machine guns in upper fuselage cowling (FU-1 only)

FEATURES:
Biplane wing layout; radial engine; headrest; wheels or floats

Vought O2U Corsair

two-seat, single-engined biplane observation land/seaplane

The first of a series of Vought types to bear the famous Corsair moniker, the O2U was designed in 1926 as a replacement for the company's UO and FU series. It was also the first Navy airplane to be built around the famous Pratt & Whitney Wasp radial engine. Some 130 O2U-1s were constructed, entering fleet service in 1927. Like its predecessors, the Corsair could be operated from land or aircraft carriers with its wheeled chassis, or from battleships and cruisers when in seaplane configuration. By mid-1928 the O2U-1 was in service with VO-3B, VO-4B, and VO-5B, these units providing Corsairs for the battleship divisions on both coasts. VS-1B, embarked in *Langley*, was also equipped with "wheeled and hooked" O2U-1s, while the Marine Corps' VO-7M gave the type its combat debut in Nicaragua in 1928. Subsequent Corsair production runs between 1928 and 1930 included 37 O2U-2s with dihedral on the lower wing and a modified rudder, 80 O2U-3s with dihedral on the upper wing, and 42 near-identical O2U-4s.

SPECIFICATION (O2U-1):

ACCOMMODATION:
Pilot and observer/gunner

DIMENSIONS:
LENGTH: 24 ft 6 in (7.47 m)
WINGSPAN: 34 ft 6 in (10.50 m)
HEIGHT: 10 ft 1.25 in (3.08 m)

WEIGHTS:
EMPTY: 2342 lb (1062 kg)
MAX T/O: 3893 lb (1766 kg)

PERFORMANCE:
MAX SPEED: 147 mph (237 kmh)
RANGE: 608 miles (980 km)
POWERPLANT: Pratt & Whitney
R-1340-88 Wasp
OUTPUT: 450 hp (336 kW)

FIRST FLIGHT DATE:
October 11, 1926

ARMAMENT:
One fixed Browning 0.30-in
machine gun above engine and
one flexibly mounted in rear
cockpit; underwing racks for
light bombs

FEATURES:
Biplane wing layout, with upper
and lower dihedral depending on
variant; radial engine; wheels or
floats; N-shaped bracing struts

Vought o3U/SU Corsair

two-seat, single-engined biplane observation/scouting land/seaplane

Building on the success enjoyed by the o2U family of observation/utility aircraft, Vought's new Corsair was initially more of the same thing, with the o3U-1 variant being identical but for an increase in sweepback and dihedral on the lower wing. The Navy received 87 examples from 1930, configured both as land and seaplanes for its observation units. The o3U-2 of 1932 had a bigger Hornet engine with low-drag cowling, revised fin shape, and simpler axle. Although ordered as the o3U-2, the 29 built were issued to the Marine Corps as SU-1s, reflecting their revised scouting role. The o3U-3 (76 built between 1933-35) reverted to the Wasp radial, while the 65 o3U-4s acquired from 1934 used the Hornet. These machines became SU-2/3s in service, while a cowled and full-canopied variant (40 built) was designated the SU-4. The last version, built in 1935, was the o3U-6, 32 of which also had partial canopies and a cowled Wasp. Although relegated to secondary duties by late 1941, 130+ Corsairs still remained in the Navy inventory.

SPECIFICATION (O3U-3):

ACCOMMODATION:
Pilot and observer/gunner

DIMENSIONS:
LENGTH: 27 ft 3 in (8.32 m)
WINGSPAN: 36 ft 0 in (10.97 m)
HEIGHT: 11 ft 6 in (3.53 m)

WEIGHTS:
EMPTY: 2938 lb (1333 kg)
MAX T/O: 4451 lb (2019 kg)

PERFORMANCE:
MAX SPEED: 164 mph (262 kmh)
RANGE: 650 miles (1040 km)
POWERPLANT: Pratt & Whitney R-1340-12 Wasp
OUTPUT: 550 hp (410 kW)

FIRST FLIGHT DATE:
1930

ARMAMENT:
One fixed Browning 0.30-in machine gun above engine and two flexibly mounted in rear cockpit; underwing racks for light bombs

FEATURES:
Biplane wing layout, with upper and lower dihedral and sweepback; radial engine (both cowled and uncowled); wheels or floats; N-shaped bracing struts; open and enclosed cockpits

Vought SBU

two-seat, single-engined biplane scout-bomber

The last biplane type to bear the Vought name, and the Navy's first 200-mph airplane, the SBU was initially designed as a two-seat fighter in 1932 in response to a Navy specification issued as a result of problems experienced in the fleet with the Curtiss F8C-4 Helldiver, which was too slow. Competing against seven other manufacturers for the Navy contract, Vought's XF3U-1 was chosen for progression to prototype form. First flown in May 1933, the design was modified into the XSBU-1 scout-bomber six months later after the Navy indicated a requirement for 27 examples. An all-new prototype was built, featuring increased fuel capacity, stronger and larger wings, and the ability to carry a 500-lb bomb. Vought received a production order for 84 airframes in January 1935, with aircraft reaching VS-3B in November of that same year. Both VS-1B and VS-2B also re-equipped with the SBU-1 in early 1936, by which time a second order for 40 SBU-2s had also been placed. Most SBUs had been retired by late 1941.

SPECIFICATION:

ACCOMMODATION:
Pilot and observer/gunner

DIMENSIONS:
LENGTH: 27 ft 10 in (8.50 m)
WINGSPAN: 33 ft 3 in (10.13 m)
HEIGHT: 11 ft 11 in (3.63 m)

WEIGHTS:
EMPTY: 3645 lb (1653 kg)
MAX T/O: 5520 lb (2504 kg)

PERFORMANCE:
MAX SPEED: 208 mph (335 kmh)
RANGE: 548 miles (880 km)
POWERPLANT: Pratt & Whitney R-1535-80 Twin Wasp Junior
OUTPUT: 750 hp (559 kW)

FIRST FLIGHT DATE:
May 1933

ARMAMENT:
One fixed Browning 0.30-in machine gun above engine and one flexibly mounted in rear cockpit; attachment for 500-lb (227-kg) bomb under fuselage and underwing racks for light bombs

FEATURES:
Biplane wing layout, with upper and lower sweepback; cowled radial engine; fixed tripod undercarriage; N-shaped bracing struts; enclosed cockpits; arrestor hook

Vought SB2U Vindicator

two-seat, single-engined scout/dive-bomber

The Navy's first monoplane scout-bomber, the Vindicator was the end result of an order placed with Vought in 1934 for two prototype carrier-based aircraft. The order called for the construction of a biplane (XSB3U-1) and a monoplane (XSB2U-1), which would then conduct comparative flight trials before a production order was placed. Both flew in early 1936, and the all-metal XSB2U-1 soon proved its superiority—the Navy purchased 54 SB2U-1s in October of that year.

Deliveries began to VB-3, embarked in *Saratoga*, in December 1937, and one year later a further 58 SB2U-2s were acquired. The latter included minor equipment changes and an increased maximum weight. Finally, in late 1940, 57 SB2U-3s were ordered, these featuring more armor protection, heavier gun armament, increased standard fuel capacity, and provision for external tanks. The SB2U-3 was the first version to be officially named the Vindicator, and this was retrospectively applied to all surviving SB2Us.

By 1940, the aircraft equipped VB-3 (*Saratoga*), VB-4, VS-41, VS-42 (*Ranger*), VS-71, and VS-72 (*Wasp*), while the bulk of the SB2U-3s had been issued to Marine Corps units VMSB-131 and VMSB-231. Both Navy and Marine Corps Vindicators saw action from land bases during the early months of the Pacific War, including participation in the pivotal Battle of Midway, when they flew from the island base. Carrier-based aircraft had been largely replaced by the superior Douglas SBD Dauntless at the end of 1941, however, and shore-based units in the Pacific duly followed suit when the SB2U's vulnerability to modern

Japanese fighters such as the A6M Zero-sen was revealed. A handful of Vindicators lingered on with training units in the USA until finally retired in 1943.

SPECIFICATION (SB2U-3):

ACCOMMODATION:
Pilot and gunner

DIMENSIONS:
LENGTH: 34 ft 0 in (10.36 m)
WINGSPAN: 42 ft 0 in (12.80 m)
HEIGHT: 10 ft 3 in (3.12 m)

WEIGHTS:
EMPTY: 5634 lb (2555 kg)
MAX T/O: 9421 lb (4273 kg)

PERFORMANCE:
MAX SPEED: 243 mph (391 kmh)
RANGE: 1120 miles (1802 km)
POWERPLANT: Pratt & Whitney R-1535-02 Twin Wasp Junior
OUTPUT: 825 hp (615 kW)

FIRST FLIGHT DATE:
January 4, 1936

ARMAMENT:
One fixed Browning 0.50-in machine gun in nose and one on flexible mount in rear cockpit; maximum load of 1000 lb (454 kg) on racks under wings and fuselage

FEATURES:
Monoplane wing; retractable undercarriage; close-cowled radial engine; fixed tailwheel; aerial mast forward of cockpit

Vultee BT-13/15 and SNV-1/2 Valiant

two-seat, single-engined monoplane basic trainer

The most-produced basic trainer in the USA during World War II, the Valiant can trace its lineage back to Vultee's BC-3 combat trainer. Tested by the USAAC in 1938, the BC-3 was fitted with a retractable landing gear and powerful 600-hp Pratt & Whitney Wasp engine. The evaluation showed that the aircraft had perfect handling characteristics, but that the landing gear need not be retractable or the powerplant so big. Vultee duly fitted oleo-pneumatic shock-struts and bolted a Pratt & Whitney Wasp Junior "up front." The end result was the BT-13 Valiant, and the USAAC ordered 300 in September 1939. A follow-on variant fitted with a different version of the Wasp Junior engine was then procured to the tune of 6407 examples. The rapidity at which these airframes were built resulted in a shortage of Wasp engines, thus forcing Vultee to create the Wright R-975-11 Whirlwind 9-powered BT-15 instead. The Navy procured well over 1500 Valiants, which it designated the SNV-1/2. By the time production ceased in 1944, 11,000+ Valiants had been built.

SPECIFICATION:

ACCOMMODATION:
Two pilots in tandem

DIMENSIONS:
LENGTH: 28 ft 10 in (8.79 m)
WINGSPAN: 42 ft 0 in (12.80 m)
HEIGHT: 11 ft 6 in (3.51 m)

WEIGHTS:
EMPTY: 3375 lb (1531 kg)
MAX T/O: 4496 lb (2039 kg)

PERFORMANCE:
MAX SPEED: 180 mph (290 kmh)
RANGE: 725 miles (1167 km)
POWERPLANT: Pratt & Whitney R-985-AN-1 Wasp Junior
OUTPUT: 450 hp (336 kW)

FIRST FLIGHT DATE:
March 24, 1939 (BT-13)

FEATURES:
Monoplane wing; fixed undercarriage; close-cowled radial engine; fixed tailwheel; aerial mast forward of cockpit

World
War II

Aeronca O-58/L-3/16 Grasshopper

two-seat, single-engined high-wing liaison/observation aircraft

In an effort to hastily acquire a light aircraft for observation/liaison duties in the frontline in the final months of peace in 1941, the Army evaluated four designs from established American manufacturers Piper, Taylorcraft, and Aeronca. The latter's offering was the Model 65, which was a modified version of its commercially available two-seat trainer. The aircraft was designated the O-58 by the USAAC, and more than 400 were purchased in three versions—in 1942 their designation changed from O (for Observation) to L (for Liaison). A further 1030 were built before production ceased in 1944, these aircraft seeing action with US forces across the globe. Postwar, more aircraft were built both for the civil and military markets, with the Army designating its variant the L-16. An engineless version of the Model 65 was also produced in 1942 when the Army expanded its glider pilot training program. Aeronca built 250 TG-5 gliders, and they played an integral part in the training of pilots who would later make assault landings in Occupied Europe.

SPECIFICATION (L-3):

ACCOMMODATION:
Pilot and passenger in tandem

DIMENSIONS:
LENGTH: 21 ft 0 in (6.40 m)
WINGSPAN: 35 ft 0 in (10.67 m)
HEIGHT: 7 ft 8 in (2.34 m)

WEIGHTS:
EMPTY: 835 lb (379 kg)
MAX T/O: 1300 lb (590 kg)

PERFORMANCE:
MAX SPEED: 87 mph (140 kmh)
RANGE: 200 miles (322 km)
POWERPLANT: Continental O-170-3
OUTPUT: 65 hp (49 kW)

FIRST FLIGHT DATE:
1941

FEATURES:
High-wing layout; tandem cockpits; fixed landing gear; extensive cockpit glazing

Beech YC/UC-43/GB-2 Traveler

four-seat, single-engined liaison/communications biplane

The first design put into production by Walter Beech, the Model 17 Staggerwing quickly established itself in the growing US civil market of the 1930s. The aircraft offered both comfort and performance to its occupants, and these attributes also appealed to senior military officers. The Navy initially acquired a handful (designated GB-1s) for the VIP transportation role in 1939, and with the outbreak of war two years later, it purchased a further 300+ examples—designated GB-2s—105 of which were supplied to the Royal Navy. The USAAC also bought three D17Ss in 1939, which were designated YC-43 Travelers. Three years later, a production order for 27 UC-43s was placed with Beech, followed by two subsequent requests for 75 and 105 Travelers, which brought total USAAF procurement to 207 aircraft. A large number of civilian Staggerwings (434 had been built by Beech up to December 7, 1941) were also impressed into military service. Production of civil Staggerwings recommenced in August 1945, and the last example left the Beech assembly line in 1948.

SPECIFICATION:

ACCOMMODATION:
Pilot and seats for up to three passengers

DIMENSIONS:
LENGTH: 26 ft 2 in (7.98 m)
WINGSPAN: 32 ft 0 in (9.75 m)
HEIGHT: 10 ft 3 in (3.12 m)

WEIGHTS:
EMPTY: 3085 lb (1399 kg)
MAX T/O: 4700 lb (2123 kg)

PERFORMANCE:
MAX SPEED: 198 mph (319 kmh)
RANGE: 500 miles (805 km)
POWERPLANT: Pratt & Whitney R-985-AN-1 Wasp Junior
OUTPUT: 450 hp (335 kW)

FIRST FLIGHT DATE:
November 4, 1932 (civilian Beech 17 Staggerwing)

FEATURES:
Staggered biplane wing layout; rectractable landing gear; close-cowled radial engine; single wing struts

Beech AT-7/11/C-45 and JRB/SNB

eight-seat, twin-engined monoplane light transportation and trainer aircraft

Like the Model 17 Staggerwing, the Beech Model 18 started life as a transport aimed squarely at the American civil market of the late 1930s. Similarities between the two Beech designs did not stop there, however, for like the Staggerwing, the first examples of the Model 18 ordered by the USAAC in 1940 operated in the staff transportation role. Designated the C-45, more than 250 were procured by the Army Air Corps, which also used them as utility transports. Some of these aircraft were passed on to the RAF/Fleet Air Arm/RCAF under Lend-Lease, the British naming them Expediter I/II/IIIs, depending on their variant state. The final transport version built for the USAAF was the C-45F, which was produced to the tune of 1137 examples—all Army Air Force C-45s were redesignated UC-45s in 1943.

Two years earlier, Beech had produced the Model 18-based AT-7 navigation trainer with positions for three trainees and a dorsal astrodome. The USAAC took delivery of 549, followed by six AT-7As with floats and a ventral fin, nine winterized AT-7Bs, and 540 AT-7Cs, fitted with different engines. Following in the AT-7's footsteps in 1941 was the AT-11 Kansan bombing/gunnery trainer, of which 1582 were built. This specialized variant had a small bomb bay, round rather than square windows in the fuselage and was armed with a 0.3-in machine gun in the nose and in the dorsal turret. Included within the bombing/gunnery trainer production run were 36 AT-11A navigation trainers.

The last wartime variant ordered by the USAAF was the F-2 photo-reconnaissance aircraft, 59 of which were acquired through the conversion of civilian Model 18ss and military C/UC-45A/FS. Finally, the Navy/Marine Corps also procured in excess of 1500 Model 18s, which it designated JRBS (equivalent to the USAAF's C-45) and SNBS (AT-7/-11).

All surviving examples were rebuilt by the Air Force and Navy in the early 1950s, resulting in USAF examples being redesignated C-45G/HS and Navy aircraft emerging as SNB-5/5PS. These machines soldiered on in the training and utility roles until the late 1960s.

SPECIFICATION (AT-11):

ACCOMMODATION:
Pilot and seats for up to seven students/passengers

DIMENSIONS:
LENGTH: 34 ft 3 in (10.4 m)
WINGSPAN: 47 ft 8 in (14.5 m)
HEIGHT: 9 ft 8 in (2.95 m)

WEIGHTS:
EMPTY: 6175 lb (2801 kg)
MAX T/O: 8727 lb (3959 kg)

PERFORMANCE:
MAX SPEED: 215 mph (346 kmh)
RANGE: 850 miles (1368 km)
POWERPLANT: two Pratt & Whitney
R-985-AN-1 Wasp Juniors
OUTPUT: 900 hp (670.6 kW)

FIRST FLIGHT DATE:
January 15, 1937 (civilian Beech 18)

ARMAMENT:
Two Browning 0.30-in machine guns in nose and in dorsal turret; maximum bomb load of 1000 lb (454 kg) in internal bomb bay

FEATURES:
Monoplane wing layout; rectractable landing gear; two close-cowled radial engines; twin-tail layout

Bell P-39 Airacobra

single-seat, single-engined monoplane fighter

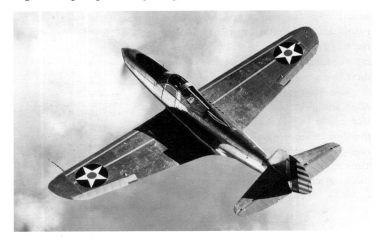

Bell's revolutionary P-39 introduced the concept of both the centrally mounted powerplant and the tricycle undercarriage to single-engined fighters, the aircraft's unusual configuration stemming from its principal armament, the propeller hub-mounted T9 37-mm cannon. In order to allow the weapon to be housed in the nose, the P-39's engine was moved aft to sit virtually over the rear half of the wing center-section, with a long shaft that ran under the pilot's seat driving the propeller through nose-mounted reduction gear. This drastically shifted the aircraft's center of gravity, thus forcing designers to adopt a tricycle undercarriage.

Unfortunately, the P-39's radical design was not matched by stunning performance, particularly at heights exceeding 14,000 ft, where its normally aspirated Allison V-1710 struggled in the "thinner" air at these altitudes. Ironically, following a service evaluation of the YP-39 in 1938-39, Bell had been told by USAAC and NACA officials that a turbocharged version of the V-1710 then available for the Airacobra was not needed! With the delivery of the first production aircraft (P-39C, 80 built) in January 1941, the wisdom of this decision was quickly called into question. In fact, so compromised was the aircraft's "combatability" in its designated role that it was relegated to close air support duties in theaters where other aircraft could be employed as fighters.

Follow-on variants included the fully militarized P-39D, with leak-proof tanks, four 0.30-in wing guns, and two 0.50-in guns, and the T-9 cannon in the nose—369 were ordered and deliveries began in April 1941. Follow-on versions were the P-39F (229 built), P-39K (250), P-39L (250), P-39M (240), and P-39N/Q (2095). The USAAF also received more than 200 Airacobras that had been repossessed from the RAF in 1942, designating these aircraft P-400s.

Seeing combat with USAAF units in North Africa and the Mediterranean, as well as the Pacific theaters, the P-39 reached its peak strength with the Army Air Force in early 1944 when 2150 examples were in frontline and training service. The aircraft also saw extensive combat with the Soviet air force, which received 4773 of the 9558 built.

SPECIFICATION (P-39L):

ACCOMMODATION:
Pilot

DIMENSIONS:
LENGTH: 30 ft 2 in (9.19 m)
WINGSPAN: 34 ft 0 in (10.36 m)
HEIGHT: 11 ft 10 in (3.61 m)

WEIGHTS:
EMPTY: 5600 lb (2540 kg)
MAX T/O: 8400 lb (3811 kg)

PERFORMANCE:
MAX SPEED: 380 mph (612 kmh)
RANGE: 650 miles (1046 km)
POWERPLANT: Allison V-1710-83
OUTPUT: 1200 hp (895 kW)

FIRST FLIGHT DATE:
April 6, 1938 (XP-39)

ARMAMENT:
One American Armaments Company T9 37-mm cannon and two Browning 0.50-in machine guns in nose and two or four Browning 0.30-in machine guns in wings; one 500-lb (227-kg) bomb on centerline rack

FEATURES:
Monoplane wing layout; rectractable, tricycle landing gear; inline engine; "car door" entry to cockpit; carburettor intake fairing behind cockpit

Bell P-63 Kingcobra

single-seat, single-engined monoplane fighter

Although the P-63 looked like an enlarged Airacobra, it was in fact an all-new design that had a superior turn of speed at all altitudes. Christened the Kingcobra, the fighter drew heavily on modifications incorporated into the P-39's original replacement, the canceled XP-39E. However, unlike the latter design, the P-63 was more than just an Airacobra fuselage with new semilaminar flow wings—the fighter was appreciably larger, and boasted an Allison V-1710-93 engine that could be boosted to 1500 hp in flight in the event of an emergency. Although 3300 P-63s were built in several different versions, by the time the first production examples reached the USAAF in October 1943, the P-51B, P-38H, and P-47C had successfully filled the Army Air Force's requirement for a frontline fighter. Most Kingcobras were therefore made available for Lend-Lease purchase, and the Soviet air force snapped up 2400. A further 300 went to Free French units in the Mediterranean, but the primary customer—the USAAF—restricted its use of the Kingcobra to training squadrons in America.

SPECIFICATION (P-63A):

ACCOMMODATION:
Pilot

DIMENSIONS:
LENGTH: 32 ft 8 in (9.96 m)
WINGSPAN: 38 ft 4 in (11.68 m)
HEIGHT: 12 ft 7 in (3.84 m)

WEIGHTS:
EMPTY: 6375 lb (2892 kg)
MAX T/O: 10,500 lb (4763 kg)

PERFORMANCE:
MAX SPEED: 410 mph (660 kmh)
RANGE: 2200 miles (3540 km)
POWERPLANT: Allison V-1710-93
OUTPUT: 1325 hp (988 kW)

FIRST FLIGHT DATE:
December 7, 1942

ARMAMENT:
One American Armaments Company T9 37-mm cannon and two Browning 0.50-in machine guns in nose and two underwing Browning 0.50-in machine guns; bomb load of up to 1500 lb (681 kg) on underwing/fuselage racks

FEATURES:
Monoplane wing layout; rectractable, tricycle landing gear; inline engine; "car door" entry to cockpit; carburettor intake fairing behind cockpit

Bell P-59 Airacomet

single-seat, twin-engined jet monoplane fighter

America's first jet fighter, the Bell P-59 was built around the revolutionary Whittle turbojet, unveiled to the US Government by Britain in September 1941. Of conventional design, the fighter was powered by two General Electric Type IAS (redesignated J31s). Flight development went smoothly, with three prototypes and 13 evaluation airframes being delivered by late 1944. It was realized at an early stage of the flight development program that the Airacomet boasted a performance inferior to many frontline piston-engined fighters of the day, so the production aircraft subsequently acquired were relegated to the fighter-trainer role. The first production P-59A was delivered to the USAAF in August 1944, and of the 20 that were built, three went to the Navy as the XF2L-1. The P-59B soon replaced the A-model in production, and a further 30 were delivered before the remaining 50 on order (plus an expected follow-on batch of 250) were canceled in October 1944. Most P-59Bs were assigned to the USAAF's 412th Fighter Group for use as drones or drone-controllers.

SPECIFICATION:

ACCOMMODATION:
Pilot

DIMENSIONS:
LENGTH: 38 ft 10 in (11.83 m)
WINGSPAN: 45 ft 6 in (13.97 m)
HEIGHT: 12 ft 4 in (3.76 m)

WEIGHTS:
EMPTY: 8165 lb (3704 kg)
MAX T/O: 13,700 lb (6214 kg)

PERFORMANCE:
MAX SPEED: 413 mph (665 kmh)
RANGE: 525 miles (845 km)
POWERPLANT: two General Electric J31-GE-3/5S
OUTPUT: 4000 lb st (18 kN)

FIRST FLIGHT DATE:
October 1, 1942

ARMAMENT:

One American Armaments Company T9 37-mm cannon and three Browning 0.50-in machine guns in nose; two underwing racks for up to 500 lb (227 kg) of bombs

FEATURES:
Monoplane wing layout; rectractable, tricycle landing gear; twin jet engines; engine intakes at wing roots

Boeing B-17 Flying Fortress

ten-seat, four-engined monoplane heavy bomber

Built as a private venture by Boeing in response to a USAAC requirement for an antishipping bomber replacement for the Martin B-10, the Model 299 was first flown on July 28, 1935. The first four-engined bomber ever built by Boeing, the Model 299 was a huge financial risk for the company. Immediately dubbed the "Flying Fortress" by the press corps in attendance for the prototype's first flight, the aircraft impressed the USAAC with its speed and high-altitude performance. However, it was not initially chosen to replace the B-10 on the grounds of cost. Nevertheless, the Model 229 had elicited enough interest for Boeing to receive an order for a batch of 13 YB-17s, followed by the signing of a second contract for 39 near-identical B-17Bs.

The latter model introduced a new nose and bigger rudder and flaps, and the aircraft that entered service in 1939-40 looked similar to the thousands of Flying Fortresses that would subsequently dominate the ranks of the USAAF in World War II. By mid-1940 the Flying Fortress had been further improved with the addition of two extra guns and the fitment of more powerful engines. Designated the B-17C, 20 were exported to Britain for service with the RAF.

Lessons learned from the European conflict saw Boeing "beef up" the armor fitted to future models of B-17, plus fit extra guns and self-sealing fuel tanks. The end result of these changes was the B-17E, 512 of which were built in 1941-42, followed by the B-17F, which had a redesigned nose to incorporate a 0.50-in machine gun, a strengthened undercarriage to cope with increased bomb loads, and Wright R-1820-97 engines. The final version to see mass-production was the chin-turreted B-17G, some 8680 examples of which

were manufactured
from 1942 through to
1945. Although both
E- and F-models had
seen combat with
bomb groups both in
the Pacific and Europe,
it was the B-17G that
really took the fight to
the Axis on a global
scale. Flying Fortresses
also saw limited service
in specialized air-sea-
rescue and transpor-
tation roles postwar.

SPECIFICATION (B-17G):

ACCOMMODATION:
Pilot and copilot, flight engineer,
navigator, bombardier/nose
gunner, radio operator/dorsal
gunner, two waist gunners, ball
turret gunner, tail gunner

DIMENSIONS:
LENGTH: 74 ft 4 in (22.66 m)
WINGSPAN: 103 ft 9 in (31.62 m)
HEIGHT: 19 ft 1 in (5.82 m)

WEIGHTS:
EMPTY: 36,135 lb (16,391 kg)
MAX T/O: 65,500 lb (29,710 kg)

PERFORMANCE:
MAX SPEED: 287 mph (462 kmh)
RANGE: 2000 miles (3219 km)
POWERPLANT: four Wright
R-1820-97 Cyclones
OUTPUT: 4800 hp (3580 kW)

FIRST FLIGHT DATE:
July 28, 1935 (Model 299)

ARMAMENT:
Twin Browning 0.50-in machine
guns in chin, dorsal, ball, and tail
turrets, plus two in nose, one in
radio compartment and one in
each waist position; maximum
bomb load of 12,800 lb (5800 kg)
in bomb bay

FEATURES:
Monoplane wing layout;
rectractable landing gear; four
radial engines; large vertical tail
surface

Boeing B-29 Superfortress

eleven-seat, four-engined monoplane heavy bomber

Boeing's timely response to the USAAC's request for a long-range strategic bomber to replace the B-17, the B-29 concept was devised soon after the Flying Fortress entered service in the late 1930s. Initially hindered by the lack of a suitable powerplant, the very long-range bomber project was resurrected in 1940 when five US manufacturers were invited to tender proposals. Eventually, only Consolidated and Boeing would produce flyable prototypes, and although the former's XB-32 Dominator flew first, it was plagued by development problems. Boeing, however, was able to convince the USAAC that it could deliver production versions of its Model 345 (designated the XB-29 by the military) by 1943, and the company duly won the contract for 1500+ bombers *before* the prototype had even flown. Boasting incredible advances in technology, including cabin pressurization, tricycle landing gear, high wing loading, and remote-controlled gun turrets, the first production B-29s were delivered in June 1943 to the 58th BW.

The incredibly complex Superfortress suffered numerous technical problems in its first months of service, including in-flight fires with its 2200-hp Wright R-3350-23 Duplex Cyclone radial engines. However, by the time the four groups that made up the 58th BW moved to India in the spring of 1944, the B-29's reliability had improved significantly. The aircraft's first combat mission was flown on June 5, 1944, and within six months all Superfortress operations were being mounted from newly built airfields in the Marianas Island chain in the western Pacific. Daily, 500 B-29s would be sent out to bomb targets on mainland Japan, these raids playing a crucial part in ending the conflict with the Japanese. The B-29 missions culminated with the two H-bomb strikes on Hiroshima and Nagasaki in August 1945. By the time production ceased in

May 1946, 3970 B-29s had been built. Postwar, the type enjoyed a long career in the USAF (including seeing considerable action in the Korean War), with 19 different variants performing numerous roles—weather reconnaissance, aerial refueling, and mothership for supersonic research aircraft—into the early 1960s.

SPECIFICATION:

ACCOMMODATION:
Pilot and copilot, flight engineer, navigator, bombardier/nose gunner, radar operator, radio operator, central fire controller/top gunner, right and left gunners, tail gunner

DIMENSIONS:
LENGTH: 99 ft 0 in (30.18 m)
WINGSPAN: 141 ft 3 in (43.05 m)
HEIGHT: 29 ft 7 in (9.02 m)

WEIGHTS:
EMPTY: 70,140 lb (31,815 kg)
MAX T/O: 124,000 lb (56,245 kg)

PERFORMANCE:
MAX SPEED: 358 mph (576 kmh)
RANGE: 3250 miles (5230 km)
POWERPLANT: four Wright R-3350-23 Duplex Cyclones
OUTPUT: 8800 hp (6564 kW)

FIRST FLIGHT DATE:
September 21, 1942

ARMAMENT:
Four turrets with four Browning 0.50-in machine guns on top/bottom of fuselage, tail turret with 20-mm cannon and two Browning 0.50-in machine guns; 20,000 lb (9072 kg) of bombs in bomb bay

FEATURES:
Monoplane wing layout; four radial engines; large vertical tail surface; heavily glazed nose

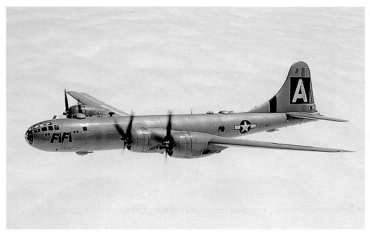

Brewster SB2A Buccaneer

two-seat, single-engined monoplane scout-bomber

One of the least successful designs to attain production in World War II, the SB2A Buccaneer was essentially a larger version of Brewster's SBA/SBN. The Navy had issued a requirement for a more effective scout-bomber with greater armament and an increased bomb load in early 1939, and Brewster responded with its Model 340. Ordered by the Navy in April of that year, the prototype XSB2A-1 flew in June 1941. By then Brewster had received a contract to build 140 for the Navy, as well as export orders from the Netherlands (162) and from the RAF (750). Although well armed, the SB2A was heavy and underpowered. Nevertheless, the Navy received an additional 80 SB2A-2s and 60 SB2A-3s in 1943-44, the latter intended for carrier operations with an arrestor hook and folding wings. The 162 ordered by the Netherlands were also taken over by the Navy, and these were issued as SB2A-4s to the Marine Corps. A total of 771 Buccaneers were eventually built, and these were used for target-towing and other secondline duties.

SPECIFICATION (SB2A-2):

ACCOMMODATION:
Pilot and gunner

DIMENSIONS:
LENGTH: 39 ft 2 in (11.94 m)
WINGSPAN: 47 ft 0 in (14.33 m)
HEIGHT: 15 ft 5 in (4.70 m)

WEIGHTS:
EMPTY: 9924 lb (4501 kg)
MAX T/O: 14,289 lb (6481 kg)

PERFORMANCE:
MAX SPEED: 274 mph (441 kmh)
RANGE: 1675 miles (2696 km)
POWERPLANT: Wright R-2600-8 Cyclone
OUTPUT: 1700 hp (1268 kW)

FIRST FLIGHT DATE:
June 17, 1941 (XSB2A-1)

ARMAMENT:
Two fixed Browning 0.50-in machine guns in upper nose, and four fixed Browning 0.30-in machine guns in wings and two flexibly mounted in rear cockpit; maximum bomb load of 1000 lb (454 kg) in bomb bay

FEATURES:
Midfuselage-mounted mono-plane wing layout; rectractable landing gear; close-cowled radial engine; enclosed cockpit

Budd RB-1 Conestoga

28-seat, twin-engined monoplane transport

Built entirely of stainless steel, the RB-1 Conestoga was the end result of a program launched by the US Government in early 1942 to encourage designers to produce noncombat types out of other materials aside from aluminum. With a history of building stainless-steel truck, bus, and rail-road car bodies, Budd secured a contract in August 1942 to produce a transportation aircraft that could match the load-carrying capacity of the C-47/R4D. It was contracted to build 600 C-93s for the Army and 200 RB-1s for the Navy, both aircraft adopting the Conestoga appellation after the pioneers' covered wagon. Featuring clamshell doors in the nose, a retractable ramp in the rear, and low tricycle landing gear, the aircraft was easier to load than the C-47. However, problems with fabricating the stainless-steel parts that made up the Conestoga delayed production, and aircraft did not reach the Navy until March 1944. By then the USAAF had canceled its order, and only 17 RB-1s were delivered to the Navy, which retired them in early 1945.

SPECIFICATION:

ACCOMMODATION:
Pilot and copilot, navigator/radio operator, loadmaster and up to 24 passengers

DIMENSIONS:
LENGTH: 68 ft 0 in (20.72 m)
WINGSPAN: 100 ft 0 in (30.48 m)
HEIGHT: 31 ft 7 in (9.66 m)

WEIGHTS:
EMPTY: 20,175 lb (9150 kg)
MAX T/O: 33,850 lb (15,354 kg)

PERFORMANCE:
MAX SPEED: 197 mph (315 kmh)
RANGE: 1617 miles (2587 km)
POWERPLANT: two Pratt & Whitney R-1830-92 Twin Wasps
OUTPUT: 2100 hp (1566 kW)

FIRST FLIGHT DATE:
October 31, 1943

FEATURES:
Shoulder-mounted monoplane wing layout; rectractable tricycle landing gear; two close-cowled radial engines; large vertical tail surface; bulbous fuselage; clamshell doors in nose; aft loading ramp

Cessna AT-8/17/UC-78 Bobcat

five-seat, twin-engined monoplane trainer and light transport

Cessna's Bobcat was the company's first twin-engined aircraft, being built as a five-seater for the civilian market. Within 12 months of the prototype flying, the Bobcat had been chosen by the Royal Canadian Air Force as a conversion trainer for pilots transitioning from single- to twin-engined aircraft. Some 550 Crane IAS (as they were designated) were supplied under Lend-Lease for the Commonwealth Joint Air Training Plan. The USAAC also acquired 33 Bobcats for service evaluation (designated AT-8s) in 1940, after which it ordered 450. These aircraft differed from the AT-8s in having Jacobs R-755-9 radials fitted in place of R-680-9s. Designated the AT-17, the trainer was ordered in batches of 223 (AT-17A), 466 (AT-17B), and 60 (AT-17C), each having different equipment fits. In 1942 the USAAF identified a role for the Cessna as a light transport, and 1287 C-78 (later UC-78) Bobcats were bought—2100 surplus AT-17C/DS were also completed in transport configuration from late 1942. Finally, the Navy procured 67 (as JRC-1S) for the transportation of ferry pilots.

SPECIFICATION (UC-78):

ACCOMMODATION:
Two pilots seated side-by-side when in training role, or one pilot and four passengers when in transport configuration

DIMENSIONS:
LENGTH: 32 ft 9 in (9.98 m)
WINGSPAN: 41 ft 11 in (12.78 m)
HEIGHT: 9 ft 11 in (3.02 m)

WEIGHTS:
EMPTY: 3500 lb (1588 kg)
MAX T/O: 5700 lb (2585 kg)

PERFORMANCE:
MAX SPEED: 195 mph (314 kmh)
RANGE: 750 miles (1207 km)
POWERPLANT: two Jacobs R-755-9S
OUTPUT: 490 hp (366 kW)

FIRST FLIGHT DATE:
1939 (civilian T-50)

FEATURES:
Monoplane wing layout; rectractable landing gear; two close-cowled radial engines; fixed tailwheel

Consolidated PB2Y Coronado

seven/ten-seat, four-engined monoplane long-range maritime patrol and transportation flying boat

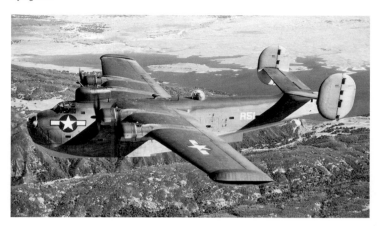

Within months of the first PBY prototype taking to the skies, the Navy instructed Sikorsky and Consolidated to produce prototypes of larger flying boats with better operational performance. First flown on December 17, 1937, Consolidated's aircraft was designated the XPB2Y-1 by the Navy. With almost all flying-boat funds being channeled into the procurement of PBYs, Consolidated had to wait until March 31, 1939 to receive a contract for six PB2Y-2s, each of which cost as much as three PBYs. A follow-on order on November 19, 1940 established the PB2Y-3 in production, and in December the first aircraft reached a frontline unit. A total of 210 PB2Y-3s were built for the Navy, with an additional ten being supplied to Britain under Lend-Lease as Coronado Is. Navy Coronados saw little in the way of combat during World War II, most being converted into transports and used for evacuating wounded troops from frontline hospitals back to Hawaii or the US. All Coronados had been withdrawn from active service before the end of 1945.

SPECIFICATION (PB2Y-3):

ACCOMMODATION:
Pilot and copilot, flight engineer, radar operator, navigator, nose, dorsal, tail, and beam gunners

DIMENSIONS:
LENGTH: 79 ft 3 in (24.15 m)
WINGSPAN: 115 ft 0 in (35.05 m)
HEIGHT: 27 ft 6 in (8.38 m)

WEIGHTS:
EMPTY: 40,935 lb (18,568 kg)
MAX T/O: 68,000 lb (30,845 kg)

PERFORMANCE:
MAX SPEED: 213 mph (343 kmh)
RANGE: 2370 miles (3814 km)
POWERPLANT: four Pratt & Whitney R-1830-88 Twin Wasps
OUTPUT: 4800 hp (3580 kW)

FIRST FLIGHT DATE:
December 17, 1937

ARMAMENT:
Twin Browning 0.50-in machine guns in nose, dorsal, and tail turrets and single gun in each beam position; maximum bomb/mine/torpedo load of 8000 lb (3629 kg) on underwing racks

FEATURES:
High-wing monoplane layout; boat-shaped hull; four radial engines; twin tail layout; retractable wingtip floats

Consolidated PBY Catalina

seven/nine-seat, twin-engined high-winged monoplane patrol bomber, amphibian and flying boat

It is extremely unlikely that the PBY Catalina's record of being the most extensively built flying boat in aviation history will ever be surpassed, Consolidated constructing (or granting the license to build in Canada and the USSR) more than 4000 examples of the robustly simple twin-engined high-winged aircraft over a ten-year period starting in 1935. Used by virtually all the Allied nations during World War II, the humble PBY flew more hours on combat patrols than any other American warplane of the period. Having beaten off a rival Douglas design, Consolidated won a highly lucrative contract in June 1935 to supply the Navy with 60 examples of its PBY-1. These were the first cantilever monoplane flying boats to see service with the US armed forces, replacing Consolidated P2Ys and Martin P3Ms. Early examples were issued to VP-11F in October 1936, and such was the pace of re-equipment that by mid-1938 14 squadrons were operating PBYs, and many more were scheduled to receive them.

Further improvements to the engine specification resulted in new variants entering service over the next four years (including 156 NAF-built PBN-1 Nomads in 1941-42), with the PBY-5A finally introducing a retractable tricycle undercarriage to the Catalina, thus making it fully amphibious. This variant, redesignated the OA-10, proved particularly popular with the USAAF, which acquired 56 directly from Navy stocks in 1943 and a further 230 from Canadian Vickers in 1944-45. Fitted with droppable lifeboats under each wing, these aircraft were used by the Air Rescue Service across the globe until 1954.

Consolidated continued to update and re-engine its tried and trusted PBY throughout the years of conflict, with improved hydrodynamics being achieved through revision of the hull shape and reworked wingtip floats.

The flying-boat's handling characteristics were also improved with the installation of a taller fin/rudder starting with the PBY-5A and this variant also featured additional fuel tankage and a higher all-up loaded weight. Although the flying boat versions of the PBY were quickly retired by the Navy postwar, amphibious PBY-6AS served until January 1957.

SPECIFICATION (PBY-5A):

ACCOMMODATION:
Pilot and copilot, flight engineer, radar/radio operator, navigator, nose gunner, two beam gunners

DIMENSIONS:
LENGTH: 63 ft 10.50 in (19.47 m)
WINGSPAN: 104 ft 0 in (31.70 m)
HEIGHT: 20 ft 2 in (6.50 m)

WEIGHTS:
EMPTY: 20,910 lb (9485 kg)
MAX T/O: 35,420 lb (16,066 kg)

PERFORMANCE:
MAX SPEED: 179 mph (288 kmh)
RANGE: 2545 miles (4096 km)
POWERPLANT: two Pratt & Whitney R-1830-92 Twin Wasps
OUTPUT: 2400 hp (1790 kW)

FIRST FLIGHT DATE:
March 21, 1935

ARMAMENT:
One Browning 0.30/0.50-in machine gun in nose, each waist blister, and in "tunnel" behind hull step; maximum bomb/mine/torpedo load of 2000 lb (907 kg) on underwing racks

FEATURES:
High-wing monoplane layout; boat-shaped hull; two radial engines; retractable wingtip floats

Consolidated B-24 Liberator

ten-seat, four-engined monoplane heavy/patrol bomber and transport

Born out of an approach made by the USAAC to Consolidated for a bomber with superior performance to the B-17, the Liberator was built in near record time. Designated the Model 32 by its manufacturer, the bomber was designed around the then-new long-span/low-drag Davis wing. The Army was so impressed with how the project was shaping up that in March 1939 it ordered 36 production examples before the prototype XB-24 had flown—a French purchasing mission also bought 120 bombers, these aircraft being issued to Britain following France's defeat by Germany in June 1940. Indeed, it was the British who coined the name "Liberator," RAF Coastal Command aircraft being the first of the type to see action, over the Atlantic, in June 1941.

That same month the USAAC received its first B-24As, although these machines were used almost exclusively by the Air Corps' Ferry Command. In fact, it was not until the advent of the B-24D in early 1942 that a true heavy bomber version of the Liberator finally went into series production. This variant featured self-sealing fuel tanks, extra defensive armor, and turbocharged Pratt & Whitney Twin Wasp R-1830-41 engines. Production soon got into full swing with the advent of the D-model, and it was this variant that was sent to the Middle East, the Pacific, and Europe in late 1942 to wage war against Axis forces. Built on five production lines by Consolidated (San Diego and Fort Worth), Douglas (Tulsa), Ford (Willow Run), and North American (Dallas), the most successful B-24 variant of them all was the J-model—no fewer than 6678 were completed between 1943-45. Some 977 Liberators were also used by the Navy as land-based patrol bombers in PB4Y form both in the Pacific and Europe. By the time production ceased on May 31, 1945, 18,475 Liberators had been built, making it the most produced American aircraft of World War II. The USAAF had declared its surviving B-24s surplus by the end of 1945, but the Navy kept its PB4Y-1PS in service until 1951.

SPECIFICATION (B-24J):

ACCOMMODATION:
Pilot and copilot, flight engineer, navigator, bombardier/nose gunner, radio operator/dorsal gunner, two waist gunners, ball turret gunner, tail gunner

DIMENSIONS:
LENGTH: 67 ft 2 in (20.47 m)
WINGSPAN: 110 ft 0 in (33.53 m)
HEIGHT: 18 ft 0 in (5.49 m)

WEIGHTS:
EMPTY: 36,500 lb (16,556 kg)
MAX T/O: 71,200 lb (32,296 kg)

PERFORMANCE:
MAX SPEED: 290 mph (467 kmh)
RANGE : 2100 miles (3380 km)
POWERPLANT: four Pratt & Whitney R-1830-65 Twin Wasps
OUTPUT: 4800 hp (3580 kW)

FIRST FLIGHT DATE:
December 29, 1939

ARMAMENT:
Nose, tail, dorsal, and ball turrets equipped with two Browning 0.50-in machine guns, and two guns in waist; maximum bomb load of 12,000 lb (5443 kg) in bomb bay/inner wing racks

FEATURES:
Large-span monoplane wing layout; rectractable landing gear; four radial engines; twin-tail layout

Consolidated PB4Y-2 Privateer

11-seat, four-engined monoplane maritime patrol bomber

Although the Navy had made much use of its PB4Y-1 Liberators starting in August 1942, these aircraft had all been configured for USAAF service when originally built. It was therefore decided in 1943 that a navalized variant would be most beneficial, and a contract was placed in May for a dedicated long-range patrol bomber based on the Liberator. Three B-24Ds were taken off the San Diego production line and rebuilt with lengthened fuselages, navalized interiors, greater defensive armament, modified engine cowlings, and a distinctive vertical tail similar to that fitted to the final Liberator transport variant. The Navy ordered 739 in a single production run, 286 of which were delivered in 1944-45. Few had reached the frontline by VJ-Day, although the Privateer-equipped VP-24 did achieve operational status in the weeks prior to Japan's surrender. The PB4Y went on to perform its best work in the Cold War as a radar and electronic countermeasures platform. After further service with the US Coast Guard, the final examples were retired in the early 1960s.

SPECIFICATION:

ACCOMMODATION:
Pilot and copilot, flight engineer, navigator, nose gunner, radar/radio operator, two dorsal gunners, two waist gunners, tail gunner

DIMENSIONS:
LENGTH: 74 ft 7 in (22.73 m)
WINGSPAN: 110 ft 0 in (33.53 m)
HEIGHT: 30 ft 1 in (9.17 m)

WEIGHTS:
EMPTY: 37,485 lb (17,003 kg)
MAX T/O: 65,000 lb (29,484 kg)

PERFORMANCE:
MAX SPEED: 237 mph (381 kmh)
RANGE: 2800 miles (4506 km)
POWERPLANT: four Pratt & Whitney R-1830-94 Twin Wasps
OUTPUT: 5400 hp (4028 kW)

FIRST FLIGHT DATE:
September 20, 1943

ARMAMENT:
Four turrets with two Browning 0.50-in machine guns and two guns in waist blisters; maximum bomb/depth charge/missile load of 6000 lb (2725 kg) in bomb bay/underwing racks

FEATURES:
Large-span monoplane wing; four radial engines; large vertical tail

Consolidated/Vought TBY/TBU Seawolf

three-seat, single-engined monoplane torpedo-bomber

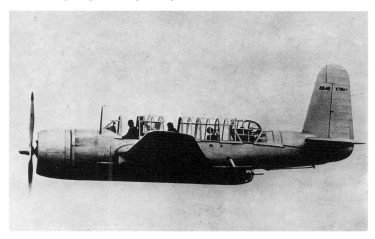

Designed by Vought but built by Consolidated, the Seawolf was a contemporary of Grumman's successful TBF/TBM Avenger. With a history of supplying aircraft to the Navy during the interwar years, Vought seemed an obvious choice to build a new monoplane torpedo-bomber for carrier service. In June 1940 the Navy contracted the company to construct a single XTBU-2 prototype, and this flew just two weeks after the attack on Pearl Harbor. Its performance seemed superior to the Avenger, and the Navy placed an order for 1100. However, Vought was already overcommitted with other contracts, especially for the F4U Corsair, and had no spare production capacity. Consolidated-Vultee was therefore subcontracted to build these machines, as the TBY-2 Seawolf, in a new production facility in Pennsylvania. The latter was not completed until mid-1944, and the first production Seawolf finally flew in August of that year. By then the Avenger had equipped every torpedo-bomber squadron in the Navy, and there was no demand for the TBY-2. Just 180 were built, and none were used operationally.

SPECIFICATION:

ACCOMMODATION:
Pilot, radar operator, gunner

DIMENSIONS:
LENGTH: 39 ft 2 in (11.95 m)
WINGSPAN: 56 ft 11 in (17.35 m)
HEIGHT: 15 ft 6 in (4.70 m)

WEIGHTS:
EMPTY: 11,366 lb (5142 kg)
MAX T/O: 18,940 lb (8590 kg)

PERFORMANCE:
MAX SPEED: 312 mph (502 kmh)
RANGE: 1025 miles (1650 km)
POWERPLANT: Pratt & Whitney R-2800-6 Double Wasp
OUTPUT: 2100 hp (1566 kW)

FIRST FLIGHT DATE:
December 22, 1941

ARMAMENT:
One fixed Browning 0.50-in machine gun in cowling, two in wings, and one in dorsal turret, and one Browning 0.30-in machine gun in ventral position; maximum bomb/torpedo load of 2000 lb (908 kg) in internal bomb bay

FEATURES:
Monoplane wing layout; retractable undercarriage; close-cowled radial engine; gun turret

Consolidated B-32 Dominator

eight-seat, four-engined monoplane bomber

Designed to the same Hemisphere Defense Weapon specification as the B-29, the B-32 Dominator shared many features with the smaller B-24. The Army Air Corps ordered the construction of the XB-32 prototype in September 1940, and this flew for the first time on September 7, 1942—two weeks before the XB-29. Although the Dominator initially featured the B-24's twin-fin arrangement, Consolidated soon opted for a single large fin/rudder. Like Boeing, Consolidated also experienced teething troubles with the XB-32's remote-controlled armament system and pressurized crew areas. These proved to be insurmountable, and delayed the B-32's service entry until November 1944. By then XX Bomber Command had had B-29s in combat for almost eight months, and the production Dominator was restricted to heights of just 30,000 ft because of its nonpressurized fuselage. Just 115 B-32s were built, and 15 became operational with the 386th BS on Okinawa—one took part in the last combat action of the war. A further 40 were configured as TB-32 trainers.

SPECIFICATION:

ACCOMMODATION:
Pilot and copilot, flight engineer, navigator/nose gunner, radar/radio operator, two dorsal gunners, tail gunner

DIMENSIONS:
LENGTH: 83 ft 1 in (25.32 m)
WINGSPAN: 135 ft 0 in (41.15 m)
HEIGHT: 33 ft 0 in (10.06 m)

WEIGHTS:
EMPTY: 60,272 lb (27,339 kg)
MAX T/O: 111,500 lb (50,576 kg)

PERFORMANCE:
MAX SPEED: 357 mph (575 kmh)
RANGE: 2800 miles (6115 km)
POWERPLANT: four Wright R-3350-23 Cyclones
OUTPUT: 8800 hp (6564 kW)

FIRST FLIGHT DATE:
September 7, 1942

ARMAMENT:
Ten Browing 0.50-in machine guns in nose, two dorsal, ventral and tail turrets; maximum bomb load of 20,000 lb (9072 kg) in twin bomb bays

FEATURES:
Large-span monoplane wing; four radial engines; large vertical tail

Culver A-8/PQ-8/TDC-2

single-seat, single-engined monoplane radio-controlled target aircraft

Developed for the training of antiaircraft gunnery batteries, the Culver A-8 was based on the company's successful LCA Cadet civil aircraft. Prior to the advent of this machine, Army gunners had had make do with firing at drogues towed some distance behind a tug aircraft. The job of flying the latter was not an enviable one, as many a pilot had endured a close shave when height and speed had been misjudged by the gunners and over/under correction made to the sighting of their weapon. In 1940 the Army selected the Cadet as a suitable platform for development as a radio-controlled target. Successful testing of the prototype XPQ-8 resulted in the follow-on purchase of 200 PQ-8s, followed by a further 200 re-engined PQ-8A (later Q-8As). The Navy also had a requirement for such a target aircraft, and after evaluating a single PQ-8A, it too ordered 200 (designated TDC-2s) from Culver in 1942. Both the Army and Navy Culvers provided valuable training to legions of gunners until war's end.

SPECIFICATION:

ACCOMMODATION:
Pilot (although usually flown unmanned)

DIMENSIONS:
LENGTH: 17 ft 8 in (5.38 m)
WINGSPAN: 26 ft 11 in (8.20 m)
HEIGHT: 5 ft 6 in (1.68 m)

WEIGHTS:
EMPTY: 720 lb (327 kg)
MAX T/O: 1305 lb (592 kg)

PERFORMANCE:
MAX SPEED: 116 mph (187 kmh)
RANGE: 420 miles (672 km)
POWERPLANT: Continental
O-200-1
OUTPUT: 125 hp (93 kW)

FIRST FLIGHT DATE:
1940

FEATURES:
Monoplane wing layout; retractable tricycle undercarriage; close-cowled flat-four piston engine; enclosed cockpit

Culver PQ-14/TD2C-1

single-seat, single-engined monoplane radio-controlled target aircraft

Culver cornered the market for unmanned aerial gunnery targets in 1940 when its Cadet light airplane was selected by the USAAC for conversion into a radio-controlled drone. Some 600 were built, 200 of which were issued to the Navy as training aids for antiaircraft gunners. As the performance of manned combat aircraft increased, so the need for a more powerful gunnery target grew. To answer this demand Culver created a purpose-built machine, which entered service in 1943 as the PQ-14. Faster than its predecessor, the new design was also more maneuverable thanks to its larger control surfaces and bigger engine. Of the 1348 PQ-14AS built, 1201 were transferred to the Navy, where they were designated TD2C-1s. The final version to enter USAAF service was the heavier PQ-14B, 1112 of which were procured. Many of these remained in military service well into the 1950s, by which time the survivors had been redesignated Q-14A/BS. Those that were not destroyed were sold into private ownership, and a number appeared on the US civil aircraft register.

SPECIFICATION:

ACCOMMODATION:
Pilot (although usually flown unmanned)

DIMENSIONS:
LENGTH: 19 ft 6 in (5.94 m)
WINGSPAN: 30 ft 0 in (9.14 m)
HEIGHT: 7 ft 11 in (2.41 m)

WEIGHTS:
EMPTY: 1500 lb (680 kg)
MAX T/O: 1830 lb (830 kg)

PERFORMANCE:
MAX SPEED: 180 mph (290 kmh)
RANGE: 512 miles (824 km)
POWERPLANT: Franklin O-300-11
OUTPUT: 150 hp (112 kW)

FIRST FLIGHT DATE:
1942

FEATURES:
Monoplane wing layout; retractable undercarriage; close-cowled inline engine

Curtiss AT-9

two-seat, twin-engined monoplane advanced trainer

The Curtiss AT-9 was ordered into production by the Army when it found that the Cessna T-50/AT-8 twin-engined trainer that it had bought "off-the-shelf" was just too stable a platform for teaching pilots destined to fly high-performance twin-engined types such as the P-38 and B-26. Curtiss had pre-empted this order by starting development of its Model 25 in advance of the Army's requirement, the purpose-built aircraft boasting both the high approach speeds and landing characteristics associated with "hot twins" then entering USAAC service. Featuring all-stressed skinning, twin Lycoming R-680-9 radial engines, and a retractable undercarriage, the Model 25 was ordered into production as the AT-9 in 1941. The first of 491 AT-9s entered service in 1942, and a further 300 near-identical AT-9As followed in 1943. Far more demanding to fly than the AT-8, the Curtiss twins were used exclusively for pilot transition training until replaced in 1944-45 by dual-control versions of frontline tactical types, which were much better suited to full crew integration training.

SPECIFICATION:

ACCOMMODATION:
Two pilots seated side-by-side in training role

DIMENSIONS:
LENGTH: 31 ft 8 in (9.65 m)
WINGSPAN: 40 ft 4 in (12.29 m)
HEIGHT: 9 ft 10 in (2.99 m)

WEIGHTS:
EMPTY: 4600 lb (2087 kg)
MAX T/O: 6000 lb (2722 kg)

PERFORMANCE:
MAX SPEED: 197 mph (317 kmh)
RANGE: 750 miles (1207 km)
POWERPLANT: two Lycoming R-680-9s
OUTPUT: 590 hp (440 kW)

FIRST FLIGHT DATE:
1941

FEATURES:
Monoplane wing layout; rectractable landing gear; two close-cowled radial engines; fixed tailwheel

Curtiss SO3C Seamew

two-seat, single-engined monoplane reconnaissance float- or landplane

Built to replace Curtiss's SOC Seagull biplane floatplane, the company's XSO3C-1 prototype beat off the rival XSO2U-1 from Vought to secure a Navy contract in late 1939. Despite being the successful design, the aircraft was found to have serious instability problems that were only solved through the adoption of upturned wingtips and tail surfaces of increased size. These problems prevented delivery of production aircraft until July 1942, when the newly commissioned cruiser USS *Cleveland* took two SO3C-1s to sea. A further 300 were built before production switched to the SO3C-2, which had additional equipment for carrier operations when fitted with a wheeled undercarriage, including arrestor gear and an underfuselage bomb rack. A total of 456 SO3C-2s were completed, followed by a further 39 lightened and re-engined SO3C-4s. The last Seamew was delivered in January 1944, and plans for a carrier-capable version of the SO3C-4 were canceled. Several months later all surviving Seamews were withdrawn from fleet use due to their poor performance. A number of surplus SO3Cs were subsequently converted into radio-controlled targets.

SPECIFICATION (SO3C-2):

ACCOMMODATION:
Pilot and observer/gunner

DIMENSIONS:
LENGTH: 36 ft 10 in (11.23 m)
WINGSPAN: 38 ft 0 in (11.58 m)
HEIGHT: 15 ft 0 in (4.57 m)

WEIGHTS:
EMPTY: 4284 lb (1943 kg)
MAX T/O: 5729 lb (2599 kg)

PERFORMANCE:
MAX SPEED: 172 mph (277 kmh)
RANGE: 1150 miles (1851 km)
POWERPLANT: Ranger SGV-770-8
OUTPUT: 600 hp (447 kW)

FIRST FLIGHT DATE:
October 6, 1939

ARMAMENT:
One fixed Browning 0.30-in machine gun in nose and one Browning 0.50-in machine gun on flexible mounting for observer; maximum bomb/depth charge load of 500 lb (227 kg) on underwing/fuselage racks

FEATURES:
Monoplane wing layout; cowled inline engine; single main float; fixed outrigger floats; upturned wingtips

Curtiss P-40 Tomahawk

single-seat, single-engined monoplane fighter

Developed simply by replacing the Twin Wasp radial of Curtiss's prewar P-36 Hawk with a supercharged Allison V-1710 inline engine, the XP-40 prototype impressed the USAAC so much that a contract for 524 aircraft was placed in early 1939. This was the largest order for military aircraft issued by the US Government to a contractor since the Great War, and the first production aircraft flew in April 1940. A large number of P-40B/Cs (no A-models were built) had been delivered to the USAAC by December 7, 1941, and these took the fight to the Japanese, but were soon shown to be inferior. Aside from USAAC use, the Curtiss design also saw action with the RAF, which christened it the Tomahawk. Some 1180 were acquired by the British through Lend-Lease, and these were flown by RAF, RCAF, RAAF, and South African units in North Africa and the Middle East in 1941-42. Around 100 of these ex-British aircraft were also issued to the American Volunteer Group in China and Myanmar (Burma) at the same time.

SPECIFICATION (P-40C):

ACCOMMODATION:
Pilot

DIMENSIONS:
LENGTH: 31 ft 8.50 in (9.66 m)
WINGSPAN: 37 ft 3.50 in (11.37 m)
HEIGHT: 10 ft 7 in (3.22 m)

WEIGHTS:
EMPTY: 5812 lb (2636 kg)
MAX T/O: 8058 lb (3655 kg)

PERFORMANCE:
MAX SPEED: 345 mph (555 kmh)
RANGE: 1230 miles (1979 km)
POWERPLANT: Allison V-1710-33
OUTPUT: 1040 hp (775 kW)

FIRST FLIGHT DATE:
October 14, 1938

ARMAMENT:
Two Browning 0.50-in machine guns in nose and two or four Browning 0.30-in machine guns in wings; maximum bomb load of 1600 lb (726 kg) on underwing/fuselage racks

FEATURES:
Monoplane wing layout; retractable undercarriage; close-cowled inline engine; radiator intake beneath propeller spinner

Curtiss P-40 Warhawk/Kittyhawk

single-seat, single-engined monoplane fighter

With the further development of the Allison V-1710, Curtiss kept pace on the airframe side by producing the P-40D/E in 1941. The primary differences between these models and the earlier Tomahawk centered on a drastically revised nose shape due to the chin radiator being moved forward, which in turn allowed the propeller thrust line to be raised, the undercarriage to be shortened, and fuselage top line to be lowered and recontoured. The modifications to the forward fuselage also meant that the nose guns were moved to the wings, changing from 0.30-in to 0.50-in Brownings in the process—the USAAC's E-model differed from the export P-40D in having six 0.50-in guns in the wings rather than four.

As with the Tomahawk, the RAF was a major export customer for the aircraft, which it christened the Kittyhawk. Despite suffering from poor performance at altitudes above 15,000 ft, the aircraft proved very successful in the fighter-bomber role, and it was used in this capacity by the RCAF, RAAF, and the South African Air Force. In US service, the aircraft received the appellation Warhawk, and subsequent variants of the fighter were powered by Packard Merlins as well as Allison V-1710s. Most of the Merlin-engined P-40Fs (1311 built) featured the lengthened fuselage adopted by the later mark Warhawks, this 20-inch extension improving directional stability at low speeds.

No fewer than 1300 V-1710-73-engined P-40Ks were built virtually alongside the F-models, followed by 600 P-40Ms, which utilized the V-1710-81 version of Allison's legendary inline engine. The P-40L (700 built) was a stripped-out Warhawk, which enjoyed improved performance through the shedding of weight by the deletion of two wing guns and fuel capacity. The final variant to attain production status was the P-40N, 1977 of which were built in 1943-44—more than 11,600 Warhawks had been completed by the time the last P-40N was delivered in December 1944. Used by the USAAF in the Pacific, China-Burma-India, North African, and Mediterranean theaters, the Warhawk was soon retired after VJ-Day.

SPECIFICATION (P-40N):

ACCOMMODATION:
Pilot

DIMENSIONS:
LENGTH: 33 ft 4 in (10.16 m)
WINGSPAN: 37 ft 4 in (11.38 m)
HEIGHT: 12 ft 4 in (3.76 m)

WEIGHTS:
EMPTY: 6200 lb (2812 kg)
MAX T/O: 8850 lb (4014 kg)

PERFORMANCE:
MAX SPEED: 343 mph (552 kmh)
RANGE: 1080 miles (1738 km) with external drop tank
POWERPLANT: Allison V-1710-81
OUTPUT: 1200 hp (895 kW)

FIRST FLIGHT DATE:
May 22, 1941

ARMAMENT:
Six Browning 0.50-in machine guns in wings; maximum bomb load of 1500 lb (680 kg) on underwing/fuselage racks

FEATURES:
Monoplane wing layout; retractable undercarriage; close-cowled inline engine; prominent radiator intake beneath propeller spinner

Curtiss sb2c Helldiver

two-seat, single-engined monoplane dive-bomber

The most numerous Allied dive-bomber of World War II, the Curtiss Helldiver endured a prolonged gestation period to mature into one of the most effective aircraft of its type. The third Curtiss design to bear the appellation "Helldiver," the aircraft had started life as the xsb2a-1 prototype. Built in response to a 1938 requirement issued by the Navy for a new scout-bomber to replace the biplane sbc Helldiver, the aircraft showed such promise that large-scale production was authorized a full 18 months before the first sb2c-1 left the Curtiss factory. Delays in the Helldiver's production were caused by the building of a new factory in Ohio and a USAAC order for 900 a-25as in April 1941. The latter machines were similar to the Navy's sb2c-1, but embodied sufficient differences to further slow progress on the aircraft. Ironically, only a handful of a-25s were delivered to the Army Air Corps, with the bulk of the order being reassigned to the Marine Corps as sb2c-1as.

Production Helldivers finally reached the Navy in November 1942 when examples were issued to vs-9, but further delays in defining the aircraft's combat configuration prevented the Helldiver from making its service debut until November of the following year over Rabaul, flying from the deck of USS *Bunker Hill*. At that time, the sb2c-1 was still inferior in many respects to the Douglas sbd Dauntless—the aircraft it was meant to replace! Some 7200 were built between 1942-45, and despite being drastically improved during its service life (880 major design changes had to be made to the sb2c-1 before production could even get underway), the Helldiver retained an unenviable reputation "around the boat," with more aircraft being lost in deck landing accidents than to enemy action. Indeed, its unpleasant flying characteristics near the stall earned it the nickname "The Beast."

Although passionately disliked by many of the myriad crews sent into combat flying it, the Helldiver was responsible for the destruction of more Japanese targets than any other US dive-bomber. Postwar, the aircraft saw Reserve service until the late 1940s.

SPECIFICATION (SB2C-4):

ACCOMMODATION:
Pilot and observer/gunner

DIMENSIONS:
LENGTH: 36 ft 8 in (11.20 m)
WINGSPAN: 49 ft 9 in (15.20 m)
HEIGHT: 16 ft 11 in (5.10 m)

WEIGHTS:
EMPTY: 10,547 lb (4784 kg)
MAX T/O: 16,616 lb (7537 kg)

PERFORMANCE:
MAX SPEED: 295 mph (475 kmh)
RANGE: 1165 miles (1875 km)
POWERPLANT: Wright R-2600-20 Cyclone
OUTPUT: 1900 hp (1417 kW)

FIRST FLIGHT DATE:
December 18, 1940

ARMAMENT:
Two 20-mm cannon or four Browning 0.50-in machine guns in wings and two flexible Browning 0.30-in machine guns in rear cockpit; maximum bomb/torpedo load of 1000 lb (454 kg) in internal bomb bay and 1000 lb (454 kg) of bombs/rockets on underwing racks

FEATURES:
Monoplane wing layout; close-cowled radial engine; large vertical tail surface

Curtiss c-46 Commando

54-seat, twin-engined monoplane transport

Built by Curtiss-Wright in an effort to recover airliner sales that had been lost to modern monoplane designs from Boeing, Douglas, and Lockheed, the c-46 started life as the cw-20 in 1936. With the prototype flying by the spring of 1940, its performance figures impressed civil and military operators alike—the USAAC ordered 200 in September of that year. To fulfill its military role, the cw-20's pressurized interior was gutted and replaced with canvas seating in an unpressurized environment, cargo doors were built into the fuselage, the floor strengthened, and uprated engines fitted. Production examples reached the USAAF's Air Transport Command in the fall of 1942, the type proving itself on long-range flights transporting men and equipment to North Africa following the Operation Torch landings. The c-46's "finest hour" came in the Far East, where India-China Wing aircraft formed the backbone of the "Hump" airlift across the Himalayas in 1943-44. More than 3000 were built, and the aircraft also served with the USAF in Korea and Vietnam.

SPECIFICATION (C-46A):

ACCOMMODATION:
Pilot and copilot, navigator/radio operator, loadmaster and up to 50 passengers

DIMENSIONS:
LENGTH: 76 ft 4 in (23.27 m)
WINGSPAN: 108 ft 1 in (32.94 m)
HEIGHT: 21 ft 9 in (6.63 m)

WEIGHTS:
EMPTY: 32,400 lb (14,696 kg)
MAX T/O: 56,000 lb (25,401 kg)

PERFORMANCE:
MAX SPEED: 269 mph (433 kmh)
RANGE: 1200 miles (1931 km)
POWERPLANT: two Pratt & Whitney R-2800-51 Double Wasps
OUTPUT: 4000 hp (2982 kW)

FIRST FLIGHT DATE:
March 26, 1940

FEATURES:
Monoplane wing layout; retractable landing gear; two close-cowled radial engines; retractable tailwheel; large vertical tail surface; bulbous fuselage

Curtiss sc Seahawk

single-seat, single-engined monoplane scout/ASW float- or landplane

In June 1942 the Navy asked Curtiss to design a
replacement for the company's Seamew and
Vought's Kingfisher, both of which had stemmed
from a similar requirement for a shipborne
scouting aircraft issued in 1937. The new aircraft
had to feature easily convertible landing gear for
wheeled operations from land bases and aircraft
carriers, or floats for when embarked aboard
battleships and cruisers. Curtiss's xsc-1 prototype
made its first flight in February 1944, the company
choosing a single-seat layout so as to save weight
and boost performance. The Navy had contracted
Curtiss to build 500 sc-1 Seahawks eight months
prior to the prototype taking to the skies, and these
were delivered as landplanes. The Navy then purchased stabilizer and Edo central floats separately,
and had them fitted when required. Production
aircraft began reaching the fleet in October 1944,
with four sc-1s joining the newly commissioned
battleship USS *Guam* to give the Seahawk its service
debut. Only 66 of a second batch of 450 had been
delivered by VJ-Day, and the rest were canceled.

SPECIFICATION:

ACCOMMODATION:
Pilot

DIMENSIONS:
LENGTH: 36 ft 4.50 in (11.09 m)
WINGSPAN: 41 ft 0 in (12.50 m)
HEIGHT: 12 ft 9 in (3.89 m)

WEIGHTS:
EMPTY: 6320 lb (2867 kg)
MAX T/O: 9000 lb (4082 kg)

PERFORMANCE:
MAX SPEED: 313 mph (504 kmh)
RANGE: 625 miles (1006 km)
POWERPLANT: Wright R-1820-62
Cyclone 9
OUTPUT: 1350 hp (1007 kW)

FIRST FLIGHT DATE:
February 16, 1944

ARMAMENT:
Two fixed Browning 0.50-in
machine guns in wings;
maximum bomb/depth charge
load of 650 lb (295 kg) on
underwing racks

FEATURES:
monoplane wing layout; cowled
radial engine; single main float;
fixed outrigger floats; four-
bladed propeller

Douglas SBD Dauntless

two-seat, single-engined monoplane scout/dive-bomber

The SBD Dauntless was the scourge of the Japanese Imperial Fleet in the crucial years of the Pacific war. Almost single-handedly, 54 SBDs from the Navy carriers *Enterprise*, *Hornet*, and *Yorktown* won the pivotal Battle of Midway on June 4, 1942, destroying four Japanese "flat tops" in just 24 hours. The SBD of 1942 could trace its origins back to rival designs penned by gifted engineers John Northrop and Ed Heinemann in the mid-1930s. Northrop produced the BT-1 for the Navy in the spring of 1938, its revolutionary all-metal stressed-skin design exhibiting airframe strength that made it an ideal candidate for adoption as a dive-bomber.

By the time the BT-1 had evolved into the BT-2, with engine and structural changes that made the revised dive-bomber virtually an all-new aircraft, Northrop had become the El Segundo Division of Douglas. The XBT-2 prototype was reworked still further by Heinemann and his team and duly redesignated the SBD-1. Production orders for 57 SBD-1s and 87 SBD-2s were placed by the Navy in April 1939, with all the "Dash-1s" going to the Marine Corps in 1940-41. The first unit to receive the Dauntless, as it was now called, was VMB-2 in late 1940, followed by VMB-1 early the next year. The SBD-2s, with extra armament and fuel capacity, had reached Navy squadrons VB-6 and VS-6 aboard *Enterprise* and VB-2 aboard *Lexington* by the end of 1941.

The definitive SBD-3, and near-identical SBD-4, entered production in the spring of 1941, these versions boasting self-sealing tanks, a bulletproof windscreen, armor protection, an uprated engine, and improved armament.

A total of 584 SBD-3s and 700 SBD-4s were built, and it was these machines that became the key combat aircraft in the Pacific in 1942-43. The SBD-5/6, 2409 examples of which were built at a new Douglas plant in Oklahoma, ended the Navy's production run for the aircraft in July 1944. The USAAC also procured nearly 900 Dauntlesses as the A-24, although they saw only limited action in the Pacific in 1942-43.

SPECIFICATION (SBD-6):

ACCOMMODATION:
Pilot and gunner

DIMENSIONS:
LENGTH: 33 ft 0 in (10.06 m)
WINGSPAN: 41 ft 6 in (12.65 m)
HEIGHT: 12 ft 11 in (3.94 m)

WEIGHTS:
EMPTY: 6535 lb (2964 kg)
MAX T/O: 9519 lb (4318 kg)

PERFORMANCE:
MAX SPEED: 255 mph (410 kmh)
RANGE: 773 miles (1244 km)
POWERPLANT: Wright R-1820-66 Cyclone 9
OUTPUT: 1350 hp (1007 kW)

FIRST FLIGHT DATE:
July 23, 1938 (XBT-2)

ARMAMENT:
Two Browning 0.50-in machine guns in nose and two flexibly mounted in rear cockpit; maximum bomb load of 2250 lb (1021 kg) on underwing/ fuselage racks

FEATURES:
Monoplane wing layout; rectractable landing gear; close-cowled radial engine; aerial mast on port side forward of cockpit; arrestor hook

Douglas C-47/R4D Skytrain

32-seat, twin-engined monoplane transport

An improved version of Douglas's revolutionary DC-1 of 1933, the C-47 was the military descendent of the Douglas Sleeper Transport, which was itself an enlarged DC-2. When the DC-3 entered civilian service in 1936, the Army Air Corps immediately contacted Douglas and advised the company of changes that needed to be made in order to render the airliner suitable for military use—these included the fitment of more powerful engines, the reinforcement of the cabin floor, and the inclusion of large cargo doors. Therefore, when the USAAC issued contracts in 1940 for the first C-47s, Douglas was able to get production immediately underway at its brand new Long Beach, California, plant. Some 963 examples of the basic C-47 were built, the first aircraft entering USAAC service in 1941.

In order to quickly increase the number of transports in USAAC service in the wake of the Pearl Habor raid, 174 civilian DC-3s were impressed into military ranks with the designations C-48 and C-49. Dedicated military versions of the Skytrain that were subsequently built through to June 1945 included the A- and B-models, which differed primarily in electrical systems and powerplant from the basic C-47. Aside from the thousands of Skytrains that served with the USAAF's Air Transport and Troop Carrier Commands in World War II, 568 aircraft were also supplied to the Navy as R4D-1/3/4/5/6/7s and issued to the Naval Air Transport Service and the South Pacific Combat Air Transport Service. The Douglas transport was a key factor in the success of the Allied war effort, fulfilling the critical "air bridge" role with men and material to virtually all theaters of conflict. Some 10,926 examples were built in the USA, and several thousand served on with the postwar Navy and USAF well into the 1970s, supporting combat operations both in Korea and Vietnam. Indeed, in the latter conflict, the minigun-equipped AC-47D actively engaged the Viet Cong in South Vietnam starting in 1965 onward. The last Skytrains in service with the Air Force and Navy were finally retired in the mid-1970s.

SPECIFICATION (C-47A):

ACCOMMODATION:
Pilot and copilot, navigator/radio operator, loadmaster, and up to 28 passengers

DIMENSIONS:
LENGTH: 64 ft 2.50 in (19.57 m)
WINGSPAN: 95 ft 0 in (28.96 m)
HEIGHT: 16 ft 11 in (5.16 m)

WEIGHTS:
EMPTY: 16,970 lb (7698 kg)
MAX T/O: 26,000 lb (11,793 kg)

PERFORMANCE:
MAX SPEED: 229 mph (369 kmh)
RANGE: 1500 miles (2414 km)
POWERPLANT: two Pratt & Whitney R-1830-93 Twin Wasps
OUTPUT: 2400 hp (1790 kW)

FIRST FLIGHT DATE:
December 17, 1935 (Douglas Sleeper Transport)

FEATURES:
Monoplane wing layout; rectractable landing gear; two close-cowled radial engines; large vertical tail surface

Douglas A-20 Havoc

three-seat, twin-engined monoplane light bomber

One of the most widely used light bombers of World War II, the A-20 evolved from a Douglas design by Jack Northrop and Ed Heinemann that was built to meet a USAAC attack specification issued in 1938. Initially known as the Model 7A, the prototype was drastically reworked and given more powerful Twin Wasp engines soon after its first flight trials in order to make the aircraft more suitable for use in Europe. Indeed, the first order for the new bomber (100 examples) came from France, not the USAAC.

The first military aircraft to attain series production with a tricycle undercarriage, DB-7 bombers began emerging from the Douglas plant in August 1939, and 60 aircraft had reached France prior to the start of the *Blitzkrieg* on May 10, 1940. A handful of undelivered DB-7s were issued to the RAF, which christened them Boston Is and used them in both training and nightfighter roles. The performance of the Douglas "twin" was far in advance of anything the British were then operating, and the Boston went on to become one of the mainstays of the RAF—1000+ aircraft were supplied through Lend-Lease.

The USAAC committed to the DB-7 (redesignated the A-20 Havoc) in May 1939, ordering 206. The first A-20As delivered were issued to units overseas in 1941, while the first to see combat were the A-20Cs of the 15th Bomb Squadron, which was sent to the UK in May 1942 and began flying missions over France alongside RAF Boston IIIs two months later. By then the definitive A-20G had entered production, and no fewer than 2850 examples (and 412 of the near-identical A-20H) would be built. Aside from its service with the Ninth and Fifteenth Air Forces in Europe, North Africa, and the Mediterranean, the Havoc also saw considerable action with the 15th Air Forces in the Pacific as a low-altitude bomber. Production ended in September 1944, by which time 7385 Havoc/ Bostons had been delivered (3125 to the Soviet Union). Most had been discarded by the USAAF by the end of 1945.

SPECIFICATION (A-20G):

ACCOMMODATION:
Pilot, navigator/bombardier, and gunner

DIMENSIONS:
LENGTH: 48 ft 0 in (14.63 m)
WINGSPAN: 61 ft 4 in (18.69 m)
HEIGHT: 17 ft 7 in (5.36 m)

WEIGHTS:
EMPTY: 15,984 lb (7250 kg)
MAX T/O: 27,200 lb (12,338 kg)

PERFORMANCE:
MAX SPEED: 317 mph (510 kmh)
RANGE: 1025 miles (1650 km)
POWERPLANT: two Wright R-2600-23 Cyclone 14S
OUTPUT: 3200 hp (2386 kW)

FIRST FLIGHT DATE:
October 26, 1938 (Douglas 7B)

ARMAMENT:
Four fixed Browning 0.50-in machine guns in nose, two in dorsal turret and one in ventral tunnel; maximum bomb load of 2600 lb (1179 kg) in bomb bay

FEATURES:
Monoplane, shoulder-mounted wing layout; rectractable tricycle landing gear; two close-cowled radial engines; large vertical tail surface

Douglas A/B-26/JD Invader

three-seat, twin-engined monoplane attack bomber

The A-26 Invader was designed as a natural successor to Douglas' successful A-20, the USAAC issuing a requirement in 1940 for an all-new multirole light bomber that could perform both fast low-level attacks and precision bombing from medium altitude. Harnessing the power of Pratt & Whitney's then new Double Wasp radial engine, prototype XP-26s were ordered by the USAAC in May 1941 in three different forms. The first featured a 75-mm gun, the second a solid radar nose and a quartet of 20-mm forward-firing weapons, plus four guns in an upper turret, and the third had optical sighting equipment in the nose and two defensive turrets. Extensive service trials in 1942-43 showed that the Douglas machine exceeded every performance specification stipulated in the USAAF requirement, being 700 lb below design weight and capable of carrying twice the specified bomb load.

The first variant to enter production was the A-26B Invader, which had a solid nose and two remote-controlled gun turrets. The Invader made its combat debut with the Ninth Air Force in the ETO on November 19, 1944, and some 1355 were eventually built, followed by 1091 C-models (which had a transparent nose, housing navigational and radar bombing equipment). Both variants saw action in the final months of World War II in Europe and the Pacific, the C-model making its combat debut in the latter theater in early 1945.

The Invader enjoyed a more active postwar career with the USAF than any of its twin-engined contemporaries, being among the first aircraft to bolster NATO forces in Europe in the late 1940s as the primary offensive weapon of the newly formed Tactical Air Command. The Navy also received 140 A-26Cs (redesignated JD-1s) for target tug duties. More than 450 B-26s (the Invader was redesignated in 1948 following the retirement of the last Marauders) split between six squadrons saw further combat in the Korean War, while the French used them in Indo-China. Following the latter's lead, the USAF employed specially converted On Mark B-26Ks in Vietnam too.

SPECIFICATION (A-26C):

ACCOMMODATION:
Pilot, navigator/bombardier, and gunner

DIMENSIONS:
LENGTH: 51 ft 3 in (15.62 m)
WINGSPAN: 70 ft 0 in (21.34 m)
HEIGHT: 18 ft 3 in (5.56 m)

WEIGHTS:
EMPTY: 22,850 lb (10,365 kg)
MAX T/O: 35,000 lb (15,876 kg)

PERFORMANCE:
MAX SPEED: 373 mph (600 kmh)
RANGE: 1400 miles (2253 km)
POWERPLANT: two Pratt & Whitney R-2800-79 Double Wasps
OUTPUT: 4000 hp (2982 kW)

FIRST FLIGHT DATE:
July 10, 1942

ARMAMENT:
Six fixed Browning 0.50-in machine guns in nose and two each in ventral and dorsal turrets; maximum bomb load of 4000 lb (1814 kg) in bomb bay and 2000 lb (907 kg) of bombs/ rockets on underwing racks

FEATURES:
Monoplane wing layout; rectractable tricycle landing gear; two close-cowled radial engines; large vertical tail surface

Douglas c-54/r5d Skymaster

52-seat, four-engined monoplane/strategic transportation aircraft

Like the Skytrain, the c-54 was a military derivative
of a civilian airliner, in this case the DC-4A.
Designed to fulfill a specification drawn up by
United Airlines for a long-range pressurized
airliner, the aircraft was ordered to the tune of 61
airframes by the US operator, followed by a buy of
71 for the USAAF —in the event, most civilian
DC-4AS were also requisitioned into military
service. The first production c-54 made its maiden
flight on March 26, 1942, and by the following
October, 24 were in service with Air Transport
Command's Atlantic Wing. The A-model was
introduced in early 1943, this aircraft having a cargo
door, stronger floor, cargo boom hoist, and larger
wing tanks. The design was further modified
during the remaining war years to suit different
USAAF requirements, 1242 c-54s of varying marks
being built. Included in this number were 183 for
the Navy, which operated them in the Pacific as
R5DS. Postwar, the c-54/R5D enjoyed a long career,
with the final examples being retired in 1974.

SPECIFICATION (c-54B):

ACCOMMODATION:
Pilot, copilot, navigator/radio
operator, loadmaster, and up to
48 passengers

DIMENSIONS:
LENGTH: 93 ft 11 in (28.63 m)
WINGSPAN: 117 ft 6 in (35.81 m)
HEIGHT: 27 ft 6.25 in (8.39 m)

WEIGHTS:
EMPTY: 38,000 lb (17,237 kg)
MAX T/O: 73,000 lb (33,112 kg)

PERFORMANCE:
MAX SPEED: 274 mph (441 kmh)
RANGE: 3900 miles (6276 km)
POWERPLANT: four Pratt &
Whitney R-2000-7 Twin Wasps
OUTPUT: 5400 hp (4028 kW)

FIRST FLIGHT DATE:
June 7, 1938 (civilian DC-4E)

FEATURES:
Monoplane wing layout;
retractable tricycle landing gear;
four close-cowled radial engines;
large vertical tail surface

Douglas BTD Destroyer

single-seat, single-engined monoplane torpedo/dive-bomber

With its SBD Dauntless proving to be a huge success in fleet service, Douglas was contracted by the Navy in June 1941 to design a replacement aircraft. The company came up with the XSB2D-1 Destroyer, which made its first flight in April 1943. Initially built as a two-seater, the aircraft had an internal bomb bay and tricycle undercarriage—the latter was a first for a carrier-capable aircraft. However, instead of being ordered into production, the aircraft was modified into a single-seater and given the added role of torpedo-bombing. With its bomb bay enlarged to allow it to carry a torpedo, dive brakes installed in each side of the fuselage, and a single 20-mm cannon in each wing, the Destroyer progressed to series production in June 1944 as the BTD-1. The Navy ordered 358 examples, but only 28 had been delivered by the time the contract was canceled in October 1945. Despite being powered by a 2300-hp Wright Cyclone 18 radial engine, the Destroyer's performance was disappointing and none were used operationally.

SPECIFICATION:

ACCOMMODATION:
Pilot

DIMENSIONS:
LENGTH: 38 ft 7 in (11.76 m)
WINGSPAN: 45 ft 0 in (13.72 m)
HEIGHT: 13 ft 7 in (4.14 m)

WEIGHTS:
EMPTY: 11,561 lb (5244 kg)
MAX T/O: 19,000 lb (8618 kg)

PERFORMANCE:
MAX SPEED: 344 mph (554 kmh)
RANGE: 1480 miles (2382 km)
POWERPLANT: Wright R-3350-14 Cyclone 18
OUTPUT: 2300 hp (1715 kW)

FIRST FLIGHT DATE:
April 8, 1943

ARMAMENT:
Two 20-mm cannon in wings; maximum bomb/torpedo load of 3200 lb (1451 kg) in internal bomb bay

FEATURES:
Cranked monoplane wing layout; rectractable tricycle landing gear; close-cowled radial engine; cannon in wings

Fairchild UC-61 Argus

four-seat, single-engined high-wing liaison/communications and instrument training aircraft

The Argus traced its lineage back to the Model 24C three-seater civilian tourer of 1933, Fairchild introducing the four-seat Model 24J in 1937. With the enlarging of the US military in the late 1930s, the Model 24 was one of the numerous civilian types impressed into service with the rapidly expanding USAAC. However, of the 163 UC-61 Forwarders (as the militarized Fairchild was designated), all bar two were passed onto the British under Lend-Lease. Christened Argus IS, the first examples arrived in the UK in 1941 and were issued to both the RAF and the Air Transport Auxiliary (ATA), which used them as "aerial taxis" for its ferry pilots. A further 364 Mk IIS followed, these machines having new radios and a 24-volt electrical system—the USAAC acquired 148 UC-61AS to this specification. The final variant built was the Ranger-engined Argus III (UC-61K), of which 306 were issued to the British. Aside from USAAC and RAF/ATA use, a small number of Fairchild 24s were also supplied to the US Navy as J2KS.

SPECIFICATION (UC-61):

ACCOMMODATION:
Pilot and three passengers

DIMENSIONS:
LENGTH: 23 ft 9 in (7.24 m)
WINGSPAN: 36 ft 4 in (11.07 m)
HEIGHT: 7 ft 7.50 in (2.32 m)

WEIGHTS:
EMPTY: 1613 lb (732 kg)
MAX T/O: 2562 lb (1162 kg)

PERFORMANCE:
MAX SPEED: 132 mph (212 kmh)
RANGE: 640 miles (1030 km)
POWERPLANT: Warner R-500
Super Scarab
OUTPUT: 165 hp (123 kW)

FIRST FLIGHT DATE:
1933 (civilian Model 24C)

FEATURES:
High-wing layout; fixed landing gear; extensive cockpit glazing; cowled radial or inline engine

Fairchild AT-21 Gunner

five-seat, twin-engined monoplane gunnery trainer

Fairchild's AT-21 was hastily designed in 1941 after the USAAC realized the importance of gun turrets to combat aircraft. When war broke out in Europe in September 1939, no US military types featured power-operated multigun turrets, but it soon became apparent that bombers would require such armament to defend themselves against attacking fighters. Lacking experience in turret gunnery, and with no training syllabus or suitable aircraft to instruct aircrew, the USAAC set to rectify this situation by establishing gunnery schools and ordering purpose-built trainers from Fairchild. The XAT-13 was intended to serve as a trainer for all bomber crews, while the XAT-14 was a specialized trainer for bomb aimers. Following testing of these prototypes, the USAAC ordered the aircraft into production as a dedicated gunnery trainer, with a two-gun dorsal turret and a single weapon in the nose. A total of 175 AT-21 Gunners were built in 1942-44, and these aircraft served with specialized gunnery schools until replaced by trainer versions of operational frontline types.

SPECIFICATION:

ACCOMMODATION:
Pilot, copilot/instructor, and three student gunners

DIMENSIONS:
LENGTH: 38 ft 0 in (11.58 m)
WINGSPAN: 52 ft 8 in (16.05 m)
HEIGHT: 13 ft 1.50 in (4 m)

WEIGHTS:
EMPTY: 8654 lb (3925 kg)
MAX T/O: 11,288 lb (5120 kg)

PERFORMANCE:
MAX SPEED: 225 mph (362 kmh)
RANGE: 910 miles (1464 km)
POWERPLANT: two Ranger V-1770-15S
OUTPUT: 1040 hp (776 kW)

FIRST FLIGHT DATE:
1941

ARMAMENT:
One Browning 0.30-in machine gun on flexible mount in nose and two in dorsal turret

FEATURES:
Monoplane wing layout; rectractable landing gear; two close-cowled inline engines; twin-tail layout

Grumman F4F/FM Wildcat

single-seat, single-engined monoplane fighter

Derived from a biplane design (XF4F-1) offered in competition to the more modern Brewster F2A Buffalo monoplane, the Wildcat was the result of a revised study into the feasibility of a single wing naval fighter undertaken by Grumman in the summer of 1936. Designated the XF4F-2, the prototype lost out to the rival Brewster in the fly-off due to the latter's superior handling qualities. However, Grumman reworked the design into the vastly superior XF4F-3, fitting a more powerful Twin Wasp engine with a two-stage supercharger, increasing the fighter's wingspan and redesigning its tail surfaces.

France provided Grumman with its first order for the aircraft, committing to 100 G-36As in early 1939. Following flight trials, the US Navy also ordered 78 Grumman fighters in August 1939. These began entering service as F4F-3 Wildcats with VF-7 and VF-41 in December 1940, followed by VF-42, VF-71, and Marine Corps squadrons VMF-121, VMF-211, and VMF-221 early the following year. By then Grumman had switched production to the F4F-4, which incorporated lessons learned from the Royal Navy's combat experience with the ex-French G-36s, which it called Martlet Is—the Fleet Air Arm used various marks from 1940 through to VE-Day. The F4F-4 (1169 built) had its armament boosted from four to six 0.50-in guns, self-sealing tanks, and wing folding.

The Wildcat proved to be a worthy opponent for the Japanese A6M Zero-sen during the battles of Coral Sea and Midway in 1942, as well as the stubborn defense of Guadalcanal. By 1943 General Motors (GM) had commenced building F4F-4s, which it redesignated FM-1s (839 built). Later that year GM switched production to the FM-2, which utilized a turbocharged Wright R-1820-56 Cyclone in place of the Twin Wasp. This swap made for an improved top speed and an optimum altitude 50 percent higher than that of the FM-1—by the time production was terminated in August 1945, 4467 FM-2s had been built. Although replaced in larger fleet carriers by the F6F Hellcat, the Wildcat served on until VJ-Day aboard escort carriers.

SPECIFICATION (F4F-4):

ACCOMMODATION:
Pilot

DIMENSIONS:
LENGTH: 28 ft 9 in (8.76 m)
WINGSPAN: 38 ft 0 in (11.58 m)
HEIGHT: 11 ft 4 in (3.45 m)

WEIGHTS:
EMPTY: 5895 lb (2674 kg)
MAX T/O: 7952 lb (3607 kg)

PERFORMANCE:
MAX SPEED: 320 mph (515 kmh)
RANGE: 770 miles (1239 km)
POWERPLANT: Pratt & Whitney
R-1830-86 Twin Wasp
OUTPUT: 1200 hp (895 kW)

FIRST FLIGHT DATE:
September 2, 1937

ARMAMENT:
Six Browning 0.50-in machine guns in wings; maximum bomb load of 200 lb (91 kg) on underwing racks

FEATURES:
Monoplane wing layout; retractable undercarriage; close-cowled radial engine; fixed tailwheel

Grumman TBF/TBM Avenger

three-seat, single-engined monoplane torpedo-bomber

Although Grumman was principally responsible for producing the majority of the Navy's fighters during World War II, the company also designed and built the best carrier-based torpedo-bomber of the conflict in the shape of the TBF/TBM Avenger. Created as a replacement for the TBD Devastator, two prototype XTBF-1s were ordered from Grumman in April 1940. Completing its maiden flight on August 1, 1941, the prototype's portly appearance was due to its capacious internal bomb bay, which was large enough to contain the biggest (22-in) torpedo in the Navy arsenal. Powered by a Wright R-2600 Cyclone radial engine, the Avenger was also well armed, with the pilot operating a forward-firing 0.50-in machine gun, a similar caliber weapon being fitted in the ventral position under the control of the bomb aimer and a 0.50-in gun in a power-operated turret, fired by the radio operator.

Flight testing proceeded rapidly, and by the end of January 1942 the first production TBF-1s were already being issued to the Navy. Like its Douglas predecessor, the Avenger was badly mauled when first exposed to the enemy at Midway in June 1942—five of the six TBF-1s of VT-8 that were sent to attack the Japanese task force from Midway Island on June 4 were shot down. One of the astounding features of the Avenger story is that the basic design of the aircraft changed very little during the course of its production life. This allowed vast quantities to be built over a very short timescale—2293 were produced between January 1942 and December 1943 alone. The Navy's demand for Avengers soon outstripped Grumman's production capacity, so General Motors (through the auspices of their Eastern Division) stepped into the breech and commenced production of the near identical TBM-1 from September 1942. Indeed, by the time the Avenger production line closed in June 1945, GM had built 7546 TBMS of various marks—a figure which far exceeded Grumman's own final build tally. Postwar, the Avenger remained in naval service well into the 1950s as an antisubmarine warfare aircraft.

SPECIFICATION (TBM-3):

ACCOMMODATION:
Pilot, bomb-aimer/gunner, and radio operator/gunner

DIMENSIONS:
LENGTH: 40 ft 0 in (12.19 m)
WINGSPAN: 54 ft 2 in (16.51 m)
HEIGHT: 16 ft 5 in (5.00 m)

WEIGHTS:
EMPTY: 10,700 lb (4853 kg)
MAX T/O: 18,250 lb (8278 kg)

PERFORMANCE:
MAX SPEED: 267 mph (430 kmh)
RANGE: 1130 miles (1819 km)
POWERPLANT: Wright R-2600-20 Cyclone 14
OUTPUT: 1750 hp (1305 kW)

FIRST FLIGHT DATE:
August 1, 1941

ARMAMENT:
Two fixed Browning 0.50-in machine guns in upper cowling and wing, as well as one in dorsal turret, and one Browning 0.30-in machine gun in ventral position; maximum bomb/torpedo load of 2000 lb (907 kg) in internal bomb bay, as well as rockets/depth charges on underwing racks

FEATURES:
Monoplane wing layout; retractable undercarriage; close-cowled radial engine; gun turret

Grumman F6F Hellcat

single-seat, single-engined monoplane fighter

The Hellcat was always destined to be a success, because it embodied the early lessons learned by users of Grumman's previous fleet fighter, the F4F Wildcat, in the Pacific, as well as general pointers from the RAF's experience in Europe. The original design for the Hellcat actually dated back to late 1940, and the Navy placed an advance order for the fighter in June 1941. Modifications to the "paper" aircraft in light of combat experience from the Battle of the Coral Sea saw Grumman lower the wing center section to enable the undercarriage to be wider splayed, the fitment of more armor-plating around the cockpit to protect the pilot and an increase in the fighter's ammunition capacity for its six 0.50-in machine guns.

Less than a year after the Navy placed its order, the prototype XF6F-1 made its first flight. It was soon realized that a more powerful engine was needed to give the fighter a combat edge, so a Pratt & Whitney R-2800-10 was installed, resulting in the F-1 being redesignated F-3. Rushed into production following successful testing of the re-engined prototype, the first squadron to see action with the F6F-3 was VF-5 aboard *Yorktown* in August 1943, and from this point on, the question of aerial supremacy in the Pacific was never in doubt. The Hellcat served aboard most fleet carriers in varying numbers, and was credited with the destruction of 4947 aircraft up to VJ-Day.

All the leading Navy aces of the war flew Hellcats, with the premier fighter squadron in the Pacific, VF-15, downing 310 enemy aircraft with the rugged Grumman. Amazingly, only four major variants of the F6F were produced—the

-3, of which 4423 were constructed between October 1942 and April 1944, the improved -5 day fighter and the specialized -3N and -5N nightfighters. By the time the last Hellcat was delivered in November 1945, 12,275 had been built. Postwar, the aircraft saw extensive service with the Navy Reserve and training units, while surplus Hellcats were converted into pilotless F6F-3/5K target drones for missile testing.

SPECIFICATION (F6F-5):

ACCOMMODATION:
Pilot

DIMENSIONS:
LENGTH: 33 ft 7 in (10.24 m)
WINGSPAN: 42 ft 10 in (13.06 m)
HEIGHT: 13 ft 6 in (4.11 m)

WEIGHTS:
EMPTY: 9153 lb (4152 kg)
MAX T/O: 15,413 lb (6991 kg)

PERFORMANCE:
MAX SPEED: 380 mph (612 kmh)
RANGE: 945 miles (1512 km)
POWERPLANT: Pratt & Whitney R-2800-10W Double Wasp
OUTPUT: 2000 hp (1491 kW)

FIRST FLIGHT DATE:
June 26, 1942

ARMAMENT:
Six Browning 0.50-in machine guns in wings; provision for six rockets under wings or up to 2000-lb (907-kg) bomb load under center section

FEATURES:
Monoplane wing layout; retractable undercarriage; close-cowled radial engine; rectractable tailwheel

Grumman OA-14/J4F Widgeon

five-seat, twin-engined high-wing utility/ASW amphibian flying boat

The Widgeon was built as a smaller and cheaper version of the successful Goose amphibian for the ever-expanding US civil market. However, fewer than 40 had reached private hands when Grumman was ordered to focus production on a militarized amphibian, which the USAAC designated the OA-14 and the Navy and Coast Guard the J4F. The latter service enjoyed its first success against the U-Boat menace in August 1942 when a J4F-1 of Coast Guard Squadron 212 sunk U-166 off the Passes of the Mississippi. Grumman received its biggest production order (131) for the J4F-2 in early 1942, the final example of which was not delivered to the Navy until February 26, 1945. The Royal Navy also received 15 J4F-2s under Lend-Lease for service in the West Indies. Grumman improved the design in 1944 with the introduction of the G-44A, which boasted a deeper keel for improved hydrodynamic performance. This variant remained in production until January 1949, by which time 76 had been built—41 were also constructed under license in France in 1948-49.

SPECIFICATION:

ACCOMMODATION:
Pilot, copilot, and three passengers

DIMENSIONS:
LENGTH: 31 ft 1 in (9.47 m)
WINGSPAN: 40 ft 0 in (12.19 m)
HEIGHT: 11 ft 5 in (3.48 m)

WEIGHTS:
EMPTY: 3189 lb (1447 kg)
MAX T/O: 4500 lb (2041 kg)

PERFORMANCE:
MAX SPEED: 153 mph (246 kmh)
RANGE: 920 miles (1481 km)
POWERPLANT: two Ranger L-440C-5s
OUTPUT: 400 hp (298 kW)

FIRST FLIGHT DATE:
June 28, 1940

ARMAMENT:
One 325-lb (147-kg) depth charge on underwing rack

FEATURES:
High-wing monoplane layout; boat-shaped hull; two close-cowled engines; fixed underwing floats

Grumman F7F Tigercat

single/two-seat, twin-engined monoplane fighter

The F7F Tigercat had only just begun to enter service by VJ-Day, despite being ordered in 1941. The fighter's long gestation period reflected the demanding Navy specification, which stipulated that the aircraft must have engines that, combined, produced in excess of 4000 hp, and a weight of fire double that of the F4F. Of all-metal construction, with a cantilever, shoulder-mounted wing, the Tigercat was a fast and well-armed fighter of considerable dimension—it appeared that only the proposed 45,000-ton *Midway* class "supercarriers" would be able to operate them. Most of the 500 F7F-1s built were allocated to the Marine Corps for use from Pacific island bases, and just as the first units were working up for deployment Japan surrendered, leaving the Tigercat untested in World War II. Aside from the -1, Grumman produced the uprated -3 and the F7F-3N/4N nightfighter, equipped with radar in a lengthened nose fairing that was operated by a second crewman. It was as a nocturnal predator that the Tigercat won its "battle spurs" over Korea in 1951.

SPECIFICATION (F7F-3):

ACCOMMODATION:
Pilot and radar operator (latter in F7F-3N/4N only)

DIMENSIONS:
LENGTH: 45 ft 4.50 in (13.83 m)
WINGSPAN: 51 ft 6 in (15.70 m)
HEIGHT: 16 ft 7 in (5.05 m)

WEIGHTS:
EMPTY: 16,270 lb (7380 kg)
MAX T/O: 25,720 lb (11,666 kg)

PERFORMANCE:
MAX SPEED: 435 mph (700 kmh)
RANGE: 1200 miles (1931 km)
POWERPLANT: two Pratt & Whitney R-2800-34W Double Wasps
OUTPUT: 4200 hp (3132 kW)

FIRST FLIGHT DATE:
November 3, 1943

ARMAMENT:
Four Browning 0.50-in machine guns in nose and four M-2 20-mm cannon in wing roots; provision for six rockets or up to 2000-lb (907-kg) bomb load on underwing racks

FEATURES:
Monoplane wing layout; retractable tricycle undercarriage; two close-cowled radial engines

Lockheed P-38 Lightning

single-seat, twin-engined monoplane fighter

The P-38 Lightning was Lockheed's first venture into the world of high-performance military aircraft. Keen to break into this lucrative military marketplace, the company had eagerly responded to the USAAC 's 1937 Request for Proposals pertaining to the acquisition of a long-range interceptor. The new machine had to have a top speed in excess of 360 mph at 20,000 ft, the ability to take-off and land over a 50-ft obstacle within 2200 ft, the reliability to fly at full throttle for over an hour nonstop, and boast an armament double that of the P-36A Hawk—the USAAC 's frontline fighter of the period. No aircraft then in service, or under development, with any air arm across the globe could match these performance figures, and Lockheed's design team, led by H. L. Hibbard and Clarence "Kelly" Johnson, soon realized that any new type proposed by them would have to be twin-engined in order to allow the fighter to attain the top speed or rate of climb stipulated by the specification. The powerplant chosen for the fighter was the 960-hp Allison V-1710, as used by its P-40 contemporary. Aside from its novel twin-boom and central nacelle layout, the prototype XP-38 utilized butt-joined and flush-riveted all-metal skins and flying surfaces—a first for a US fighter.

The XP-38's test program progressed well, and aside from some minor adjustments to the flying surfaces and the introduction of progressively more powerful Allison engines, frontline P-38s differed little from the prototype throughout the aircraft's six-year production run. The appellation "Lightning" was bestowed upon the P-38 by the RAF and adopted by the Americans with the advent of the E-model in mid-1941. The definitive P-38 models—namely the E, F, H, J, and L—fitted with supercharged Allison engines, improved Fowler flaps and extra fuel, proved more than a match for Axis fighters across the globe.

In fact, the Lightning was credited with more kills in the Pacific theater than any other USAAF type, and the two top-scoring American pilots of World War II claimed all their victories flying P-38s.

SPECIFICATION (P-38J):

ACCOMMODATION:
Pilot

DIMENSIONS:
LENGTH: 37 ft 10 in (11.53 m)
WINGSPAN: 52 ft 0 in (15.85 m)
HEIGHT: 9 ft 10 in (3.00 m)

WEIGHTS:
EMPTY: 12,780 lb (5797 kg)
MAX T/O: 21,600 lb (9798 kg)

PERFORMANCE:
MAX SPEED: 414 mph (666 kmh)
RANGE: 475 miles (764 km)
POWERPLANT: two Allison
V-1710-89/91S
OUTPUT: 2850 hp (2126 kW)

FIRST FLIGHT DATE:
January 27, 1939

ARMAMENT:
One AN-M2 "C" 20-mm cannon
and four Browning 0.50-in
machine guns in nose; maximum
bomb/rocket load of 3200 lb
(1451 kg) under wings

FEATURES:
Monoplane wing layout;
rectractable, tricycle
undercarriage; twin inline
engines; twin boom/tail layout;
radiator housings on booms

Lockheed A-28/29/AT-18 and PBO Hudson

four/five-seat, twin-engined monoplane trainer and maritime patrol-bomber

Developed from the Model 14 Super Electra airliner in response to a British Purchasing Commission order for 200 aircraft in June 1938, Lockheed's Hudson was created to perform the long-range reconnaissance mission. Lockheed had to drastically expand its Burbank, California, plant in order to manufacture these aircraft, and the first example flew on December 10, 1938. Deliveries began two months later, and by the time the final Hudson was produced for the RAF in June 1943, 2000 had been received by the British. The USAAC also received several hundred repossessed British Hudsons in 1941-42, designating them A-28/29s. With their dorsal turrets deleted, these aircraft were used as bomber crew trainers and on antisubmarine patrols in 1942-43 along the eastern and western seaboards. The Army also acquired 217 turreted AT-18s as air gunnery trainers and target tugs, and 83 nonturreted AT-18As for navigation training. In August 1941 the Navy requisitioned 20 British Hudsons, which were designated PBO-1s and used on antisubmarine patrols.

SPECIFICATION (A-29):

ACCOMMODATION:
Pilot, copilot, navigator/bombardier, and turret gunner

DIMENSIONS:
LENGTH: 44 ft 4 in (13.51 m)
WINGSPAN: 65 ft 6 in (19.96 m)
HEIGHT: 11 ft 11 in (3.63 m)

WEIGHTS:
EMPTY: 12,825 lb (5817 kg)
MAX T/O: 20,500 lb (9299 kg)

PERFORMANCE:
MAX SPEED: 253 mph (407 kmh)
RANGE: 1550 miles (2494 km)
POWERPLANT: two Wright GR-1820-87 Cyclone 9s
OUTPUT: 2400 hp (1790 kW)

FIRST FLIGHT DATE:
December 10, 1938 (Hudson I)

ARMAMENT:
Two fixed Browning 0.30-in machine guns in nose, two in dorsal turret, and one in ventral hatch; maximum bomb/depth charge/rocket load of 1600 lb (726 kg) in bomb bay and under wings

FEATURES:
Monoplane wing layout; close-cowled twin radial engines; twin-tail layout; dorsal turret

Lockheed Model 18 Lodestar

17-seat, twin-engined monoplane transportation aircraft

The final twin-engined commercial transporter designed by Lockheed, the Model 18 Lodestar was basically a larger version of the Model 14. Capable of accommodating up to 14 passengers in high-speed comfort in civilian guise, the Lodestar was produced in a number of versions that differed primarily in the type of engines fitted. The first military interest in the aircraft came in 1940 from the Navy, which ordered three versions of Lodestar—the R50-4 (executive transportation), R50-5 (personnel transportation), and R50-6 (troop transportation). The following year Lockheed built 13 Lodestars for the USAAC, these being designated C-57s. A number of civilian Lodestars were also requisitioned by the Army Air Corps following Pearl Harbor, and these were designated C-56s. The USAAF made further purchases in 1942-43, acquiring almost 350 C-60s, some of which were passed onto the RAF and Commonwealth air forces, who operated them as Lodestar Is, IAs and IIs. Postwar, many surplus Lodestars reverted to their civilian role of airliner/cargo hauler.

SPECIFICATION (C-56):

ACCOMMODATION:
Pilot and copilot, navigator, and 14 passengers

DIMENSIONS:
LENGTH: 49 ft 10 in (15.19 m)
WINGSPAN: 65 ft 6 in (19.96 m)
HEIGHT: 11 ft 1 in (3.38 m)

WEIGHTS:
EMPTY: 11,650 lb (5284 kg)
MAX T/O: 17,500 lb (7938 kg)

PERFORMANCE:
MAX SPEED: 253 mph (407 kmh)
RANGE: 1600 miles (2575 km)
POWERPLANT: two Wright R-1820-71s
OUTPUT: 2400 hp (1790 kW)

FIRST FLIGHT DATE:
September 21, 1939

FEATURES:
Monoplane wing layout; rectractable landing gear; close-cowled twin radial engines; twin-tail layout

Lockheed B-34/37 Lexington and PV Ventura/Harpoon

four/five-seat, twin-engined monoplane bomber/reconnaissance aircraft

Spurred on by the success of the Hudson, Lockheed designed a more advanced "bombing twin" for the RAF based on the Model 18 Lodestar. The new aircraft (designated the Ventura I by the RAF) was not only larger than its predecessor, but had more powerful engines, a ventral gun position, and could carry more bombs. The first examples of 675 ordered by the British made their debut with Bomber Command on November 3, 1942. Serious losses during subsequent daylight raids revealed the Ventura's vulnerability, so the survivors were passed on to Coastal Command and the balance of 350+ airframes still on order canceled. These surplus aircraft were acquired by the USAAF, entering service as B-34s in the maritime patrol role. The Navy also showed interest in the aircraft, receiving some 1600 as PV-1 Venturas. The improved PV-2 Harpoon was ordered in June 1943, 500 being built from March 1944. Like the PV-1, most PV-2s saw action in the Pacific, with a number remaining in service with the Reserve until the late 1940s.

SPECIFICATION (PV-1):

ACCOMMODATION:
Pilot, copilot, navigator, dorsal and ventral gunners

DIMENSIONS:
LENGTH: 51 ft 9 in (15.81 m)
WINGSPAN: 65 ft 6 in (19.96 m)
HEIGHT: 11 ft 11 in (3.63 m)

WEIGHTS:
EMPTY: 20,197 lb (9161 kg)
MAX T/O: 31,077 lb (14,097 kg)

PERFORMANCE:
MAX SPEED: 312 mph (499 kmh)
RANGE: 1660 miles (2656 km)
POWERPLANT: two Pratt & Whitney R-2800-31 Double Wasps
OUTPUT: 4000 hp (2982 kW)

FIRST FLIGHT DATE:
July 31, 1941

ARMAMENT:
Two fixed Browning 0.50-in machine guns in nose, two in dorsal turret and two in ventral hatch; maximum bomb/depth charge/torpedo load of 3000 lb (1360 kg) in bomb bay, plus 2000 lb (907 kg) on underwing racks

FEATURES:
Monoplane wing; close-cowled twin radial engines; twin-tail layout

Martin PBM Mariner

nine-seat, twin-engined maritime patrol-bomber, antisubmarine flying boat/amphibian

The PBM Mariner served the Navy well primarily in the Pacific, where it performed a variety of missions including antisubmarine warfare, maritime patrol, transportation, and air-sea rescue. Although 20 production aircraft were ordered by the Navy in December 1937, it was not until 1941 that the first PBM-1s entered service with VP-74. Initially fitted with stabilizing floats, which retracted inward into the wings, the advent of the PBM-3 the following year saw Martin revert to fixed outrigger floats, as well as the adoption of lengthened engine nacelles. The major Mariner production model was the PBM-5 of 1944, 631 of which were built. The PBM-5A amphibian was derived from this variant, featuring a retractable tricycle undercarriage. Just 36 examples were built, and these were used in the air-sea rescue role by the US Coast Guard. RAF Coastal Command received 25 PBM-3Bs in August 1943, but they were soon returned to the US, while the RAAF operated 12 PBM-3Rs. A total of 1405 PBMs had been built by the time production ended in 1949.

SPECIFICATION (PBM-3D):

ACCOMMODATION:
Pilot, copilot, flight engineer, radar/radio operator, navigator, nose, dorsal and tail turret gunners, beam gunner

DIMENSIONS:
LENGTH: 79 ft 10 in (24.33 m)
WINGSPAN: 118 ft 0 in (35.97 m)
HEIGHT: 27 ft 6 in (8.40 m)

WEIGHTS:
EMPTY: 33,175 lb (15,048 kg)
MAX T/O: 58,000 lb (26,308 kg)

PERFORMANCE:
MAX SPEED: 211 mph (340 kmh)
RANGE: 2240 miles (3605 km)
POWERPLANT: two Pratt & Whitney R-2600-22 Cyclones
OUTPUT: 3800 hp (2834 kW)

FIRST FLIGHT DATE:
February 18, 1939

ARMAMENT:
Two Browning 0.50-in machine guns in nose, dorsal, and tail turrets, single gun in waist windows; maximum bomb/mine load of 4000 lb (1814 kg) in engine nacelles

FEATURES:
High-wing monoplane; boat-shaped hull; two radial engines; twin-boom/-tail layout

Martin B-26/JM Marauder

five/seven-seat, twin-engined bomber

Martin relied on its previous experience as a successful bomber builder for the USAAC when it entered its Model 179 in the widely contested 1939 Medium Bomber competition. The Army was looking for an aircraft that had good speed, range, and ceiling performance, was armed with four 0.30-in guns, and could carry 2000 lb of bombs. It did not specify optimum landing speeds, and understood that long takeoff runs would be required. In order to meet the specifications stipulated by the requirement, Martin built its Model 179 around a wing optimized for high-speed cruising rather than moderate landing speeds.

Far in advance of its competitors in terms of performance and potential production, the Martin bomber easily won the competition in September 1939 and 201 examples were ordered straight "off the drawing board." However, the manufacturer's decision to plump for high wing loading resulted in an aircraft that initially proved difficult for novice pilots to fly safely. The B-26 (as it was designated by the USAAC upon its entry into service in the spring of 1941) soon earned an unenviable reputation as a "widow maker." Converting crews onto the aircraft proved a lengthy, and often dangerous, process, and despite Martin improving the bomber's handling characteristics (starting with the 641st B-model onward) through the fitment of a greater wingspan and taller tail, the "widow maker" sobriquet remained with the B-26 throughout its service career.

In the light of this, it is therefore ironic that the Marauder enjoyed the lowest loss rate of any USAAF bomber to see action in the European theater—B-26s equipped eight bomb groups in the ETO and MTO between 1943-45. The Marauder was also a key Allied weapon in the Pacific, the type having made its combat debut in this theater in April 1942. Although not seeing combat with its 272 Marauders, the Navy used the aircraft (designated JM-1/2s) extensively in the training role as target tugs. The 550+ AT-23 Marauder trainers built by Martin also saw widespread use with the USAAF in 1943-45. The last of 5157 B-26s constructed in World War II was delivered on April 28, 1945.

SPECIFICATION (B-26G):

ACCOMMODATION:
Pilot, copilot, bombardier/nose gunner, radio operator, navigator, dorsal, and tail turret gunners

DIMENSIONS:
LENGTH: 56 ft 1 in (17.09 m)
WINGSPAN: 71 ft 0 in (21.64 m)
HEIGHT: 20 ft 4 in (6.20 m)

WEIGHTS:
EMPTY: 25,300 lb (11,476 kg)
MAX T/O: 38,200 lb (17,327 kg)

PERFORMANCE:
MAX SPEED: 283 mph (455 kmh)
RANGE: 1100 miles (1770 km)
POWERPLANT: two Pratt & Whitney R-2800-43 Double Wasps
OUTPUT: 3840 hp (2684 kW)

FIRST FLIGHT DATE:
November 25, 1940

ARMAMENT:
Four fixed Browning 0.50-in machine guns on fuselage sides, one in nose, pairs in dorsal and tail turrets, and two in ventral positions; maximum bomb load of 4000 lb (1814 kg) in bomb bay

FEATURES:
Monoplane wing layout; rectractable landing gear; close-cowled twin radial engines; dorsal and tail turrets

North American BC/AT-6/SNJ Texan

two-seat, single-engined monoplane advanced trainer

For decades known simply as the "pilot maker," the AT-6/SNJ Texan was *the* global trainer during World War II. Derived from the NA-26, which was itself a variant of the prewar NA-16, the Texan was initially designated the BC-1. This aircraft had won the USAAC's March 1937 design competition, held at Wright Field, to find a new trainer in the "basic combat" category. The aircraft had to have the equipment and attributes of a frontline combat type, and in order to meet this criteria the North American design featured a retractable undercarriage, provision for armament, representative navigation and engine instruments, and a two-way radio. None of these things had previously been seen in training aircraft, and the Army Air Corps awarded the manufacturer a contract to build 180 BC-1s.

In 1940 the USAAC revised its designation policy, and the BC-1/1A became the AT-6/6A Texan. The aircraft's name originated in 1941 when North American established a second production line in Dallas, Texas, for its now in-demand trainer. Starting with the AT-6B onward, all Texans would be built in Dallas. The refinement of the aircraft coincided with a rapid expansion of the US armed forces, and orders flowed in ranging in size from 94 AT-6s requested in 1939 to an accumulated total of 3404 AT-6Ds less than five years later. In total, 15,109 airframes were built between 1938-45 to train combat pilots across the continental USA.

Aside from its widespread use with the USAAF, the Navy also relied on 4500 SNJ Texans to provide its pilots with basic training both ashore and at sea aboard aircraft carriers—arrestor hooks were fitted as standard to many SNJS. Close to 3000 Texans remained in service with the US armed forces postwar, and 2068 of them were eventually remanufactured as T-6G/SNJ-7S in the late 1940s. A number of USAF T-6F/GS saw combat in the Korean War as spotting aircraft for UN troops, while at home, both Air Force and Navy Texans served on as primary, basic, and instrument trainers well into the 1950s.

SPECIFICATION (AT-6A):

ACCOMMODATION:
Two pilots in tandem

DIMENSIONS:
LENGTH: 29 ft 0 in (8.83 m)
WINGSPAN: 42 ft 0.25 in (12.80 m)
HEIGHT: 11 ft 9 in (3.58 m)

WEIGHTS:
EMPTY: 3900 lb (1769 kg)
MAX T/O: 5300 lb (2338 kg)

PERFORMANCE:
MAX SPEED: 210 mph (336 kmh)
RANGE: 629 miles (1006 km)
POWERPLANT: Pratt & Whitney
R-1340-49 Wasp
OUTPUT: 600 hp (448 kW)

FIRST FLIGHT DATE:
April 1936 (NA-26)

ARMAMENT:
One fixed Browning 0.30-in machine gun in wing root and one on flexible mounting in rear cockpit

FEATURES:
Monoplane wing layout; retractable undercarriage; close-cowled radial engine; fixed tailwheel

North American B-25/PBJ Mitchell

four/six-seat, twin-engined monoplane medium bomber

North American's response to a prewar USAAC request for a twin-engined medium bomber, the B-25 Mitchell proved to be one of the most venerable, and versatile, combat aircraft to see action in World War II. Tailored to fit USAAC Circular Proposal 38-385, the prototype carried out successful flight trials, but North American was encouraged to further improve its design by the Army, which now stated that any future medium bomber would have to carry a payload of 2400 lb—twice that originally stipulated in 38-385. Re-engineered and considerably enlarged, the definitive production airframe was designated the NA-62. So impressed with what it saw on the drawing board, the USAAC ordered 184 aircraft (to be designated the B-25) before metal had even been cut on the revised design.

The first production standard machine was flown on August 19, 1940, by which point it had been christened the Mitchell after maverick Army bomber proponent William "Billy" Mitchell. Like a number of other Army Air Corps types then entering service, the B-25 benefited from the lessons being bitterly learned by the combatants in Europe, and crew armor-plating and self-sealing tanks were quickly fitted into production machines by North American—these aircraft were designated B-25As. Gaining early fame in the Doolittle Raid on Tokyo in April 1942, the Mitchell went on to fight not only with the USAAF in the Pacific, but also with Marine Corps, British, Dutch, and Australian units.

The Marine Corps designated its Mitchells PBJ-1s, and more than 700 were received in 1943-45. These aircraft equipped eight frontline units within the

Marine Medium Bombardment Group, the latter waging war against the Japanese from islands in the South Pacific in the final 18 months of the conflict. By war's end the veteran Mitchell was still in production, having outlasted its rivals from Douglas and Martin to become the most prolific American medium bomber of World War II—built to the tune of 9889 air-frames. Postwar, TB-25 pilot/aircrew trainers, based on the prolific B-25J, served on with the USAF until 1959.

SPECIFICATION (B-25J):

ACCOMMODATION:
Pilot, copilot, bombardier/nose gunner, navigator, dorsal and tail turret gunners

DIMENSIONS:
LENGTH: 52 ft 11 in (16.13 m)
WINGSPAN: 67 ft 7 in (20.60 m)
HEIGHT: 16 ft 4 in (4.98 m)

WEIGHTS:
EMPTY: 19,480 lb (8836 kg)
MAX T/O: 35,000 lb (15,876 kg)

PERFORMANCE:
MAX SPEED: 272 mph (438 kmh)
RANGE: 1350 miles (2173 km)
POWERPLANT: two Wright R-2600-92 Cyclones
OUTPUT: 3400 hp (2535 kW)

FIRST FLIGHT DATE:
January 1939

ARMAMENT:
Four fixed Browning 0.50-in machine guns on fuselage sides, two on flexible mounts in nose, two in dorsal and tail turrets and two in waist; maximum bomb load of 3000 lb (1361 kg) in bomb bay, plus wing racks for rockets

FEATURES:
Monoplane wing layout; rectractable, tricycle landing gear; close-cowled twin radial engines; dorsal and tail turrets; twin-tail layout

North American P-51B/C Mustang

single-seat, single-engined monoplane fighter

Derived from the Allison-engined P-51A Mustang, which had been built in record time to a British requirement for a new fighter type, the Rolls-Royce Merlin-powered P-51B proved a revelation when first flown in October 1942. The original North American design had suffered from poor performance in the high-altitude dogfights that characterized air combat in Europe. However, the airframe itself was more than sound, so the RAF quickly searched for a replacement powerplant and came up with the Merlin 61. Once mated with this battle-proven engine, the aircraft began to realize its full potential as a fighter—a communiqué of the findings was immediately sent to North American, and the rest is history. Car manufacturer Packard was granted a license to build the 1300-hp Merlin as the Packard V-1650-3, and North American followed the British lead in refitting two surplus P-51A airframes with the "new" powerplants.

Flight testing, which began in November 1942, soon revealed a 50-mph increase in the fighter's top speed at optimum altitude—the fighter, designated the P-51B, was capable of 439 mph at 30,000 ft, compared to the P-51A's 387 mph at 15,000 ft. P-51Bs made their combat debut over Europe with the 354th FG in December 1943, just when the Eighth Air Force's much-vaunted daylight bomber campaign had begun to falter due to unsustainable losses. Here was the "Mighty Eighth's" "knight in shining armor," capable of escorting B-17s and B-24s throughout their hazardous missions over occupied Europe. Soon, the P-51B had proven itself to be the best long-range fighter in the Allied arsenal (the aircraft had a range of 2080 miles when equipped with 110-gallon wing drop tanks), and VIII Fighter Command clamored for additional Mustangs to be allocated to its fighter groups.

Aside from the 1988 B-models produced by the parent company at its Inglewood, California, plant, in 1943-44, an additional 1750 near-identical c-models were also completed in a new factory in Dallas, Texas. P-51B/CS saw combat with USAAF fighter groups in the ETO, MTO, and China-Burma-India well into 1945.

SPECIFICATION (P-51B):

ACCOMMODATION:
Pilot

DIMENSIONS:
LENGTH: 32 ft 3 in (9.83 m)
WINGSPAN: 37 ft 0 in (11.28 m)
HEIGHT: 13 ft 8 in (4.16 m)

WEIGHTS:
EMPTY: 6980 lb (3166 kg)
MAX T/O: 11,800 lb (5352 kg)

PERFORMANCE:
MAX SPEED: 439 mph (702 kmh)
RANGE: 400 miles (640 km)
POWERPLANT: Packard V-1650-3
OUTPUT: 1380 hp (1019 kW)

FIRST FLIGHT DATE:
October 13, 1942

ARMAMENT:
Four/six Browning 0.50-in machine guns in wings; maximum bomb/rocket load of 2000 lb (454 kg) on underwing racks

FEATURES:
Monoplane wing layout; rectractable landing gear; close-cowled inline engine; ventral air intake; four-bladed propeller

North American P-51D/K Mustang

single-seat, single-engined monoplane fighter

In an effort to further improve the already superb Merlin-engined Mustang, North American set about reworking the P-51's fuselage in early 1943. The end result was the XP-51D, which first flew on November 17, 1943. The most striking feature of this aircraft was its cut-down rear fuselage decking and sliding "teardrop" canopy, which gave the pilot an unrestricted view aft—crucial for a fighter pilot striving to keep his tail clear of enemy aircraft. The P-51D also boasted six Browning 0.50-cal machine guns as standard armament, and had a strengthened wing to allow greater external loads to be carried. The fighter's internal fuel capacity was also increased, and a fin fillet added on all but the earliest production D-models to compensate for the reduced fuselage side area as a result of the cut-down decking.

Production of the P-51D commenced in early 1944, and the first examples arrived in the UK for service with the Eighth Air Force's VIII Fighter Command just prior to D-Day. North American's Inglewood plant would complete a total of 6502 P-51Ds, while a second production line in Dallas built a further 1337 P-51Ks. The latter variant differed from the D-model in having an Aeroproducts rather than a Hamilton-Standard propeller. North American also built 299 camera-equipped F-6D/K Mustangs, and these saw service alongside photoreconnaissance F-6Cs (ex-P-51B/Cs) in both Europe and the Pacific. Aside from its service escorting bombers in the ETO and MTO from mid-1944 through to VE-Day, the P-51D/K also saw action as a bomb/bazooka tube-equipped fighter-bomber in the China-Burma-India theater, as well as on Very

Long Range missions from Iwo Jima, in the Pacific, protecting B-29s sent to bomb Japan. Postwar, Mustangs served on in the frontline with the USAF until 1949, by which time they had been redesignated F-51D/KS.

Surplus aircraft were then passed onto Reserve and Air National Guard units, many of which were activated during the Korean War in 1950 and instructed to supply Mustangs and pilots to three frontline bomb groups fighting the communist forces. Surviving F-51s were eventually retired from US service in 1957.

SPECIFICATION:

ACCOMMODATION:
Pilot

DIMENSIONS:
LENGTH: 32 ft 3 in (9.83 m)
WINGSPAN: 37 ft 0 in (11.28 m)
HEIGHT: 12 ft 2 in (3.71 m)

WEIGHTS:
EMPTY: 7635 lb (3463 kg)
MAX T/O: 12,100 lb (5488 kg)

PERFORMANCE:
MAX SPEED: 437 mph (703 kmh)
RANGE: 950 miles (1520 km)
POWERPLANT: Packard V-1650-7
OUTPUT: 1720 hp (1283 kW)

FIRST FLIGHT DATE:
November 17, 1943

ARMAMENT:
Six Browning 0.50-in machine guns in wings; maximum bomb/rocket load of 2000 lb (454 kg) on underwing racks

FEATURES:
Monoplane wing layout; rectractable landing gear; close-cowled inline engine; ventral air intake; four-bladed propeller; "teardrop" canopy

North American P-51A/A-36 Mustang

single-seat, single-engined monoplane fighter

The Mustang has its origins in a British Purchasing Commission deal struck with North American in April 1940 for an advanced fighter to supplant the Spitfire, the company having a completed prototype —tailored to the British specifications—ready for flight within 120 days of the original submission. North American had already made a start independently of the British deal, its NA-73X design incorporating lessons gleaned from aerial combat in Europe. The prototype was completed just three days short of the required date, the aircraft (christened the "Mustang I" by the British) handling beautifully in testing thanks to its revolutionary semilaminar-flow airfoil wing. However, it was soon realized that the fighter's Allison V-1710 performed poorly above 17,000 ft due to its lack of supercharging, so RAF Mustang Is were fitted with cameras and relegated to low-level tactical reconnaissance and army cooperation roles. The USAAF, seeing that the Mustang I was no good as a fighter above medium altitude, ordered just 500 A-36AS and 310 P-51AS for ground attack tasks instead.

SPECIFICATION:

ACCOMMODATION:
Pilot

DIMENSIONS:
LENGTH: 32 ft 3 in (9.83 m)
WINGSPAN: 37 ft 0 in (11.28 m)
HEIGHT: 12 ft 2 in (3.71 m)

WEIGHTS:
EMPTY: 6550 lb (2971 kg)
MAX T/O: 8800 lb (3992 kg)

PERFORMANCE:
MAX SPEED: 387 mph (622 kmh)
RANGE: 1250 miles (2010 km) with
external tanks
POWERPLANT: Allison V-1710-39
OUTPUT: 1150 hp (858 kW)

FIRST FLIGHT DATE:
October 26, 1940

ARMAMENT:
Six fixed Browning 0.50-in
machine guns or four 20-mm
cannon in wings; maximum
bomb load of 2000 lb (454 kg)
on underwing racks

FEATURES:
Monoplane wing layout;
rectractable landing gear;
close-cowled inline engine;
ventral air intake

Northrop P-61 Black Widow

three-seat, twin-engined monoplane fighter

The first aircraft to be purposely designed as a radar-equipped nightfighter, Northrop's P-61 Black Widow was heavily influenced by early RAF combat experiences with radar-equipped fighters in 1940-41. Built to fulfill a 1940 USAAC requirement, the P-61 was designed around the bulky Radiation Laboratory SCR-720 radar, which was mounted in the aircraft's nose. The company's design was accepted the following year, and Northrop immediately commenced building two XP-61 prototypes and 13 YP-61 evaluation aircraft. The largest fighter ever procured for frontline service by the USAAF, the P-61's airframe was capable of housing a dorsal barbette of four 0.50-in machine guns and four ventrally mounted 20-mm cannon. After initial structural and radar problems, the aircraft was issued to a frontline unit in March 1944, and both ETO and Pacific squadrons saw action that spring. Some 706 P-61s were built in three variants by Northrop, and the type also saw action as a night intruder against ground targets as well as in its designated nightfighter role.

SPECIFICATION (P-61A):

ACCOMMODATION:
Pilot, front gunner, and radio operator/rear gunner

DIMENSIONS:
LENGTH: 48 ft 11 in (14.91 m)
WINGSPAN: 66 ft 0 in (20.12 m)
HEIGHT: 14 ft 2 in (4.32 m)

WEIGHTS:
EMPTY: 20,965 lb (9510 kg)
MAX T/O: 32,400 lb (14,696 kg)

PERFORMANCE:
MAX SPEED: 369 mph (594 kmh)
RANGE: 1000 miles (1600 km)
POWERPLANT: two Pratt & Whitney R-2800-65 Double Wasps
OUTPUT: 4500 hp (3356 kW)

FIRST FLIGHT DATE:
May 26, 1942

ARMAMENT:
Four fixed Browning 0.50-in machine guns in lower forward fuselage and four AN-M2 20-mm cannon in remote-controlled dorsal turret; maximum bomb/rocket load of 6400 lb (2903 kg) on underwing racks

FEATURES:
Monoplane wing layout; close-cowled twin radial engines; dorsal turret; twin boom/tail layout

Piper O-59/L-4/L-18/L-21 Grasshopper

two-seat, single-engined high-wing liaison/observation aircraft

As with the Aeronca L-3 and Taylorcraft L-2 described elsewhere in this section, Piper's L-4 Grasshopper was also heavily used by the USAAC in the artillery spotting and frontline liaison roles in World War II. Like its contemporaries, the L-4 was essentially a militarized version of a successful civilian design of the previous decade—in this case the exceptional Taylor Aircraft Company (later Piper) J-3 Cub of the mid-1930s. The Army Air Corps first came to realize the usefulness of the design during large-scale military maneuvers held in Louisiana in August 1941, which saw 44 hastily camouflaged Cubs employed in the field. In the aftermath of the exercise, the USAAC ordered 948 O-59As (redesignated L-4As soon after they entered service), which embodied certain changes over the civilian J-3, including an improved tandem cockpit arrangement, increased glazing that offered better all-round visibility and the installation of two-way military radios.

Following the attack on Pearl Harbor, hundreds of ex-civilian Cubs were also impressed into military service. Indeed, by 1945 the combined total of civil and military Cubs/Grasshoppers built was nearing the 10,000 mark—including a contract for 1301 L-4Hs, which proved to be the largest single order placed by the US military for liaison aircraft in World War II. First seeing action with the Army in late 1942 during the Operation Torch invasion of North Africa, L-4s, flying alongside Taylorcraft L-2s and Aeronca L-3s (all officially named Grasshoppers), supported American forces in every campaign on every front until war's end.

In an odd move, Piper also received a request by the USAAC to produce a training glider utilizing the Grasshopper's airframe minus its engine and undercarriage. This it duly did, and the Army subsequently purchased 250 examples with the designation TG-8. The L-4 remained in service postwar, and 838 examples of the improved L-18 variant were also acquired by the Army in 1949-50, followed by 718 L-21A/BS in 1951-52. Piper Grasshoppers saw further action with the Army in Korea in the early 1950s, and the last L-21s were not retired until the 1960s.

SPECIFICATION (L-4H):

ACCOMMODATION:
Pilot and passenger in tandem

DIMENSIONS:
LENGTH: 22 ft 0 in (6.71 m)
WINGSPAN: 35 ft 3 in (10.74 m)
HEIGHT: 6 ft 8 in (2.03 m)

WEIGHTS:
EMPTY: 730 lb (331 kg)
MAX T/O: 1220 lb (533 kg)

PERFORMANCE:
MAX SPEED: 85 mph (137 kmh)
RANGE: 190 miles (306 km)
POWERPLANT: Continental
O-170-3
OUTPUT: 65 hp (48 kW)

FIRST FLIGHT DATE:
1937 (Cub trainer) and 1941
(YO-59 military derivative)

FEATURES:
High-wing layout; tandem
cockpits; fixed landing gear;
extensive cockpit glazing

Republic P-47 Thunderbolt

single-seat, single-engined monoplane fighter

The original P-47 design was produced to meet a 1940 USAAC requirement for a lightweight interceptor similar in size and stature to the Spitfire and Bf 109. Powered by Allison's V-1710-39 1150-hp inline engine, the XP-47A had just two 0.50-in machine guns as armament and lacked protective armor or self-sealing tanks. However, combat reports from Europe proved the folly of a lightweight fighter, and the USAAC modified its design requirements to include an eight-gun fitment, heavy armor-plating, and a self-sealing fuel system. Republic responded with an all-new design, powered, crucially, by a turbocharged R-2800 Double Wasp radial engine. Despite initial reliability problems with its powerplant, production of the Republic design forged ahead.

In late 1942, the 56th FG gave the P-47B its combat debut with the Eighth Air Force, performing vital escort missions for B-17 bombers. Initial encounters with German fighters were not encouraging for Thunderbolt pilots, as their mount was outmaneuvered at low-to-medium altitudes, and its engine performance was lackluster—the aircraft's short range was also criticized. The arrival of the C-model in mid-1943 addressed these problems, and as combat tactics evolved, pilots learnt how best to fly the Thunderbolt in order to effectively counter the more nimble Luftwaffe fighters.

By the end of 1943, the first D-models had arrived in the UK, followed five months later by "bubble top" Thunderbolts, which became the favoured mount thanks to their superior rearward visibility. Aside from its use as a bomber escort, the Thunderbolt had also performed great work as a fighter-bomber in the ETO, MTO, and the Pacific. The ultimate Thunderbolt was the P-47N, whose uprated turbocharged R-2800-61 engine was capable of producing 2800 hp in combat configuration at 32,500 ft.

Some 1816 P-47NS were built (out of a total of 15,677 Thunderbolts), the majority of which were put to use escorting B-29s on bombing raids on the Japanese home islands in 1945. A number of P-47NS soldiered on with the Air National Guard, and a handful of other air arms, into the early 1950s.

SPECIFICATION
(P-47D-25):

ACCOMMODATION:
Pilot

DIMENSIONS:
LENGTH: 36 ft 1.75 in (11.02 m)
WINGSPAN: 40 ft 9.25 in (12.43 m)
HEIGHT: 14 ft 2 in (4.32 m)

WEIGHTS:
EMPTY: 10,000 lb (4536 kg)
MAX T/O: 19,400 lb (8800 kg)

PERFORMANCE:
MAX SPEED: 428 mph (688 kmh)
RANGE: 475 miles (760 km)
POWERPLANT: Pratt & Whitney
R-2800-59 Double Wasp
OUTPUT: 2300 hp (1715 kW)

FIRST FLIGHT DATE:
May 6, 1941 (XP-47B)

ARMAMENT:
Eight Browning 0.50-in machine guns in wings; maximum bomb/rocket load of 2000 lb (908 kg) on underwing racks

FEATURES:
Monoplane wing layout; rectractable landing gear; close-cowled radial engine; four-bladed propeller

Stinson uc-81/at-19 Reliant

four-seat, single-engined high-wing navigation/radio trainer and communications aircraft

Derived from the successful high-wing cabin monoplane of the 1930s, the first militarized Reliants were indeed 47 ex-civilian aircraft impressed into USAAC service at the outbreak of World War II—these aircraft were designated uc-81s and used as communication hacks. Two Reliants had been acquired by the Navy in 1935, one of which was passed onto the Coast Guard. The latter was designated a rq-1, while the Navy machine was identified as an xr3q-1. Maintaining the nautical flavor, the largest customer for the Reliant was in fact the Royal Navy, which purchased 500 Reliant is (the USAAF designated them at-19s) under Lend-Lease agreements for the Fleet Air Arm. The first examples arrived in Britain in the summer of 1943, and the aircraft subsequently served in the radio, navigational, and photographic training roles, as well as performing general utility flights. A total of 12 faa units operated Reliant is until war's end, when around 350 were returned to the USA, reconditioned by Stinson and sold to civilian buyers.

SPECIFICATION:

ACCOMMODATION:
Pilot and three passengers

DIMENSIONS:
LENGTH: 30 ft 0 in (9.14 m)
WINGSPAN: 41 ft 10.50 in (12.76 m)
HEIGHT: 8 ft 7 in (2.62 m)

WEIGHTS:
EMPTY: 2810 lb (1275 kg)
MAX T/O: 4000 lb (1814 kg)

PERFORMANCE:
MAX SPEED: 141 mph (227 kmh)
RANGE: 810 miles (1303 km)
POWERPLANT: Lycoming R-680
OUTPUT: 290 hp (216 kW)

FIRST FLIGHT DATE:
1933 (SR/SR-2 civilian variant)

FEATURES:
High-wing layout; fixed landing gear; close-cowled radial engine

Stinson O-49/L-1 Vigilant

two-seat, single-engined high-wing liaison/observation aircraft

One of three manufacturers to submit designs in response to a requirement issued by the USAAC in 1940 for a new light observation aircraft, Stinson was awarded a contract for 142 O-49s. To achieve the low-speed and high-lift performance stipulated, it fitted the leading edge of the aircraft's wing with automatically operating slats, while the trailing edge boasted wide-span slotted flaps and large slotted ailerons. By the time Vigilant (as it was known in RAF service) production had begun, Stinson had been acquired by Vultee. A follow-on contract for 182 Vigilants saw the aircraft modified with a lengthened fuselage, resulting in a designation change to O-49A. The RAF received 100 Vigilants in 1941-42 and used them for light liaison and artillery spotting in Tunisia, Sicily, and Italy. All O-49/O-49As became L-1/L-1As in 1942, while aircraft modified into air ambulances (L-1B/C), glider pickup trainers (L-1D), and floatplanes (L-1E/FS) also received designation changes. Only two batches of L-1s were acquired, as the Grasshopper family proved more effective in the observation role.

SPECIFICATION (L-1A):

ACCOMMODATION:
Pilot and observer/passenger in tandem

DIMENSIONS:
LENGTH: 34 ft 3 in (10.44 m)
WINGSPAN: 50 ft 11 in (15.52 m)
HEIGHT: 10 ft 2 in (3.10 m)

WEIGHTS:
EMPTY: 2670 lb (1211 kg)
MAX T/O: 3400 lb (1542 kg)

PERFORMANCE:
MAX SPEED: 122 mph (196 kmh)
RANGE: 280 miles (451 km)
POWERPLANT: Lycoming R-680-9
OUTPUT: 295 hp (220 kW)

FIRST FLIGHT DATE:
Summer 1940

FEATURES:
High-wing layout; fixed landing gear; close-cowled radial engine

Stinson o-62/L-5/oY Sentinel

two-seat, single-engined high-wing light liaison aircraft

The Stinson L-5 Sentinel was derived from the successful civilian Voyager design evaluated by the USAAC in 1941, although it was not part of the Army trial held that year. Six aircraft were initially acquired (designated YO-54S), and after minor modifications had been carried out to "militarize" them (cabin layout change from three to two seats, improving visibility out of the cockpit, and fuselage/undercarriage strengthening), an initial order for 275 o-62s (as they were redesignated) was placed. A follow-on purchase of 1456 machines was received by the manufacturer in 1942, and by the time the first of these aircraft reached the USAAC, all o-62s had been redesignated L-5s. During the type's career, modifications were carried out which made it more suited to specific missions—an upward-hinged door was fitted to allow the L-5B to carry a stretcher, while the L-5C was fitted with a K-20 reconnaissance camera. More than 3000 Sentinels were eventually built for the Army, while the Marine Corps acquired 306 as OY-1s. Postwar, L-5/OY-1s saw further action in Korea.

SPECIFICATION (L-5):

ACCOMMODATION:
Pilot and observer/passenger in tandem

DIMENSIONS:
LENGTH: 24 ft 1 in (7.34 m)
WINGSPAN: 34 ft 0 in (10.36 m)
HEIGHT: 7 ft 11 in (2.41 m)

WEIGHTS:
EMPTY: 1550 lb (703 kg)
MAX T/O: 2020 lb (916 kg)

PERFORMANCE:
MAX SPEED: 130 mph (209 kmh)
RANGE: 420 miles (676 km)
POWERPLANT: Lycoming o-435-1
OUTPUT: 185 hp (138 kW)

FIRST FLIGHT DATE:
1940

FEATURES:
High-wing layout; fixed landing gear; close-cowled engine; extensive cockpit glazing

Taylorcraft O-57/L-2 Grasshopper

two-seat, single-engined high-wing light liaison aircraft

The third design in the triumvirate of civilian two-seaters trialed by the Army in August 1941, the original Taylorcraft YO-57s were standard production Model DS hastily camouflaged in drab olive paint. Christened Grasshopper, this aircraft was similarly modified to improve visibility for the crew and airframe durability. An initial USAAC order for 336 O-57As was received by Taylorcraft, followed by a further 140 in 1942. By the time delivery of the second batch had commenced, the reclassification of aircraft of this type from observation to liaison had taken place, resulting in all O-57/57As becoming L-2/2As. The two remaining batches ordered from Taylorcraft comprised 490 L-2Bs optimized for field artillery spotting and 900 L-2Ms, which had cowled engines and wing spoilers. Taylorcraft was also involved in producing a small number (253) of engineless gliders based on the L-2 design. Designated ST-100s, these machines were used to train future glider pilots. Many L-2s ended up on the US civilian register postwar, while others were supplied to foreign air arms.

SPECIFICATION:

ACCOMMODATION:
Pilot and observer/passenger in tandem

DIMENSIONS:
LENGTH: 22 ft 9 in (6.93 m)
WINGSPAN: 35 ft 5 in (10.79 m)
HEIGHT: 8 ft 0 in (2.44 m)

WEIGHTS:
EMPTY: 875 lb (397 kg)
MAX T/O: 1300 lb (590 kg)

PERFORMANCE:
MAX SPEED: 88 mph (142 kmh)
RANGE: 230 miles (370 km)
POWERPLANT: Continental O-170-3
OUTPUT: 65 hp (48 kW)

FIRST FLIGHT DATE:
1937

FEATURES:
High-wing layout; fixed landing gear; close-cowled engine; extensive cockpit glazing

Vought F4U/FG-1 Corsair

single-seat, single-engined monoplane fighter

Designed as a lightweight fighter built around the most powerful piston engine then available, Vought's prototype XF4U-1 was ordered by the Navy in June 1938 following a study of the company's V-166 proposal. In order to harness the immense power of the Pratt & Whitney XR-2800 Double Wasp engine, the largest diameter propeller fitted to a fighter up to then had to be used by the prototype—sufficient ground clearance for the propeller was achieved through the use of an inverted gull wing. The future looked rosy for the aircraft, but modifications incorporated into the design as a result of lessons learned in combat over Europe left the Corsair unfit for carrier use. It was therefore left to the Marine Corps to debut the aircraft in combat from Pacific island bases in February 1943, when VMF-124 made its first patrols from Guadalcanal in F4U-1 "birdcage" aircraft.

Just 688 framed canopy "Dash-1s" were built before production switched to the more familiar "bubble" canopy F4U-1A, this aircraft featuring a raised cockpit, strengthened landing gear, and a small spoiler near the leading edge of the starboard wing to improve directional stability when the wheels touched the ground. All these modifications were deemed necessary to render the Corsair suitable for carrier use. Nevertheless, the Navy remained leery about sending F4Us to sea until mid-1944, by which time the Royal Navy's Fleet Air Arm had been operating Corsairs from its carriers for more than six months. Ashore, a clutch of Navy squadrons had been taking the fight to the Japanese, flying alongside similarly equipped Marine Corps units. Aside from the 4675 F4U-1A/C/DS built by Vought, Brewster constructed 735 and Goodyear 4014 (the latter designated FG-1S).

The final production version of the Corsair built in World War II was the F4U-4, which featured a bigger engine and four-bladed propeller. The Corsair enjoyed a prosperous postwar career that lasted beyond the Korean War. Indeed, the final F4U-7 did not roll off the Vought production line until January 31, 1952, this aircraft being the 12,571st, and last, Corsair built.

SPECIFICATION (F4U-4):

ACCOMMODATION:
Pilot

DIMENSIONS:
LENGTH: 33 ft 8 in (10.26 m)
WINGSPAN: 40 ft 11 in (12.47 m)
HEIGHT: 14 ft 9 in (4.50 m)

WEIGHTS:
EMPTY: 9205 lb (4175 kg)
MAX T/O: 14,670 lb (6654 kg)

PERFORMANCE:
MAX SPEED: 446 mph (718 kmh)
RANGE: 1005 miles (1617 km)
POWERPLANT: Pratt & Whitney R-2800-18W Double Wasp
OUTPUT: 2450 hp (1827 kW)

FIRST FLIGHT DATE:
May 29, 1940

ARMAMENT:
Six Browning 0.50-in machine guns in wings; provision for eight rockets under wings or up to 2000-lb (907-kg) bomb load under fuselage center section

FEATURES:
Inverted gull-wing monoplane layout; retractable undercarriage; close-cowled radial engine; rectractable tailwheel; arrestor hook

Timm N2T Tutor

two-seat, single-engined monoplane primary trainer

The Timm Aircraft Corporation of Van Nuys, California, succeeded in securing a single order from the Navy for its PT-160K primary trainer principally because the aircraft used nonconventional materials in its construction. The US Government was greatly concerned in 1942 that the aircraft industry would suffer from a shortage of light alloys such as aluminum due to the increased war output, so it encouraged manufacturers to seek out alternatives. The previous year, Timm's PT-160K had become the first aircraft made of plastic-bonded plywood (a process patented under the name Aeromold by Timm) to achieve an Approved Type Certificate by the Federal Aviation Authority, and in early 1942 the Navy acquired two (designated XN2T-1S) for evaluation. Fitted with a Continental R-670 radial engine, the trainer proved a success during its flight trials and Timm received a contract to build 262 as the N2T-1 Tutor. The first Tutors reached the Navy in 1943, and these machines saw little more than a year of service prior to being declared surplus in late 1944.

SPECIFICATION:

ACCOMMODATION:
Two pilots in tandem

DIMENSIONS:
LENGTH: 24 ft 10 in (7.57 m)
WINGSPAN: 36 ft 0 in (10.97 m)
HEIGHT: 10 ft 8 in (3.25 m)

WEIGHTS:
EMPTY: 1940 lb (880 kg)
MAX T/O: 2725 lb (1236 kg)

PERFORMANCE:
MAX SPEED: 144 mph (232 kmh)
RANGE: 400 miles (644 km)
POWERPLANT: Continental R-670-4
OUTPUT: 220 hp (164 kW)

FIRST FLIGHT DATE:
April 2, 1941 (S-160K)

FEATURES:
Monoplane wing layout; fixed undercarriage; exposed radial engine; tandem open cockpits

Vought OS2U Kingfisher

two-seat, single-engined monoplane reconnaissance float- or landplane

Serving as the Navy's standard scout-observation floatplane in World War II, the Kingfisher was designed for either inshore use or launching by catapult from capital ships. Developed in 1937 as a replacement for earlier biplanes built by Vought to serve the Navy in the same observation capacity, the Kingfisher embodied tried and tested techniques employed by the company in previous designs. The prototype XOS2U-1 made its first flight in July 1938, and production examples reached the fleet in August 1940. The definitive Kingfisher in terms of numbers built was the OS2U-3, 1006 of which were delivered before production ended in 1942. The Naval Aircraft Factory also built 300 OS2N-1 landplanes that were used for training and coastal patrols. Kingfishers saw action with the Navy across the globe, being used for reconnaissance, antisubmarine patrols, air-sea rescue, dive-bombing, and artillery spotting. A small number of aircraft were also exported, with the largest customer being Britain, which was supplied with 100 under Lend-Lease. A total of 1519 Kingfishers were built.

SPECIFICATION:

ACCOMMODATION:
Pilot and observer/gunner

DIMENSIONS:
LENGTH: 33 ft 10 in (10.31 m)
WINGSPAN: 35 ft 11 in (10.95 m)
HEIGHT: 15 ft 1.50 in (4.61 m)

WEIGHTS:
EMPTY: 4123 lb (1870 kg)
MAX T/O: 6000 lb (2722 kg)

PERFORMANCE:
MAX SPEED: 164 mph (264 kmh)
RANGE: 805 miles (1295 km)
POWERPLANT: Pratt & Whitney R-985-AN-2 Wasp Junior
OUTPUT: 450 hp (335 kW)

FIRST FLIGHT DATE:
July 20, 1938

ARMAMENT:
One fixed Browning 0.30-in machine gun in nose and one on flexible mounting for observer; maximum bomb load of 650 lb (295 kg) on underwing racks

FEATURES:
Monoplane wing layout; cowled radial engine; single main float and fixed outrigger floats (seaplane), or fixed undercarriage (landplane)

Vultee A-31/35 Vengeance

two-seat, single-engined monoplane dive-bomber

Production of the Vengeance was instigated in 1940 when the British Purchasing Commission placed an order for 700 examples following bitter experience of the effectiveness of the Ju 87 Stuka. Designed to a British specification, the Vultee dive-bomber was the successor to the company's V-11/12 light attack aircraft that it had sold to export customers in the late 1930s. The first production example flew in July 1941, by which point a further 300 had been ordered through the USAAC as A-31s as part of the newly established Lend-Lease arrangement between the British and American governments. Deliveries were still in progress when Pearl Harbor was bombed, and the USAAC immediately commandeered 243 A-31s for its own use, redesignating them V-72s. A further 930 were also ordered by the USAAC, these aircraft being equipped to Army standards with five 0.50-in guns. Designated A-35A/BS, at least 562 of these machines eventually reached the RAF. Deemed obsolescent, the A-35s saw little service with the USAF other than as target tugs and general hacks.

SPECIFICATION (A-35B):

ACCOMMODATION:
Pilot and observer/gunner

DIMENSIONS:
LENGTH: 39 ft 9 in (12.12 m)
WINGSPAN: 48 ft 0 in (14.63 m)
HEIGHT: 15 ft 4 in (4.67 m)

WEIGHTS:
EMPTY: 10,300 lb (4672 kg)
MAX T/O: 16,400 lb (7439 kg)

PERFORMANCE:
MAX SPEED: 279 mph (449 kmh)
RANGE: 600 miles (966 km)
POWERPLANT: Wright R-2600-13 Cyclone 14
OUTPUT: 1700 hp (1268 kW)

FIRST FLIGHT DATE:
July 1941

ARMAMENT:
Four Browning 0.50-in machine guns in wings and two flexibly mounted in rear cockpit; maximum bomb load of 2000 lb (908 kg) on underwing racks

FEATURES:
Monoplane wing layout; close-cowled radial engine; large vertical tail surface

Postwar

Beech T-34 Mentor

two-seat, single-engined primary trainer

Based on the hugely successful civilian Beech Model 35 Bonanza, the Model 45 Mentor was built in 1948 in response to an expected demand by the USAF for a new primary tuitional trainer to replace the veteran T-6 Texan. Five years were to pass, however, before the Beech trainer was chosen to fill the role, the USAF undertaking a fly-off that saw a wide variety of designs trialed. As part of this evaluation, three pre-production Mentors were acquired by the Air Force, which designated them YT-34s. Once selected, Beech supplied Training Command with 350 T-34As from its Wichita plant (plus a further 100 from Canadian Car & Foundry), deliveries commencing in 1954. That same year also saw the Navy select the Mentor as its basic trainer, 423 T-34Bs being acquired. The Mentor was replaced in Air Force ranks from 1960 onward following the adoption of an all-through jet training syllabus, while the Navy continued to use its T-34Bs until the late 1970s, when the T-34C Turbo Mentor entered service.

SPECIFICATION (T-34A):

ACCOMMODATION:
Two pilots in tandem

DIMENSIONS:
LENGTH: 25 ft 10 in (7.87 m)
WINGSPAN: 32 ft 10 in (10.01 m)
HEIGHT: 10 ft 0.25 in (3.04 m)

WEIGHTS:
EMPTY: 2055 lb (932 kg)
MAX T/O: 2900 lb (1315 kg)

PERFORMANCE:
MAX SPEED: 188 mph (302 kmh)
RANGE: 770 miles (1238 km)
POWERPLANT: Continental O-470-13
OUTPUT: 225 hp (168 kW)

FIRST FLIGHT DATE:
December 2, 1948

FEATURES:
Straight-wing layout; tandem seating; extensive cockpit glazing; rectractable tricycle landing gear

Beech T-34C Turbo Mentor

two-seat, single-engined primary trainer

The T-34C was chosen by the Navy as the ideal aircraft for its Long-Range Pilot Training Syllabus, which had been devised so that a single type could be bought as a replacement for both the T-34B Mentor and the more advanced North American T-28B/C Trojan. Two prototype YT-34CS were built, these machines combining the airframe of the T-34B with a derated Pratt & Whitney PT6A-25 turboprop engine. Following extended flight testing in 1973-74, which strived to achieve satisfactory spin-recovery characteristics, production was initiated with an order for 334 T-34CS in April 1975. The last of these was delivered in April 1984, and a follow-on batch of 19 was acquired in 1989-90. Aside from a change in powerplant, the T-34C differed from the B-model by having a greater wingspan, additional ventral fins, a larger dorsal fin, and strakes forward of the tailplane leading edge roots. The Turbo Mentor is still currently serving as the Navy's primary trainer, although it is being progressively replaced by Raytheon's T-6A Texan II.

SPECIFICATION:

ACCOMMODATION:
Two pilots in tandem

DIMENSIONS:
LENGTH: 28 ft 9 in (8.70 m)
WINGSPAN: 33 ft 4 in (10.16 m)
HEIGHT: 9 ft 11 in (3.02 m)

WEIGHTS:
EMPTY: 2630 lb (1193 kg)
MAX T/O: 4274 lb (1938 kg)

PERFORMANCE:
MAX SPEED: 257 mph (411 kmh)
RANGE: 810 miles (1296 km)
POWERPLANT: Pratt & Whitney
Canada PT6A-25
OUTPUT: 400 shp (300 kW)

FIRST FLIGHT DATE:
September 21, 1973

FEATURES:
Straight-wing layout; tandem seating; turboprop engine; extensive cockpit glazing; rectractable tricycle landing gear; ventral fins

Beech L-23/U-8 Seminole

six-seat, twin-engined staff transportation/battlefield surveillance aircraft

Beech's six-seater Model 50 Twin Bonanza was the first twin-engined light aircraft to achieve production quantity in the US after World War II. Flown in prototype form on November 15, 1949, a single example of the Model 50 was supplied to the Army as the YL-23 in January 1952 for flight testing. The aircraft would subsequently perform liaison and light utility roles as the L-23A Seminole, 55 examples being ordered in 1952, followed by a further 40 near-identical L-23BS. In November 1956 the Army began to receive the first of 85 L-23DS, which were based on the civil Model E50 Twin Bonanza. This variant featured more powerful Lycoming O-480-1 engines, and the surviving 93 L-23A/BS were also remanufactured to this standard. In 1962 all L-23DS were redesignated U-8DS, the U standing for Utility. More than 30 Seminoles were also kitted out for the radar observation/ photography and battlefield surveillance mission in 1958-60, these aircraft being designated RL-23D/RU-8D. All U-8DS were replaced by larger U-8FS (ex-civilian Queen Air 65s) in the early 1980s.

SPECIFICATION (L-23D):

ACCOMMODATION:
Two pilots and four passengers

DIMENSIONS:
LENGTH: 31 ft 6.50 in (9.64 m)
WINGSPAN: 45 ft 3.50 in (13.82 m)
HEIGHT: 11 ft 4 in (3.47 m)

WEIGHTS:
EMPTY: 4974 lb (2256 kg)
MAX T/O: 7000 lb (2134 kg)

PERFORMANCE:
MAX SPEED: 233 mph (373 kmh)
RANGE: 1355 miles (2168 km)
POWERPLANT: two Lycoming O-480-1S
OUTPUT: 680 hp (507 kW)

FIRST FLIGHT DATE:
January 1952 (YL-23)

FEATURES:
Straight-wing layout; rectractable tricycle landing gear; twin, close-cowled engines

Beech U-21 Ute and T-44 Pegasus

12-seat, twin-engined staff transportation/battlefield surveillance/training aircraft

In May 1963 Beech started flight trials of a Queen Air fitted with two Pratt & Whitney PT6A-6 turboprop engines. Early the following year, the company released the new Model 65-90 King Air, which was a re-engineered version of the unique PT6A-powered Queen Air of 1963. The Army selected the new aircraft for production in October 1966, the unpressurized Beech being designated the U-21A Ute. A total of 166 were delivered in 1967-68, and these aircraft found gainful employment shuttling senior officers between bases across the globe. As with the L-23/U-8, the Army modified 50+ Utes (as RU-21s) to perform electronic reconnaissance duties, primarily in Vietnam. The Navy also acquired Beech's King Air 90 in 1976 after it chose the aircraft to fulfill its requirement for an advanced turboprop training platform. Designated the T-44 Pegasus, a total of 61 aircraft were delivered to VT-28 and VT-31 at NAS Corpus Christi in 1977. The last Utes were retired in 1994, but 27 T-44s soldier on in the advanced maritime training role with VT-31.

SPECIFICATION (U-21A):

ACCOMMODATION:
Two pilots and ten passengers

DIMENSIONS:
LENGTH: 35 ft 6 in (10.85 m)
WINGSPAN: 45 ft 10.50 in (13.74 m)
HEIGHT: 14 ft 2 in (4.32 m)

WEIGHTS:
EMPTY: 5235 lb (2275 kg)
MAX T/O: 9650 lb (4377 kg)

PERFORMANCE:
MAX SPEED: 248 mph (397 kmh)
RANGE: 960 miles (1536 km)
POWERPLANT: two Pratt & Whitney PT6A-20S
OUTPUT: 1100 shp (820 kW)

FIRST FLIGHT DATE:
March 1967

FEATURES:
Straight-wing layout; rectractable tricycle landing gear; twin, close-cowled turboprop engines

Beech T-42 Cochise

six-seat, twin-engined training aircraft

In the early 1960s the Army was searching for an "off-the-shelf" civil type to use as a fixed-wing twin-engined instrument trainer for pilots destined to fly larger aircraft in frontline service. In February 1965 it chose the B55 Baron as the platform best suited to this role, the Beech "twin" having evolved from the Model 95 Travel Air of the 1950s. The Baron 55 was the first model made available in 1960, and the Army ordered 70 examples of the near-identical B55 variant (which featured a longer nose and increased takeoff weight) five years later. The aircraft was designated the T-42A Cochise in military service, and 65 examples were issued to the Army Aviation School and five delivered to Turkey as part of the Military Assistance Program. These aircraft served in a training capacity with the Army until the late 1980s, when more than half of the surviving airframes were sold to civilian buyers. The remaining T-42s were withdrawn from use and placed in storage in the mid-1990s.

SPECIFICATION:

ACCOMMODATION:
Two pilots and four passengers

DIMENSIONS:
LENGTH: 29 ft 0 in (8.84 m)
WINGSPAN: 37 ft 9.75 in (11.52 m)
HEIGHT: 9 ft 3 in (2.82 m)

WEIGHTS:
EMPTY: 3075 lb (1395 kg)
MAX T/O: 5300 lb (2404 kg)

PERFORMANCE:
MAX SPEED: 242 mph (390 kmh)
RANGE: 1143 miles (1840 km)
POWERPLANT: two Teledyne Continental IO-520-C
OUTPUT: 570 hp (412 kW)

FIRST FLIGHT DATE:
February 29, 1960 (Baron 55)

FEATURES:
Straight-wing layout; rectractable tricycle landing gear; twin, close-cowled engines

Beech U/QU-22

single-seat, single-engined electronic surveillance aircraft

Based on the commercial Bonanza 36, the U-22 was ordered by the USAF for use in Vietnam as an electronic intelligence-gathering (Elint) drone as part of the Pave Eagle project. The aircraft acquired was effectively a standard single-finned Bonanza 36, but with an engine that was fitted with a reduction gear in a bulged housing atop the nose that drove a large slow-running propeller. A further bulge on the right side of the cowling covered an outsize electric generator that helped power the myriad intelligence gathering receivers and recorders stuffed into the fuselage behind the solitary pilot's seat. The USAF initially trialed six YQU-22AS as it strived to finalize the aircraft's mission fit, and once this had been settled, 27 QU-22BS were delivered in 1970. Fitted out with Elint and drone-control equipment by Sperry Rand Univac, the aircraft made its combat debut from bases in Thailand. Although usually controlled by an operator sitting in a DC-130, the QU-22s normally carried a pilot to monitor operations and fly the aircraft in an emergency.

SPECIFICATION:

ACCOMMODATION:
Pilot

DIMENSIONS:
LENGTH: 26 ft 4 in (8.04 m)
WINGSPAN: 32 ft 10 in (9.78 m)
HEIGHT: 8 ft 5 in (2.59 m)

WEIGHTS:
EMPTY: 2315 lb (1050 kg)
MAX T/O: 3600 lb (1633 kg)

PERFORMANCE:
MAX SPEED: 199 mph (318 kmh)
RANGE: 980 miles (1568 km)
POWERPLANT: Continental
IO-520-B
OUTPUT: 285 hp (213 kW)

FIRST FLIGHT DATE:
September 14, 1959 (Model 33 Bonanza)

FEATURES:
Straight-wing layout; rectractable tricycle landing gear; single close-cowled engine; tip tanks

Beech C/UC-12 Huron

ten-seat, twin-engined staff transportation/battlefield surveillance aircraft

Used by all four services, the C-12 Huron is a militarized version of Beech's Super King Air 200. The aircraft was selected in 1974 to perform the staff transportation role for the Army, Navy, Marine Corps, and Air Force, the C-12 providing an "off-the-shelf" solution for this requirement. The Army received the first of its 60 C-12As in July 1975, followed by 30 identical aircraft for the Air Force. Follow-on purchases saw the aircraft re-engined and fitted with a cargo door. In the late 1970s the Army also started development of the RC-12D/K, the Huron being modified to perform the battlefield reconnaissance and electronic intelligence missions. The final C-12 variant to enter service with the USAF's Air National Guard was the stretched J-model, based on the Beech 1900C. The 85 UC-12Bs delivered to the Navy and Marine Corps featured cargo doors and bigger engines from the outset. An additional 12 UC-12Fs, with better avionics and bigger engines, followed, and today more than 140 Hurons remain in service with the US military.

SPECIFICATION (UC-12F):

ACCOMMODATION:
Two pilots and six/eight passengers

DIMENSIONS:
LENGTH: 43 ft 9 in (13.38 m)
WINGSPAN: 54 ft 6 in (16.64 m)
HEIGHT: 15 ft 0 in (4.57 m)

WEIGHTS:
EMPTY: 7538 lb (3419 kg)
MAX T/O: 12,500 lb (5670 kg)

PERFORMANCE:
MAX SPEED: 339 mph (542 kmh)
RANGE: 1600 miles (2560 km)
POWERPLANT: two Pratt & Whitney Canada PT6A-42S
OUTPUT: 1700 shp (1270 kW)

FIRST FLIGHT DATE:
October 1972 (Super King Air 200)

FEATURES:
Straight-wing layout; rectractable tricycle landing gear; twin, close-cowled turboprop engines; T-tail

Beech T-1A Jayhawk

seven-seat, twin-engined tanker/transportation aircrew training aircraft

An "off-the-shelf" development of the Beechjet 400A business jet, the T-1A was acquired to meet a USAF requirement for a Tanker/Training System (TTTS) aircraft. Beating off rival designs, the Jayhawk provides tailored training for student pilots destined to fly transports such as the C-5, C-17, KC-135, and KC-10. The first of 168 T-1As was delivered in January 1992, with the final example being received in 1997. The acquisition of the Jayhawk meant that future Air Mobility Command pilots no longer trained on the overworked T-38 Talon, which was now used exclusively for those destined to fly fast jets. The militarized T-1A differed from the Beechjet 400A in having six fewer cabin windows, strengthened undercarriage, increased fuel capacity with single-point refueling, strengthened wing leading edges and windshield for low-level birdstrike protection, and cabin-mounted avionics (moved from the nose). The T-1A presently equips four wings within Air Education and Training Command, these aircraft being operated in Specialized Undergraduate Pilot Training configuration.

SPECIFICATION:

ACCOMMODATION:
Two pilots and five passengers

DIMENSIONS:
LENGTH: 48 ft 5 in (14.75 m)
WINGSPAN: 43 ft 6 in (13.25 m)
HEIGHT: 13 ft 9 in (4.19 m)

WEIGHTS:
EMPTY: 10,115 lb (4588 kg)
MAX T/O: 15,780 lb (7157 kg)

PERFORMANCE:
MAX SPEED: 542 mph (867 kmh)
RANGE: 2222 miles (3575 km)
POWERPLANT: two Pratt & Whitney Canada JT15D-5BS
OUTPUT: 5800 lb st (26 kN)

FIRST FLIGHT DATE:
September 1989 (Beechjet 400A)

FEATURES:
Swept-wing layout; rectractable tricycle landing gear; twin, podded engines on rear fuselage; T-tail

Boeing C/KC-97 Stratofreighter/Stratotanker

102-seat, four-engined transportation/air-refueling tanker aircraft

The transport derivative of Boeing's B-29, the C-97 was appreciably bigger than the Superfortress due to the addition of a second fuselage of greater diameter on top of the existing structure. Three pre-production examples of the aircraft were designated the XC-97 by the USAAF, and although they had been ordered simultaneously with the B-29 in January 1942, the latter type took precedence in respect to its development. Boeing commenced flight trials with the XC-97 in 1944, and an order for 50 C-97As was placed. Although designed as a transporter of people and freight, it was in the role of aerial tanker for Strategic Air Command (SAC) that the C-97 achieved its greatest success. In fact, 811 KC-97 tankers in three different variants were built. The combination of the aircraft's capacious cargo hold and Boeing's Flying Boom refueling system allowed the Stratotanker to transfer fuel to SAC's fleet of fighters and bombers. Following their replacement by jet-powered KC-135s, KC-97s were passed on to Air National Guard units, which continued to use them into the 1970s.

SPECIFICATION (KC-97G):

ACCOMMODATION:
Pilot and copilot, navigator, flight engineer, boom operator, crew chief, and up to 96 passengers

DIMENSIONS:
LENGTH: 110 ft 4 in (33.64 m)
WINGSPAN: 141 ft 3 in (43.05 m)
HEIGHT: 38 ft 3 in (11.75 m)

WEIGHTS:
EMPTY: 82,500 lb (37,422 kg)
MAX T/O: 175,000 lb (78,980 kg)

PERFORMANCE:
MAX SPEED: 375 mph (600 kmh)
RANGE: 4300 miles (6920 km)
POWERPLANT: four Pratt & Whitney R-4360-59B Wasp Majors
OUTPUT: 14,000 hp (10,440 kW)

FIRST FLIGHT DATE:
November 15, 1944

FEATURES:
Monoplane-wing layout; four radial engines; "double bubble" fuselage; tricycle undercarriage; external refueling boom (KC-97 only)

Boeing B/RB-47 Stratojet

three-seat, six-engined medium bomber

Strongly influenced by the postwar discovery of swept-wing jet aircraft in Germany, Boeing abandoned its work on conventional straight-winged designs and produced the Model 450. This was ordered by the USAAF in 1945, and flight test results proved that the jet exceeded the claims made for it by Boeing, with drag proving to be 25 percent lower than estimated. Although the XB-47 (USAF designation) could not fly the long missions requested by SAC, the jet was still ordered in quantity in 1949—the first B-47As reached the frontline in late 1950. The more refined B-47B was the first large-scale production variant, and three factories churned these out following the escalation of hostilities in Korea. The B-47E of 1951 featured bigger engines, 20-mm guns in the tail turret, a new radar bombing system, ejection seats, and a refueling receptacle. In service with SAC throughout the 1950s, the B-47 equipped 28 bomb wings, each with 45 aircraft. Some 2042 Stratojets were built, including 300+ RB-47E and ERB-47H reconnaissance and electronic countermeasures aircraft.

SPECIFICATION (B-47E):

ACCOMMODATION:
Pilot, copilot/tail gunner, and bombardier/navigator

DIMENSIONS:
LENGTH: 109 ft 10 in (33.50 m)
WINGSPAN: 116 ft 0 in (35.36 m)
HEIGHT: 27 ft 11 in (8.52 m)

WEIGHTS:
EMPTY: 80,756 lb (36,631 kg)
MAX T/O: 206,700 lb (93,759 kg)

PERFORMANCE:
MAX SPEED: 606 mph (980 kmh)
RANGE: 4000 miles (6400 km)
POWERPLANT: six General Electric J47-GE-25AS
OUTPUT: 36,000 lb st (160 kN)

FIRST FLIGHT DATE:
December 17, 1947

ARMAMENT:
Two M-3 20-mm cannon in remote-controlled tail turret; 22,000 lb (9979 kg) of bombs in bomb bay

FEATURES:
Monoplane, swept-wing layout; six turbojets in underwing pods; "double bubble" fuselage; fuselage-mounted undercarriage, with wing outriggers; fighter-style bubble cockpit

Boeing B-52 Stratofortress

five-seat, eight-engined strategic bomber

For many years the biggest, heaviest, and most powerful bomber ever built, the B-52 may have been eclipsed by the Russian Tu-160 in terms of offensive potential, but it is likely to remain a viable frontline weapon of war long after the Tupolev bomber has been consigned to history. Originally planned by Boeing in 1946 as a B-50 replacement, the aircraft was to have been a straight-winged bomber that relied on turboprop engines due to the lack of available powerplants capable of propelling an intercontinental bomber. However, the B-52 became a direct beneficiary of Pratt & Whitney's more fuel-efficient J57 turbojet, which was far superior to its rivals both in terms of performance and economy. Redesigned with eight engines housed in four double pods beneath swept wings, the prototype YB-52 completed its first flight on April 15, 1952.

Initially built with tandem seating for the pilot and copilot, production B-52As had a revised side-by-side layout in an airliner-style cockpit. Re-equipping B-50 squadrons from March 1955, the B-52 was produced to the tune of 744 airframes in eight subtypes. Numerically, the most important of these was the B-52D (170), which played a key role in the Vietnam War and was the backbone of the SAC's Cold War nuclear bomber force into the 1970s, and the B-52G (193 built), with its smaller fin and remote-controlled tail guns.

The final production variant was the B-52H (102 built), which was similar to the G-model except for its eight Pratt & Whitney TF33 turbofan engines and 20-mm cannon in the tail turret, rather than four 0.50-in machine guns. The B-52G saw extensive combat in Operation Desert Storm in 1991, because it was capable of employing conventional cruise missiles and iron bombs. The G-models were retired from USAF service soon afterward, leaving just 90 B-52Hs equipping frontline units. Like the B-52Gs, these aircraft are now capable of employing both nuclear and conventional bombs, as well as cruise missiles, and have dropped/fired the latter in combat in Iraq, Kosovo, and Afghanistan. Surviving B-52Hs are set to serve until 2040.

SPECIFICATION (B-52H):

ACCOMMODATION:
Pilot, copilot, navigator, bombardier/radar navigator, and ECM operator

DIMENSIONS:
LENGTH: 160 ft 11 in (49.05 m)
WINGSPAN: 185 ft 0 in (56.39 m)
HEIGHT: 40 ft 8 in (12.40 m)

WEIGHTS:
EMPTY: 195,000 lb (88,450 kg)
MAX T/O: 505,000 lb (229,088 kg)

PERFORMANCE:
MAX SPEED: 598 mph (957 kmh)
RANGE: 10,059 miles (16,095 km)
POWERPLANT: eight Pratt & Whitney TF33-P-3s
OUTPUT: 110,000 lb st (488 kN)

FIRST FLIGHT DATE:
April 15, 1952

ARMAMENT:
60,000 lb (27,216 kg) of bombs/missiles split between bomb bay and two underwing stores pylons

FEATURES:
Monoplane, shoulder-mounted swept-wing; eight turbojets in underwing pods; fuselage-mounted undercarriage, with wing outriggers

Boeing B/KB-50 Superfortress

11-seat, four-engined strategic bomber

SAC's frontline strategic bomber from the late 1940s until the early 1950s, the B-50 started life as the B-29D. Some 5152 D-models were on order when World War II ended, but only 50 survived cancelation to be built. Although based on the original B-29, the D-model was powered by four new and very powerful Pratt & Whitney Wasp Major engines, and also featured a lighter and stronger alloy airframe and taller tailfin. The new bomber had been redesignated the B-50 by the time the prototype flew on June 25, 1947, and the USAF bought 80 A-models, 45 B-models, 222 D-models, and 24 TB-50H dual-control trainers. A number of these were converted into WB-50s for weather reconnaissance and KB-50s for aerial refueling following their service as bombers, and this ensured their employment with USAF and Air National Guard units until 1968. The KB-50J proved particularly successful, 112 being utilized as tankers following the fitment of the hose-reel system or Boeing's Flying Boom—these aircraft also had two podded J47 turbojets.

SPECIFICATION (B-50D):

ACCOMMODATION:
Pilot, copilot, engineer, navigator, radar operator, bombardier, radio/electronic countermeasures operator, left/right side gunners, and top and tail gunners

DIMENSIONS:
LENGTH: 99 ft 0 in (30.17 m)
WINGSPAN: 141 ft 3 in (43.05 m)
HEIGHT: 32 ft 8 in (9.99 m)

WEIGHTS:
EMPTY: 80,609 lb (36,564 kg)
MAX T/O: 173,000 lb (78,471 kg)

PERFORMANCE:
MAX SPEED: 380 mph (608 kmh)
RANGE: 4900 miles (7886 km)
POWERPLANT: four Pratt & Whitney R-4360-35 Wasp Majors
OUTPUT: 14,000 hp (10,440 kW)

FIRST FLIGHT DATE:
June 25, 1947

ARMAMENT:
Four turrets with two/four Browning 0.50-in machine guns, and tail turret with three machine guns; bomb load of 28,000 lb (12,701 kg) in bomb bay

FEATURES:
Monoplane wing layout; four radial engines; very large vertical tail surface

Boeing C-22

93-seat, three-engined transportation aircraft

Although one of the world's most successful airliners, Boeing's 727 failed to see widespread service with the US armed forces. In fact, only six second-hand examples were acquired by the Air Force in 1986 for use as VIP transports with the Air National Guard (ANG) and US Southern Command. These machines were sourced from Lufthansa, Pan Am, and Singapore Airlines, with four of the jets initially being flown as C-22BS by Detachment 1 of the 121st TFW District of Columbia ANG, based at Andrews AFB. This unit was later raised to squadron level as the 201st Military Airlift Squadron (MAS), with its ex-Pan Am Series 100 jets configured to carry 24 VIPs and 66 regular passengers—the unit routinely transported ANG inspection and training teams across the country. Southern Command's ex-Lufthansa 727-030 was designated a C-22A, and this was eventually replaced by a newer ex-Singapore Airlines 727-212 and designated a C-22C. Operated from Andrews AFB by the 310th MAS, this jet was finally retired, along with the last of the four C-22BS, in 2004.

SPECIFICATION (C-22C):

ACCOMMODATION:
Pilot, copilot, engineer, and up to 90 passengers depending on configuration

DIMENSIONS:
LENGTH: 153 ft 2 in (46.69 m)
WINGSPAN: 108 ft 0 in (32.92 m)
HEIGHT: 34 ft 0 in (10.36 m)

WEIGHTS:
EMPTY: 102,900 lb (46,675 kg)
MAX T/O: 209,500 lb (95,027 kg)

PERFORMANCE:
MAX SPEED: 622 mph (1001 kmh)
RANGE: 2720 miles (4392 km)
POWERPLANT: three Pratt & Whitney JT8D-9AS
OUTPUT: 43,500 lb st (193 kN)

FIRST FLIGHT DATE:
July 27, 1967 (727-200)

FEATURES:
Monoplane, swept-wing layout; three turbojets grouped around tail; T-tail

Boeing C/EC/KC-135

194-seat, four-engined transportation/tanker/special missions/AWACS aircraft

Sired by the Boeing-funded 367-80 civilian jet transport, the C-135 family of military aircraft was ordered into production for the USAF following an evaluation of the prototype soon after its first flight in July 1954. Just three months later Boeing received an order for 29 aircraft to serve in the dual roles of tanker for Strategic Air Command and logistic support for the Military Air Transport Service. Joining the USAF starting in August 1956, the aircraft were rarely used in the dual role as production of the C-135 was large enough to allow KC-135 variants to operate exclusively as aerial refuelers. The system at the heart of the Stratotanker is the high-speed Boeing Flying Boom, which is flown into the receiving aircraft's refueling receptacle by the boom operator aboard the KC-135.

The USAF bought 732 KC-135s between June 1957 and January 1965, while a further 88 were delivered as C-135 transports. The KC-135 fleet has been the subject of two major re-engining programs (beginning in the 1970s and continuing on beyond 2000), with more than 160 Air Force Reserve and Air National Guard A-models being fitted with TF33 turbofans from retired 707 airliners. During the 1980s and into the 1990s, a further 400+ KC-135As were re-engined with CFM56 turbofans and redesignated KC-135R/Ts.

More than 28 different variants of C-135 have been flown by the USAF over the years on all manner of reconnaissance, transportation and command post duties, and further examples have operated with the Navy as E-6 Mercury (16 built) submarine communications and airborne command aircraft since 1989.

Also utilizing the basic c-135/707 airframe is the Airborne Warning & Control System e-3 Sentry (34 built for the USAF), which was developed in the early 1970s as a replacement for the USAF's piston-engined ec-121 force. The eyes of the e-3's detection system is its Westinghouse apy-1/2 radar, mounted in a rotodome above the rear fuselage. The final c-135/707 variant to enter USAF service was the e-8 Joint Strategic Target Attack Radar System (J-STARS) battlefield reconnaissance platform. Fitted with mission avionics developed by Northrop-Grumman, a total of 20 were delivered in 1996-98, these being converted 707 airliners.

SPECIFICATION (KC-135R):

ACCOMMODATION:
Pilot, copilot, navigator, boom operator (as tanker), and various other crew/passenger configurations depending on role

DIMENSIONS:
LENGTH: 136 ft 3 in (41.53 m)
WINGSPAN: 130 ft 10 in (39.88 m)
HEIGHT: 41 ft 8 in (12.70 m)

WEIGHTS:
EMPTY: 106,305 lb (48,220 kg)
MAX T/O: 322,500 lb (146,285 kg)

PERFORMANCE:
MAX SPEED: 614 mph (982 kmh)
RANGE: 2897 miles (4635 km)
POWERPLANT: four CFM International F108s
OUTPUT: 88,000 lb st (392 kN)

FIRST FLIGHT DATE:
July 15, 1954

FEATURES:
Monoplane, swept-wing layout; four turbofans in underwing pods; tall tailfin; external refueling boom (KC-135 only)

Boeing C-17 Globemaster III

157-seat, four-engined strategic and intratheater transportation aircraft

Chosen by the USAF in August 1981 to meet its C-X requirement for a heavy airlifter, the C-17 suffered a long and troublesome development but has gone on to enjoy great success in service. The McDonnell Douglas design had to be able to perform both strategic and intratheater missions and boast good short field performance for operations from semi-prepared runways. It also needed good ground maneuverability and a capacious cargo hold capable of housing an M1 Abrams main battle tank or up to three AH-64 Apaches. Embodying classic military transportation aircraft features such as a high wing and rear-fuselage loading ramp, the C-17 also has advanced-technology features—winglets, supercritical wing section, high-performance turbo-fan engines, and externally blown flaps. Following prolonged development, production aircraft began reaching the USAF in 1993. The C-17 has since then seen service across the globe, supporting US military efforts in Iraq and Afghanistan. The USAF's total buy numbers 180 Globemaster IIIs.

SPECIFICATION:

ACCOMMODATION:
Pilot, copilot, loadmaster, and up to 154 passengers

DIMENSIONS:
LENGTH: 174 ft 0 in (53.04 m)
WINGSPAN: 169 ft 10 in (51.76 m)
HEIGHT: 55 ft 1 in (16.79 m)

WEIGHTS:
EMPTY: 277,000 lb (125,645 kg)
MAX T/O: 585,000 lb (265,350 kg)

PERFORMANCE:
MAX SPEED: 521 mph (833 kmh)
RANGE: 2663 miles (4260 km)
POWERPLANT: four Pratt & Whitney F117-PW-100s
OUTPUT: 166,800 lb st (742 kN)

FIRST FLIGHT DATE:
September 15, 1991

FEATURES:
Shoulder-mounted swept-wing layout; winglets; four podded turbofan engines; tall T-tail

Boeing T/CT-43 and C-40 Clipper

21-seat, twin-engined navigation training aircraft and 140-seat transport

In May 1971 the USAF announced that it had selected the Boeing 737-253 as an "off-the-shelf" platform to meet its needs for a navigation trainer to replace the piston-engined Convair T-29. Designated the T-43A, 19 examples were delivered from mid-1973. Featuring a standard two-crew flight deck, the aircraft had their main cabins configured for 12 student navigators, four advanced students, and three instructors. All were initially operated as trainers, but eight were later converted into transports (designated CT-43AS) for use by ANG units, and as shuttles for personnel working at secret test sites in Nevada. The second 737 variant to enter US military service was the C-40, which the Navy chose as its Unique Fleet Essential Airlift Replacement Aircraft in 1997. Based on the 737-700, the Clipper can be configured either for passengers only or in a "combi" freight/passenger fit. Eight have been delivered to the Navy Reserve to date to replace its fleet of 29 C-9 Skytrain IIs. The USAF has also received four C-40B/Cs as C-137/22 replacements, with more to follow.

SPECIFICATION (T-43A):

ACCOMMODATION:
Pilot, copilot, and 19 students/instructors

DIMENSIONS:
LENGTH: 100 ft 0 in (30.48 m)
WINGSPAN: 93 ft 0 in (28.35 m)
HEIGHT: 37 ft 0 in (11.28 m)

WEIGHTS:
EMPTY: 60,210 lb (27,311 kg)
MAX T/O: 115,500 lb (52,391 kg)

PERFORMANCE:
MAX SPEED: 628 mph (1010 kmh)
RANGE: 2994 miles (4818 km)
POWERPLANT: two Pratt & Whitney JT8D-9s
OUTPUT: 29,000 lb st (129 kN)

FIRST FLIGHT DATE:
August 8, 1967 (737-200)

FEATURES:
Monoplane, swept-wing layout; two turbojet engines in underwing pods; tall tailfin

Boeing F/A-18E/F Super Hornet

single/two-seat, twin-engined fighter-bomber

Initially developed by McDonnell Douglas (which was acquired by Boeing in December 1996), the single-seat F/A-18E and two-seat F/A-18F can trace their history back to 1987 and the Hornet 2000 project. The latter was prompted by a Naval Air Systems Command study for future evolutionary upgrades to the successful F/A-18A/C Hornet, which was then entering service with the Navy's light strike community. McDonnell Douglas was quick to offer the Super Hornet as an alternative to the stillborn A-12A Avenger, which was canceled in 1991 due to huge budget overruns.

The manufacturer was awarded a development contract for seven aircraft in 1992, and the first prototype (F/A-18E) completed its maiden flight in November 1995. Compared with the earlier F/A-18C, the F/A-18E is 4 feet (1.30 m) longer, has a wing span that is 7 feet (2.19 m) greater and an overall wing area that is increased by 100 square feet (9.3 m²). Thanks to its larger airframe, the jet's fuel capacity has been significantly increased to the point where the Super Hornet's range is 40 percent greater than the original Hornet. The aircraft's engine intakes were also redesigned to increase the airflow to its more powerful F414 engines, which were uprated derivatives of the F/A-18A/C's F404 turbofan.

Following service trials, the first production aircraft was delivered to fleet replacement squadron VFA-122 in September 1999. VFA-115 became the first unit to deploy with the Super Hornet in 2002, the squadron giving the jet its combat debut over Iraq during Operation Southern Watch/Iraqi Freedom.

Seen as a replacement for both the F-14 Tomcat and early-build F/A-18CS, the F/A-18E/F is currently in full-scale production at Boeing. A true multirole aircraft, the Super Hornet performs fighter, strike, tanking, and photoreconnaissance missions when embarked aboard one of the Navy's 12 aircraft carriers.

Further proof of the jet's adaptability came in December 2002 when the Navy chose the EA-18G Growler electronic surveillance and attack aircraft as a direct replacement for the venerable EA-6B Prowler. Using the same technologies embodied in the latter jet, the first of 90 Growlers will be delivered in 2009.

SPECIFICATION (F/A-18E):

ACCOMMODATION:
Pilot, or pilot and weapon-systems officer in tandem (F/A-18F/EA-18G)

DIMENSIONS:
LENGTH: 60 ft 1 in (18.31 m)
WINGSPAN: 44 ft 9 in (13.62 m)
HEIGHT: 16 ft 0 in (4.88 m)

WEIGHTS:
EMPTY: 29,574 lb (13,387 kg)
MAX T/O: 66,000 lb (29,937 kg)

PERFORMANCE:
MAX SPEED: 1197 mph (1915 kmh)
RANGE: 903 miles (1445 km)
POWERPLANT: two General Electric F414-GE-400S
OUTPUT: 44,000 lb st (196 kN)

FIRST FLIGHT DATE:
November 18, 1995

ARMAMENT:
One M61A1 Vulcan 20-mm cannon in nose; 17,750 lb (8050 kg) of bombs/rockets/missiles on six underwing, two wingtip (missiles) and one underfuselage stores pylons; two missiles in two semi-recessed underfuselage troughs

FEATURES:
Shoulder-mounted, swept wing; fighter-type bubble canopy; twin fins; long leading edge root ex-tensions; squared engine intakes

Boeing E-4/VC-25

94-seat, four-engined VIP transportation/command post/strategic transportation aircraft

The USAF selected Boeing's 747-200 to serve as the basis for its E-4A Advanced Airborne National Command Post/National Emergency Airborne Command Post aircraft in the early 1970s, with the first of three airframes being delivered in 1974. The jet's primary mission is to provide a platform from which the President and senior government officials can operate during war. Featuring a comprehensive command, control, and communications suite, the aircraft also boasts a "flying White House Situation Room," a second conference room, and battle staff areas. A single upgraded E-4B was acquired in 1979, this machine having more powerful engines, a super high-frequency communications aerial, and the ability to break into civilian radio/television networks for direct broadcasting. The older E-4As were all upgraded to B-model specification in the 1980s. The USAF also bought two VC-25s in 1990 to serve as presidential transports, these modified 747-200s featuring state-of-the-art communications links, and a presidential stateroom.

SPECIFICATION (E-4B):

ACCOMMODATION:
Two complete flight crews, consisting of pilot, copilot, navigator, and flight engineer, and various other crew/passenger configurations depending on role

DIMENSIONS:
LENGTH: 231 ft 4 in (70.51 m)
WINGSPAN: 195 ft 8 in (59.64 m)
HEIGHT: 63 ft 5 in (19.33 m)

WEIGHTS:
EMPTY: 380,800 lb (172,730 kg)
MAX T/O: 800,000 lb (362,874 kg)

PERFORMANCE:
MAX SPEED: 602 mph (969 kmh)
RANGE: 7830 miles (12,600 km)
POWERPLANT: four General Electric F103-GE-100s
OUTPUT: 210,000 lb st (934 kN)

FIRST FLIGHT DATE:
February 9, 1969 (747-100)

FEATURES:
Monoplane, swept-wing layout; four turbofans in underwing pods; tall tailfin

Cavalier F-51D Mustang Mk 2

single/two-seat, single-engined monoplane fighter-bomber

The Cavalier Mustang was born out of Florida newspaper magnet David Breed Lindsay Jr.'s desire to convert surplus ex-military F-51s into high-performance executive transports. The first such modified aircraft were ex-RCAF F-51Ds, which were rebuilt by Lindsay's company Trans Florida Aviation Inc. in the late 1950s and early 1960s. Having sold the RCAF aircraft, Lindsay expanded his business and acquired other surplus airframes and parts. In 1966 the US Department of Defense decided that the Cavalier Mustang would be ideal as a Counter Insurgency platform for "friendly" countries in South America, and duly contracted the company to refurbish Mustangs as part of Project Peace Condor. These aircraft, supplied to Bolivia, El Salvador, the Dominican Republic, Guatemala, and Indonesia, featured Merlin 620 engines taken from ex-RCAF C-54GM transports, a taller fin, strengthened wings for additional weapons pylons, and optional tip-tanks. The last of the refurbished Mustangs was retired (by the *Fuerza Aerea Dominicana*) in 1984.

SPECIFICATION (CAVALIER MUSTANG MK 2):

ACCOMMODATION:
Pilot (dual controls optional)

DIMENSIONS:
LENGTH: 32 ft 9.50 in (9.81 m)
WINGSPAN: 40 ft 1 in (12.10 m)
HEIGHT: 14 ft 8 in (4.51 m)

WEIGHTS:
EMPTY: 7635 lb (3466 kg)
MAX T/O: 10,500 lb (4762 kg)

PERFORMANCE:
MAX SPEED: 457 mph (731 kmh)
RANGE: 2000 miles (3200 km)
POWERPLANT: Merlin 620
OUTPUT: 1725 hp (1285 kW)

FIRST FLIGHT DATE:
December 1967

ARMAMENT:
Six Browning 0.50-in machine guns in wings; maximum bomb/rocket load of 5000 lb (2268 kg) on underwing stores pylons

FEATURES:
Monoplane wing; close-cowled inline engine; ventral air intake; four-bladed propeller; optional wingtip tanks; tall vertical fin/rudder

Cessna L-19/O-1 Bird Dog

two-seat, single-engined high-wing liaison/Forward Air Control aircraft

Winner of an Army competition in June 1950 for a two-seat observation and liaison aircraft, the Cessna Model 305 was loosely based on the company's successful Model 170 of the late 1940s. Built to replace the World War II-vintage Grasshopper family of aircraft, the Cessna L-19 (Army designation) was powered by a Continental O-47-11 213-hp engine, as opposed to the Continental C145-2 145-hp unit of its civil predecessor. This meant that the aircraft was better suited to military service, and particularly the Forward Air Control (FAC) role that it made its own in the early years of the Vietnam War. Redesignated the O-1 in 1962, Cessna had delivered 3431 by the time production ceased that year. Most of these were O-1As (L-19As), with later variants introducing uprated equipment and wing stores such as target-marking rockets. The exploits of the O-1 over Vietnam are legendary, USAF and South Vietnamese pilots pinpointing enemy troop locations through communication with "friendlies" on the ground, prior to calling in air strikes to hit targets marked with smoke rockets.

SPECIFICATION (O-1E):

ACCOMMODATION:
Pilot and observer/passenger in tandem

DIMENSIONS:
LENGTH: 25 ft 9 in (7.85 m)
WINGSPAN: 36 ft 0 in (10.97 m)
HEIGHT: 7 ft 4 in (2.22 m)

WEIGHTS:
EMPTY: 1614 lb (732 kg)
MAX T/O: 2400 lb (1087 kg)

PERFORMANCE:
MAX SPEED: 151 mph (243 kmh)
RANGE: 530 miles (853 km)
POWERPLANT: Continental O-47-11
OUTPUT: 213 hp (159 kW)

FIRST FLIGHT DATE:
December 1949

ARMAMENT:
Maximum bomb/rocket load of 500 lb (226 kg) on underwing stores pylons

FEATURES:
High-wing layout; single-wing bracing strut; fixed undercarriage; flat-six engine; extensive cockpit glazing

Cessna O-2 Super Skymaster

two-seat, twin-engined high-wing observation/Forward Air Control aircraft

Although the war in Vietnam had provided the O-1 with its "finest hour" in military service, it also highlighted the need for a more advanced FAC aircraft capable of greater speeds and increased weapons carriage. Once again Cessna provided the answer in the form of a "militarized" version of the Model 337 Skymaster, known as the O-2 Super Skymaster. Its unique "push/pull" layout gave the O-2 twin-engined performance and reliability, and allowed the USAF to fit military specification radios and four weapons pylons under the wings. Further FAC modifications included the addition of extra windows in the fuselage for the observer in the right-hand seat. More than 350 O-2As were delivered to the USAF by Cessna in 1967-68, the type serving as a temporary replacement for the O-1 until the dedicated North American OV-10 Bronco was produced. Aside from their FAC use, O-2s were also produced in Bravo configuration for psychological warfare operations. Surviving Super Skymasters were retired from ANG service in the 1980s.

SPECIFICATION:

ACCOMMODATION:
Pilot and observer/passenger seated side-by-side

DIMENSIONS:
LENGTH: 29 ft 9 in (9.07 m)
WINGSPAN: 38 ft 0 in (11.58 m)
HEIGHT: 9 ft 4 in (2.84 m)

WEIGHTS:
EMPTY: 2848 lb (1292 kg)
MAX T/O: 5400 lb (2449 kg)

PERFORMANCE:
MAX SPEED: 199 mph (320 kmh)
RANGE: 1060 miles (1706 km)
POWERPLANT: two Teledyne Continental IO-360C/DS
OUTPUT: 420 hp (314 kW)

FIRST FLIGHT DATE:
March 30, 1964 (Super Skymaster)

ARMAMENT:
Underwing stores pylons for gun pods and rockets of undisclosed weight

FEATURES:
High-wing layout; single-wing bracing strut; retractable, tricycle undercarriage; "push-pull" engine layout; twin tail booms

Cessna L-27/U-3

five/six-seat, twin-engined communications aircraft

Cessna's first post-World War II light twin-engined aircraft was the Model 310, which completed its maiden flight in January 1953. A sleek, modern design, the aircraft was selected "off-the-shelf" by the Air Force in 1957 to perform utility and communications roles. The USAF purchased 160 unmodified 310s using the original designation L-27A, which it later changed to U-3A. An additional 35 upgraded U-3Bs were delivered in 1960-61, these aircraft being equipped with the more powerful engines used in the 310C, extra cabin windows, a longer nose, and swept vertical fin. Often referred to by pilots as "Blue Canoes" when in USAF service due to their dark blue color scheme, surplus U-3s were passed on to Air National Guard units that had been given the FAC mission in 1969—these aircraft were replaced by O-2s when they became available. The Army National Guard and Reserve also received ex-USAF U-3A/Bs in the early 1970s, and these were the last examples of the Cessna light twin to be retired in the late 1980s.

SPECIFICATION (U-3A):

ACCOMMODATION:
One pilot and four/five passengers

DIMENSIONS:
LENGTH: 29 ft 6 in (8.99 m)
WINGSPAN: 36 ft 11 in (11.25 m)
HEIGHT: 9 ft 11 in (3.02 m)

WEIGHTS:
EMPTY: 3125 lb (1418 kg)
MAX T/O: 5200 lb (2360 kg)

PERFORMANCE:
MAX SPEED: 237 mph (381 kmh)
RANGE: 777 miles (1248 km)
POWERPLANT: two Teledyne Continental IO-470-VOS
OUTPUT: 520 hp (388 kW)

FIRST FLIGHT DATE:
January 3, 1953 (Cessna Model 310)

FEATURES:
Straight-wing layout; rectractable tricycle landing gear; twin, close-cowled engines; wingtip tanks

Cessna U-17 Skywagon

six-seat, single-engined high-wing utility/Forward Air Control aircraft

The Model 185 Skywagon was built as a multi-purpose aircraft that was inexpensive both to produce and to operate. These attributes made it ideally suited to the Department of Defense's Military Assistance Program (MAP), and examples were supplied to Bolivia, Costa Rica, Laos, and South Vietnam. Operators appreciated the aircraft's strengthened structure, which allowed it to be stripped out and converted into a cargo hauler that could get into and out of the most modest of landing strips—an optional fiberglass belly Cargo-Pack could also be bolted to the Skywagon to further boost its carrying capability. The 185 was selected by the USAF for MAP in 1963, the Air Force redesignating the aircraft the U-17. Some 262 A-models were built, followed by 205 Bravos with derated engines. Model 185s were also procured directly from Cessna by several non-MAP countries, including South Africa and Australia. Aside from its use in the general utility role, the Skywagon carried on the Cessna tradition of FAC—a task still occasionally undertaken today by Turkish 185s.

SPECIFICATION (U-17B):

ACCOMMODATION:
Pilot and up to five passengers

DIMENSIONS:
LENGTH: 25 ft 9 in (7.85 m)
WINGSPAN: 35 ft 10 in (10.92 m)
HEIGHT: 7 ft 9 in (2.36 m)

WEIGHTS:
EMPTY: 1585 lb (719 kg)
MAX T/O: 3350 lb (1519 kg)

PERFORMANCE:
MAX SPEED: 178 mph (286 kmh)
RANGE: 1035 miles (1665 km)
POWERPLANT: Teledyne Continental IO-520-D
OUTPUT: 300 hp (224 kW)

FIRST FLIGHT DATE:
July 1960

FEATURES:
High-wing layout; single-wing bracing strut; fixed under-carriage; flat-six engine; extensive cockpit glazing

Cessna T-41 Mescalero

four-seat, single-engined high-wing primary training aircraft

In 1961 the USAF adopted an "all-through" jet training syllabus following the introduction of the Cessna T-37. However, it soon found that it was wasting money using this aircraft to eliminate unsuitable pilot trainees, so the Air Force decided to reintroduce a piston-engined primary trainer for initial flight screening. The Air Force chose Cessna's popular Model 172 to perform this task, 170 aircraft being ordered as the T-41 Mescalero in July 1964—an additional 30 were bought in 1967. The initial batch of T-41s had all been delivered by July 1965, and they went into service with eight civilian contract flight schools located near to one of Air Training Command's Undergraduate Pilot Training bases. The USAF subsequently bought a further 52 T-41Cs (whose engines were more powerful and supercharged for altitude) for use at the Air Force Academy in Colorado, while the Army acquired 255 T-41Bs for training and support duties. The USAF replaced its Mescaleros with Slingsby T-3 Fireflies in the early 1990s, by which time the Army had also disposed of its T-41Bs.

SPECIFICATION (T-41A):

ACCOMMODATION:
Pilot and three passengers

DIMENSIONS:
LENGTH: 26 ft 11 in (8.20 m)
WINGSPAN: 35 ft 7.50 in (10.86 m)
HEIGHT: 8 ft 9.50 in (2.68 m)

WEIGHTS:
EMPTY: 1245 lb (565 kg)
MAX T/O: 2300 lb (1043 kg)

PERFORMANCE:
MAX SPEED: 139 mph (224 kmh)
RANGE: 615 miles (990 km)
POWERPLANT: Teledyne
Continental O-300-C
OUTPUT: 145 hp (108 kW)

FIRST FLIGHT DATE:
November 1955 (Model 172)

FEATURES:
High-wing layout; single-wing
bracing strut; fixed tricycle
undercarriage; close-cowled
engine; extensive cockpit glazing;
swept tailfin

Cessna T-47A/UC-35 Citation

five-seat, twin-engined jet radar training/transportation aircraft

Seeing only brief service with the Navy in the 1980s, the T-47A was procured specifically to serve as a radar navigation and airborne radar-intercept trainer for naval flight officers destined to fly the F-14 Tomcat. The Navy acquired 15 modified versions of the commercial Citation II to replace earlier T-39D Sabreliners in this role. Changes incorporated into the aircraft included the fitment of an APQ-159 nose radar, which simulated systems included in the F-14's AWG-9, shorter wings, and the installation of Pratt & Whitney Canada JT15D-5 engines. The first T-47A made its maiden flight on February 15, 1984, and aircraft entered service with VT-86 at NAS Pensacola later that same year. The T-47As soon began to show signs of structural stress, and they did not perform well at high altitude. Following their replacement by seven T-39Ns in the early 1990s, all but one of the T-47As was destroyed in a hangar fire in Kansas in July 1993. The Army acquired 20 Citation II-based UC-35A/B/Cs as VIP transports from 1997, the Marine Corps following suit with a dozen UC-35C/Ds in 1999.

SPECIFICATION (T-47A):

ACCOMMODATION:
Pilot, instructor, and three students

DIMENSIONS:
LENGTH: 47 ft 10.75 in (8.92 m)
WINGSPAN: 46 ft 6 in (14.18 m)
HEIGHT: 14 ft 9.75 in (4.51 m)

WEIGHTS:
EMPTY: 9035 lb (4098 kg)
MAX T/O: 15,000 lb (6804 kg)

PERFORMANCE:
MAX SPEED: 484 mph (779 kmh)
RANGE: 1958 miles (3151 km)
POWERPLANT: two Pratt & Whitney Canada JT15D-5s
OUTPUT: 5800 lb st (26 kN)

FIRST FLIGHT DATE:
September 15, 1969 (Model 500 Citation)

FEATURES:
Straight-wing layout; side-by-side cockpit; tricycle landing gear; rear-mounted podded engines

Cessna T-37 Tweet and A/OA-37 Dragonfly

two-seat, twin-engined jet trainer/light attack aircraft

In 1952 the USAF identified a requirement for an "all-through" jet trainer that could be used to instruct pilots from basic through to wings standard. Several manufacturers put forward designs and the winner of the contest was Cessna with its Model 318. Powered by two 920-lb st Continental J69s, and with side-by-side seating, the straight-winged Cessna completed its maiden flight on October 12, 1954. Designated the T-37 in USAF service, the first of 534 A-models was delivered to the Air Force in 1957. This variant was followed by the more powerful T-37B in 1959, which also featured better navigation and communications equipment and provision for the fitment of wingtip tanks. A further 449 were built, and all surviving A-models were also upgraded to this standard. The final trainer version to be built was the T-37C, 269 of which were constructed specially for export.

Still soldiering on in frontline service today, the venerable T-37 was to have been replaced in the 1980s by the stillborn Fairchild T-46A. However, cost overruns with the latter design forced its abandonment, and it was not until 1999 that the first examples of the Raytheon-built piston-engined T-6 Texan II began to enter service with the USAF's Air Education and Training Command as a T-37 replacement.

The Tweet trainer was not the only version of the T-37 flown by the USAF, for its more muscular sibling in the form of the A-37 Dragonfly also saw 24 years of service with both the Air Force and the ANG. In 1960 Cessna had made the decision to build a combat-capable version of the Tweet, fitting more powerful 2850-lb st General Electric J85 turbojets into the aircraft. The airframe was also restressed for combat, and the first A-37AS (converted T-37BS) were evaluated in Vietnam in mid-1967. The definitive A-37B, with bigger engines, eight underwing pylons, armored protection, and a minigun in the forward fuselage, was put into production in 1968. In all, 577 B-models were built, many of these serving with the USAF —130+ were later modified into OA-37B FAC platforms.

SPECIFICATION (A-37B):

ACCOMMODATION:
Two pilots side-by-side

DIMENSIONS:
LENGTH: 29 ft 3.50 in (8.92 m)
WINGSPAN: 35 ft 10.50 in (10.93 m)
HEIGHT: 8 ft 10.50 in (2.71 m)

WEIGHTS:
EMPTY: 6211 lb (2817 kg)
MAX T/O: 14,000 lb (6350 kg)

PERFORMANCE:
MAX SPEED: 507 mph (816 kmh)
RANGE: 1012 miles (1628 km)
POWERPLANT: two General Electric J85-GE-17AS
OUTPUT: 5700 lb st (25 kN)

FIRST FLIGHT DATE:
October 12, 1954 (T-37A)

ARMAMENT:
One GAU-2B/A 7.62-mm minigun in nose; up to 5680 lb (2576 kg) of bombs/rockets/gun pods on eight underwing stores pylons

FEATURES:
Straight-wing layout; side-by-side cockpit; extensive cockpit glazing; tricycle landing gear; wing root engine intakes; wingtip tanks (A-37 only)

Convair L-13

three-seat, single-engined high-wing liaison/observation aircraft

Consolidated Vultee developed the L-13 in the final months of World War II as a replacement for the various Grasshopper types then in service with the USAAF. Capable of general liaison, observation, and photographic reconnaissance, the aircraft could also be quickly converted into an aerial ambulance. The L-13 was designed by Stinson of Wayne, Michigan, and the first of two XL-13 prototypes flew in late 1945. Although Consolidated sold its Stinson division to Piper in late 1948, the company kept the rights to the L-13 and put the aircraft into production at its Convair plant in San Diego, California. A total of 300 L-13As were eventually built for the newly formed USAF in 1947-48, and 48 of these were supplied directly to the ANG. The latter machines had a more powerful engine, folding wings, and seating for six. An additional 28 L-13Bs were also built in 1949, these aircraft being "winterized" A-models fitted with skis, floats, or wheels for use in the Arctic. Surviving L-13s were sold into civilian ownership in the 1950s.

SPECIFICATION (L-13A):

ACCOMMODATION:
Pilots and two passengers

DIMENSIONS:
LENGTH: 31 ft 9 in (9.68 m)
WINGSPAN: 40 ft 6 in (12.35 m)
HEIGHT: 13 ft 10 in (4.22 m)

WEIGHTS:
EMPTY: 2100 lb (953 kg)
MAX T/O: 3500 lb (1588 kg)

PERFORMANCE:
MAX SPEED: 115 mph (184 kmh)
RANGE: 368 miles (589 km)
POWERPLANT: Franklin O-425-5
OUTPUT: 245 hp (183 kW)

FIRST FLIGHT DATE:
Late 1945

FEATURES:
High-wing layout; tandem cockpits; fixed landing gear; extensive cockpit glazing

Convair R3Y Tradewind

108-seat, four-engined monoplane long-range troop transportation/ambulance flying boat

In 1945 the Navy contracted Convair to build a sleek flying boat powered by four newly developed Allison T40 turboprop engines driving contra-rotating propellers. Two were constructed in the late 1940s as XP5Y-1S, and the first was flown in April 1950. On-going problems with the aircraft's engines slowed progress, and in an attempt to speed things up the Navy abandoned the P5Y armed patrol version of the Tradewind and focused on the R3Y transportation/tanker variant instead. In troop transportation/ambulance configuration, the aircraft could carry 103 fully armed troops or 92 stretcher patients and 12 medics. The first of five R3Y-1s delivered to the Navy completed its maiden flight in February 1954, and the follow-on R3Y-2 (six built) took to the skies eight months later. Featuring a nose-loading door that allowed vehicles to discharge directly onto landing beaches, a solitary R3Y-2 was converted into a four-point aerial tanker. Engine problems continued to plague the Tradewind throughout its brief service life to the point where the Navy ordered them to be grounded and sold for scrap in 1958.

SPECIFICATION:

ACCOMMODATION:
Pilot, copilot, flight engineer, navigator, loadmaster, and 103 passengers

DIMENSIONS:
LENGTH: 139 ft 8 in (42.26 m)
WINGSPAN: 145 ft 9 in (44.42 m)
HEIGHT: 51 ft 5 in (15.68 m)

WEIGHTS:
EMPTY: 71,824 lb (32,579 kg)
MAX T/O: 145,500 lb (65,998 kg)

PERFORMANCE:
MAX SPEED: 388 mph (624 kmh)
RANGE: 2785 miles (4482 km)
POWERPLANT: four Allison T40-A-4S
OUTPUT: 20,400 shp (15,224 kW)

FIRST FLIGHT DATE:
April 18, 1950

FEATURES:
High-wing monoplane layout; boat-shaped hull; four turboprop engines; tall tailfin; fixed outer wing floats

Convair T-29/R4Y/C-131

52-seat, twin-engined trainer/transportation aircraft

The T-29, R4Y, and C-131 were the military versions of Convair's 240/340/440 series of twin-engined airliners. The T-29 (based on the Convair 240) entered service with the USAF in 1949 as a navigator, bombardier, and radio-operator trainer. Some 48 unpressurized T-29As were bought, followed by 105 T-29Bs and 119 T-29Cs. Both the B- and C-models featured pressurized fuselages, while the follow-on T-29D had a bombsight and camera-scoring capability—93 D-models were built starting in August 1953. The C-131 was an improved version of the T-29, 46 of which entered service in 1950-51. Dubbed the "Samaritan" because of its medical evacuation role, the first of 26 C-131As reached Military Air Transport Service in December 1954. Major follow-on variants included the C-131B (36 built), C-131D (ten for European-based MATS units), VC-131D (16 for staff/VIP transportation), R4Y-1 (Navy variant, redesignated C-131F in 1962—36 built), and the C-131E (SAC ECM trainer—11 built). The USCG also received 22 ex-USAF C-131As. The last C-131s were retired by ANG and Navy units in 1990.

SPECIFICATION (T-29B):

ACCOMMODATION:
Pilot, copilot, engineer, navigator, and 16 students

DIMENSIONS:
LENGTH: 74 ft 8 in (22.79 m)
WINGSPAN: 91 ft 9 in (28.01 m)
HEIGHT: 26 ft 11 in (7.95 m)

WEIGHTS:
EMPTY: 29,000 lb (13,154 kg)
MAX T/O: 43,575 lb (19,766 kg)

PERFORMANCE:
MAX SPEED: 296 mph (474 kmh)
RANGE: 1500 miles (2400 km)
POWERPLANT: two Pratt & Whitney R-2800-97s
OUTPUT: 4800 hp (3579 kW)

FIRST FLIGHT DATE:
September 22, 1949 (T-29A)

FEATURES:
Straight-wing layout; two close-cowled radial engines; tall fin/rudder; square fuselage windows

Convair B-36 Peacemaker

15-seat, ten-engined strategic bomber

Designed to be able to operate against Nazi-held Europe from bases in North America should Britain have fallen to the Germans in World War II, Convair's B-36 had to be able to carry a 10,000-lb bomb load to a target 5000 miles away after taking off from a 5000-ft runway. The prototype's development program was initially slowed by material shortages due to the demands being placed on the US aviation industry to keep pace with wartime production quotas. In fact, it was only after VJ-Day that work gathered momentum, and when the XB-36 made its first flight on August 8, 1946, it was the world's largest aircraft. The unarmed B-36A entered service with SAC in 1947, the first production models being used as crew trainers in advance of armed B/D-models, which equipped bomb groups from 1948. In an effort to increase the bomber's over-target height and speed, the B-36D was fitted with two twin-jet pods. A total of 386 B-36s were built, and many were stripped of their armament and used as reconnaissance platforms.

SPECIFICATION (B-36D):

ACCOMMODATION:
Pilot, copilot, radar/bombardier, navigator, flight engineer, two radio operators, three forward, and five rear gunners

DIMENSIONS:
LENGTH: 162 ft 1 in (49.40 m)
WINGSPAN: 230 ft 0 in (70.14 m)
HEIGHT: 46 ft 8 in (14.26 m)

WEIGHTS:
EMPTY: 158,843 lb (72,051 kg)
MAX T/O: 357,500 lb (162,200 kg)

PERFORMANCE:
MAX SPEED: 439 mph (707 kmh)
RANGE: 7500 miles (12,070 km)
POWERPLANT: six Pratt & Whitney R-4360-41 Wasp Majors and four General Electric J47-GE-19s
OUTPUT: 21,000 hp (15,659 kW) and 20,800 lb st (91 kN)

FIRST FLIGHT DATE:
August 8, 1946

ARMAMENT:
16 20-mm cannon in eight remote-controlled turrets; 72,000 lb (32,659 kg) bomb load in bomb bay

FEATURES:
Swept-wing; radial engines

Convair B-58 Hustler

three-seat, four-engined bomber

Convair's B-58 Hustler was the first aircraft of its type to reach Mach 2. To achieve this, the manufacturer included many structural firsts within the Hustler's airframe, including widespread use of the stainless-steel honeycomb sandwich. It was also the first bomber to have a slim body and large payload pod (housing ordnance/fuel), the latter allowing the B-58 to become significantly smaller once jettisoned. Numerous technical difficulties created by the bomber's state-of-the-art design were rapidly overcome by Convair, and the prototype took to the skies on November 11, 1956. Production B-58As reached SAC in 1959, and the 43rd and 305th BWs illustrated the Hustler's high-speed potential by setting world speed records between New York and Paris, and Tokyo and London. Despite its outstanding performance, only 116 B-58s were built, as SAC had shifted its nuclear weapons focus from manned bombers to intercontinental ballistic missiles. Aside from the B-58A, Convair also built a number of TB-58 trainers. The last Hustlers were retired in January 1970.

SPECIFICATION:

ACCOMMODATION:
Pilot, navigator, and defense-systems operator

DIMENSIONS:
LENGTH: 96 ft 9 in (29.50 m)
WINGSPAN: 56 ft 10 in (17.31 m)
HEIGHT: 31 ft 5 in (9.60 m)

WEIGHTS:
EMPTY: 55,560 lb (25,200 kg)
MAX T/O: 163,000 lb (73,930 kg)

PERFORMANCE:
MAX SPEED: 1385 mph (2125 kmh)
RANGE: 5125 miles (8248 km)
POWERPLANT: four General Electric J79-GE-5Bs
OUTPUT: 62,400 lb st (279 kN)

FIRST FLIGHT DATE:
November 11, 1956

ARMAMENT:
One T-171 20-mm cannon in remote-controlled tail barbette; 19,450 lb (882o kg) of bombs in bomb bay and 7000 lb (3175 kg) on four underwing stores pylons

FEATURES:
Delta-wing layout; four turbojets in underwing pods; no horizontal tailplane; thin, tapered fuselage; large payload pod beneath fuselage

Convair F-102 Delta Dagger

single-seat, single-engined fighter

The end result of a 1950 USAF design competition for an integral all-weather interceptor weapon system, the Convair F-102 Delta Dagger had at its heart the Hughes MX-1179 weapons system, which comprised a radar, computer, and Falcon missiles. Convair had experimented with delta-wing designs in the late 1940s, and its prototype YF-102 completed its first flight on October 24, 1953. A further nine were built for test and evaluation purposes, and it soon became obvious that the aircraft was under-powered and incapable of level supersonic flight. Chastened by the poor performance of their design, Convair engineers applied the "area rule" principal to the revised YF-102A, which was created in just 117 days. Cambered wings, a new canopy, and a more powerful engine were also introduced, resulting in the aircraft at last meeting USAF expectations. Some 875 F-102As were built in 1955-56, and these served with 27 Air Defense Command (ADC) units well into the late 1960s. Replaced in ADC service by the F-106, Delta Daggers then served with 23 Air National Guard squadrons until retired in 1976.

SPECIFICATION:

ACCOMMODATION:
Pilot

DIMENSIONS:
LENGTH: 68 ft 4.50 in (20.84 m)
WINGSPAN: 38 ft 1.50 in (11.62 m)
HEIGHT: 21 ft 2.50 in (6.46 m)

WEIGHTS:
EMPTY: 20,160 lb (9144 kg)
MAX T/O: 31,276 lb (14,187 kg)

PERFORMANCE:
MAX SPEED: 825 mph (1327 kmh)
RANGE: 1350 miles (2173 km)
POWERPLANT: Pratt & Whitney J57-P-23A
OUTPUT: 17,200 lb st (79 kN)

FIRST FLIGHT DATE:
October 24, 1953 (YF-102)

ARMAMENT:
Six Hughes AIM-4 Falcon guided missiles in weapons bay

FEATURES:
Delta-wing layout; no horizontal tailplane; "area rule" fuselage; triangular tailfin

Convair F-106 Delta Dart

single-seat, single-engined fighter

Originally designated the F-102B, the Delta Dart was the successor to the Delta Dagger. Featuring a more powerful Pratt & Whitney J75 engine and the Hughes MA-1 integrated fire-control system, the F-106 mated the F-102's delta wing with a redesigned fuselage. The bigger engine and neater airframe gave the Delta Dart a top speed near double that of the F-102. In November 1955 the USAF ordered 17 F-102Bs, and by the time the first prototype flew on December 26, 1956, the aircraft had been redesignated the F-106. The fighter had to be able to intercept Soviet bombers in all weather up to 70,000 ft over a radius of 430 miles. Part of an integrated defense system, the F-106 was data-linked to the semiautomatic ground environment air defense network protecting North America. Early F-106s failed to meet ADC expectations and the USAF reduced its order from 1000 to 360. Production aircraft entered service in October 1959, and 15 ADC units received F-106s. Replaced by F-15s in the late 1970s, Delta Darts soldiered on with the Air National Guard until 1988.

SPECIFICATION:

ACCOMMODATION:
Pilot

DIMENSIONS:
LENGTH: 70 ft 8.50 in (21.55 m)
WINGSPAN: 38 ft 3.50 in (11.67 m)
HEIGHT: 20 ft 3.50 in (6.18 m)

WEIGHTS:
EMPTY: 23,814 lb (10,802 kg)
MAX T/O: 38,250 lb (17,350 kg)

PERFORMANCE:
MAX SPEED: 1487 mph (2393 kmh)
RANGE: 1950 miles (3138 km)
POWERPLANT: Pratt & Whitney J75-P-17
OUTPUT: 24,500 lb st (110 kN)

FIRST FLIGHT DATE:
December 26, 1956

ARMAMENT:
One M61A1 20-mm cannon in forward fuselage and four Hughes AIM-4 Falcon and two AIM-2 Genie guided missiles in weapons bay

FEATURES:
Delta-wing layout; no horizontal tailplane; "area rule" fuselage; squared-off fin/tail

Douglas A3D/A-3 Skywarrior

seven-seat, twin-engined bomber/electronic warfare aircraft

The A3D (as it was originally designated) Skywarrior was the world's first carrier-based strategic bomber. Designed around the predicted size of future thermonuclear bombs and the strength and length of the *Forrestal* class "supercarriers," the jet boasted a large bomb bay, blind bombing radar, and a remote tail turret. Douglas was contracted to build 280 Skywarriors, with the last of these being completed in January 1961. Performing the heavy bomber mission for a decade, the Skywarrior was replaced in its intended role by the more agile, and more survivable, A-6 Intruder in the mid-1960s, although the A-3's fleet service continued for another 25 years. Thanks to its size, the Skywarrior could perform other tasks such as aerial refueling (KA-3B), reconnaissance (RA-3B), radar/navigation training (TA-3B), and electronic countermeasures (EA-3B). Seeing action in the Vietnam War, the Skywarrior disappeared from carrier decks in the late 1980s, although a handful of EA-3Bs flew from shore bases in Operation Desert Storm in 1991.

SPECIFICATION (A-3B):

ACCOMMODATION:
Pilot, copilot, and bombardier

DIMENSIONS:
LENGTH: 76 ft 4 in (21.10 m)
WINGSPAN: 72 ft 5 in (22.10 m)
HEIGHT: 22 ft 9.50 in (6.99 m)

WEIGHTS:
EMPTY: 39,409 lb (17,875 kg)
MAX T/O: 82,000 lb (37,195 kg)

PERFORMANCE:
MAX SPEED: 610 mph (982 kmh)
RANGE: 2000 miles (3220 km)
POWERPLANT: two Pratt & Whitney J57-P-10s
OUTPUT: 24,800 lb st (110 kN)

FIRST FLIGHT DATE:
October 28, 1952

ARMAMENT:
Two remote-controlled 20-mm cannon in tail turret; provision for up to 15,000 lb (6804 kg) of bombs in bomb bay

FEATURES:
Shoulder-mounted swept wing; retractable tricycle undercarriage; two podded engines below wings; arrestor hook

Douglas AD/A-1 Skyraider

single/four-seat, single-engined attack/AEW/transportation aircraft

Initially dubbed the "Dauntless II," the XBT2D-1 had the overwhelming reputation of the wartime Douglas dive-bomber to live up to. That the aircraft went on to break all records for frontline longevity for a piston-engined attack type, and served with distinction in both the Korean and Vietnamese conflicts, proves that the renamed Skyraider's own reputation as a tough workhorse was equal to its initial Dauntless sobriquet. Reputedly designed in 24 hours in the Statler Hotel in Washington, D.C., in June 1944, the success of the Skyraider was due as much to its engine—the Wright R-3350 radial—as to its rugged aerodynamics.

That very same engine delayed the Skyraider's entry into service long enough for the aircraft to miss World War II. In fact, for a number of years it seemed that the new Douglas attack aircraft was destined to remain unproven in action with the Navy, just like Grumman's Bearcat of the same period. However, unlike the latter aircraft, the Skyraider refused to become obsolete, and fought throughout the Korean War. Capable of employing rockets, bombs, napalm, mines, torpedoes, and depth charges, as well as its 20-mm cannon, the AD-1 was described as the world's best close-support aircraft by the Navy's ranking admiral in-theater during the Korean campaign.

In 1955 the Skyraider's frontline strength peaked at 29 Navy and 13 Marine Corps squadrons, after which its numbers began to drop as more modern jet types reached the fleet. With the aircraft's best years seemingly behind it, the A-1 (redesignated in 1962) was given a new lease of life when conflict broke out in Vietnam in 1964-65—so much so that both the USAF and South Vietnamese Air Force used surplus Navy A-1s in action from 1964 until the fall of Saigon in 1975. The Navy had, in the meantime, finally retired its last Skyraiders in April 1968 following four hard years of combat over Vietnam. Aside from the numerous attack variants, the Skyraider also performed ECM (AD-2/3/4/5Q), airborne early warning (AD-3/4/5W), and carrier on-board delivery missions for the Navy. A total of 3180 Skyraiders were built between 1946-57.

SPECIFICATION (A-1J):

ACCOMMODATION:
Pilot

DIMENSIONS:
LENGTH: 40 ft 1 in (12.19 m)
WINGSPAN: 50 ft 9 in (15.47 m)
HEIGHT: 15 ft 10 in (4.83 m)

WEIGHTS:
EMPTY: 12,313 lb (5585 kg)
MAX T/O: 25,000 lb (11,340 kg)

PERFORMANCE:
MAX SPEED: 311 mph (501 kmh)
RANGE: 3000 miles (4828 km)
POWERPLANT: Wright R-3350-26WB
OUTPUT: 3050 hp (2271 kW)

FIRST FLIGHT DATE:
March 18, 1945

ARMAMENT:
Four 20-mm cannon in outer wings; provision for up to 8000 lb (3630 kg) of ordnance on 14 underwing and one center fuselage stores pylons

FEATURES:
Straight-wing layout; close-cowled radial engine; retractable undercarriage; bubble canopy; arrestor hook

Douglas A4D and A/TA-4 Skyhawk

single/two-seat, single-engined attack/advanced training aircraft

Bucking the trend for ever larger combat aircraft when built in the early 1950s, the Douglas A-4 was the brainchild of company chief engineer Ed Heinemann, who had also been responsible for the A-26 and A-1 almost a decade before. Weighing significantly less than half the specified weight (of 30,000 lb) stipulated by the Navy for its new jet attack bomber, yet still capable of undertaking all the missions required of it, the A4D, as it was designated until 1962, was quickly dubbed "Heinemann's Hot Rod" thanks to its outstanding performance.

The first A4D-1s entered fleet service in September 1956, and a total of 165 had been built when production switched to the re-engined A4D-2 in 1958. By the time the Vietnam War escalated into all-out conflict in 1965, most carrier air wings included at least two squadrons of Skyhawks. The B-, C-, and E-models had all seen the capabilities (and weight) of the A-4 increase since the first examples were built, and the aircraft played a central part in the air war fought by the Navy and Marine Corps over the jungles of South-East Asia through to 1973.

The final combat-capable Skyhawks bought by the Navy were 167 A-4Fs, acquired in 1967-69. The Marine Corps continued to receive newly built A-4Ms (162 delivered) until 1979, however, this variant equipping frontline light attack units well into the late 1980s. By then, the Navy's A-4s were being exclusively used as adversary trainers for fleet fighter units. The final single-seat Skyhawks (of which 2405 were built between 1954 and 1979) were retired by the Navy and

Marine Corps in the early 1990s, leaving only two-seat TA-4 trainers to soldier on until 2001. The latter could trace their ancestry to 1964, when Douglas was contracted to produce a trainer variant of the Skyhawk as a replacement for the TF-9J. No fewer than 555 were subsequently built for the Navy/Marine Corps and export markets. Aside from performing intermediate and advanced tuitional roles, TA-4s were also used for FAC, electronic warfare, and adversary pilot training.

SPECIFICATION (A-4E):

ACCOMMODATION:
Pilot, or two pilots in tandem
(TA-4)

DIMENSIONS:
LENGTH: 40 ft 1.50 in (12.22 m)
WINGSPAN: 27 ft 6 in (8.38 m)
HEIGHT: 15 ft 0 in (4.57 m)

WEIGHTS:
EMPTY: 9284 lb (4211 kg)
MAX T/O: 24,500 lb (11,113 kg)

PERFORMANCE:
MAX SPEED: 685 mph (1102 kmh)
RANGE: 920 miles (1480 km)
POWERPLANT: Pratt & Whitney
J52-P-6
OUTPUT: 8500 lb st (38 kN)

FIRST FLIGHT DATE:
June 22, 1954

ARMAMENT:
Two Mk 12 20-mm cannon in wing roots; 8200 lb (3720 kg) of bombs/rockets/missiles on four underwing/one center fuselage stores pylons

FEATURES:
Delta-wing; delta tailplane; bubble canopy; arrestor hook; engine air intakes on fuselage sides

Douglas B-66 Destroyer

seven-seat, twin-engined bomber/electronic warfare/weather reconnaissance aircraft

Built at Douglas's Long Beach, California, plant, the B-66 started life as a slightly modified Skywarrior that was tailored to meet a USAF requirement for a tactical attack bomber. Yet, despite looking outwardly similar, the Destroyer had hardly a single airframe part or system common with the A-3. This in turn meant that the B-66 was expensive both to construct and maintain. Built as reconnaissance tactical/nuclear bombers, 145 RB-66BS were produced for the USAF's Tactical Air Command, followed by 72 B-66BS. Although the reconnaissance bomber variant saw only brief service, the electronic intelligence-optimized RB-66C proved far more successful, the Destroyer's bomb bay having been replaced by a pressurized compartment for electronic warfare (EW) systems. Some 36 RB-66CS were built, and an identical number of WB-66D weather reconnaissance jets were also delivered to the USAF. The Destroyer saw considerable combat over Vietnam, with EW-configured EB-66C/ES (rebuilt B/RB-66S) providing much-needed electronic countermeasures.

SPECIFICATION (B-66B):

ACCOMMODATION:
Pilot, copilot, and bombardier

DIMENSIONS:
LENGTH: 75 ft 2 in (22.90 m)
WINGSPAN: 72 ft 6 in (22.10 m)
HEIGHT: 23 ft 7 in (7.19 m)

WEIGHTS:
EMPTY: 42,369 lb (19,218 kg)
MAX T/O: 83,000 lb (37,648 kg)

PERFORMANCE:
MAX SPEED: 594 mph (950 kmh)
RANGE: 1500 miles (2400 km)
POWERPLANT: two Allison J71-A-13S
OUTPUT: 20,000 lb st (44 kN)

FIRST FLIGHT DATE:
June 28, 1954

ARMAMENT:
Two remote-controlled 20-mm cannon in tail turret; provision for up to 15,000 lb (6804 kg) of bombs in bomb bay

FEATURES:
Shoulder-mounted swept wing; retractable tricycle undercarriage; two podded engines below wings

Douglas R4D-8/C-117 Dolphin

41-seat, twin-engined transportation aircraft

Dubbed the Super DC-3 by manufacturer Douglas, the R4D-8 was the military version of the reworked transportation classic that had so revolutionized both civil and military air transportation. Rather than produce an all-new design, Douglas was convinced that all the market wanted was another variant of the Dakota. Accordingly, the aircraft was revised through the fitment of a squared-off tail section and a more aerodynamic wing (slightly swept and squared off). Further streamlining was achieved by fully enclosing the main gear legs, while the aircraft's performance was improved through the fitment of more powerful Wright Cyclones. Despite an exhaustive American sales tour, the Super DC-3 evoked little interest—indeed, if it had not been for the Navy ordering 100 examples as the R4D-8 (only 17 were built, with the remainder being converted from standard R4DS), it is unlikely that the Super DC-3 would have entered series production. In military service, the R4D-8 (redesignated the C-117D in 1962) was employed in cargo hauling and VIP tasks.

SPECIFICATION:

ACCOMMODATION:
Pilot, copilot, navigator, and 38 passengers

DIMENSIONS:
LENGTH: 71 ft 1 in (21.67 m)
WINGSPAN: 93 ft 0 in (28.34 m)
HEIGHT: 18 ft 11 in (5.51 m)

WEIGHTS:
EMPTY: 21,470 lb (9738 kg)
MAX T/O: 30,500 lb (13,834 kg)

PERFORMANCE:
MAX SPEED: 270 mph (432 kmh)
RANGE: 2125 miles (3420 km)
POWERPLANT: two Wright R-1820-80 Cyclones
OUTPUT: 3070 hp (2290.22 kW)

FIRST FLIGHT DATE:
June 1949

FEATURES:
Straight-wing layout, but with swept leading edge; two close-cowled radial engines; tall tailfin; low-set tailplane, fully retractable undercarriage

Douglas R6D/C-118 Liftmaster

78-seat, four-engined transportation aircraft

The C-118 was the end result of a USAAF requirement for a C-54 Skymaster successor that provided the advantages of a greater payload, higher performance, and most importantly, full pressurization so that the aircraft could attain higher altitudes, and thus be flown over adverse weather. Initially designated the XC-112A, the transport completed its first flight in February 1946. However, with World War II now over, the USAAF had lost interest in the new aircraft, and it duly became the civil DC-6 airliner instead. Essentially an enlarged version of the DC-4/C-54, the DC-6 initially shared its wing and fuselage structure, although later A/B models were twelve feet longer. The first DC-6 to enter military service was the 26th production example built, which the USAAF bought in 1947 for use as a presidential transport for President Harry S. Truman. Designated a C-118, this aircraft paved the way for future orders from both the Air Force and the Navy, the former buying 101 C-118As and the latter 65 R6D-1s (which were redesignated C-118Bs in 1962) for personnel and logistic transportation.

SPECIFICATION:

ACCOMMODATION:
Pilot, copilot, navigator, engineer, and 74 passengers

DIMENSIONS:
LENGTH: 105 ft 7 in (32.21 m)
WINGSPAN: 117 ft 6 in (35.81 m)
HEIGHT: 28 ft 8 in (8.77 m)

WEIGHTS:
EMPTY: 49,767 lb (22,574 kg)
MAX T/O: 107,000 lb (48,535 kg)

PERFORMANCE:
MAX SPEED: 315 mph (504 kmh)
RANGE: 4720 miles (7552 km)
POWERPLANT: four Pratt & Whitney R-2800-52WS
OUTPUT: 10,000 hp (7457 kW)

FIRST FLIGHT DATE:
February 15, 1946

FEATURES:
Straight-wing layout; tricycle landing gear; four close-cowled radial engines; tall tailfin; low-set tailplane

Douglas C-124 Globemaster

205-seat, four-engined strategic transportation aircraft

Using the DC-4 as a base, Douglas commenced work on a giant military transport in 1942 after securing an order for a prototype from the USAAF. Designated the XC-74, the prototype flew on September 3, 1945. With the war now all but over, the emphasis for the aircraft shifted to civil transoceanic employment. Pan American ordered 26, but then pulled out of the project, while a large-scale USAAF buy was reduced to 14 aircraft. These were delivered in 1946-47, and had almost circular-section fuselages due to the fact that the civilian C-74 was to have been pressurized. This proved impractical on the military variant because of the large freight doors, so the pressurization was deleted and the C-74 redesigned with a fuselage that offered twice the internal volume. The nose was fitted with clamshell doors for loading vehicles and heavy freight. Designated the YC-124 Globemaster, the first prototype flew on November 27, 1949, and production examples reached the USAF in May 1950. A total of 204 C-124AS and 243 C-124CS were built, and they saw service into the 1970s.

SPECIFICATION (C-124C):

ACCOMMODATION:
Pilot, copilot, navigator, engineer, loadmaster, and 200 passengers

DIMENSIONS:
LENGTH: 130 ft 5 in (39.75 m)
WINGSPAN: 174 ft 1.50 in (53.08 m)
HEIGHT: 48 ft 3.50 in (14.70 m)

WEIGHTS:
EMPTY: 101,165 lb (45,887 kg)
MAX T/O: 194,500 lb (88,223 kg)

PERFORMANCE:
MAX SPEED: 304 mph (489 kmh)
RANGE: 6820 miles (10,975 km)
POWERPLANT: four Pratt & Whitney R-4360-20WAS
OUTPUT: 14,000 hp (10,440 kW)

FIRST FLIGHT DATE:
November 27, 1949 (YC-124)

FEATURES:
Straight-wing layout; tricycle landing gear; four close-cowled radial engines; tall tailfin; large, double-deck fuselage; clamshell doors in nose

Douglas C-133 Cargomaster

five/six-seat, four-engined heavy logistic freighter

Developed by Douglas to fulfill a USAF requirement for a logistic transporter capable of lifting strategic cargo that could not be easily "broken down" for carriage in the C-124 or C-130, the C-133 went straight into production from the drawing board. The first C-133A doubled as the prototype, the aircraft's pressurized fuselage of circular section being able to accept the new Atlas and Titan ICBMS through full-width rear cargo doors. The first of 35 A-models was delivered to the USAF in August 1957, and these were followed by 15 C-133BS from 1959, the latter variant boasting a more powerful version of the T34 engine and a revised rear fuselage combining clamshell doors. It was estimated at the time that roughly 96 percent of all US military equipment could be carried by the Cargomaster. This was put to the test during the American build-up in South Vietnam in the mid-1960s. The advent of the C-5 Galaxy in 1969 eased the overworked C-133's burden, the Lockheed transporter eventually replacing the Cargomaster. The last C-133s were retired in 1979.

SPECIFICATION (C-133A):

ACCOMMODATION:
Pilot, copilot, navigator, two flight engineers, loadmaster

DIMENSIONS:
LENGTH: 157 ft 6.5 in (48.02 m)
WINGSPAN: 179 ft 8 in (54.75 m)
HEIGHT: 48 ft 3 in (14.7 m)

WEIGHTS:
EMPTY: 120,000 lb (54,432 kg)
MAX T/O: 275,000 lb (124,740 kg)

PERFORMANCE:
MAX SPEED: 331 mph (530 kmh)
RANGE: 3975 miles (6360 km)
POWERPLANT: four Pratt & Whitney T34-P-7WAS
OUTPUT: 26,000 shp (19,388 kW)

FIRST FLIGHT DATE:
April 23, 1956

FEATURES:
Shoulder-mounted straight-wing; tricycle landing gear; four close-cowled turboprop engines; tall tailfin; rear cargo doors

Douglas F3D/F-10 Skynight

two-seat, twin-engined all-weather fighter

On April 3, 1946 Douglas received a contract from the Navy to produce an all-weather jet fighter for use from its new large aircraft carriers. Designated the XF3D-1, the prototype made its first flight on March 23, 1948, after which work commenced on 28 F3D-1 Skynights. Production aircraft reached VC-3 in 1951, by which time testing of the F3D-2 had begun. This version became the definitive Skynight variant, with 237 built. Deemed unsuitable for carrier operations, most F3D-2s were passed on to the Marine Corps, which sent Skynights into action in Korea. Thanks to its radar equipment and all-weather interception capabilities, the jet proved successful in the nightfighter role, downing MiG-15s and a Po-2 in 1952-53. A number of F3D-2s were modified for different tasks in the 1950s, 35 receiving electronic reconnaissance and counter-measures equipment as F3D-2Qs and 55 being converted into F3D-2T radar-controller trainers. Surviving Skynights became F/TF/EF-10BS in September 1962, and the latter variant was the first tactical EW jet aircraft to see service in Vietnam.

SPECIFICATION (F3D-2):

ACCOMMODATION:
Pilot and radar operator

DIMENSIONS:
LENGTH: 45 ft 6 in (13.87 m)
WINGSPAN: 50 ft 0 in (15.24 m)
HEIGHT: 16 ft 1 in (4.92 m)

WEIGHTS:
EMPTY: 18,160 lb (8237 kg)
MAX T/O: 26,850 lb (12,179 kg)

PERFORMANCE:
MAX SPEED: 600 mph (960 kmh)
RANGE: 1200 miles (1920 km)
POWERPLANT: two Westinghouse J34-WE-36s
OUTPUT: 6800 lb st (15 kN)

FIRST FLIGHT DATE:
March 23, 1948

ARMAMENT:
Four 20-mm cannon under nose and four Sparrow missiles on four underwing stores pylons

FEATURES:
Straight wing; tricycle landing gear; engines located under wing center section

Douglas F4D/F-6 Skyray

single-seat, single-engined fighter

Influenced by wartime work carried out by German scientists on delta-winged aircraft, the Navy issued a proposal for a short-range interceptor with a similar layout. Two XF4D-1 prototypes were ordered in December 1948, although development was delayed by problems with the aircraft's ill-fated Westinghouse J40 turbojet. Using an Allison J35 instead, the prototype made its first flight on January 23, 1951. By the time production aircraft began to be assembled at Douglas in late 1954, the Skyray featured a Pratt & Whitney J57-P-8. Further flight-test problems delayed delivery of jets to the Navy until April 1956, after which large numbers were handed over in a short space of time. All 420 aircraft on order had been built by December 1958, and all to F4D-1 standard. Flown by eleven Navy and six Marine Corps fighter squadrons, as well as three reserve units and several specialized squadrons, the Skyray enjoyed only a brief career due to its modest armament and engine performance. Redesignated the F-6A in September 1962, final examples were retired 18 months later.

SPECIFICATION:

ACCOMMODATION:
Pilot

DIMENSIONS:
LENGTH: 45 ft 8.50 in (13.90 m)
WINGSPAN: 33 ft 6 in (10.20 m)
HEIGHT: 13 ft 0 in (3.96 m)

WEIGHTS:
EMPTY: 16,030 lb (7250 kg)
MAX T/O: 25,000 lb (11,340 kg)

PERFORMANCE:
MAX SPEED: 695 mph (1112 kmh)
RANGE: 1200 miles (1920 km)
POWERPLANT: Pratt & Whitney J57-P-8B
OUTPUT: 10,500 lb st (46 kN)

FIRST FLIGHT DATE:
January 23, 1951

ARMAMENT:
Four 20-mm cannon in outer wings; provision for up to 4000 lb (1814 kg) of bombs/rockets on six underwing/fuselage stores pylons

FEATURES:
Delta wing; no horizontal tailplane; tricycle landing gear; arrestor hook; engine air intakes on fuselage sides aft of cockpit

Fairchild C-123 Provider

65-seat, twin-engined transportation aircraft

The Provider was developed from the Chase Aircraft XG-20 all-metal troop/cargo glider of 1949. The USAF expressed interest in a powered version of the design, so the company fitted two Double Wasp engines to the second prototype glider and redesignated it the XC-123 Avitruc. In 1953 a contract for 300 C-123BS was awarded to Kaiser-Frazer, although the latter company soon ran into production difficulties and Fairchild stepped in to fulfill the order. Production aircraft reached the USAF in 1954, and the C-123's rugged build and excellent handling characteristics made it popular with aircrew. The Provider became the first USAF transport committed to the Vietnam War, and aside from hauling troops and cargo, UC-123B variants were also used to spray pesticides. The C-123's performance was greatly improved with the fitment of two podded J85 turbojets during the reworking of B-models into K-specification aircraft in the early 1960s, while the specialist H/J version received a similar boost in power, but with Fairchild J44 turbojets fitted in wingtip pods.

SPECIFICATION (C-123B):

ACCOMMODATION:
Pilot, copilot, flight engineer, loadmaster, and up to 61 troops

DIMENSIONS:
LENGTH: 75 ft 3 in (23.25 m)
WINGSPAN: 110 ft 0 in (33.35 m)
HEIGHT: 34 ft 1 in (10.38 m)

WEIGHTS:
EMPTY: 29,900 lb (13,563 kg)
MAX T/O: 60,000 lb (27,240 kg)

PERFORMANCE:
MAX SPEED: 245 mph (392 kmh)
RANGE: 1470 miles (2365 km)
POWERPLANT: two Pratt & Whitney R-2800-99W Cyclones
OUTPUT: 4600 hp (3430 kW)

FIRST FLIGHT DATE:
October 14, 1949 (XC-123)

FEATURES:
Shoulder-mounted straight wing; tricycle landing gear; two close-cowled radial engines; tall tail; rear-loading ramp

Fairchild A-10 Thunderbolt II

single-seat, twin-engined close-support attack aircraft

Conceived during the Vietnam War, the A-10 was designed to operate in low-intensity conflicts as a close-support aircraft for troops on the ground. The Fairchild jet was the winner of the USAF's AX competition, which called for a jet with good endurance, a potent weapons suite, and exceptional survivability. Designs from Northrop and Fairchild Republic were chosen to compete in a fly-off in 1972, and the YA-10 from the latter company duly beat its YA-9 rival and secured a production contract.

The Thunderbolt II had been constructed with survivability foremost in mind. For example, the jet's low-set straight wing not only made the A-10 highly maneuverable, it also shielded the aircraft's twin, podded, General Electric TF34 turbofan engines from ground fire—the engines were also widely spaced so that damage to one would not knock out the other. Finally, the pilot was sat in a titanium armor "bathtub." Aside from being able to carry up to 16,000 lb of bombs, rockets, and missiles, the A-10 boasts the awesome General Electric GAU-8 seven-barrel 30-mm cannon buried in its forward fuselage.

The first of 715 A-10As was delivered to the USAF in March 1976, with the aircraft remaining in production until 1983. Very few changes were made to the Thunderbolt II during this period, which was unusual for a modern combat aircraft built in such quantity. Although built to oppose communist aggression in Europe, the A-10 made its combat debut Iraq in 1991. Inflicting heavy losses on enemy tank divisions, Thunderbolt II units flew more than 8500 sorties in Operation Desert Storm. Sent into action over Iraq once again in 2003, the jet continues to play an active role in the Global War on Terror both in the Middle East and in Afghanistan. A number of aircraft were also redesignated as OA-10s in the late 1980s to perform the forward air-controlling mission in place of the elderly OV-10 Bronco. Both the A-10 and OA-10 remain key types in Air Force, Air National Guard and Air Force Reserve ranks.

SPECIFICATION:

ACCOMMODATION:
Pilot

DIMENSIONS:
LENGTH: 53 ft 4 in (16.26 m)
WINGSPAN: 57 ft 6 in (17.53 m)
HEIGHT: 14 ft 8 in (4.47 m)

WEIGHTS:
EMPTY: 21,451 lb (9730 kg)
MAX T/O: 50,000 lb (22,680 kg)

PERFORMANCE:
MAX SPEED: 518 mph (835 kmh)
RANGE: 620 miles (1000 km)
POWERPLANT: two General Electric
TF34-GE-100S
OUTPUT: 18,130 lb st (80.6 kN)

ARMAMENT:
One General Electric GAU-8
Avenger 30-mm cannon in nose;
provision for up to 16,000 lb
(7257 kg) of bombs/rockets/
missiles on 11 underwing and
underfuselage stores pylons

FIRST FLIGHT DATE:
April 5, 1972

FEATURES:
Low "plank" unswept wing;
tricycle landing gear; podded
turbofan engines; bubble canopy;
twin tailfins

Fairchild C-82 Packet and C-119/R4Q Flying Boxcar

46/68-seat, twin-engined tactical transportation aircraft

Fairchild's C-82 transportation aircraft was developed to meet an Army requirement issued in 1941, its distinctive twin-boom layout being adopted as the solution to a design concept championed by the manufacturer that saw the aircraft built around a large uninterrupted cargo hold that could be loaded/unloaded at near-ground level. Contracted to build 100 C-82A Packets, Fairchild's prototype flew in September 1944 and production aircraft reached the USAAF in late 1945. Further orders were placed for an additional 892 Packets, but in the wake of VJ-Day just 220 C-82As were built in total. These aircraft served with Troop Carrier units into the 1950s, when they were finally replaced by Fairchild's follow-on tactical transport, the C-119 Flying Boxcar. The latter maintained its predecessor's highly valued near-ground level loading/unloading attributes, but had its flightdeck moved ahead of the cargo hold rather than sitting on top of it. The Flying Boxcar also had a wider fuselage, strengthened wings (which allowed it to operate to higher weights), and more powerful R-3350 engines fitted in place of the C-82's R-2800s.

Flown in prototype form as the XC-82B in November 1947, the first C-119Bs began to enter service with the USAF in December 1949. By the time production ceased in 1955, 946 had been accepted into the USAF, with a further 99 also being delivered to the Marine Corps as R4Q-1/2s in 1950-53. A further 141 were sold overseas through various assistance programs.

The aircraft saw action in the Korean and Vietnam Wars, with heavily armed nocturnal interdiction variants fitted with Gatling guns and night sensors giving the Flying Boxcar an offensive role in the latter conflict—26 AC-119G Shadows and a similar number of jet-assisted AC-119K Stingers were converted from standard C-119s in 1966-67. Relegated to the Air National Guard by the early 1970s, many early C-119s had been upgraded to J-model specification (featuring a "beaver-tail" rear door, which could be opened in flight) by this stage. The aircraft was finally retired by the Marine Corps in 1972 and by the ANG three years later.

SPECIFICATION (C-119G):

ACCOMMODATION:
Pilot, copilot, navigator, radio operator, flight engineer, loadmaster, and up to 62 troops

DIMENSIONS:
LENGTH: 86 ft 6 in (26.36 m)
WINGSPAN: 109 ft 3 in (33.30 m)
HEIGHT: 26 ft 6 in (8.07 m)

WEIGHTS:
EMPTY: 40,785 lb (18,500 kg)
MAX T/O: 72,700 lb (32,977 kg)

PERFORMANCE:
MAX SPEED: 281 mph (450 kmh)
RANGE: 1630 miles (2608 km)
POWERPLANT: two Wright R-3350-89A Cyclones
OUTPUT: 7000 hp (5220 kW)

FIRST FLIGHT DATE:
November 1947

FEATURES:
Shoulder-mounted straight wing; tricycle landing gear; two close-cowled radial engines; twin boom/tail layout; rear-loading ramp

General Dynamics F-16 Fighting Falcon

single/two-seat, single-engined multirole fighter

Developed as the Model 401 in the early 1970s by General Dynamics for inclusion in the USAF's Lightweight Fighter Program, the YF-16 was pitched against designs from four other manufacturers. First flown in prototype form on January 20, 1974, the aircraft beat the rival Northrop YF-17 (forerunner to the F/A-18) in a fly-off that lasted almost a year. The aircraft was duly chosen to fulfill the USAF's air combat fighter program requirement, and the first of eight development F-16As performed its maiden flight in December 1976. Production jets (2795 A-models would be built for the Air Force) began reaching the 388th Tactical Fighter Wing in January 1979, and aircraft were quickly issued to other fighter wings in the USA, Europe, and Asia.

Aside from the single-seat jets, the USAF also acquired 204 F-16B two-seaters, which featured full mission avionics and weapons but 17 percent less fuel. In 1980 the USAF launched the Multi Stage Improvement Program, which it hoped would increase the F-16's multirole all-weather attack capability through the addition of bolt-on targeting pods. The F-16 would also be made beyond visual range missile-capable. The new aircraft was designated the F-16C/D, and production jets started reaching the USAF in late 1984. Fitted with an AN/APG-68 radar in place of the AN/APG-66, the new Fighting Falcon (or "Viper," as it is unofficially known) had improved self-protection jammers and an ability to employ a wider range of munitions. Subsequent variants featured bigger engines and HARM missile-capability in order to perform the anti-SAM "Wild Weasel" mission. The Navy also received 26 stripped-out F/TF-16Ns in 1985-86 to act as adversary trainers. With new F-16Cs entering USAF service, older F-16As were passed onto the ANG and Reserve, and 272 of these were upgraded to Air Defense Fighter standard in the late 1980s so that they could employ AIM-7 Sparrow missiles in defense of the USA. Blooded in combat in Operation Desert Storm in 1991, USAF F-16s have seen much combat over the past 15 years. The 2231st, and last, F-16 built for the USAF was delivered in 2005.

SPECIFICATION (F-16C BLOCK 30/40):

ACCOMMODATION:
Pilot

DIMENSIONS:
LENGTH: 49 ft 4 in (15.03 m)
WINGSPAN: 32 ft 10 in (10 m)
HEIGHT: 16 ft 5 in (5.01 m)

WEIGHTS:
EMPTY: 19,100 lb (8665 kg)
MAX T/O: 42,300 lb (19,190 kg)

PERFORMANCE:
MAX SPEED: 1328 mph (2125 kmh)
RANGE: 2431 miles (3890 km)
POWERPLANT: General Electic
F110-GE-100
OUTPUT: 27,600 lb st (123 kN)

FIRST FLIGHT DATE:
January 20, 1974

ARMAMENT:
One M61A1 Vulcan 30-mm cannon in fuselage; provision for up to 12,000 lb (5435 kg) of bombs/ rockets/missiles on six underwing, one under fuselage and two wingtip stores pylons

FEATURES:
Midmounted swept wings; bubble canopy; tricycle landing gear; chin air intake; ventral strakes

General Dynamics F/FB/EF-111

two-seat, twin-engined strategic/tactical strike/electronic warfare aircraft

The F-111 was originally developed to meet a bold Department of Defense edict that the USAF's requirement for a new fighter-bomber and the Navy's need for a new fleet air defense fighter should be met by a single aircraft—the TFX. Designated the F-111 by General Dynamics, the prototype flew for the first time on December 21, 1964. Although the overweight F-111B naval fighter was canceled in 1968, the USAF's F-111A showed far greater promise. Battling an airframe that was both overweight and underpowered, General Dynamics persisted with the design and eventually handed over the first of 141 A-models in late 1967. Even then the USAF had to deal with persistent problems with the complex wing-sweep system and ineffective engine air inlets.

Although the jet made an inauspicious combat debut in Vietnam in 1968, the F-111 evolved into the most capable medium-range strike bomber of its generation. The A-model was followed into service by 94 F-111ES, with revised inlets and better engines, 96 F-111DS, with improved avionics, and finally 106 F-111FS, which boasted new engines and still better weapons systems. Strategic Air Command (SAC) also received 76 FB-111s beginning in 1969, these aircraft combining the F-111A's fuselage with the longer-span wings of the stillborn F-111B.

Capable of carrying a staggering 40,000 lb of ordnance, the FB-111 was bought as an interim replacement for both the B-58 and early-build B-52s. SAC initially intended to buy 210 jets, but with numbers drastically scaled back, only two wings received FB-111s. These aircraft later became F-111GS when their nuclear strike role was removed in the early 1990s. The USAF also acquired 42 EF-111A Ravens from 1981, these aircraft having previously seen service as F-111AS. The USAF had contracted Grumman in the early 1970s to fit the Tactical Jamming System from its EA-6B Prowler into the F-111, and the resulting aircraft remained in service until 1998. Both the F-111F and the EF-111 saw extensive combat in Operation Desert Storm, and both types soldiered on with the USAF until the late 1990s.

SPECIFICATION (F-111A):

ACCOMMODATION:
Pilot and weapons systems officer seated side-by-side

DIMENSIONS:
LENGTH: 73 ft 6 in (22.40 m)
WINGSPAN: 63 ft 0 in (19.20 m)
HEIGHT: 17 ft 0.50 in (5.22 m)

WEIGHTS:
EMPTY: 46,172 lb (20,943 kg)
MAX T/O: 91,500 lb (41,500 kg)

PERFORMANCE:
MAX SPEED: 1450 mph (2335 kmh)
RANGE: 3165 miles (5093 km)
POWERPLANT: two Pratt & Whitney TF30-P-3S
OUTPUT: 37,000 lb st (164 kN)

FIRST FLIGHT DATE:
December 21, 1964

ARMAMENT:
4000 lb (1814 kg) of bombs in bomb bay and 31,500 lb (14,290 kg) of bombs/rockets/ missiles on four underwing stores pylons

FEATURES:
Midmounted variable-geometry wings; bubble canopy; tricycle landing gear; wing root engine intakes; wide, sleek nose

Gates c-21 Learjet

ten-seat, twin-engined priority airlift/medevac aircraft

The Gates Learjet Model 35A was chosen in 1983 by the USAF as an "off-the-shelf" replacement for its fleet of cт-39 Sabreliner light transports. The latter had been operated by Military Airlift Command (MAC) on priority passenger/cargo and medevac duties since the 1960s, and the Air Force entered into an agreement with Gates to replace these jets with 80 brand new Learjet 35As. Designated c-21As, the machines were delivered to MAC units as Operational Support Aircraft between April 1984 and October 1985. Procured under a five-year lease deal with the manufacturer, the Air Force subsequently bought the aircraft outright. In 1986 four more were purchased for use by the Air National Guard. The c-21A can carry up to eight passengers or 3153 lb of cargo, and has a quickly convertible interior for employment in the medical evacuation of stretcher patients. The c-21A currently equips the 375th Airlift Wing at Scott AFB, Illinois, which controls Airlift Flights at four bases in the USA. The jet is also used by the Germany-based 86th Airlift Wing, as well as a solitary squadron.

SPECIFICATION:

ACCOMMODATION:
Two pilots and up to eight passengers

DIMENSIONS:
LENGTH: 48 ft 8 in (14.83 m)
WINGSPAN: 39 ft 6 in (12.04 m)
HEIGHT: 12 ft 3 in (3.73 m)

WEIGHTS:
EMPTY: 9838 lb (4462 kg)
MAX T/O: 18,300 lb (8301 kg)

PERFORMANCE:
MAX SPEED: 542 mph (867 kmh)
RANGE: 2662 miles (4260 km)
POWERPLANT: two Garrett TFE731-2-2BS
OUTPUT: 7000 lb st (31 kN)

FIRST FLIGHT DATE:
August 22, 1973 (Learjet 35)

FEATURES:
Swept-wing layout; rectractable tricycle landing gear; twin, podded engines on rear fuselage; т-tail; wingtip tanks

Grumman F8F Bearcat

single-seat, single-engined fighter-bomber

The last piston-engined Grumman fighter, the Bearcat bucked the unwritten law of the day that stated that a new fighter had to be larger in order to be better than its predecessor. The Bearcat was shorter and lighter than the F6F Hellcat it replaced, and although both types were powered by the R-2800 Double Wasp engine, the Bearcat could easily out-perform the F6F thanks to its compact design. The Navy was so pleased with the F8F that it ordered 2023, with delivery commencing in January 1945. VF-19 was the first unit to receive Bearcats, and it was just completing workups when the A-bomb attacks on Hiroshima and Nagasaki brought the war to a dramatic end. Postwar, the contract was slashed by 1258, and production ceased in May 1949 following the delivery of 1266 F8Fs. Included in this number were cannon-armed F8F-1/B2S, nightfighter F8F-1/2NS, and photo-reconnaissance F8F-2PS. Although 24 units flew Bearcats with the Navy, not a single one saw combat with the aircraft. The last F8Fs were retired from frontline service in late 1952.

SPECIFICATION (F8F-1):

ACCOMMODATION:
Pilot

DIMENSIONS:
LENGTH: 28 ft 3 in (8.61 m)
WINGSPAN: 35 ft 10 in (7.87 m)
HEIGHT: 13 ft 10 in (4.20 m)

WEIGHTS:
EMPTY: 7070 lb (3206 kg)
MAX T/O: 12,947 lb (5873 kg)

PERFORMANCE:
MAX SPEED: 421 mph (680 kmh)
RANGE: 1105 miles (1775 km)
POWERPLANT: Pratt & Whitney R-2800-34W Double Wasp
OUTPUT: 2800 hp (2087 kW)

FIRST FLIGHT DATE:
August 21, 1944

ARMAMENT:
Four Colt-Browning 0.50-in machine guns in wings; up to 2000 lb (907 kg) of bombs/rockets on six underwing and one underfuselage stores pylons

FEATURES:
Straight wing; close-cowled radial engine; rectractable undercarriage; arrestor hook; bubble canopy

Grumman F9F Panther

single-seat, single-engined fighter-bomber

As Grumman's first jet fighter, the F9F was originally designed to be powered by four small axial-flow Westinghouse 19XB (J30) engines identical to those slated for fitment into the AF-2's predecessor, the XTB3F-1. However, the Navy had been monitoring the performance of the Rolls-Royce Nene, and duly had two examples shipped to the Naval Air Center in Philadelphia for bench testing. The engine's performance was so revelatory that it was soon placed in license-production by Pratt & Whitney as the J42. The prototype XF9F-1 Panther made use of one of the "imports" to complete its flight trials in 1947-48.

A conventional design with straight wings and excellent low speed handling for carrier operations, the first of 567 F9F-2s reached fleet squadron VF-51 in May 1949. Unlike the prototypes, all production aircraft had permanent wingtip tanks fitted. Following the interim "Dash-3" and "-4," Grumman commenced production of the definitive F9F-5 (725 built, including 109 modified F9F-4s) in late 1950, this variant introducing a longer fuselage, taller tail, and more powerful J48 turbojet. These modifications went some way to improving the Panther's poor straightline speed, although this problem was not totally addressed until the advent of the swept-wing F9F-6 Cougar in 1951.

The first carrier-based jet to see action over Korea on August 6, 1950, the Panther performed almost half the attack missions flown during the conflict by Navy/Marine Corps units—no fewer than 24 squadrons saw action with F9Fs from carriers off Korea. Although principally used as an attack jet, the Panther was also a successful photoreconnaissance platform, with oblique and vertical cameras fitted in the lengthened nose section of the F9F-2/5P. These aircraft also saw extensive use over Korea throughout the war. Following their replacement in the fleet by swept-wing Cougars and Furies soon after the Korean War had ended in mid-1953, surviving Panthers were converted into pilotless target drones (F9F-2/5KD), or manned drone controllers. The handful of surviving F9F-5KDs were redesignated DF-9ES in 1962.

SPECIFICATION (F9F-5):

ACCOMMODATION:
Pilot

DIMENSIONS:
LENGTH: 35 ft 10 in (10.69 m)
WINGSPAN: 38 ft 0 in (11.58 m)
HEIGHT: 12 ft 3 in (3.74 m)

WEIGHTS:
EMPTY: 10,147 lb (4603 kg)
MAX T/O: 18,721 lb (8492 kg)

PERFORMANCE:
MAX SPEED: 579 mph (926 kmh)
RANGE: 1300 miles (2080 km)
POWERPLANT: Pratt & Whitney J42-P-6A
OUTPUT: 6250 lb st (30 kN)

FIRST FLIGHT DATE:
November 24, 1947

ARMAMENT:
Four M-2 20-mm cannon in nose; provision for up to 2000 lb (907 kg) of bombs/rockets on six underwing stores pylons

FEATURES:
Straight wing; engine air intakes on fuselage sides below cockpit; high-mounted horizontal tailplane; bubble canopy; arrestor hook; wingtip tanks

Grumman F9F/F-9 Cougar

single/two-seat, single-engined fighter-bomber/advanced trainer

Proving the soundness of Grumman's original jet fighter design, the F9F Panther was developed into the swept-wing F9F-8 Cougar and remained in production for a further seven years. Grumman had first proposed making a swept-wing Panther in 1950, and in March of the following year the Navy contracted for three prototypes to be built. The "new" aircraft, designated the XF9F-6, comprised a Panther fuselage and tail unit, an uprated J48-P-8 engine and a new wing with 35 degrees sweepback. The prototype made its maiden flight in September 1951, and 646 F9F-6s, 168 near-identical F9F-7s, and 60 F9F-6P photoreconnaissance aircraft were built. The F9F-8 introduced a lengthened fuselage, modified canopy, and larger wings. Of the 711 built, 110 were configured as F9F-8P photo-reconnaissance jets. The final variant produced by Grumman was the stretched two-seat F9F-8T advanced trainer, 399 of which were delivered in 1956-59. Redesignated F/RF/TF-9s in 1962, Cougars served with numerous frontline, training, and Reserve units until 1974.

SPECIFICATION (F9F-8):

ACCOMMODATION:
Pilot, or two pilots in tandem (F9F-8T/TF-9)

DIMENSIONS:
LENGTH: 41 ft 9 in (12.77 m)
WINGSPAN: 34 ft 6 in (10.54 m)
HEIGHT: 12 ft 3 in (3.74 m)

WEIGHTS:
EMPTY: 11,866 lb (5382 kg)
MAX T/O: 19,738 lb (8953 kg)

PERFORMANCE:
MAX SPEED: 647 mph (1035 kmh)
RANGE: 1200 miles (1920 km)
POWERPLANT: Pratt & Whitney J48-P-8A
OUTPUT: 7250 lb st (32 kN)

FIRST FLIGHT DATE:
September 20, 1951

ARMAMENT:
Four M-2 20-mm cannon in nose; provision for up to 4000 lb (1814 kg) of bombs/rockets/missiles on six underwing stores pylons

FEATURES:
Swept wing; engine air intakes in wing root; high-mounted horizontal tailplane; bubble canopy; arrestor hook

Grumman S2F/S-2 Tracker, C-1 Trader and E-1 Tracer

four/eleven-seat, twin-engined ASW/AEW/utility aircraft

Built as a replacement for the "hunter/killer" Guardian, the Tracker was developed over an incredibly short time span. Despite being of modest dimensions, the S-2's airframe nevertheless proved more than capable of housing all the ASW radar, sensor equipment, and weaponry deemed necessary to locate and destroy submarines. A combination of fuel-efficient Wright Cyclone radials and long-span wings gave the aircraft a superb loitering ability. With space at a premium aboard ship, all the S-2's mission equipment was installed in such a way so as to allow its retraction back into the fuselage when not in use—the APS-38 was housed in a ventral "bin," the MAD boom retracted into the tail and eight sonobuoys were stored in each of the rear engine nacelles. The first S2F-1 (redesignated S-2A in 1962) entered fleet service in February 1954, and when production ceased in 1968, Grumman had built 1181 Trackers/Traders. The Tracker also formed the basis for the E-1B Tracer AEW aircraft (88 built), which served from 1958-76 and the C-1A Trader Carrier On-board Delivery transport (87 built).

SPECIFICATION (S-2E):

ACCOMMODATION:
Pilot, copilot/tactical operator, and two radar operators (S-2/E-1), or pilot, copilot, and nine passengers (C-1)

DIMENSIONS:
LENGTH: 43 ft 6 in (13.26 m)
WINGSPAN: 69 ft 8 in (21.23 m)
HEIGHT: 16 ft 7 in (5.06 m)

WEIGHTS:
EMPTY: 18,750 lb (8505 kg)
MAX T/O: 29,150 lb (13,222 kg)

PERFORMANCE:
MAX SPEED: 267 mph (430 kmh)
RANGE: 1300 miles (2095 km)
POWERPLANT: two Wright R-1820-82WA Cyclones
OUTPUT: 3050 hp (2274 kW)

FIRST FLIGHT DATE:
December 4, 1952

ARMAMENT:
Provision for up to 4810 lb (2181 kg) of torpedoes/depth charges/rockets in weapons bay and on six underwing stores pylons

FEATURES:
Shoulder-mounted straight wing; two close-cowled radial engines; rectractable undercarriage; arrestor hook

Grumman AF-2 Guardian

two/four-seat, single-engined ASW/strike aircraft

Built to counter the Soviet submarine threat, the AF-2 entered production in two separate variants, which combined to perform the ASW mission. The AF-2W (153 built) was the "hunter" element of the team, its four-man crew searching for submarines with the aircraft's belly-mounted APS-20 radar and other dedicated sensors, calling in the two-man AF-2S "killer" when a contact was encountered. The latter aircraft would then "locally acquire" the target using APS-31 radar, an AVQ-2 searchlight and sonobuoys, before despatching the submarine with bombs/torpedo/depth charges—all of which could be carried in the aircraft's weapon bay (which contained the APS-20 radar equipment in the -2W). An initial run of 193 AF-2SS was undertaken by Grumman, with the first examples reaching the fleet in October 1950. A follow-on batch of 40 MAD-equipped S-models completed the production run in 1953. Replaced in the fleet by a single ASW platform in the form of the S-2 Tracker, the Guardian had been consigned to the Navy Reserve by 1955.

SPECIFICATION (AF-2S):

ACCOMMODATION:
Pilot and navigator (AF-2S), or pilot, navigator, and two radar operators (AF-2W)

DIMENSIONS:
LENGTH: 43 ft 4 in (13.2 m)
WINGSPAN: 60 ft 8 in (18.49 m)
HEIGHT: 16 ft 2 in (4.93 m)

WEIGHTS:
EMPTY: 14,580 lb (6613 kg)
MAX T/O: 25,500 lb (11,567 kg)

PERFORMANCE:
MAX SPEED: 317 mph (510 kmh)
RANGE: 1500 miles (2415 km)
POWERPLANT: Pratt & Whitney R-2800-48W Double Wasp
OUTPUT: 2400 hp (1789 kW)

FIRST FLIGHT DATE:
December 19, 1946

ARMAMENT:
(AF-2S only) up to 4000 lb (1814 kg) of bombs/torpedo/ depth charges in bomb bay

FEATURES:
Straight wing; close-cowled radial engine; rectractable undercarriage; arrestor hook

Grumman UF-1/2 and U-16 Albatross

four/six-seat, twin-engined rescue, utility and ASW amphibian

Having gained a wealth of experience building amphibians thanks to the huge number of JRF Goose aircraft supplied to the Allies in World War II, Grumman decided to embark on a study to replace its earlier machine with an all-new type that was three times the size of its predecessor. The result was the G-64 Albatross, which retained a link with previous Grumman amphibians through the employment of a trademark cantilever high wing and main gear retraction into the fuselage sides. Both the Navy and the USAF were so impressed by the Albatross prototype that they each ordered their own variants into series production. While the Air Force adopted the designation SA-16A, which later changed to HU-16, the Navy opted initially for JR2F-1 and then UF-1/2 (also later redesignated to U-16). The first of 418 production aircraft entered service in July 1949, and the improved SA-16B/UF-2 followed in 1955. USAF, Navy, and US Coast Guard aircraft saw combat in Korea and Vietnam, and surviving HU-16s remained in the inventory well into the 1970s.

SPECIFICATION (UF-2):

ACCOMMODATION:
Pilot, copilot, navigator, crew chief, and radar operator

DIMENSIONS:
LENGTH: 61 ft 3 in (18.68 m)
WINGSPAN: 96 ft 8 in (29.46 m)
HEIGHT: 25 ft 10 in (7.87 m)

WEIGHTS:
EMPTY: 22,883 lb (10,380 kg)
MAX T/O: 35,700 lb (16,194 kg)

PERFORMANCE:
MAX SPEED: 236 mph (379 kmh)
RANGE: 2850 miles (4587 km)
POWERPLANT: two Wright R-1820-76AS
OUTPUT: 2850 hp (2125 kW)

FIRST FLIGHT DATE:
October 24, 1947

FEATURES:
High-mounted straight wing; two close-cowled radial engines; rectractable undercarriage; boat-shaped hull; fixed outriggers

Grumman A-6 Intruder

two-seat, twin-engined bomber

The requirement for a carrier-based aircraft capable of all-weather long-range bombing strikes was formulated during the final months of the Korean War. Following refinement of the specification in the mid-1950s, an industry competition was held by the Navy in 1957. Later that same year, Grumman's G-128 Intruder was duly chosen to fill this requirement over nine other designs from seven rival manufacturers. The first of six A2F-1 development aircraft flew on April 19, 1960, and by the time production aircraft began to reach to VA-42 in February 1963, the jet's designation had changed to A-6A (482 built).

Making its combat debut over Vietnam in 1965, the Intruder would see much action in the conflict both from carriers in the Gulf of Tonkin and ashore from Marine Corps bases in South Vietnam. The Marine Corps had received its first A-6As in October 1964, and seven all-weather attack squadrons would operate them until the early 1990s. Capable of carrying up to 18,000 lb of bombs (both dumb and precision) and missiles, the Intruder's usefulness was further enhanced by its all-weather attack navigation equipment.

Following limited production of the A-6B (19 A-models capable of carrying HARM antiradar missiles), A-6C (12 A-6As fitted with improved targeting systems) and the KA-6D (78 A-6As reconfigured as dedicated aerial tankers through the fitment of the Sergeant Fletcher hose/drogue refueling system), Grumman switched its attention to the vastly improved A-6E. Featuring more powerful engines and a better and more reliable navigation/attack radar and computer, the first E-model flew in February 1970. Of the 445 acquired, 240 were newly built jets (the last was not delivered until 1989) and 205 refurbished A-6As. The A-6E's weapons systems were periodically upgraded during its 26-year career in the fleet, allowing the Intruder to remain a viable all-weather bomber right up until its retirement in early 1997. Aside from its war of attrition in Vietnam, the jet also saw combat over Libya, Lebanon, and the Persian Gulf in the 1980s, and over Iraq and Kuwait during Operation Desert Storm in 1991.

SPECIFICATION (A-6E):

ACCOMMODATION:
Pilot and bombardier-navigator

DIMENSIONS:
LENGTH: 54 ft 9 in (16.69 m)
WINGSPAN: 53 ft 0 in (16.15 m)
HEIGHT: 16 ft 2 in (4.93 m)

WEIGHTS:
EMPTY: 27,613 lb (12,525 kg)
MAX T/O: 58,600 lb (26,580 kg)

PERFORMANCE:
MAX SPEED: 685 mph (1037 kmh)
RANGE: 1077 miles (1733 km)
POWERPLANT: two Pratt & Whitney J52-P-8Bs
OUTPUT: 18,600 lb st (82.8 kN)

FIRST FLIGHT DATE:
April 19, 1960

ARMAMENT:
Up to 18,000 lb (8165 kg) of bombs/missiles in four underwing/one centerline stores pylons

FEATURES:
Midmounted swept wing; engine air intakes on fuselage sides, either side of cockpit; low-mounted horizontal tailplane; bubble canopy; arrestor hook; refueling probe immediately in front of cockpit

Grumman F-14 Tomcat

two-seat, twin-engined fighter-bomber

Emerging from the failed F-111B fleet fighter program, the F-14 Tomcat was for many years the world's best long-range defense fighter. Grumman, as lead contractor for the Navy's version of the F-111, had independently begun work on the G-303 air defense fighter long before the cancelation of the General Dynamics project, and this was duly selected in January 1969. Built to replace the F-4, the aircraft featured key systems from the F-111B, including the AWG-9 radar, AIM-54 Phoenix missile, TF30 engines, and variable-sweep wings. Designated the F-14 by the Navy, the prototype undertook its maiden flight on December 12, 1970, and the first of 556 production aircraft reached VF-124 at NAS Miramar, in San Diego, in 1972.

VF-1 and VF-2 conducted the first operational deployment with the jet aboard USS *Enterprise* in 1974-75, and during the course of the cruise the units covered the evacuation of Saigon. The delivery of jets peaked in the early 1980s, by which time 12 Atlantic Fleet and 10 Pacific Fleet units had re-equipped with F-14s, along with single training squadrons on both coasts. Four Reserve units were also issued with Tomcats in the mid-1980s. The F-14A experienced its first combat in August 1981, when two VF-41 jets shot down two Libyan Su-22s over the Mediterranean—the Libyans would lose two more MiG-23s to VF-32 in January 1989.

Selected Tomcat squadrons picked up the photoreconnaissance mission from the early 1980s following the introduction of the Tactical Air Reconnaissance Pod System, which was carried beneath the fuselage of the jet.

Fifty A-models were re-engined and redesignated as F-14B/DS in the late 1980s and 76 new build jets delivered. Both the B- and D-models featured the General Electric F110 engine, while the F-14D also boasted all-new radar and digital avionics.

With its principal fighter mission disappearing with the ending of the Cold War, the Tomcat saw much combat in Operations Enduring Freedom and Iraqi Freedom as a precision bomber that was capable of employing both laser-guided bombs and GPS-guided J-weapons.

SPECIFICATION (F-14A):

ACCOMMODATION:
Pilot and radar intercept officer in tandem

DIMENSIONS:
LENGTH: 62 ft 8 in (19.10 m)
WINGSPAN: 64 ft 2 in (19.54 m)
HEIGHT: 16 ft 0 in (4.88 m)

WEIGHTS:
EMPTY: 40,105 lb (18,190 kg)
MAX T/O: 74,349 lb (33,724 kg)

PERFORMANCE:
MAX SPEED: 1553 mph (2485 kmh)
RANGE: 2012 miles (3220 km)
POWERPLANT: two Pratt & Whitney TF30-P-412S
OUTPUT: 41,800 lb st (186 kN)

ARMAMENT:
One M61A1 Vulcan 20-mm cannon in forward fuselage; up to eight air-to-air missiles on four wing glove and four fuselage stores pylons, or 14,500 lb (6577 kg) of bombs

FIRST FLIGHT DATE:
December 12, 1970

FEATURES:
Variable-sweep wings; low-mounted horizontal tailplane; bubble canopy; arrestor hook; twin fins; underfuselage strakes

Grumman F11F/F-11 Tiger

single-seat, single-engined fighter

Intended to be a development of the Panther/Cougar family, the Tiger eventually became an all-new fighter. Taking shape with incredible speed, Grumman's G-98 prototype completed its first flight on July 30, 1954. Christened the Tiger, the fighter featured a waisted body to allow for the volume of the wing as per NACA's area rule for minimum transonic and supersonic drag. Powered by a Wright J65 turbojet with afterburner, and designated the F11F-1 by the Navy, the jet entered production in 1956. Delayed by engine performance and reliability issues, only 42 short-nose F11F-1s were built, and the first of these entered fleet service with VA-156 (a day fighter unit, despite its attack designation) in March 1957. The radar-capable (but never fitted) long-nose F11F-1 variant soon followed, and 157 had been delivered to the Navy by the time production ended in December 1958. Although only five fighter units made brief use of the Tiger in fleet service, the Navy's Blue Angels formation display team was equipped with the redesignated F-11A until 1968.

SPECIFICATION (F11F-1 LONG NOSE):

ACCOMMODATION:
Pilot

DIMENSIONS:
LENGTH: 44 ft 11 in (13.70 m)
WINGSPAN: 31 ft 7.50 in (9.63 m)
HEIGHT: 13 ft 3 in (4.05 m)

WEIGHTS:
EMPTY: 13,428 lb (6092 kg)
MAX T/O: 22,160 lb (10,052 kg)

PERFORMANCE:
MAX SPEED: 890 mph (1432 kmh)
RANGE: 700 miles (1130 km)
POWERPLANT: Wright J65-W-18
OUTPUT: 11,000 lb st (49.2 kN)

FIRST FLIGHT DATE:
July 30, 1954

ARMAMENT:
Four M-2 20-mm cannon in fuselage and up to four AIM-9 Sidewinder missiles on four underwing stores pylons

FEATURES:
Midmounted swept wing; engine air intakes on fuselage either side of cockpit; low-mounted horizontal tailplane; bubble canopy; arrestor hook

Grumman EA-6A/B Prowler

two/four-seat, twin-engined electronic warfare aircraft

The Navy and Marine Corps' standard tactical electronic warfare (EW) aircraft, the EA-6B traces its lineage back to the EF-10 Skynight of the early 1960s. The latter type was initially replaced in Marine Corps service by the EA-6A Intruder, 27 of which were built for service in Vietnam. This interim EW aircraft, which was little more than a converted A-6A, sired the purpose-built Prowler in the late 1960s, which the Navy used to replace its EKA-3B Skywarriors on carrier decks. Based on the A-6, the EA-6B has a stretched forward fuselage for a four-man crew consisting of a pilot and three electronic warfare officers. EW antenna are fitted into a bulbous fin tip fairing, while radar jamming equipment is carried in underwing pods. This EW mission equipment combines to form the Tactical Jamming System. First flown on May 25, 1968, production Prowlers began reaching the fleet in 1971. Some 170 aircraft were built in a production run that lasted until 1991. One of the most highly valued assets in the US armed forces, the Prowler remains in the forefront of current combat operations.

SPECIFICATION (EA-6B):

ACCOMMODATION:
Pilot and three electronic-warfare officers

DIMENSIONS:
LENGTH: 59 ft 10 in (18.24 m)
WINGSPAN: 53 ft 0 in (16.15 m)
HEIGHT: 16 ft 3 in (4.95 m)

WEIGHTS:
EMPTY: 31,572 lb (14,320 kg)
MAX T/O: 65,000 lb (29,895 kg)

PERFORMANCE:
MAX SPEED: 599 mph (958 kmh)
RANGE: 1106 miles (1770 km)
POWERPLANT: two Pratt & Whitney J52-P-408s
OUTPUT: 22,400 lb st (99.6 kN)

FIRST FLIGHT DATE:
May 25, 1968

ARMAMENT:
Up to four AGM-88 HARM anti-radar missiles on four underwing stores pylons

FEATURES:
Midmounted swept wing; engine air intakes on fuselage either side of cockpit; low-mounted horizontal tailplane; bubble canopy; arrestor hook; refueling probe immediately in front of cockpit; bulbous fin tip fairing

Grumman OV-1 Mohawk

two-seat, twin-engined battlefield surveillance aircraft

The OV-1 Mohawk was built to fulfill the Army's need for a dedicated battlefield observation platform. Boasting STOL (short takeoff and landing) capability, crew armor, and systems redundancy in order to allow it to remain operational after having been hit by small-arms fire, the Mohawk proved itself to be the ideal aircraft for the task. Its twin turboprop engines combined with the aircraft's short high-lift wings to make the OV-1 an agile battlefield interdictor, while its long-stroke undercarriage allowed for rough-field operations. The first OV-1AS entered Army service in February 1961, and by the time of the Vietnam War, more than 150 had been delivered. The final OV-1s were delivered in 1970, bringing production to a close after the 375th airframe had been completed. The Mohawk's passive electronic intelligence role saw the D-model become an important weapon in the Cold War arsenal, aircraft being converted to carry infrared linescan and side-looking radar. The surviving OV-1D/RV-1s were retired from Army service in 1996 when fatigue lives were reached.

SPECIFICATION (OV-1D):

ACCOMMODATION:
Pilot and observer, seated side-by-side

DIMENSIONS:
LENGTH: 41 ft 0 in (12.50 m)
WINGSPAN: 48 ft 0 in (14.63 m)
HEIGHT: 12 ft 8 in (3.86 m)

WEIGHTS:
EMPTY: 11,067 lb (5020 kg)
MAX T/O: 19,230 lb (8722 kg)

PERFORMANCE:
MAX SPEED: 299 mph (478 kmh)
RANGE: 1237 miles (1980 km)
POWERPLANT: two Lycoming T53-L-15s
OUTPUT: 2200 shp (1640 kW)

FIRST FLIGHT DATE:
April 14, 1959

ARMAMENT:
Gun/rocket pods and grenade launchers occasionally fitted on two underwing stores pylons

FEATURES:
Midmounted straight-wing; two turboprop engines mounted atop wings; bulged, side-by-side canopy; triple tailfin

Grumman E-2 Hawkeye

five-seat, twin-engined airborne early warning aircraft

The E-2 Hawkeye was developed to replace Grumman's E-1 Tracer, which was an AEW derivative of the S-2. The Navy announced in March 1957 that it had chosen the Grumman design, combined with the digital processors and the General Electric APS-96 surveillance radar. The resulting W2F-1 (redesignated the E-2 in 1962) featured the radar housed in a rotodome above the fuselage. Tailored to fit within a carrier hangar deck, the aircraft had high-mounted, folding wings and a four-finned tailplane with significant dihedral. The first of 59 E-2AS was delivered to the Navy in 1961, and the aircraft saw much service during the Vietnam War. E-2AS were upgraded to E-2B standard from 1969, while the definitive E-2C made its fleet debut in 1971. The latter variant was initially fitted with APS-125 radar and improved signal-processing equipment, and over the years the aircraft has been upgraded with better radar. Still in production for the Navy today, more than 170 E-2CS have been built to date. Export versions of the aircraft have also been sold to seven countries.

SPECIFICATION (E-2C):

ACCOMMODATION:
Pilot, copilot, combat information center officer, air control operator, and radar operator

DIMENSIONS:
LENGTH: 57 ft 7 in (17.54 m)
WINGSPAN: 80 ft 7 in (24.56 m)
HEIGHT: 18 ft 4 in (5.58 m)

WEIGHTS:
EMPTY: 39,373 lb (17,860 kg)
MAX T/O: 53,267 lb (24,160 kg)

PERFORMANCE:
MAX SPEED: 390 mph (625 kmh)
RANGE: 1784 miles (2855 km)
POWERPLANT: two Allison T56-A-425S
OUTPUT: 10,200 shp (7610 kW)

FIRST FLIGHT DATE:
October 21, 1960

FEATURES:
Straight, high-mounted wings; two turboprop engines mounted beneath wings; four tailfins; radome atop fuselage; arrestor hook

Grumman C-2 Greyhound

42-seat, twin-engined Carrier Onboard Delivery aircraft

Grumman's tradition of building Carrier Onboard Delivery (COD) aircraft for the Navy stretched back to its cargo-carrying Avenger of World War II and similarly configured C-1 Trader version of the S-2 of the 1950s. The final example of Grumman's COD "craft" came in the form of the C-2 Greyhound, which was derived from the E-2. Whereas the Avenger and the C-1 had simply been passenger/cargo-configured versions of frontline types, the Greyhound was significantly different from its donor airframe. Although retaining the E-2's powerplants and wings, its fuselage was much broader, and featured a rear-loading cargo ramp and upturned tail. The first of two YC-2A prototypes completed its maiden flight on November 18, 1964, after which a follow-on batch of 17 C-2AS was built. Entering fleet service in 1966, the Greyhound has been a constant feature on Navy carrier decks across the globe ever since. An additional 39 C-2s were built in 1985-89 as replacements for the recently retired C-1 Traders. The Greyhound is set to remain in Navy service for the foreseeable future.

SPECIFICATION:

ACCOMMODATION:
Pilot, copilot, crew chief, and 39 passengers

DIMENSIONS:
LENGTH: 56 ft 10 in (17.32 m)
WINGSPAN: 80 ft 7 in (24.56 m)
HEIGHT: 15 ft 11 in (4.84 m)

WEIGHTS:
EMPTY: 36,345 lb (16,485 kg)
MAX T/O: 57,500 lb (26,080 kg)

PERFORMANCE:
MAX SPEED: 359 mph (575 kmh)
RANGE: 1806 miles (2890 km)
POWERPLANT: two Allison T56-A-425S
OUTPUT: 9824 shp (7330 kW)

FIRST FLIGHT DATE:
November 18, 1964

FEATURES:
Straight, high-mounted wings; two turboprop engines mounted beneath wings; four tailfins; rear-loading cargo ramp; arrestor hook

Grumman TC/VC-4 Academe/Gulfstream I

ten-seat, twin-engined bombardier/navigator trainer and VIP transportation aircraft

The Navy had originally planned to procure a militarized version of the Gulfstream I executive transportation aircraft in 1962 for use as a navigation trainer and transport. However, a lack of funding saw the purchase deferred, and it was left to the US Coast Guard (USCG) to give the type its service debut when a solitary Gulfstream I was acquired in 1963 for use as a VIP transport. Designated a VC-4A, this aircraft still remains in use today at Opa Locke, Miami. In 1966 the Navy ordered nine Gulfstream Is to serve as TC-4C Academe bombardier/navigator trainers for aircrew destined to fly A-6s. A simulated Intruder cockpit was installed in the rear of the cabin, an A-6 nose grafted onto the front of the aircraft, and four identical radar/navigation training consoles filled the fuselage. Shared between three A-6 training units, these aircraft were periodically upgraded to keep abreast with new systems installed in the A-6E bomber. Redesignated TC-4Cs, the Academe were retired in 1996. The Army also had a second-hand Gulfstream I for VIP transportation in the 1980s.

SPECIFICATION (TC-4C):

ACCOMMODATION:
Pilot, copilot, and eight instructors/students

DIMENSIONS:
LENGTH: 67 ft 10.75 in (20.69 m)
WINGSPAN: 78 ft 4 in (23.88 m)
HEIGHT: 23 ft 4 in (7.11 m)

WEIGHTS:
EMPTY: 24,575 lb (11,114 kg)
MAX T/O: 36,000 lb (16,330 kg)

PERFORMANCE:
MAX SPEED: 365 mph (587 kmh)
RANGE: 1980 miles (3186 km)
POWERPLANT: two Rolls-Royce Dart RDA7/2 Mk 529-8xs
OUTPUT: 4420 shp (3296 kW)

FIRST FLIGHT DATE:
August 14, 1958

FEATURES:
Straight, low-mounted wings; two turboprop engines mounted above wings; bulbous A-6 nose; tall tailfin

Gulfstream c-11/20/37

16/26-seat, twin-engined priority airlift/VIP transportation/freight aircraft

Used in small numbers by the Air Force, Navy, Army, Marine Corps, and US Coast Guard, the Gulfstream family of jet-powered transports entered military service with the USCG in July 1968 when a solitary Gulfstream II was acquired and given the designation vc-11a. In 1981 the Army leased a second-hand Gulfstream II for VIP use as a c-20j. The Air Force bought 13 Gulfstream IIIs (designated c-120a/b/cs) in 1983-86 as replacements for its vc-140a/b Special Mission Support aircraft, followed by two Gulfstream IVs (c-20hs) in 1990. Finally, in 1997 it ordered six Gulfstream vs (c-37as) to perform the priority airlift mission—this variant is capable of nonstop transatlantic flight. The Navy bought two Gulfstream IIIs (c-20ds) in 1987 to serve as staff transports, with seating for 14, followed by five c-20gs (one is operated by the Marine Corps) in 2000, which are employed as Operational Support Aircraft. Shared between two Navy Reserve units, the c-20gs have a freight door on their starboard forward fuselage and a convertible interior for either passengers or cargo.

SPECIFICATION (C-20G):

ACCOMMODATION:
Two pilots and up to 26 passengers

DIMENSIONS:
LENGTH: 88 ft 3.50 in (26.91 m)
WINGSPAN: 77 ft 10.75 in (23.74 m)
HEIGHT: 24 ft 3.50 in (7.40 m)

WEIGHTS:
EMPTY: 42,400 lb (19,232 kg)
MAX T/O: 74,600 lb (33,838 kg)

PERFORMANCE:
MAX SPEED: 589 mph (943 kmh)
RANGE: 4611 miles (7377 km)
POWERPLANT: two Rolls-Royce Tay Mk 611-8 engines
OUTPUT: 27,700 lb st (123 kN)

FIRST FLIGHT DATE:
October 2, 1966 (Gulfstream II)

FEATURES:
Swept-wing layout; rectractable tricycle landing gear; twin, podded engines on rear fuselage; T-tail; oval-shaped fuselage windows

Helio AU-24 Stallion

six-seat, single-engined, high-winged light utility aircraft

A military derivative of Helio's STOL family of civil utility aircraft, the Kaman-developed Stallion was built specifically for the counterinsurgency role in South-East Asia. To achieve its incredible short-field performance, the aircraft was equipped with full-span automatic leading-edge slats, an augmented lateral control system and slotted flaps. Unlike Helio's H-250 and H-395 Courier, the Stallion relied on a turboprop engine to offset its increased all-up weight. Much of the latter took the form of six underwing hardpoints and 1900 lb of assorted weaponry (rockets, bombs, flares, and other "goodies"), plus a cabin-mounted machine gun or M197 20-mm cannon. Designated the H-550A by Helio, 15 were ordered as the AU-24A by the USAF with 1972 funds, these aircraft being sent to South Vietnam and evaluated during Project Credible Chase. Fourteen unarmed Stallions were subsequently handed over to the Khmer (Cambodian) Air Force in 1973.

SPECIFICATION:

ACCOMMODATION:
Pilot and five passengers

DIMENSIONS:
LENGTH: 39 ft 7 in (12.07 m)
WINGSPAN: 41 ft 0 in (12.50 m)
HEIGHT: 9 ft 3 in (2.81 m)

WEIGHTS:
EMPTY: 2860 lb (1297 kg)
MAX T/O: 6300 lb (2857 kg)

PERFORMANCE:
MAX SPEED: 216 mph (348 kmh)
RANGE: 1090 miles (1755 km)
POWERPLANT: Pratt & Whitney
(UACL) PT6A-27
OUTPUT: 680 shp (507 kW)

FIRST FLIGHT DATE:
June 5, 1964

ARMAMENT:
Cabin-mounted M197 20-mm
cannon or machine gun; up to
1900 lb (862 kg) of bombs/
rockets/flares on six underwing
stores pylons

FEATURES:
High-mounted, unbraced
straight wing; fixed taildragger
undercarriage; three-bladed
propeller; close-cowled
turboprop engine

Lockheed F-80/TO/TV Shooting Star

single-seat, single-engined fighter-bomber/reconnaissance aircraft

Lockheed's first jet was designed by chief engineer Clarence L. "Kelly" Johnson and built within a 180-day time limit in 1943 after the company had been approached by the USAAF to construct an all-new fighter type. Lacking a suitable American engine, the prototype XP-80 was powered by a Halford (de Havilland) H 1 Goblin supplied by the British. The aircraft completed its first flight on January 8, 1944, and by January of the following year two YP-80AS had been sent to Italy to operate in combat conditions. More would also be despatched to the UK for frontline trials, but production P-80AS failed to reach fighter squadrons until December 1945.

Contracts for 5000+ Shooting Stars had been placed with Lockheed and North American in 1944, but 3000 of these were canceled soon after VJ-Day. Nevertheless, 1718 F-80A/B/CS (as the type was designated in June 1948) were built, and these equipped units in the continental USA, Europe, and the Far East. It was the latter groups based in Japan that initially bore the brunt of the early fighting in Korea in 1950-51, with units flying 15,000 sorties in the first four months of the war. A Shooting Star also shot down the first MIG-15 to fall to the USAF on November 8, 1950 in the world's first jet-versus-jet combat. F-80s remained in the frontline through to the end of the war in July 1953.

A number of photoreconnaissance Shooting Stars were also produced by Lockheed, starting with 152 RP-80AS (later redesignated RF-80AS) in 1946-47 and 70 RF-80CS shortly afterward. These aircraft had cameras fitted in their lengthened and deepened noses in place of the six 0.50-in machine guns.

Having served with 13 fighter groups in the frontline, surviving F-80s were relegated to the ANG post-Korea following the introduction of the F-84 and F-86. The last F-80s were retired by the ANG in 1958, although a handful of RF-80s survived until 1961. The Navy also acquired 50 F-80CS in 1948, which it designated TO-1s (later changed to TV-1). These were used as advanced jet trainers into the 1950s.

SPECIFICATION (F-80C):

ACCOMMODATION:
Pilot

DIMENSIONS:
LENGTH: 34 ft 5 in (10.49 m)
WINGSPAN: 38 ft 9 in (11.81 m)
HEIGHT: 11 ft 3 in (3.43 m)

WEIGHTS:
EMPTY: 8420 lb (3819 kg)
MAX T/O: 16,856 lb (7646 kg)

PERFORMANCE:
MAX SPEED: 594 mph (956 kmh)
RANGE: 825 miles (1328 km)
POWERPLANT: Allison J33-A-35
OUTPUT: 5400 lb st (24 kN)

FIRST FLIGHT DATE:
January 8, 1944

ARMAMENT:
Six fixed Browning 0.50-in machine guns in nose; up to 2000 lb (908 kg) of bombs/rockets on four underwing pylons

FEATURES:
Straight-wing layout; retractable landing gear; wingtip tanks; low lateral engine intakes; bubble canopy

Lockheed T-33/TV-2

two-seat, single-engined trainer

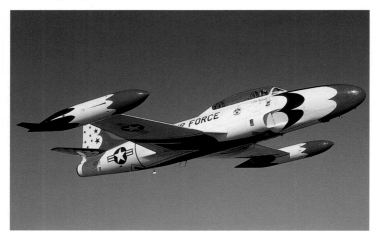

Boasting the title of the world's most populous jet trainer, the T-33 was built to a total of 6750 airframes during the 1950s. Sired by the F-80, the prototype T-33 was a stretched F-80C fitted with a second seat and a long canopy. First examples were designated TF-80Cs, and these entered service with the USAF in the late 1940s as replacements for the veteran T-6 Texan. Dubbed the "T-Bird" following the type's redesignation as the T-33, the trainer proved to be so successful that production of the two-seater soon outstripped that of the F-80— almost 4000 entered Air Force service. Although the last T-33s were retired from the USAF's Training Command in 1974, "T-Birds" remained in use with Tactical Air Command, ANG, and Reserve units as General Utility Support aircraft until 1988. The Navy and Marine Corps also procured 699 T-33s from 1949, these aircraft (initially designated TO/TV-2s, and then T-33Bs from 1962) being used for advanced/instrument training and utility roles. A number of surplus T-33s (both Navy and Air Force) were also converted into target drones in the 1960s.

SPECIFICATION (T-33A):

ACCOMMODATION:
Two pilots in tandem

DIMENSIONS:
LENGTH: 37 ft 9 in (11.48 m)
WINGSPAN: 38 ft 10.50 in (11.85 m)
HEIGHT: 11 ft 8 in (3.55 m)

WEIGHTS:
EMPTY: 8084 lb (3667 kg)
MAX T/O: 14,442 lb (6551 kg)

PERFORMANCE:
MAX SPEED: 543 mph (869 kmh)
RANGE: 1100 miles (1760 km)
POWERPLANT: Allison J33-A-35
OUTPUT: 5200 lb st (23 kN)

FIRST FLIGHT DATE:
March 22, 1948 (TF-80C)

FEATURES:
Straight-wing layout; retractable landing gear; wingtip tanks; low lateral engine intakes; long bubble canopy

Lockheed T2V/T-1 Seastar

two-seat, single-engined trainer

Following the Navy's procurement of 53 F-80CS for advanced training in 1948, dedicated two-seat TF-80CS were acquired in quantity in 1949. These aircraft were identical to the USAF's T-33, and they proved unsuitable for carrier operations due to a lack of forward visibility for the instructor in the rear cockpit—they were also deemed to be too fragile for arrested deck landings. In order to overcome these problems, Lockheed took a standard TV-2 in late 1953 and fitted a humped cockpit to give the rear seat occupant a better view. The lower landing and takeoff speeds necessary for carrier operation were achieved through the fitment of leading- and trailing-edge flaps and a blown-flaps system of boundary layer control. Built as a private venture, the prototype also featured a more powerful J33-A-24 engine and strengthened airframe (almost 4000 lb heavier than a standard T-33). First flown on December 16, 1953, the T2V-1 was ordered into production and the first of 150 delivered in 1956. Redesignated the T-1A in 1962, the jet was retired from service in the early 1970s.

SPECIFICATION:

ACCOMMODATION:
Two pilots in tandem

DIMENSIONS:
LENGTH: 38 ft 6.50 in (11.70 m)
WINGSPAN: 42 ft 10 in (12.83 m)
HEIGHT: 13 ft 4 in (4.08 m)

WEIGHTS:
EMPTY: 11,965 lb (5427 kg)
MAX T/O: 15,800 lb (7167 kg)

PERFORMANCE:
MAX SPEED: 580 mph (928 kmh)
RANGE: 970 miles (1552 km)
POWERPLANT: Allison J33-A-24
OUTPUT: 6100 lb st (27 kN)

FIRST FLIGHT DATE:
December 16, 1953

FEATURES:
Straight-wing layout; retractable landing gear; wingtip tanks; low lateral engine intakes; long, humped bubble canopy

Lockheed C-69/C-121 Constellation/Warning Star

93-seat, four-engined transportation and airborne early-warning aircraft

Developed for Howard Hughes' Trans World Airlines, the majestic Constellation donned drab olive rather than red and white airliner trim as the first production aircraft were requisitioned as strategic transports for the USAAF, which designated them C-69s. Just 22 were taken on charge, but these aircraft made a big impression, and a number of longer-range C-121s were bought postwar. With the development of the stretched Super Constellation in 1950, the full military potential of the aircraft was realized, as specialist AEW (dubbed Warning Stars) and Elint variants were procured by the USAF and the Navy—20 distinct subtypes would eventually see operational service. The aircraft's "finest hour" came during the Vietnam War, when seven different variants of C-121 were used for radar/electronic surveillance, airborne early warning and fighter control, airborne radio relay, weather reconnaissance, and conventional troop transportation. The Navy was the final US military operator of the aircraft, the last of its 142 Warning Star surveillance aircraft being retired in 1982.

SPECIFICATION (EC-121D):

ACCOMMODATION:
Pilot, copilot, navigator, flight engineer, and 64 (C-69) or 88 passengers (C-121), or 22-26 systems operators (EC-121)

DIMENSIONS:
LENGTH: 116 ft 2 in (35.41 m)
WINGSPAN: 123 ft 0 in (37.49 m)
HEIGHT: 27 ft 0 in (8.1 m)

WEIGHTS:
EMPTY: 80,611 lb (36,275 kg)
MAX T/O: 143,600 lb (64,620 kg)

PERFORMANCE:
MAX SPEED: 321 mph (517 kmh)
RANGE: 4600 miles (7405 km)
POWERPLANT: four Wright R-3350-34s
OUTPUT: 13,000 hp (9694 kW)

FIRST FLIGHT DATE:
January 9, 1943

FEATURES:
Straight-wing layout; retractable landing gear; four close-cowled radial engines; wingtip tanks; three-finned tail; large radomes above and below fuselage (AEW variants only)

Lockheed P2V/P-2 Neptune

seven-seat, twin-engined maritime patrol and antisubmarine warfare aircraft

Designed with extreme range and endurance in mind, the Neptune was the end result of development work carried out by Lockheed subsidiary Vega into an aircraft combining a high aspect ratio wing with two then new R-3350 radial engines. With Lockheed focusing its efforts on other high-priority designs like the P-38 and Ventura, it was not until the last months of the war that the prototype XP2V-1 Neptune finally flew. Aside from the previously mentioned features, the aircraft also had large Fowler flaps for good short-field performance, a capacious weapons bay, and two defensive turrets. The first of 838 P2V Neptunes was delivered to the Navy in March 1947, and the aircraft went on to become the staple ASW platform for many Western countries into the 1960s. Redesignated the P-2 in 1962, the Neptune was built in seven subtypes that saw the aircraft evolve into a superb maritime patrol machine. Modified OP-2E Elint and AP-2H "gunship" versions were also employed to great effect by the USAF and Army in Vietnam. The Navy retired its last SP-2H Neptunes in April 1978.

SPECIFICATION (P2V-3):

ACCOMMODATION:
Pilot, copilot, navigator, engineer, three sensor operators/turret gunners

DIMENSIONS:
LENGTH: 77 ft 10 in (23.70 m)
WINGSPAN: 100 ft 0 in (30.48 m)
HEIGHT: 28 ft 1 in (8.58 m)

WEIGHTS:
EMPTY: 34,875 lb (15,833 kg)
MAX T/O: 64,100 lb (29,075 kg)

PERFORMANCE:
MAX SPEED: 337 mph (539 kmh)
RANGE: 3930 miles (6288 km)
POWERPLANT: two Wright R-3350-26WS
OUTPUT: 6400 hp (4772 kW)

FIRST FLIGHT DATE:
May 17, 1945

ARMAMENT:
Six fixed and two turret-mounted 20-mm cannon and two Browning 0.50-in machine guns; up to 8000 lb (3629 kg) of bombs/rockets/depth charges in bomb bay and on underwing pylons

FEATURES:
Straight-wing layout; retractable landing gear; two close-cowled radial engines; wingtip tanks

Lockheed c-130/kc-130/ec-130 Hercules

97-seat, four-engined tactical transport aircraft

The Hercules was developed expressly to fulfill a 1951 USAF requirement for a new turboprop-engined tactical transport to equip squadrons within the Military Air Transport Service. The prototype yc-130 conducted its maiden flight on August 23, 1954, and the first of 204 a-models entered service with the USAF's Troop Carrier Command and Tactical Air Command units in December 1956. With 27 c-130as delivered, Lockheed changed the nose profile of the aircraft by fitting a radar into a new radome. The latter replaced the transport's original bluff nose shape, and all Hercules have featured radar noses ever since.

The improved c-130b (123 built for the USAF), with bigger engines driving four-bladed propellers, more fuel, and a strengthened undercarriage, entered service in mid-1959. In 1961 production switched to the c-130e (377 built for the USAF), which offered better performance, increased takeoff weight, and more fuel. Finally, in 1965, Lockheed commenced production of the definitive H-model, which was effectively an improved c-130e. The USAF received more than 400 H-models over a 35-year period, and the aircraft still form the backbone of Air Mobility Command's tactical transport fleet today. Numerous special missions variants of the c-130a-h have also been used by the USAF, ANG, and Reserve over the past four decades, conducting electronic warfare (ec-130), special forces insertion/extraction (mc-130), search and rescue (hc-130), gunship (ac-130), and weather (wc-130) missions.

The Navy, Marine Corps, and Coast Guard have all used examples of the

Hercules since 1960. The Marine Corps received its aircraft first, putting 43 KC-130F tanker/transports into service in 1960-61. A further 14 KC-130RS were ordered in the mid-1970s, followed by ten KC-130TS in 1983. The Navy initially bought seven C-130FS without refueling gear, followed by four ski-equipped C-130BLS for use in support of operations in the Antarctic—six more were purchased in the mid-1960s. A total of 22 EC-130G/QS were also acquired, these being fitted out for use as radio communication relay aircraft in support of worldwide Fleet Ballistics Missile submarine operations. Finally, the Coast Guard acquired no fewer than 42 HC-130B/HS for air/sea rescue patrols.

SPECIFICATION (C-130H):

ACCOMMODATION:
Pilot, copilot, navigator, flight engineer, loadmaster, and up to 92 passengers

DIMENSIONS:
LENGTH: 97 ft 9 in (29.79 m)
WINGSPAN: 132 ft 7 in (40.41 m)
HEIGHT: 38 ft 3 in (11.66 m)

WEIGHTS:
EMPTY: 76,470 lb (34,685 kg)
MAX T/O: 175,000 lb (79,380 kg)

PERFORMANCE:
MAX SPEED: 376 mph (602 kmh)
RANGE: 4918 miles (7870 km)
POWERPLANT: four Allison T56-A-15S
OUTPUT: 18,032 shp (13,448 kW)

FIRST FLIGHT DATE:
August 23, 1954

ARMAMENT:
Two M61 Vulcan 20-mm cannon, two 7.62-mm miniguns, two 40-mm Bofors cannon, and a 105-mm howitzer, all mounted on left side of fuselage (AC-130 variants only)

FEATURES:
Shoulder-mounted straight wing; retractable landing gear in fairings; four close-cowled turboprop engines

Lockheed Martin C-130J Hercules

95-seat, four-engined tactical transportation aircraft

The C-130J is the latest addition to the Hercules family, the aircraft being procured by the USAF as a replacement for its aging C-130ES. The J-model has also been bought by the Marine Corps in KC-130J configuration and by the Coast Guard, which used the HC-130J designation for its six aircraft. The most comprehensive update of the classic Hercules so far, the C-130J features a state-of-the-art cockpit with multifunction displays, new generation Allison/Rolls-Royce turboprop engines driving six-bladed propellers, and numerous systems improvements designed to reduce manpower requirements, lower operating and support costs, and provide life-cycle cost savings over earlier C-130s. In respect to performance, the J-model climbs faster and higher, flies farther at a higher cruise speed, and takes off and lands in a shorter distance than previous versions of the Hercules. The C-130J was developed as a private venture by Lockheed, with the prototype completing its maiden flight in April 1996 and the Air Force receiving its first example in January 1999.

SPECIFICATION:

ACCOMMODATION:
Pilot, copilot, loadmaster, and 92 passengers

DIMENSIONS:
LENGTH: 97 ft 9 in (29.79 m)
WINGSPAN: 132 ft 7 in (40.41 m)
HEIGHT: 38 ft 9 in (11.81 m)

WEIGHTS:
EMPTY: 75,562 lb (34,274 kg)
MAX T/O: 175,000 lb (79,379 kg)

PERFORMANCE:
MAX SPEED: 403 mph (645 kmh)
RANGE: 3279 miles (5247 km)
POWERPLANT: four Allison
AE 2100D3S
OUTPUT: 18,364 shp (14,772 kW)

FIRST FLIGHT DATE:
April 5, 1996

FEATURES:
Shoulder-mounted straight wing; retractable landing gear in fairings; four close-cowled turboprop engines; five-bladed propellers

Lockheed F-94 Starfire

two-seat, single-engined fighter

The ultimate development of the long-lived F-80/T-33 series, the F-94 Starfire was the best-known all-weather interceptor of the 1950s. Equipped with APG-33 radar in the nose and a Sperry Zero-reader flight director, the prototype YF-94 (a modified TF-80C) made its first flight on April 16, 1949. Driven by the threat of Soviet long-range bombers attacking North America under the cover of darkness, Lockheed completed the maiden flight of the first production F-94A just five months later. Equipping Air Defense Command units starting in December 1949, 110 F-94As and 357 F-94Bs served with 24 frontline squadrons in the USA and Alaska. Despite fears of a radar-equipped jet coming down over enemy territory, the jet made its combat debut over Korea in late 1952. The revised F-94C was effectively an all-new aircraft, featuring a bigger engine, thinner wing, redesigned fuselage with a longer rear section, stepped cockpits, and a swept tailplane. Some 387 C-models were built, and the last of 21 ANG fighter squadrons to be equipped with Starfires retired its F-94Cs in July 1959.

SPECIFICATION (F-94C):

ACCOMMODATION:
Pilot and radar observer in tandem

DIMENSIONS:
LENGTH: 44 ft 6 in (13.56 m)
WINGSPAN: 42 ft 5 in (12.93 m)
HEIGHT: 14 ft 11 in (4.55 m)

WEIGHTS:
EMPTY: 12,700 lb (5760 kg)
MAX T/O: 24,200 lb (10,980 kg)

PERFORMANCE:
MAX SPEED: 646 mph (1040 kmh)
RANGE: 1250 miles (2000 km)
POWERPLANT: Pratt & Whitney J48-P-5
OUTPUT: 8750 lb st (38 kN)

FIRST FLIGHT DATE:
April 16, 1949

ARMAMENT:
Four fixed Browning 0.50-in machine guns in nose (F-94A/B), or 24/48 2.75-in Mighty Mouse air-to-air rocket projectiles in nose and in wing pods (F-94C)

FEATURES:
Straight-wing layout; retractable landing gear; wingtip tanks; low lateral engine intakes; bubble canopy; swept tailplane (F-94C)

Lockheed C-141 Starlifter

210-seat, four-engined strategic transportation aircraft

The USAF's first purpose-designed jet transport, the C-141 gave the Air Force the ability to airlift large numbers of troops, and their equipment, to war zones across the globe in just a matter of hours. The C-141 was designed in response to the USAF's Specific Operational Requirement 182 for a turbofan-powered freighter for Military Airlift Command. Featuring the fuselage cross-section of the C-130, high-mounted wings with lifting devices for good short-field performance, and a rear-loading ramp, the first C-141A completed its maiden flight in December 1963. Entering service in 1965, 285 Starlifters were built as replacements for piston-engined C-97s and C-124s, as well as turbo-jet-engined C-135s. C-141s saw extensive service on the transpacific route supporting the war in Vietnam, and the USAF's experience with the Starlifter during the conflict resulted in the jet being "stretched" by 23 ft to produce the C-141B—271 aircraft were modified in 1977-82. The "glass-cockpit" C-141C (64 modified) entered service in 1998, and these were the last examples retired in May 2006.

SPECIFICATION (C-141B):

ACCOMMODATION:
Pilot, copilot, flight engineer, navigator, loadmaster, and up to 205 passengers

DIMENSIONS:
LENGTH: 168 ft 4 in (51.29 m)
WINGSPAN: 159 ft 11 in (48.74 m)
HEIGHT: 39 ft 3 in (11.96 m)

WEIGHTS:
EMPTY: 148,120 lb (67,185 kg)
MAX T/O: 343,000 lb (155,580 kg)

PERFORMANCE:
MAX SPEED: 569 mph (910 kmh)
RANGE: 6424 miles (10,279 km)
POWERPLANT: four Pratt & Whitney TF33-P-7s
OUTPUT: 84,000 lb st (374 kN)

FIRST FLIGHT DATE:
December 17, 1963

FEATURES:
Shoulder-mounted swept wing; retractable landing gear in fairings; four podded turbofan engines under wings; T-tail

Lockheed F-104 Starfighter

single-seat, single-engined fighter

Designed by Clarence L. "Kelly" Johnson, the XF-104 Starfighter compromised everything (primarily maneuverability, weapons carriage, and endurance) in search of superior flight performance. To achieve Mach 2.2, and an impressive initial rate of climb, the Starfighter combined the power of the afterburning J79 with a wing of minuscule span and razor-thin chord. With such features, the Starfighter was pushing the limits of available technology, which caused delays in the development of production aircraft. The first of 153 F-104As reached Air Defense Command (ADC) in 1958, followed by an additional 26 two-seat F-104Bs. The aircraft's poor range restricted its frontline use, and all Starfighters were retired by ADC in 1960. The tactically optimized c-model (77 built) and two-seat F-104D (21 built) were also procured in 1958-59, this variant featuring an inflight refueling probe and ground attack mission-optimized avionics and stores pylons. The 479th TFW took the Starfighter to war in 1965 when it briefly flew combat missions over South Vietnam. The ANG retired the last F-104s in service in 1975.

SPECIFICATION (F-104C):

ACCOMMODATION:
Pilot

DIMENSIONS:
LENGTH: 54 ft 9 in (16.69 m)
WINGSPAN: 21 ft 11 in (6.68 m)
HEIGHT: 13 ft 6 in (4.11 m)

WEIGHTS:
EMPTY: 13,277 lb (6022 kg)
MAX T/O: 23,590 lb (10,700 kg)

PERFORMANCE:
MAX SPEED: 1450 mph (2330 kmh)
RANGE: 850 miles (1360 km)
POWERPLANT: General Electric J79-GE-7
OUTPUT: 10,000 lb st (45 kN)

FIRST FLIGHT DATE:
February 7, 1954

ARMAMENT:
One fixed T171E5 20-mm Vulcan cannon in fuselage; up to 2000 lb (907 kg) of bombs/rockets/ missiles on six underwing and three underfuselage pylons, or two missiles on wingtip rails

FEATURES:
Small, unswept wings with anhedral; retractable landing gear; wingtip tanks; lateral engine intakes; bubble canopy; T-tail

Lockheed F-117 Nighthawk

single-seat, single-engined precision strike fighter

The end result of the USAF's Have Blue program launched in the mid-1970s, the F-117 was developed by Lockheed's legendary Advanced Development Company—better known as the "Skunk Works." The latter had been tasked by the Air Force to secretly design an attack aircraft that was difficult to detect with radar. Two XST (Experimental Stealth Technology) Have Blue prototypes were built, and the first of these flew in December 1977. Similar in appearance to the follow-on F-117, both XSTs were lost in crashes soon after they had been built. In November 1978 the green light was given to Lockheed by the USAF to construct the first of five full-scale development aircraft as part of the Senior Trend program. The prototype successfully flew for the first time on June 18, 1981, and the first of 59 production aircraft was delivered to the USAF in August 1982.

Issued to the newly formed, and top secret, 4450th Tactical Group at Tonopah, in Nevada, the unit achieved operational capability in October 1983. The group flew the jet exclusively at night for the first five years of its existence in order retain the veil of secrecy surrounding the F-117A. It also operated a fleet of A-7 Corsair IIs from Tonopah, ostensibly as part of an avionics test program, so as to legitimize the 4450th's existence. It was not until November 1988 that the F-117A was revealed to the world by the Department of Defense. The last Nighthawk was delivered to the USAF in mid-1990, and six months later the jet saw combat with the 49th TFG over Baghdad as the group led the opening strikes of Operation Desert Storm. The aircraft's faceted airframe construction, radar absorbent material, and platypus exhausts, combined with stealthy flight profiles, rendered the F-117 near invisible to enemy radar throughout the campaign.

Used in combat since then in the Balkans in 1999 (where one was shot down by a Serbian SAM) and again over Iraq in 2003, the Nighthawk is slated for retirement by the USAF in 2008.

SPECIFICATION:

ACCOMMODATION:
Pilot

DIMENSIONS:
LENGTH: 65 ft 11 in (20.08 m)
WINGSPAN: 43 ft 4 in (13.20 m)
HEIGHT: 12 ft 5 in (3.78 m)

WEIGHTS:
EMPTY: 29,500 lb (13,380 kg)
MAX T/O: 52,500 lb (23,815 kg)

PERFORMANCE:
MAX SPEED: 650 mph (1040 kmh)
RANGE: 659 miles (1055 km)
POWERPLANT: two General Electric F404-GE-F1D2S
OUTPUT: 21,600 lb st (96 kN)

FIRST FLIGHT DATE:
June 18, 1981

ARMAMENT:
Up to 4000 lb (1814 kg) of bombs/missiles in internal weapons bay

FEATURES:
Sharply swept wings; faceted airframe construction; platypus exhaust; all-black radar absorbent material coating overall; outward-canted tailplanes

Lockheed P-3 Orion

ten-seat, four-engined maritime patrol and antisubmarine warfare aircraft

The Navy began its search for a Neptune replacement in August 1957, when it called for design proposals for a new high-performance antisubmarine warfare (ASW) aircraft. In order to speed up the acquisition process, and save money, the Navy suggested to manufacturers that they should consider modifying an existing type to meet its requirement. Lockheed duly adapted its Electra turboprop airliner, retaining its wings, tail unit, powerplant, most of the fuselage, and numerous other major components. Designated the Model 185, the aircraft's fuselage was shorter than the Electra's by seven feet, had a weapons bay built in, and was filled with ASW-related avionics. It also boasted a distinctive MAD tail "stinger." The Lockheed design won the contest, and the full prototype completed its maiden flight in November 1959.

The first of 157 P-3As entered Navy service in August 1962, this variant duly being followed by the improved B-model (124) in 1965. The B-model boasted uprated engines and the provision to carry the Bullpup missile. The final ASW version built was the P-3C, which made its frontline debut in 1969. Close to 300 of these were built for the Navy during a production run that lasted until 1990, these aircraft having been progressively improved over the intervening three decades to Upgrade III status.

The most effective maritime patrol and ASW platform in today's Navy, the Orion has recently become a crucial weapon in the Global War on Terror over landlocked Afghanistan and also Iraq. Capable of employing Maverick, Slam-Er, and Harpoon missiles with deadly accuracy thanks to the antisurface warfare improvement plan of 1998-99, the Orion's mix of weaponry, long loiter time on station, and sophisticated electronic detection/warfare suite have made it an invaluable asset. The Navy's P-3Cs are at present flown by 13 frontline and seven Reserve units. Specialist EP-3 Elint/Sigint platforms have also served the Navy well since the 1960s, as have the handful of VP/UP-3A VIP/troop transport and NP-3D test-bed/special mission aircraft. The veteran Orions look set to soldier on with the Navy until at least 2020.

SPECIFICATION:

ACCOMMODATION:
Pilot, copilot, navigator, flight engineer, tactical coordinator, three sensor operators, and two observers/sonobuoy loaders

DIMENSIONS:
LENGTH: 116 ft 10 in (35.61 m)
WINGSPAN: 99 ft 8 in (30.37 m)
HEIGHT: 33 ft 9 in (10.27 m)

WEIGHTS:
EMPTY: 61,491 lb (27,890 kg)
MAX T/O: 142,000 lb (64,410 kg)

PERFORMANCE:
MAX SPEED: 473 mph (761 kmh)
RANGE: 5591 miles (8945 km)
POWERPLANT: four Allison T56-A-14s
OUTPUT: 19,640 shp (14,640 kW)

FIRST FLIGHT DATE:
November 25, 1959

ARMAMENT:
Internal bomb bay and ten underwing pylons can carry up to 20,000 lb (9072 kg) of torpedoes/depth charges/mines/missiles

FEATURES:
Low tapered wing; four wing-mounted turboprop engines, tail MAD boom

Lockheed C-5 Galaxy

355-seat, four-engined heavylift strategic transportation aircraft

The world's largest aircraft for more than a decade, the C-5 Galaxy was created by Lockheed following the USAF's issuing of its Cargo Experimental Heavy Logistics System requirement which stipulated that the aircraft had to be capable of airlifting payloads of 250,000 lb over 3019 miles without flight refueling. Powered by newly designed engines from General Electric, the prototype C-5 made its first flight in June 1968 and production aircraft entered service in December 1969. A total of 81 C-5As were built between 1969-73, and 77 were rewinged in the 1980s due to structural problems. An additional 50 C-5Bs (with simplified landing gear and better flight controls) were delivered in 1986-89. A heavily utilized asset, the 111-strong Galaxy fleet has suffered from increasing engine and avionics reliability issues in recent years. In order to prolong the C-5's life, the USAF launched the Avionics Modernization and Re-Engine and Reliability programs in 2005. Reworked aircraft will be redesignated C-5Ms once upgraded.

SPECIFICATION (C-5B):

ACCOMMODATION:
Pilot, copilot, flight engineer, two loadmasters, and 350 passengers

DIMENSIONS:
LENGTH: 247 ft 10 in (75.54 m)
WINGSPAN: 222 ft 9 in (67.88 m)
HEIGHT: 65 ft 2 in (19.85 m)

WEIGHTS:
EMPTY: 374,000 lb (169,643 kg)
MAX T/O: 837,000 lb (379,655 kg)

PERFORMANCE:
MAX SPEED: 575 mph (920 kmh)
RANGE: 6506 miles (10,410 km)
POWERPLANT: four General Electric TF39-GE-1CS
OUTPUT: 172,000 lb st (765 kN)

FIRST FLIGHT DATE:
December 17, 1963

FEATURES:
Shoulder-mounted swept wing; retractable landing gear in fairings; four podded turbofan engines under wings; T-tail; upward-lifting nose freight door

Lockheed U-2/TR-1

single-seat, single-engined reconnaissance aircraft

The U-2 was designed by Lockheed's secretive "Skunk Works" department in response to a request by the US government for a purpose-built reconnaissance aircraft that would hopefully be immune from interception by communist fighters. It would achieve its immunity by flying at extremely high altitudes (90,000 ft). The "black" nature of the program resulted in the aircraft's U-2 designation (U for utility, rather than R for reconnaissance). Resembling a powered glider, the first prototype completed its maiden flight in complete secrecy on August 1, 1955, and production U-2As were delivered to remote Watertown Strip, in Nevada, where Central Intelligence Agency (CIA) pilots converted onto them and prepared to fly missions over communist countries. Others were issued to the USAF, Lockheed building a total of 48 U-2A/B/Cs and five two-seat DS. Flown extensively throughout the 1950s and 60s, additional, larger, U-2Rs (12 built from 1967) were followed by 37 TR-1s in 1979. These were redesignated U-2Rs in the 1980s, and the survivors remain in service with the USAF and NASA.

SPECIFICATION (U-2R):

ACCOMMODATION:
Pilot

DIMENSIONS:
LENGTH: 62 ft 9 in (19.13 m)
WINGSPAN: 103 ft 0 in (31.39 m)
HEIGHT: 16 ft 0 in (4.88 m)

WEIGHTS:
EMPTY: 10,000 lb (4355 kg)
MAX T/O: 41,300 lb (18,735 kg)

PERFORMANCE:
MAX SPEED: 431 mph (690 kmh)
RANGE: 3019 miles (4830 km)
POWERPLANT: Pratt & Whitney J75-P-13B
OUTPUT: 17,000 lb st (76 kN)

FIRST FLIGHT DATE:
August 1, 1955

FEATURES:
Shoulder-tapered, unswept, long-span wings; retractable landing gear on fuselage centerline; wing pods on some aircraft; engine air intakes on fuselage sides aft of cockpit; long nose

Lockheed C-140 JetStar

12-seat, four-engined VIP transportation aircraft

The Lockheed Model 1329 light jet transport was built to participate in a competition being staged by the USAF to find a general Utility Transport Category airplane. The twin-engined JetStar flew in prototype form for the first time on September 4, 1957, only 241 days after design completion. The aircraft was beaten in the competition by the rival North American Saberliner, but all was not lost for Lockheed as the Kennedy White House chose the re-engined JetStar (fitted with four JT12A-6s) as a Presidential/VIP transport to augment the first Boeing VC-135s then being used as Air Force One aircraft. Designated C-140A/BS, the USAF bought 16 JetStars, the first of which was delivered in late 1961. Five C-140AS were assigned to Air Force Communications Command for use in evaluating military navigation aids and operations, and the remaining eleven C-140BS were issued to Miltary Airlift Command for operational support airlift. Six of the latter jets were flown as VC-140BS on special government and White House airlift missions. All were retired by the early 1990s.

SPECIFICATION:

ACCOMMODATION:
Pilot, copilot, and ten passengers

DIMENSIONS:
LENGTH: 60 ft 5 in (18.42 m)
WINGSPAN: 53 ft 8 in (16.37 m)
HEIGHT: 20 ft 5 in (6.23 m)

WEIGHTS:
EMPTY: 18,450 lb (8376 kg)
MAX T/O: 38,940 lb (17,678 kg)

PERFORMANCE:
MAX SPEED: 575 mph (920 kmh)
RANGE: 2865 miles (4585 km)
POWERPLANT: four Pratt & Whitney JT12A-6s
OUTPUT: 13,200 lb st (59 kN)

FIRST FLIGHT DATE:
September 4, 1957

FEATURES:
Low-mounted swept wings; midwing external fuel tanks; four podded engines attached to rear fuselage

Lockheed SR-71

two-seat, twin-engined reconnaissance aircraft

The ultimate high-speed manned reconnaissance aircraft, the SR-71 was unique in being able to cruise at a sustained Mach 3. The jet evolved from the CIA-sponsored A-12 program, which was created in secrecy by Lockheed's "Skunk Works" under the direction of Clarence L. "Kelly" Johnson. Eighteen A-12s were built in the early 1960s, and following flight testing, the USAF committed to the creation of the larger SR-71. The first of 31 A-models (including three SR-71B trainers) flew on December 22, 1964, and these served exclusively with the 9th Strategic Reconnaissance Wing at Beale AFB, California—detachments were also maintained at Mildenhall, in Suffolk, and Kadena, on Okinawa. Involved in numerous Cold War missions across the USSR, Eastern Europe, China, North Africa, and the Middle East, the SR-71 was eventually retired in 1990 due to budgetary constraints. NASA continued to operate several jets for research purposes, and in 1995 two were briefly brought back into USAF service to plug a gap in US reconnaissance capabilities. They were permanently retired once again in 1996, however.

SPECIFICATION:

ACCOMMODATION:
Pilot and reconnaissance systems operator

DIMENSIONS:
LENGTH: 107 ft 5 in (37.74 m)
WINGSPAN: 55 ft 7 in (16.95 m)
HEIGHT: 18 ft 6 in (5.64 m)

WEIGHTS:
EMPTY: 60,000 lb (27,215 kg)
MAX T/O: 170,000 lb (77,110 kg)

PERFORMANCE:
MAX SPEED: 2012 mph (3220 kmh)
RANGE: 3018 miles (4830 km)
POWERPLANT: two Pratt & Whitney J58-1s
OUTPUT: 65,000 lb st (291 kN)

FIRST FLIGHT DATE:
December 22, 1964

FEATURES:
Low-mounted delta-shaped wings; engines built into wings; angular fuselage; inward-canted twin fins

Lockheed S-3 Viking

four-seat, twin-engined maritime patrol, antisubmarine warfare and aerial tanking aircraft

In 1967 the Navy issued a requirement for a replacement for the S-2. Five manufacturers submitted designs, and in 1969 the YS-3A Viking from the Lockheed/Ling Temco Vought team was selected as the winner. The first of eight service-evaluation aircraft made its maiden flight on January 21, 1972. Powered by two turbofan engines slung beneath a shoulder-mounted wing, the Viking featured a large internal weapons bay, seating for four crewmen and an extensive ASW suite. The S-3A entered fleet service in July 1974, and 187 examples were built. The upgraded S-3B variant was created in the mid-1980s, the aircraft featuring improved avionics and air-to-surface missile capability. All surviving S-3As were upgraded to this specification. Aside from four US-3A Carrier Onboard Delivery aircraft, the only other variant was the short-lived ES-3A EW aircraft, 16 of which were converted from S-3As in the 1990s—these were retired in 1999. Today, a handful of S-3Bs remain in service in the surface search and control and aerial tanking roles. All S-3s will be retired by 2008.

SPECIFICATION (S-3B):

ACCOMMODATION:
Pilot, copilot, tactical coordinator, and sensor operator

DIMENSIONS:
LENGTH: 49 ft 5 in (15.06 m)
WINGSPAN: 68 ft 8 in (20.93 m)
HEIGHT: 22 ft 9 in (6.93 m)

WEIGHTS:
EMPTY: 26,650 lb (12,088 kg)
MAX T/O: 52,540 lb (23,832 kg)

PERFORMANCE:
MAX SPEED: 521 mph (833 kmh)
RANGE: 3803 miles (6085 km)
POWERPLANT: two General Electric TF34-GE-400BS
OUTPUT: 18,550 lb st (83 kN)

FIRST FLIGHT DATE:
January 21, 1972

ARMAMENT:
Internal bomb bay and two underwing pylons can carry up to 7000 lb (3175 kg) of torpedoes/depth charges/bombs/mines/missiles

FEATURES:
Shoulder-mounted swept wings; two podded turbofan engines under wings; arrestor hook; tall folding tail

Lockheed YO-3A

six-seat, single-engined, monoplane observation aircraft

Contracted by the Army to build an ultraquiet light aircraft for use in Vietnam as a carrier of sensors for tracking Viet Cong guerrillas operating in South Vietnam, Lockheed's Missiles and Space Company commenced development on the project in July 1967. It initially rebuilt two Schweizer X-32A tandem-seat sailplanes into QT-2 aircraft, powered by silenced 100-hp engines and fitted with numerous night sensors. These were trialed in Vietnam in February 1968 as part of Project Prize Crew, and the aircraft proved to be generally undetectable down to heights as low as 100 ft. In 1969 Lockheed was contracted to build 11 larger YO-3AS, which featured a new low-wing airframe, a nose-mounted engine and retractable main landing gear. Nine were operated in South Vietnam in 1970-72 by the 1st Army Security Agency Company, and the aircraft flew with various engine/propeller combinations on a wide range of missions. Thanks to its large wingspan, the aircraft would often glide over enemy positions searching for Viet Cong with its side-looking airborne radar.

SPECIFICATION:

ACCOMMODATION:
Pilot and observer seated in tandem

DIMENSIONS:
LENGTH: 30 ft 0 in (9.14 m)
WINGSPAN: 57 ft 0 in (17.37 m)
HEIGHT: 9 ft 2 in (2.80 m)

WEIGHTS:
EMPTY: 3130 lb (1420 kg)
MAX T/O: 3800 lb (1724 kg)

PERFORMANCE:
MAX SPEED: 138 mph (179 kmh)
RANGE: 400 miles (640 km)
POWERPLANT: Continental IO-360D
OUTPUT: 210 hp (157 kW)

FIRST FLIGHT DATE:
1969

FEATURES:
Glider-type straight wing; retractable undercarriage; close-cowled piston engine; bubble canopy

Lockheed Martin F-35 Lightning II

single-seat, single-engined multirole fighter

The winning design in the US Joint Strike Fighter (JSF) program, the F-35 is scheduled to be built in three variants—conventional takeoff and landing F-35A for the USAF; short takeoff vertical landing F-35B for the Marine Corps; and carrier-based F-35C for the Navy. These variants are destined to replace the AV-8 Harrier II, A-10 Thunderbolt II, F/A-18 Hornet, and F-16 Fighting Falcon. Designed in conjunction with British Aerospace, Lockheed Martin commenced work on an X-35 prototype in November 1996. Completing its first flight on October 24, 2000, the X-35 subsequently beat Boeing's rival X-32 in a series of concept demonstration flights conducted over the next 12 months. Dogged by development problems since then centering on excessive weight, cost overruns, and technology transfer wrangling between the US manufacturer and its overseas partners, the F-35 is creeping toward service introduction. In fact, the USAF's first F-35A was rolled out in February 2006. The first A-models are scheduled to enter service in 2009.

SPECIFICATION (F-35A):

ACCOMMODATION:
Pilot

DIMENSIONS:
LENGTH: 50 ft 6 in (15.37 m)
WINGSPAN: 35 ft 0 in (10.65 m)
HEIGHT: 17 ft 4 in (5.28 m)

WEIGHTS:
EMPTY: 26,000 lb (12,000 kg)
MAX T/O: 42,000 lb (19,000 kg)

PERFORMANCE:
MAX SPEED: 1200 mph (2000 kmh)
RANGE: 620 miles (1000 km)
POWERPLANT: Pratt & Whitney F135
OUTPUT: 37,000 lb st (165 kN)

FIRST FLIGHT DATE:
October 24, 2000

ARMAMENT:
One fixed 25-mm GAU-12/U cannon in fuselage; up to 2000 lb (910 kg) of bombs/ missiles in internal weapons bay, and additional weaponry on four underwing and two wingtip pylons

FEATURES:
Shoulder-mounted swept wings; twin fins; intakes beneath leading edge root extensions; internal weapons carriage

Martin P4M Mercator

16-seat, twin-engined maritime patrol and electronic intelligence aircraft

Designed in the final months of World War II, the Mercator featured mixed piston engine and jet powerplants housed in unique combined nacelles. Jet propulsion gave the aircraft an impressive top speed of 411 mph, while the piston engines meant that the aircraft boasted an impressive 3000-mile range when the jets were not in use. The latter would only be used fleetingly during a typical patrol mission. The Allison centrifugal turbojets were installed in the large engine nacelles beneath two Pratt & Whitney Wasp Major radials. The prototype XP4M-1 made its first flight in September 1946, and the Navy ordered 19 production aircraft. These entered service with VP-21 in June 1950. Quickly replaced by Neptunes in the patrol bomber role, surplus Mercators were converted into P4M-1Q electronic intelligence (Elint) aircraft and issued to VQ-1 in the Pacific and VQ-2 in the Mediterranean. For ten years these aircraft flew dangerous Elint missions along the Chinese borders and over the USSR, and one aircraft was shot down in August 1956. All had been retired by May 1960.

SPECIFICATION:

ACCOMMODATION:
Pilot, copilot, navigator, engineer, two turret gunners, and ten mission specialists

DIMENSIONS:
LENGTH: 85 ft 3 in (25.98 m)
WINGSPAN: 114 ft 0 in (34.75 m)
HEIGHT: 29 ft 9 in (9.07 m)

WEIGHTS:
EMPTY: 43,420 lb (19,695 kg)
MAX T/O: 83,378 lb (37,820 kg)

PERFORMANCE:
MAX SPEED: 411 mph (661 kmh)
RANGE: 3100 miles (5000 km)
POWERPLANT: two Pratt & Whitney Wasp Major R-4360-20AS and two Allison J-33-10AS
OUTPUT: 6500 hp (4847 kW) and 9200 lb st (41 kN)

FIRST FLIGHT DATE:
September 20, 1946

ARMAMENT:
Four turret-mounted 20-mm cannon and four 0.50-in machine guns; up to 16,000 lb (7258 kg) of bombs/mines/depth charges in bomb bay

FEATURES:
Straight-wing layout; two close-cowled radial engines, with jet engines slung underneath

Lockheed Martin F-22 Raptor

single-seat, twin-engined air superiority fighter

The most advanced, and expensive, fighter currently fielded by any air force in the world, the Lockheed Martin F-22 Raptor finally entered USAF service in December 2005 following 15 years of testing and development. The winning design to emerge from the Air Force's Advanced Tactical Fighter (ATF) program (which was launched in October 1986 to find an F-15 replacement), the YF-22 beat off the rival Northrop McDonnell Douglas YF-23 in 1991. Lockheed teamed up with General Dynamics and Boeing during the design phase of the project, the prototype YF-22 making its maiden flight in September 1990. Built to defeat all current and projected manned fighter types in air-to-air combat, and thus achieve "air dominance," the F-22 endured a long and costly gestation that saw the airframe significantly redesigned and overall production numbers drastically cut as the aircraft failed to meet Air Force expectations.

The first of nine engineering and manufacturing development aircraft performed its maiden flight in September 1997, the new fighter having been officially named the Raptor several months prior to this. The USAF originally planned to buy 750 aircraft as part of the ATF program, but this figure has been drastically reduced over the past two decades, and it now appears that just 183 aircraft will be delivered at a cost of $338 million a piece. Although hugely expensive, the F-22A is truly a state-of-the-art fighter, boasting the most capable radar fitted in an aircraft of its size, Mach 1 capability without afterburner and a top speed in excess of Mach 2.42, internal weapons carriage, stealth capabilities, and unrivaled maneuverability thanks to thrust vectoring. The aircraft also possesses enormous development potential, particularly as a swing-mission strike aircraft. Indeed, the Raptor's designation was changed to F/A-22 in September 2002 by the Air Force in an attempt to highlight the jet's ground attack capabilities, and thus deflect criticism that it was receiving at the time about the aircraft's single mission status. The Raptor's designation reverted back to F-22A in December 2005 upon the jet's introduction into service with the 1st FW's 27th FS.

SPECIFICATION:

ACCOMMODATION:
Pilot

DIMENSIONS:
LENGTH: 62 ft 1 in (18.90 m)
WINGSPAN: 44 ft 6 in (13.56 m)
HEIGHT: 16 ft 8 in (5.08 m)

WEIGHTS:
EMPTY: 31,670 lb (14,365 kg)
MAX T/O: 80,000 lb (36,288 kg)

PERFORMANCE:
MAX SPEED: 1600 mph (2570 kmh)
RANGE: 2000 miles (3200 km)
POWERPLANT: two Pratt & Whitney F119-PW-100S
OUTPUT: 70,000 lb st (311 kN)

FIRST FLIGHT DATE:
September 29, 1990

ARMAMENT:
One fixed 20-mm M61A1 Vulcan cannon in wing root; up to 7000 lb (3174 kg) of bombs/ missiles in internal weapons bay and on four underwing pylons

FEATURES:
Shoulder-mounted swept wings; twin fins; intakes beneath leading edge root extensions; internal weapons carriage

Martin JRM Mars

186-seat, four-engined long-range maritime transportation flying boat

The original Mars was ordered on August 23, 1938 by the Navy as a flying-boat patrol bomber. However, progress was slowed by war priorities, and the first XPB2M-1 did not fly until July 1942. By that time the aircraft's long-range patrol mission was being performed by navalized Liberators (PB4YS) and the PBY Catalina, forcing Martin to convert the huge flying boat into a troop transport. Redesignated the JRM-1, 20 Mars were ordered by the Navy in January 1945, but only five were built before VJ-Day, followed by a sixth JRM-2 powered by uprated R4360 Wasp Major engines. The earlier aircraft were also subsequently re-engined, and all six machines given the designation JRM-3. Production JRMs differed from the XPB2M by having a longer nose and a single tailfin in place of the traditional Martin endplate-type fins and rudders. The aircraft were issued to Navy Air Transport Service unit VR-2, and the four survivors (one was lost in an accident in 1945 and another in a fire in 1950) were declared obsolete in 1956.

SPECIFICATION (JRM-2):

ACCOMMODATION:
Pilot, copilot, flight engineer, radio operator, navigator, crew chief, and 180 passengers

DIMENSIONS:
LENGTH: 120 ft 3 in (36.66 m)
WINGSPAN: 200 ft 0 in (60.96 m)
HEIGHT: 47 ft 11 in (14.35 m)

WEIGHTS:
EMPTY: 77,920 lb (35,344 kg)
MAX T/O: 165,000 lb (74,844 kg)

PERFORMANCE:
MAX SPEED: 220 mph (352 kmh)
RANGE: 3315 miles (5304 km)
POWERPLANT: four Pratt & Whitney R4360 Wasp Majors
OUTPUT: 14,000 hp (10,439 kW)

FIRST FLIGHT DATE:
July 21, 1945 (JRM-1)

FEATURES:
High-wing monoplane; boat-shaped hull; four radial engines; large single tailfin/rudder; fixed outrigger floats

Martin P5M/P-5 Marlin

11-seat, twin-engined maritime patrol flying boat

A postwar evolution of Martin's PBM Mariner, the Marlin proved to be the Navy's last operational flying boat. Indeed, Martin made use of the Mariner's distinctive gull wing and upper fuselage, combined with a new lower hull, when it built the prototype XP5M-1. The latter flew on May 30, 1948, and featured Wright R-3350 engines with twice the horsepower of the Mariner's R-2600s. The Marlin also had radar-operated nose/tail turrets, as well as a power-operated dorsal turret. By the time production commenced in 1951, the Marlin had had its nose turret replaced by an APS-80 search radar, the dorsal turret had been removed, and the flight deck raised for better visibility. The first of 114 P5M-1s reached the frontline on April 23, 1952. The following year Martin redesigned the Marlin in P5M-2 form, the aircraft featuring a T-tail, lower bow chine, and more powerful engines. By the time production of the aircraft ended in 1960, 145 had been built. Redesignated the P-5B in 1962, the Marlin remained in frontline service until 1966.

SPECIFICATION (P-5B):

ACCOMMODATION:
Pilot, copilot, flight engineer, radio operator, navigator, crew chief, three sensor operators, two observers/sonobuoy loaders

DIMENSIONS:
LENGTH: 100 ft 7 in (30.66 m)
WINGSPAN: 118 ft 2 in (36.02 m)
HEIGHT: 32 ft 8.50 in (9.97 m)

WEIGHTS:
EMPTY: 50,485 lb (22,900 kg)
MAX T/O: 85,000 lb (38,555 kg)

PERFORMANCE:
MAX SPEED: 251 mph (404 kmh)
RANGE: 2050 miles (3300 km)
POWERPLANT: two Wright R-3350-32WS
OUTPUT: 7400 hp (5518 kW)

FIRST FLIGHT DATE:
May 30, 1948

ARMAMENT:
Internal bomb bay and two underwing stores pylons capable of carrying up to 8000 lb (3629 kg) of bombs/torpedoes/depth charges/mines/rockets

FEATURES:
High-wing monoplane; boat-shaped hull; two radial engines; large single tailfin (P5M-1), or T-tail (P5M-2/P-5B)

Martin AM Mauler

single-seat, single-engined attack aircraft

Built as a rival to the far more successful AD Skyraider, the Mauler was designed as a single type capable of performing both scout/dive- and torpedo-bombing missions. Crewed by just a pilot, rather than the two/three-man crews of previous designs, the Martin XBTM-1 was ordered in prototype form by the Navy on May 31, 1944 and flown for the first time on August 26, that same year. Flight trials proved successful, and 750 BTM-1s (redesignated AM-1s prior to entering service) were ordered on January 15, 1945. The first production aircraft completed its maiden flight on December 16, 1946, but problems in testing and carrier qualification of the aircraft meant it did not attain service entry (with VA-17A) until March 1948. By late 1949 several other units were flying Maulers, but production was ended in October of that year following the delivery of 151 aircraft. The Navy had decided to standardize its fleet squadrons on the far superior AD Skyraider, and the Maulers were relegated to Reserve units. Disliked by those that flew it, all AM-1s were retired in the early 1950s.

SPECIFICATION:

ACCOMMODATION:
Pilot

DIMENSIONS:
LENGTH: 41 ft 2 in (12.55 m)
WINGSPAN: 50 ft 0 in (15.20 m)
HEIGHT: 16 ft 10 in (5.10 m)

WEIGHTS:
EMPTY: 14,500 lb (6575 kg)
MAX T/O: 23,386 lb (10,605 kg)

PERFORMANCE:
MAX SPEED: 367 mph (590 kmh)
RANGE: 1800 miles (2898 km)
POWERPLANT: Pratt & Whitney
R-3350-4
OUTPUT: 2975 hp (2218 kW)

FIRST FLIGHT DATE:
August 26, 1944

ARMAMENT:
Four 20-mm cannon in outer wings; provision for up to 4500 lb (2041 kg) of ordnance on 14 underwing and one center fuselage stores pylons

FEATURES:
Straight-wing layout; close-cowled radial engine; retractable undercarriage; bubble canopy; arrestor hook

Martin B-57 Canberra

two-seat, twin-engined reconnaissance bomber

When the USAF selected the English Electric Canberra to serve as a tactical attack bomber in the late 1940s, it was the first time a foreign combat aircraft had been chosen for frontline service with the US military in large numbers since 1918. Martin was given the contract to manufacture the British jet under license, and the moderately Americanized B-57A entered service in late July 1953. The bulk of the 75 A-models were being re-rolled as RB-57 photoreconnaissance platforms as soon as they entered service. Martin heavily modified the follow-on B-57B in order to make it a more adaptable attack aircraft. Featuring a fighter-style canopy, the aircraft had additional underwing pylons, a rotary bomb-bay door, and improved avionics. A total of 202 B-57Bs were built, followed by 38 B-57C trainers, 20 RB-57D high-altitude reconnaissance platforms, and 68 B-57E target tugs. Seeing extensive combat in Vietnam, the final modified B-57G precision bombers were retired in 1974, but specialist electronic warfare, weather reconnaissance, and target tug variants served on with the ANG until 1982.

SPECIFICATION (B-57B):

ACCOMMODATION:
Pilot and navigator

DIMENSIONS:
LENGTH: 65 ft 6 in (19.96 m)
WINGSPAN: 64 ft 0 in (19.50 m)
HEIGHT: 15 ft 7 in (4.75 m)

WEIGHTS:
EMPTY: 26,800 lb (12,200 kg)
MAX T/O: 55,000 lb (24,950 kg)

PERFORMANCE:
MAX SPEED: 582 mph (937 kmh)
RANGE: 2100 miles (3380 km)
POWERPLANT: two Wright J65-5s
OUTPUT: 14,440 lb st (33 kN)

FIRST FLIGHT DATE:
July 20, 1953

ARMAMENT:
Provision for four 20-mm cannon or eight 0.50-in machine guns in outer wings; bomb bay load of 5000 lb (2268 kg), plus rockets/ bombs on eight underwing and two wingtip stores pylons

FEATURES:
Straight-wing; tricycle landing gear; two midwing mounted engines; fighter-type bubble canopy

McDonnell FD/FH Phantom

single-seat, twin-engined fighter

In August 1943 the McDonnell Aircraft Corporation was asked by the Navy to develop a new carrier-based fighter that would be powered by jet engines then under development by Westinghouse. McDonnell was a newcomer to aviation, having been founded in 1939. It had yet to produce aircraft in quantity, and it was for this very reason that the Navy chose it to work on the first jet-powered naval fighter—all major manufacturers were busily churning out aircraft for the war effort. Having toyed with the idea of fitting six jet engines in each wing, McDonnell settled on two Westinghouse 19 XB-2BS instead. The first prototype XFD-1 made its maiden flight on January 26, 1945, and on July 19, 1946 the second prototype conducted operations from a carrier for the first time. Production aircraft reached VF-17A in July 1947 (the FD-1 being redesignated the FH-1 at this time), and Marine Corps squadron VMF-122 also received Phantoms. Just 60 FH-1s were eventually built, and although phased out of frontline service in July 1950, they served with seven Reserve units for a further three years.

SPECIFICATION:

ACCOMMODATION:
Pilot

DIMENSIONS:
LENGTH: 38 ft 9 in (11.85 m)
WINGSPAN: 40 ft 9 in (12.42 m)
HEIGHT: 14 ft 2 in (4.32 m)

WEIGHTS:
EMPTY: 6683 lb (3031 kg)
MAX T/O: 12,035 lb (5459 kg)

PERFORMANCE:
MAX SPEED: 479 mph (766 kmh)
RANGE: 980 miles (1580 km)
POWERPLANT: two Westinghouse J30-WE-20S
OUTPUT: 3200 lb st (15 kN)

FIRST FLIGHT DATE:
January 26, 1945

ARMAMENT:
Four 0.50-in Browning machine guns in nose

FEATURES:
Straight wing; tricycle landing gear; engines housed within wing roots; fighter-type bubble canopy

McDonnell F2H/F-2 Banshee

single-seat, twin-engined fighter

Derived from the McDonnell's pioneering FD-1 Phantom jet fighter, the Banshee retained the former's unswept wing and two Westinghouse axial engines housed within fattened wing roots. The Phantom had been the world's first operational naval jet fighter to operate from an aircraft carrier, although its service life had been restricted by a limited production run of just 60 jets due to the modest power produced by its J30 engines. The J34 cured these problems, and the Navy ordered 56 F2H-1s following the successful testing of the prototype XF2D-1 in 1947. The first examples reached the fleet in March 1949, by which time McDonnell had commenced development of the improved F2H-2, with its longer fuselage for extra fuel and 200-gallon wingtip tanks. Some 188 were built, followed by 146 F2H–2N/2P nightfighters and photoreconnaissance aircraft. Seeing action in the Korean War with both the Navy and Marine Corps, the Banshee remained in naval service into the late 1950s. The final frontline variants were the radar-equipped F2H-3 (250 built) and re-engined F2H-4 (150 built).

SPECIFICATION (F2H-3):

ACCOMMODATION:
Pilot

DIMENSIONS:
LENGTH: 47 ft 6 in (14.48 m)
WINGSPAN: 44 ft 10 in (13.67 m)
HEIGHT: 14 ft 6 in (4.40 m)

WEIGHTS:
EMPTY: 12,790 lb (5800 kg)
MAX T/O: 22,312 lb (10,270 kg)

PERFORMANCE:
MAX SPEED: 610 mph (982 kmh)
RANGE: 2000 miles (3220 km)
POWERPLANT: two Westinghouse J34-WE-34S
OUTPUT: 6500 lb st (30 kN)

FIRST FLIGHT DATE:
January 11, 1947

ARMAMENT:
Four M-2 20-mm cannon in nose; up to 4000 lb (1814 kg) of bombs/rockets/missiles on eight underwing pylons

FEATURES:
Straight, folding wing; tricycle landing gear; engines housed within wing roots; fighter-type bubble canopy; arrestor hook; wingtip tanks

McDonnell F3H/F-3 Demon

single-seat, single-engined fighter

Designed as the first naval jet aircraft to be equal in performance to the fastest land-based fighters, the Demon promised to be the most advanced machine of its generation. However, in reality, the aircraft was badly let down by its original engine, the unreliable Westinghouse J40. The F3H had been designed around the J40, and the prototype XF3H-1 flew with the XJ40-WE-6 engine in place on August 7, 1951. By the time production aircraft were being built, the fighter's weight had increased to the point where the more powerful J40-WE-24 was needed, but this proved unreliable, and the underpowered J40-WE-22 was used instead. The Navy responded by cutting its order from 529 F3H-1s to 56, and these were issued to training units only. McDonnell reworked the jet to allow the Allison J71 to be fitted, and the first of 459 F3H-2s entered fleet service in 1956. This variant could carry both the AIM-7C and AIM-9C air-to-air guided missiles, and featured an APG-51 radar. Redesignated the F-3B in 1962, the Demon remained in frontline service until 1965.

SPECIFICATION (F3H-2):

ACCOMMODATION:
Pilot

DIMENSIONS:
LENGTH: 58 ft 11 in (17.95 m)
WINGSPAN: 35 ft 4 in (10.76 m)
HEIGHT: 14 ft 7 in (4.45 m)

WEIGHTS:
EMPTY: 22,300 lb (10,115 kg)
MAX T/O: 33,900 lb (15,376 kg)

PERFORMANCE:
MAX SPEED: 647 mph (1040 kmh)
RANGE: 1370 miles (2200 km)
POWERPLANT: Allison J71-A-2E
OUTPUT: 14,250 lb st (33 kN)

FIRST FLIGHT DATE:
August 7, 1951

ARMAMENT:
Four M-2 20-mm cannon in nose; up to 6600 lb (2994 kg) of bombs/rockets/missiles on four underwing pylons

FEATURES:
Midmounted, swept wing; tricycle landing gear; engines housed within wing roots; fighter-type bubble canopy; arrestor hook; swept tail

McDonnell Douglas F-15E Strike Eagle

two-seat, twin-engined strike fighter

Although procured as an air superiority fighter, the F-15 was designed by McDonnell Douglas with the capability to field air-to-ground weapons. In July 1980 the Eagle's bombing potential was realized when the company's F-15E proposal was accepted by the USAF as a contender for its dual-role fighter requirement. In May 1984 the F-15E was chosen ahead of the F-16XL from General Dynamics, the prototype Strike Eagle making its first flight in December 1986. Built to replace the F-111 in USAF service, the F-15E featured an APG-70 radar, permanent conformal fuel tanks, improved F100 engines, and bolt-on Lockheed Martin targeting pods. The first examples reached the frontline in April 1988, and by mid-1994 204 F-15Es had been delivered. The aircraft made its combat debut over Iraq in Operation Desert Storm in 1991, and it has since seen combat in every conflict that the USAF has been committed to. An additional 17 F-15Es were acquired in 1999-2000, and the fleet of 200+ jets is presently split between seven frontline and two training squadrons.

SPECIFICATION:

ACCOMMODATION:
Pilot and weapon systems operator in tandem

DIMENSIONS:
LENGTH: 63 ft 9 in (19.43 m)
WINGSPAN: 42 ft 9.75 in (13.05 m)
HEIGHT: 18 ft 5.50 in (5.63 m)

WEIGHTS:
EMPTY: 31,700 lb (14,379 kg)
MAX T/O: 81,000 lb (36,741 kg)

PERFORMANCE:
MAX SPEED: 1659 mph (2654 kmh)
RANGE: 2778 miles (4445 km)
POWERPLANT: two Pratt & Whitney F100-PW-229S
OUTPUT: 58,300 lb st (258 kN)

FIRST FLIGHT DATE:
December 11, 1986

ARMAMENT:
One M61A1 20-mm cannon in right wing root; up to 24,500 lb (11,115 kg) of bombs/missiles on 16 wing/fuselage stores pylons

FEATURES:
Shoulder-mounted swept wing; fuselage air intakes below cockpit; fighter-type bubble canopy; twin fins; prominent nose radome; conformal fuel tanks on intake sides

McDonnell F/RF-101 Voodoo

single/two-seat, twin-engined fighter-bomber/reconnaissance aircraft

Easily the biggest and most powerful fighter of its day, the F-101 was developed from the XF-88 Voodoo prototype of 1948. A very promising design, with swept wings and cutting-edge technology, it was let down by its Westinghouse J34 engines. Once war had broken out in Korea in June 1950, the dormant XF-88 was resurrected once again as a long-range escort for Strategic Air Command's heavy bomber force. Fitted with all-new Pratt & Whitney J57 afterburning turbojets and an extra fuel cell, the resulting F-101A Voodoo was one of the heaviest single-seat fighters ever built. Although designed as an escort for B-47s and B-52s, the F-101A evolved into an attack aircraft for Tactical Air Command (TAC). The first A-model flew on September 29, 1954, and when SAC dropped its requirement for the Voodoo, all 77 A-models were issued to TAC starting in May 1957 onward.

The F-101A was followed by 47 near-identical C-models, which were capable of carrying a tactical nuclear weapon. The jet's impressive performance at medium to low altitude meant that the Voodoo was a prime candidate for the reconnaissance mission, and McDonnell duly built 35 RF-101As and 166 RF-101Cs between 1956-60. These aircraft had lengthened noses for downward or oblique cameras and other reconnaissance sensors. RF-101A/Cs saw combat with the USAF over Cuba and Vietnam, and in the latter conflict no fewer than 32 were lost in action. A number of surplus F-101A/Cs were converted into RF-101G/Hs in the mid-1960s for ANG use. The definitive Voodoo in terms of production quantities was the all-weather capable F-101B (and F-101F operational trainer), which sacrificed the fuel of the single-seat aircraft for a radar operator to work the MG-13 fire-control radar.

No fewer than 478 two-seat Voodoos were built for Air Defense Command (ADC), with deliveries beginning in March 1959. A total of 16 ADC squadrons defended North America with the F-101B in the 1960s, and some of these were issued to the ANG from 1969 following relegation from frontline service. The final F-101B/FS were retired in 1981.

SPECIFICATION (F-101B):

ACCOMMODATION:
Pilot, and pilot and radar operator (F-101B/F)

DIMENSIONS:
LENGTH: 67 ft 4.75 in (20.55 m)
WINGSPAN: 39 ft 8 in (12.09 m)
HEIGHT: 18 ft 0 in (5.49 m)

WEIGHTS:
EMPTY: 28,000 lb (12,700 kg)
MAX T/O: 51,000 lb (23,133 kg)

PERFORMANCE:
MAX SPEED: 1220 mph (1963 kmh)
RANGE: 1550 miles (2500 km)
POWERPLANT: two Pratt & Whitney J57-PW-53s
OUTPUT: 29,980 lb st (129 kN)

FIRST FLIGHT DATE:
September 29, 1954 (F-101A)

ARMAMENT:
Three M-39 20-mm cannon in fuselage (F-101A/C); up to 2000 lb (907 kg) of bombs/rockets/ missiles on four underwing/ underfuselage pylons, or in semi-recessed underfuselage troughs

FEATURES:
Low-mounted swept wing; tricycle landing gear; air intakes at wing roots; fighter-type bubble canopy; swept tail, with high-mounted tailplane

McDonnell Douglas F-4 Phantom II (Navy and Marine Corps)

two-seat, twin-engined fighter-bomber/reconnaissance aircraft

The F-4 Phantom II can trace its lineage back to October 1954, when the Navy sent a letter of intent to McDonnell, which had commenced work on a twin-engined attack fighter the previous year. Initially designed as an attack aircraft, its role changed to that of a long-range high-altitude fighter in 1955. Powered by two General Electric J79 engines, and featuring a two-crew cockpit, the prototype F4H-1 made its maiden flight in May 1958. By the end of the year the McDonnell design had been selected ahead of the Vought F8U-3 Crusader III as the new Navy fleet fighter. Further minor changes were made to the jet to make it more suitable for carrier operations, and deck trials were completed in February 1960. An initial batch of 24 F4H-1 trial aircraft was delivered in 1960-61, and these were redesignated F-4AS in 1962. By then the definitive F-4B had begun to enter service with fleet squadrons, the first example having flown on March 25, 1961. A total of 649 B-models (which equipped 29 frontline squadrons) would be built for the Navy and Marine Corps until production switched to the F-4J in 1966.

Based on the B-model, the photo-reconnaissance RF-4B was also produced during this period, its lengthened nose featuring cameras rather than a fire-control radar—46 were built exclusively for the Marine Corps.

The follow-on J-model (522 built up to January 1972) featured better bomb-delivery avionics, an improved radar, data link equipment, a more powerful version of the J79 engine, and bigger wheels. Like the B-model, the F-4J saw extensive service in Vietnam.

In January 1971 the Navy commenced an upgrade program for its F-4BS, some 228 airframes being fitted with more modern avionics and structural strengthening—they were redesignated F-4NS following rework. A similar upgrade was undertaken on 248 F-4JS in 1977-80, these aircraft being fitted with smokeless engines, improved radar, and leading edge slats. Redesignated F-4SS, these jets were the last Phantom IIS to be retired by the Navy in 1987 and the Marine Corps in 1990.

SPECIFICATION (F-4J):

ACCOMMODATION:
Pilot and radar intercept officer in tandem

DIMENSIONS:
LENGTH: 58 ft 3.75 in (17.79 m)
WINGSPAN: 38 ft 4.75 in (11.72 m)
HEIGHT: 16 ft 3 in (4.96 m)

WEIGHTS:
EMPTY: 30,770 lb (13,957 kg)
MAX T/O: 56,000 lb (25,401 kg)

PERFORMANCE:
MAX SPEED: 1415 mph (2264 kmh)
RANGE: 1900 miles (3040 km)
POWERPLANT: two General Electric J79-GE-10S
OUTPUT: 23,940 lb st (104 kN)

FIRST FLIGHT DATE:
May 27, 1958 (F4H-1)

ARMAMENT:
Up to 16,000 lb (7257 kg) of bombs/rockets/missiles on five underwing/fuselage pylons, or in four semirecessed under-fuselage troughs (missiles only)

FEATURES:
Low-mounted swept wing with dihedral on outer panels; fuselage air intakes below cockpit; fighter-type bubble canopy; swept tail and tailplane with anhedral

McDonnell Douglas F/RF-4/Phantom II (Air Force)

two-seat, twin-engined fighter-bomber/reconnaissance aircraft

The backbone of Tactical Air Command (TAC), the F-4 Phantom II first came to the attention of the USAF in 1961, just as early examples of the fighter were entering service with the Navy. Air Force trials showed that the jet was superior to any fighter then in the USAF inventory, so in March 1962 it was chosen for service with TAC. Bought to perform close air support, interdiction, and counter air, the Phantom II was barely modified for Air Force service. Indeed, the only significant changes incorporated into the F-4C centered on the fitment of a flying-boom refueling receptacle, dual controls for the crew, inertial navigation, and an improved weapon-aiming system.

The first of 583 F-4Cs reached the USAF in November 1963, by which time the prototype RF-4C reconnaissance Phantom II had also made its maiden flight. This aircraft was 33 inches longer than the standard C-model, and featured forward, oblique, and panoramic cameras in its nose. Production of 503 RF-4Cs commenced in May 1964 and continued through to December 1973.

The F-4C was replaced in production by the D-model in early 1966, this variant boasting systems that improved the jet's weapon accuracy in both air-to-air and air-to-ground missions. Following the construction of 793 F-4Ds, McDonnell Douglas incorporated lessons learned in combat over Vietnam into the E-model Phantom II, which was fitted with a 20-mm M61A1 cannon in the nose immediately beneath an AN/APQ-120 fire-control radar. A total of 831 F-4Es would be built between 1967 and 1976, and like the C/D-models before them, they saw action in Vietnam until the withdrawal of US troops in early

1973. The final Phantom II variant to enter USAF service was the F-4G "Wild Weasel," which was used to kill enemy radar and surface-to-air missile sites with specialized antiradar weapons—116 E-models were converted into F-4GS in 1975-79, and a small number of these aircraft helped defeat Iraqi radar sites in Operation Desert Storm in 1991. Relegated to ANG and Reserve service in the 1980s, the last USAF Phantom IIs were retired in 1996.

SPECIFICATION (F-4E):

ACCOMMODATION:
Pilot and weapon-systems officer in tandem

DIMENSIONS:
LENGTH: 63 ft 0 in (19.20 m)
WINGSPAN: 38 ft 8 in (11.77 m)
HEIGHT: 16 ft 6 in (5.02 m)

WEIGHTS:
EMPTY: 30,328 lb (13,757 kg)
MAX T/O: 61,795 lb (28,030 kg)

PERFORMANCE:
MAX SPEED: 1494 mph (2390 kmh)
RANGE: 1991 miles (3185 km)
POWERPLANT: two General Electric J79-GE-17AS
OUTPUT: 23,620 lb st (105 kN)

FIRST FLIGHT DATE:
May 27, 1958

ARMAMENT:
One M61A1 20-mm cannon in nose (F-4E only); up to 16,000 lb (7257 kg) of bombs/rockets/missiles on five underwing/fuselage pylons, or in four semirecessed underfuselage troughs (missiles only)

FEATURES:
Low-mounted swept wing with dihedral outer panels; fuselage air intakes below cockpit; fighter-type bubble canopy; swept tail, with anhedral tailplane; gun in nose

McDonnell Douglas F-15A-D Eagle

single/two-seat, twin-engined air superiority fighter

The world's pre-eminent air superiority fighter since its introduction into service in the mid-1970s, the F-15 was the end result of the USAF's F-X requirement launched ten years earlier to find a replacement for the F-4 Phantom II. Embodying lessons learned from air combat in Vietnam, the F-X called for an aircraft that had a thrust-to-weight ratio in excess of unity, and that was able to out-turn any opponent in order to bring its missiles to bear first. McDonnell Douglas' F-15 beat off rivals from Fairchild-Republic and North American Rockwell, and the prototype was first flown on July 27, 1972. Powered by purpose-built Pratt & Whitney F100 turbofans, and featuring the Hughes APG-63 radar, the Eagle was a compelling package.

The first production aircraft entered service with the 58th Tactical Fighter Training Wing at Luke AFB in November 1974, the unit being issued with early-build TF-15As (soon redesignated F-15Bs). A total of 57 two-seat F-15Bs would be acquired by the USAF, along with 355 single-seat F-15As. The first operational unit to be issued with A-model jets was the 1st TFW in January 1976—the wing finally swapped its Eagles for Raptors in early 2006. In June 1979 production switched to the F-15C/D, this aircraft initially differing from the A-model only through the addition of featuring moderately improved avionics and equipment, as well as the ability to carry conformal fuel tanks.

From February 1983 onward, C-model jets were subject to the Multi Stage Improvement Program, which saw the Hughes APG-70 radar installed and compatibility with new weapons such as the AIM-120 AMRAAM achieved—

A/B models were also upgraded in due course. Production of the F-15C/D ceased in 1992 following the construction of 622 jets. The previous year, USAF Eagle pilots had proven themselves in combat by shooting down 32 Iraqi aircraft without loss while protecting Coalition jets during Operation Desert Storm. Additional action was seen over Serbia in 1999, when more kills were achieved. Today, significant numbers of Eagles still serve with frontline units in the USA, Europe, and the Pacific, as well as the ANG.

SPECIFICATION (F-15C):

ACCOMMODATION:
Pilot, or two pilots in tandem (F-15B/D)

DIMENSIONS:
LENGTH: 63 ft 9 in (19.43 m)
WINGSPAN: 42 ft 9.75 in (13.05 m)
HEIGHT: 18 ft 5.50 in (5.63 m)

WEIGHTS:
EMPTY: 28,600 lb (12,973 kg)
MAX T/O: 68,000 lb (30,844 kg)

PERFORMANCE:
MAX SPEED: 1678 mph (2685 kmh)
RANGE: 1228 miles (1965 km)
POWERPLANT: two Pratt & Whitney F100-PW-220S
OUTPUT: 47,660 lb st (211 kN)

FIRST FLIGHT DATE:
July 27, 1972

ARMAMENT:
One M61A1 20-mm cannon in right wing root; up to 16,000 lb (7257 kg) of missiles in four semi-recessed underfuselage troughs and on three wing/fuselage stores pylons

FEATURES:
Shoulder-mounted swept wing; fuselage air intakes below cockpit; fighter-type bubble canopy; twin fins; prominent nose radome

McDonnell Douglas/BAe T-45 Goshawk

two-seat, single-engined advanced trainer

Winner of the Navy's VTXTS program to find a replacement for the TA-4J and T-2 trainers in November 1981, the BAe Hawk then spent many years being navalized by McDonnell Douglas to make the jet capable of withstanding carrier operations. Both its airframe and undercarriage were strengthened, the latter featuring twin-wheel nose gear that retracted into an enlarged forward fuselage. Side-mounted airbrakes were installed, as was an arrestor hook and ventral fin. Navy standard cockpit displays and radios were also fitted. Designated the T-45 Goshawk, the first full-scale development aircraft flew for the first time in April 1988, and deliveries were scheduled for 1989. However, stability problems and poor engine performance delayed this until January 1992. The first 82 jets were built as T-45As, while the remaining 86 were completed to T-45C standard. The latter featured the multifunction display-dominated "Cockpit 21" glass cockpit—all A-models will be upgraded to this standard. The T-45 is a key component in the Goshawk Training System.

SPECIFICATION:

ACCOMMODATION:
Two pilots in tandem

DIMENSIONS:
LENGTH: 39 ft 4 in (11.99 m)
WINGSPAN: 30 ft 10 in (9.40 m)
HEIGHT: 13 ft 6 in (4.11 m)

WEIGHTS:
EMPTY: 9394 lb (4261 kg)
MAX T/O: 13,500 lb (6123 kg)

PERFORMANCE:
MAX SPEED: 648 mph (1037 kmh)
RANGE: 810 miles (1296 km)
POWERPLANT: Rolls-Royce
F405-RR-401
OUTPUT: 5527 lb st (25 kN)

FIRST FLIGHT DATE:
April 1988 (T-451A)

FEATURES:
Low swept wing; tandem cockpit; air intakes either side of cockpit; arrestor hook; nose leg catapult strut

McDonnell Douglas C-9 Skytrain II/Nightingale

117-seat, twin-engined transportation and medical evacuation aircraft

In August 1967 the USAF selected the DC-9-30 version of McDonnell Douglas's successful civil twin-jet airliner to meet its requirement for an "off-the-shelf" aircraft capable of performing aeromedical evacuations. Designated the C-9A Nightingale, the first of 21 aircraft entered service with the 375th Aeromedical Airlift Wing in August 1968. Featuring a large forward freight door, therapeutic oxygen supply and an isolated care section, these aircraft gave sterling service to the USAF until finally retired in 2004. Three C-9Cs fitted out as VIP transports remain in daily use at Andrews AFB, however. The Navy and Marine Corps also chose the DC-9-30 for Operational Support Airlift, procuring 15 C-9B Skytrain IIs in 1973-74. Like the USAF's C-9AS, these aircraft featured a cargo door for palletized freight, while a follow-on buy of 12 DC-9-30s had no such freight-loading capability. Used as an intratheater logistics-support aircraft by Reserve units within the Fleet Logistics Support Wing, the Navy started to replace its C-9s with C-40 Clippers in 2001.

SPECIFICATION (C-9B):

ACCOMMODATION:
Pilot, copilot, and up to 115 passengers depending on configuration

DIMENSIONS:
LENGTH: 119 ft 3 in (36.35 m)
WINGSPAN: 93 ft 3 in (28.42 m)
HEIGHT: 27 ft 6 in (8.38 m)

WEIGHTS:
EMPTY: 59,706 lb (27,082 kg)
MAX T/O: 108,000 lb (48,988 kg)

PERFORMANCE:
MAX SPEED: 568 mph (909 kmh)
RANGE: 2937 miles (4700 km)
POWERPLANT: two Pratt & Whitney JT8D-9s
OUTPUT: 29,000 lb st (129 kN)

FIRST FLIGHT DATE:
February 25, 1965 (DC-9)

FEATURES:
Monoplane, swept-wing layout; two podded turbojets on either side of rear fuselage; T-tail

McDonnell Douglas F/A-18A-D Hornet

single/two-seat, twin-engined fighter-bomber

Following the cancelation of the Navy's VFAX lightweight multirole fighter program by US Congress in 1974, the latter recommended that the service should focus on a navalized General Dynamics YF-16 or Northrop YF-17, which had been built for the USAF-sponsored Lightweight Fighter project. Neither of these companies had any experience constructing naval aircraft, so McDonnell Douglas paired up with Northrop and Vought went into partnership with General Dynamics. Being twin-engined, the Northrop design had a clear advantage over the YF-16, because the Navy has always favored twin-engined combat aircraft when given the choice.

Selected to develop their YF-17 prototype into a frontline aircraft on May 2, 1975, Northrop and McDonnell Douglas were initially instructed to build separate F-18 fighter and A-18 attack jets. However, these designs were combined into a single airframe in an effort to cut costs, resulting in production of the F/A-18A Hornet. The first of 11 development jets made its maiden flight on November 18, 1978, this machine differing significantly from the lightweight YF-17. Bigger and heavier than the latter, the Hornet was powered by two F404 turbofans and featured a Hughes APG-65 radar. It had also been navalized, which meant that a strengthened undercarriage and arrestor hook had been fitted and a folding mechanism installed in the wings.

Production aircraft reached the Navy in May 1980, with the Marine Corps receiving its first Hornets two years later. A total of 371 A-models and 40 two-seat F/A-18Bs were delivered to the Navy/Marine Corps up to 1986, when production switched to the F/A-18C/D. The latter featured improved avionics, a new central computer, and greater weapons compatibility, and 464 had been built for the Navy/Marine Corps by the time production ended in 1999. Some 161 of these were two-seat D-models, including 96 Night Attack jets used in the Forward Air Controller (Airborne) mission by the Marine Corps. In 2002-03 200 F/A-18AS were upgraded to A+ specification with C-model avionics and returned to frontline service. Making its combat debut over Libya in 1986, the Hornet has seen considerable action from both carrier decks and shore bases with the Navy and the Marine Corps.

SPECIFICATION (F/A-18C):

ACCOMMODATION:
Pilot, or two pilots in tandem (F/A-18B/D)

DIMENSIONS:
LENGTH: 56 ft 0 in (17.07 m)
WINGSPAN: 37 ft 6 in (11.43 m)
HEIGHT: 15 ft 3.50 in (4.66 m)

WEIGHTS:
EMPTY: 29,619 lb (13,435 kg)
MAX T/O: 51,900 lb (23,541 kg)

PERFORMANCE:
MAX SPEED: 1197 mph (1915 kmh)
RANGE: 2084 miles (3335 km)
POWERPLANT: two General Electric F404-GE-402S
OUTPUT: 35,550 lb st (158 kN)

FIRST FLIGHT DATE:
June 9, 1974 (YF-17)

ARMAMENT:
One M61A1 20-mm cannon in nose; 17,000 lb (7711 kg) of bombs/rockets/missiles on four underwing, two wingtip (missiles), and one underfuselage stores pylons; two missiles in two semirecessed underfuselage troughs

FEATURES:
Shoulder-mounted swept wing; fighter-type bubble canopy; twin fins; long leading edge root extensions

McDonnell Douglas/BAe AV-8 Harrier I/II

single-seat, single-engined strike aircraft

The world's first practical vertical takeoff and landing fixed-wing aircraft, the Harrier was developed from the Hawker P 1127. The jet was powered by the Rolls-Royce Pegasus engine, which was able to vector thrust through 90° from the horizontal via its four pivoting exhaust nozzles. Six P 1127s were built to prove the concept, followed by nine preproduction Kestrel aircraft. Six of the latter were transferred to the USA for testing, and by the late 1960s the Kestrel had evolved into the Harrier strike aircraft. In 1969 the Marine Corps placed an order with Hawker Siddeley for 102 single-seat AV-8As and eight two-seat TAV-8As.

The Harrier's ability to operate from rudimentary landing sites and the decks of ships (not exclusively aircraft carriers) appealed to the Marine Corps, which needed a strike aircraft to support its beach-head assaults. The first AV-8As arrived in the USA in January 1971, and VMA-513 began workups with the jet four months later. Two more frontline squadrons (and a training unit) would swap their Phantom IIs for AV-8s in the next two years. Between 1979-84, 47 AV-8s were upgraded to AV-8C standard, these jets featuring better avionics and improved lift devices.

By the time these original Harriers had been retired in 1987, McDonnell Douglas and BAe had already started delivering AV-8B Harrier II replacements to the Marine Corps. Similar in configuration to the earlier AV-8A/C, this aircraft had an enlarged carbonfibre wing, a raised cockpit, lift improvement devices, an uprated Pegasus engine, and more weapons pylons. The first of four full-scale development AV-8Bs completed its maiden flight on November 5, 1981, and frontline aircraft began reaching the Marine Corps in January 1984. The two-seat TAV-8B trainer variant made its first flight in October 1986. A total of 280 AV-8Bs and 27 TAV-8Bs would eventually be acquired by the Marine Corps. The jet made its combat debut in Operation Desert Storm in 1991, and since then a considerable number of AV-8Bs have been reworked as night-attack Harrier IIs with nose-mounted FLIR or as APG-65 radar-equipped Harrier II(Plus) aircraft. The jet has been a key weapon in the Global War on Terror, seeing considerable action over Iraq and Afghanistan since 2003.

SPECIFICATION (AV-8B):

ACCOMMODATION:
Pilot

DIMENSIONS:
LENGTH: 46 ft 4 in (14.12 m)
WINGSPAN: 30 ft 4 in (9.25 m)
HEIGHT: 11 ft 8 in (3.55 m)

WEIGHTS:
EMPTY: 13,968 lb (6336 kg)
MAX T/O: 31,000 lb (14,060 kg)

PERFORMANCE:
MAX SPEED: 666 mph (1065 kmh)
RANGE: 2275 miles (3640 km)
POWERPLANT: Rolls-Royce F402-RR-408A
OUTPUT: 23,800 lb st (106 kN)

FIRST FLIGHT DATE:
October 21, 1960 (P 1127)

ARMAMENT:
One GAU-12/A 25-mm cannon in underfuselage pod; up to 13,235 lb (6003 kg) of rockets/ bombs/missiles split between seven underwing/fuselage stores pylons

FEATURES:
Shoulder-mounted swept wing layout; centerline main undercarriage with wingtip outriggers; large air intakes either side of cockpit; engine nozzles mounted on central fuselage

McDonnell Douglas κc-10 Extender

80-seat, three-engined strategic tanker/transportation aircraft

Based on the DC-10-30CF convertible freighter, the κc-10 Extender was selected by the USAF in December 1977 as the winning design in its Advanced Tanker/Cargo Aircraft (ATCA) competition. The ATCA program had been created so that the Air Force could purchase an "off-the-shelf" civil airliner capable of strategic transportation and air-to-air refueling. The first κc-10A flew on July 12, 1980 and a total of 60 Extenders were bought, the aircraft retaining 88 percent commonality with the civilian DC-10-30CF in terms of systems. It was, however, fitted with military avionics, satellite communications equipment, a McDonnell Douglas Advanced Aerial Refueling Boom, a hose-and-drogue refueling system, a boom operator's station, and its own inflight refueling receptacle. Twenty of the κc-10As also have hose-and-reel refueling units beneath their outer wings. Aside from their basic fuel tanks, each aircraft has additional fuel stored in seven bladder tanks fitted in the lower cargo hold. Freight and 75 passengers can also be carried in the main deck.

SPECIFICATION:

ACCOMMODATION:
Pilot, copilot, navigator, flight engineer, boom operator, and up to 75 passengers

DIMENSIONS:
LENGTH: 181 ft 7 in (55.35 m)
WINGSPAN: 155 ft 4 in (47.35 m)
HEIGHT: 58 ft 1 in (17.70 m)

WEIGHTS:
EMPTY: 240,065 lb (108,890 kg)
MAX T/O: 590,000 lb (267,620 kg)

PERFORMANCE:
MAX SPEED: 614 mph (982 kmh)
RANGE: 11,566 miles (18,505 km)
POWERPLANT: three General Electric F103-GE-100S
OUTPUT: 157,500 lb st (700 kN)

FIRST FLIGHT DATE:
August 29, 1970 (DC-10)

FEATURES:
Monoplane, swept-wing layout; two podded turbojets under each wing, with third engine built into tailfin; refueling boom beneath rear fuselage

North American AJ/A-2 Savage

three-seat, three-engined bomber/tanker

On August 13, 1945, just a week after the first atomic bomb was dropped on Hiroshima, the Navy initiated a design competition for a carrier-based attack aircraft that could deliver a 10,000-lb payload—the weight of the plutonium-based "Fat Man" Nagasaki bomb. North American's NA-146 design was selected as the winner of the comp-etition, and the Navy ordered it into production in June 1946. Equipped with two 2400-hp Pratt & Whitney R-2800 engines as well as a 4600-lb thrust Allison J33 auxiliary jet in the tail, the first AJ Savages were delivered three years later. With the completion of carrier suitability trials in 1950, the AJ-1 was introduced into service with the fleet as the largest (at the time) nuclear strike aircraft ever to fly from a carrier. In addition to the nuclear strike role, the Savage was also modified for use as a carrier-based flight-refueling tanker. Some 55 AJ-1S, 55 AJ-2S, and 30 AJ-2PS were built, and they were replaced by A3D Skywarriors in the late 1950s—the tanker variant (redesignated KA-2 in 1962) served on into the mid-1960s.

SPECIFICATION (AJ-1):

ACCOMMODATION:
Pilot, copilot, navigator/engineer

DIMENSIONS:
LENGTH: 63 ft 10 in (19.46 m)
WINGSPAN: 75 ft 2 in (22.90 m)
HEIGHT: 20 ft 5 in (6.23 m)

WEIGHTS:
EMPTY: 29,203 lb (13,246 kg)
MAX T/O: 52,862 lb (23,978 kg)

PERFORMANCE:
MAX SPEED: 472 mph (760 kmh)
RANGE: 2475 miles (3960 km)
POWERPLANT: two Pratt & Whitney R-2800-44W radials and one Allison J33-A-10 turbojet
OUTPUT: 4600 hp (3430 kW) and 4600 lb st (20.47 kN)

FIRST FLIGHT DATE:
July 3, 1948

ARMAMENT:
Up to 10,500 lb (4763 kg) of bombs in bomb bay and on underwing stores pylons

FEATURES:
Straight, shoulder-mounted wing layout; retractable landing gear; two close-cowled radial engines under wings, with turbojet in rear fuselage; wingtip tanks; arrestor hook; heavily glazed canopy

North American F/RF/86A-H Sabre

single-seat, single-engined fighter-bomber

Aside from the Bell UH-1 Huey, no other postwar Western combat aircraft has been built in as great a number as the F-86. Total production amounted to 9502 airframes covering no less than 13 separate land- and sea-based variants. The first contracts for the fighter were placed jointly by the USAAF and Navy in 1944, although the initial design featured unswept wings and a fuselage of greater diameter to allow it to house the Allison J35-2 engine. Following examination of captured German jet aircraft, and related documentation, North American radically altered the fighter's shape to produce the vastly superior XP-86. Featuring wings with a 35-degree sweep angle, a lengthened fuselage, pressurized cockpit, power-boosted ailerons, and automatic leading edge slots, the XP-86 made its maiden flight on October 1, 1947.

The Air Force ordered 221 P-86As (designation changed to F-86A in June 1948 – 554 eventually built) in December 1947, and these began reaching squadrons in February 1949. Several US-based wings had swapped their F-80s for F-86As by the time the Sabre was committed to combat in Korea in December 1950. Going head-to-head with the equally impressive Soviet-built MiG-15, the F-86 soon proved its superiority during numerous dogfights with the communist fighter. Combat duly ushered in further improvements to the aircraft, with the F-86E (393 built between 1950-52) featuring an all-flying tail to boost the jet's maneuverability at high speeds.

The definitive Korean War era Sabre was the F-86F (700 built between 1952-56), which was fitted with a revised profile "6-3" wing, which had its full span leading edge slabs removed and the bare leading edge extended by six inches at the root and three inches at the top to improve the jet's handling at high altitude. This variant also had a more powerful engine, and the ability to carry bombs. The final production variant of the Sabre built for the USAF was the F-86H (473 built in 1954-55), this aircraft embodying many new features including a J73 engine, increased wingspan, longer and deeper fuselage, larger tailplane, and four 20-mm cannon. All air superiority Sabres had been transferred from frontline units to the ANG by mid-1958, and the Guard retired its last examples (F-86HS) in 1970.

SPECIFICATION (F-86A):

ACCOMMODATION:
Pilot

DIMENSIONS:
LENGTH: 37 ft 6.50 in (11.44 m)
WINGSPAN: 37 ft 1.50 in (11.32 m)
HEIGHT: 14 ft 8 in (4.47 m)

WEIGHTS:
EMPTY: 10,093 lb (4578 kg)
MAX T/O: 16,223 lb (7359 kg)

PERFORMANCE:
MAX SPEED: 679 mph (1093 kmh)
RANGE: 660 miles (1060 km)
POWERPLANT: General Electric
J47-GE-13
OUTPUT: 5200 lb st (22 kN)

FIRST FLIGHT DATE:
October 1, 1947 (XP-86)

ARMAMENT:
Six Browning M-2 0.50-in machine guns in nose; maximum bomb/rocket load of 2000 lb (908 kg) on two underwing stores pylons

FEATURES:
Low-mounted swept-wing layout; tricycle landing gear; engine air intake in nose; fighter-type bubble canopy; swept tail; low-mounted tailplane

North American B-45 Tornado

four-seat, four-engined bomber/reconnaissance aircraft

At the end of 1944, the USAAF announced a design competition for a jet-powered bomber, and the end result was the B-45 Tornado—the Air Force's first effective jet bomber. Although in effect little more than a conventional medium bomber fitted with jet rather than piston engines, the Tornado proved to be a tough and reliable workhorse for the USAF. The first of 96 B-45As entered service between February 1948 and June 1949, and these were followed by ten B-45Cs and 33 RB-45Cs. The B-45 served as a reconnaissance aircraft during the Korean War, while several units were also based in Europe with USAFE into the 1950s. Although the bomber version never saw combat, the photoreconnaissance variant —assigned to Strategic Air Command—performed classified, deep penetration photographic intelligence missions over many Cold War communist countries from bases in Europe, Asia, and North America. In fact, the RB-45 was the forerunner of the U-2 and SR-71 surveillance aircraft. Surviving Tornadoes, some of which had been converted into target tugs, were retired in the late 1950s.

SPECIFICATION (B-45C):

ACCOMMODATION:
Pilot, copilot, bombardier/ navigator, and tail gunner

DIMENSIONS:
LENGTH: 75 ft 4 in (22.98 m)
WINGSPAN: 96 ft 0 in (29.26 m)
HEIGHT: 25 ft 2 in (7.68 m)

WEIGHTS:
EMPTY: 48,903 lb (22,182 kg)
MAX T/O: 112,952 lb (51,235 kg)

PERFORMANCE:
MAX SPEED: 580 mph (933 kmh)
RANGE: 1910 miles (3056 km)
POWERPLANT: four General Electric J45-GE-13s
OUTPUT: 20,800 lb st (93.25 kN)

FIRST FLIGHT DATE:
March 17, 1947

ARMAMENT:
Two Browning 0.50-in machine guns in tail turret; maximum bomb load of 22,000 lb (9979 kg) in bomb bay

FEATURES:
Shoulder-mounted straight wing; tricycle landing gear; engines mounted in pairs beneath wings; manned tail turret; glazed nose; tailplane with dihedral

North American F-82 Twin Mustang

two-seat, twin-engined monoplane fighter

Although often referred to simply as two P-51s joined by a single wing, the F-82 was a wholly new design that used the twin-boom configuration to achieve long range and good endurance. Created in 1943 as an escort fighter for long-range bombing missions in the Pacific War, the two-man P-82 (as then designated) would have a navigator who could also help fly the aircraft for brief periods in order to allow the pilot to rest during the course of eight-hour missions. When built, the XP-82 featured new fuselages (booms), which differed significantly from the P-51 they were based on. The prototype first flew on April 15, 1945, and only 20 P-52Bs had been built by war's end. Postwar, North American reconfigured the aircraft as a night-fighter, equipped with a search radar in a central pod. This proved highly successful, with 100 F-82E day escort fighters and 100 F-82F and 50 F-82G nightfighters being built. The F-82 saw brief action in the early weeks of the Korean War, prior to being retired in the mid-1950s.

SPECIFICATION (F-82G):

ACCOMMODATION:
Pilot and navigator

DIMENSIONS:
LENGTH: 42 ft 5 in (12.93 m)
WINGSPAN: 51 ft 3 in (11.28 m)
HEIGHT: 13 ft 10 in (4.22 m)

WEIGHTS:
EMPTY: 15,997 lb (7256 kg)
MAX T/O: 25,591 lb (11,608 kg)

PERFORMANCE:
MAX SPEED: 461 mph (742 kmh)
RANGE: 2240 miles (3605 km)
POWERPLANT: two Allison V-1710-143
OUTPUT: 3800 hp (2834 kW)

ARMAMENT:
Six Browning 0.50-in machine guns in wings; maximum bomb/rocket load of 4000 lb (1816 kg) on underwing stores pylons

FIRST FLIGHT DATE:
April 15, 1945

FEATURES:
Monoplane wing layout; rectractable landing gear; two close-cowled inline engines; twin fuselages ("booms"); central radar pod

North American F-86D/K/L Sabre Dog

single-seat, single-engined all-weather interceptor

Fitted with a distinctive radome above the engine intake, the gunless F-86D Sabre "Dogship" was developed by North American to provide the USAF with an all-weather interceptor for homeland defense. Using a standard F-86A airframe as a base, the manufacturer widened the fuselage and increased it in length to 40 ft 4 in. The fighter's J47 engine was fitted with an afterburner and the six 0.50-in guns deleted in favor of a retractable tray carrying 24 2.75-in unguided rockets. Finally, the forward fuselage was packed with avionics associated with the APG-36 search radar housed in the radome, and their poor reliability caused severe problems, which greatly delayed the jet's service entry. The prototype YF-86D made its first flight in December 1949, but Air Defense Command (ADC) did not receive examples until April 1953. A total of 2504 D-models were built, and 981 of these were upgraded to F-86L specification (with H-model wings and improved avionics) from 1956. All ADC "Dogships" had been passed on to the ANG by 1960, which retired its last F-86Ls five years later.

SPECIFICATION (F-86L):

ACCOMMODATION:
Pilot

DIMENSIONS:
LENGTH: 40 ft 4 in (12.31 m)
WINGSPAN: 39 ft 9.50 in (11.93 m)
HEIGHT: 16 ft 2.50 in (4.94 m)

WEIGHTS:
EMPTY: 13,822 lb (6270 kg)
MAX T/O: 20,276 lb (9197 kg)

PERFORMANCE:
MAX SPEED: 693 mph (1115 kmh)
RANGE: 550 miles (885 km)
POWERPLANT: General Electric J47-GE-33
OUTPUT: 7650 lb st (32 kN)

FIRST FLIGHT DATE:
December 22, 1949 (XP-86)

ARMAMENT:
24 2.75-in rockets in under-fuselage tray

FEATURES:
Low-mounted swept-wing layout; tricycle landing gear; engine air intake in nose; radar radome above intake; fighter-type bubble canopy; swept tail; tailplane without anhedral

North American T-39 Sabreliner

ten-seat, twin-engined crew trainer/VIP transport

The T-39 was developed by North American as a private venture to meet a USAF requirement announced in 1956 for an "off-the-shelf" utility and combat-readiness trainer. Although eight companies submitted proposals, the NA 246 Sabreliner was the only one to actually be flown in prototype form (starting on September 16, 1958 onward), and the USAF informed North American that it had won the competition. A total of 143 T-39As, six T-39Bs, and three T-39Fs were built for the USAF. The A-models were used as radar trainers for pilots destined to fly the F-105D, while the T-39Fs provided specialist F-105F "Wild Weasel" training. Others were used as staff transports. The Navy ordered 42 navalized T-39Ds in 1961, these serving as trainers for pilots and radar intercept officers chosen to fly fighters. A further 17 were bought in the late 1960s for fleet support missions, being designated CT-39E/GS. Finally, 17 ex-civilian T-39Ns were acquired by the Navy for advanced strike/radar training in 1991. Although the USAF retired the last of its Sabreliners in 2002, around 30 are still used by the Navy.

SPECIFICATION (T-39A):

ACCOMMODATION:
Pilot, copilot, and eight passengers

DIMENSIONS:
LENGTH: 43 ft 9 in (13.34 m)
WINGSPAN: 44 ft 5 in (13.53 m)
HEIGHT: 16 ft 0 in (4.88 m)

WEIGHTS:
EMPTY: 9895 lb (4488 kg)
MAX T/O: 18,340 lb (8319 kg)

PERFORMANCE:
MAX SPEED: 567 mph (907 kmh)
RANGE: 2199 miles (3519 km)
POWERPLANT: two Pratt & Whitney JT12A-8s
OUTPUT: 6600 lb st (29 kN)

FIRST FLIGHT DATE:
September 16, 1958

FEATURES:
Low-mounted swept wing; tricycle landing gear; twin podded engines attached to rear fuselage; triangular windows in fuselage

North American FJ/F-1 Fury

single-seat, single-engined fighter-bomber

Designed by North American in response to a joint Navy and Army Air Force request for a jet-powered fighter, the NA-134 (redesignated the FJ-1 Fury in Navy service) featured unswept wings and a fuselage of large diameter—the latter had to be able to house the General Electric J35 axial flow turbojet. The prototype XFJ-1 completed its first flight on November 27, 1946, and production examples began reaching the Navy in March 1948. By then the original order for 100 FJ-1s (placed in January 1945) had been slashed to 30, as more promising fighter types influenced by German wartime jet research began to take flight. Only VF-5A received FJ-1s, and it became the first jet fighter unit to serve at sea (aboard USS *Boxer*) in 1948. By late 1949 all surviving Furies had been passed on to the Reserve.

With the FJ-1 still some while away from reaching the fleet, North American radically altered the NA-134's shape and produced the XP-86. Entering service with the USAF less than a year after the FJ-1, the F-86A was a far superior machine in all respects. The Navy duly ordered a navalized F-86 as the FJ-2 in early 1951, and 200 were built in 1953-54 for Marine Corps use only. Effectively a navalized F-86, these aircraft featured folding wings, AN/APG-30 radar, an increased wheel track, and four 20-mm cannon.

The revised FJ-3 Fury followed in 1954, this aircraft being better suited to carrier operations than the FJ-2 thanks to its enlarged intake and more powerful J65-W-4 engine. A total of 538 were built up to August 1956, and these equipped 17 Navy and four Marine Corps units from September 1954.

The final Fury variants built were the FJ-4 and FJ-4B, which had drastically redesigned fuselages, 50 percent more fuel capacity, and air-to-air missile compatibility. Built between 1955-58, 372 late model Furies equipped both Navy and Marine Corps units into the early 1960s (by which time they had been redesignated F-1s).

SPECIFICATION (FJ-4):

ACCOMMODATION:
Pilot

DIMENSIONS:
LENGTH: 36 ft 4 in (11.09 m)
WINGSPAN: 39 ft 1 in (11.91 m)
HEIGHT: 13 ft 11 in (3.99 m)

WEIGHTS:
EMPTY: 13,210 lb (5992 kg)
MAX T/O: 23,700 lb (10,750 kg)

PERFORMANCE:
MAX SPEED: 680 mph (1088 kmh)
RANGE: 2020 miles (3232 km)
POWERPLANT: Wright J65-W-16A
OUTPUT: 6000 lb st (26 kN)

FIRST FLIGHT DATE:
November 27, 1946 (XFJ-1)

ARMAMENT:
Four 20-mm cannon in nose; maximum bomb/rocket/missile load of 3000 lb (1361 kg) on six underwing stores pylons (FJ-4B)

FEATURES:
Low-mounted straight (FJ-1) or swept-wing layout (FJ-2/3/4); tricycle landing gear; engine air intake in nose; fighter type bubble canopy; low-mounted tailplane

North American F-100 Super Sabre

single/two-seat, single-engined fighter-bomber

The natural successor to the F-86, the F-100 Super Sabre was larger and more powerful than its famous forebear. It was also capable of breaking the sound barrier in level flight, which was a first for any combat aircraft. Development on the F-100 had commenced as early as February 1949, and the overall size and shape of the fighter was barely influenced by air combat over Korea. In fact, had lessons from that conflict been incorporated into the aircraft, it would have been a less complex design with the best possible rate of climb and performance at high altitude. Known as the Model 180, the aircraft adhered to the F-86's configuration to the point where it was initially called the Sabre 45 due to the angle of wing sweepback.

In November 1951 the Air Force ordered two prototypes and 110 production aircraft, which it designated F-100A Super Sabres. The prototype YF-100 made its first flight on May 25, 1953, and flight testing progressed so rapidly that production F-100As (203 built up to March 1954) started leaving North American's Inglewood plant just five months later. Although the 479th TFW was declared operational in September 1954, a series of flight control-related crashes saw the F-100A grounded two months later. North American quickly rectified these problems by lengthening both the jet's wings and vertical fin, and the Super Sabre's handling was never an issue again.

Production switched to the F-100C fighter bomber in September 1955, and a staggering 476 examples were built for the USAF in less than 18 months. The definitive F-100D followed, this variant having an enlarged fin/rudder and additional underwing pylons. No fewer than 1264 D-models were built, and more than 500 of these were written off in crashes from mid-1956 through to the mid-1970s. North American also built 339 F-100F two-seat Super Sabres between March 1957 and October 1959.

F-100C/D/FS saw action in Vietnam throughout the conflict, with four fighter wings being based in-theater. The ANG also received its fair share of F-100s, with 23 units flying them from 1958 through to 1979.

SPECIFICATION (F-100D):

ACCOMMODATION:
Pilot, or two pilots in tandem (F-100F)

DIMENSIONS:
LENGTH: 49 ft 6 in (15.09 m)
WINGSPAN: 38 ft 9.50 in (11.81 m)
HEIGHT: 16 ft 2.75 in (4.96 m)

WEIGHTS:
EMPTY: 21,000 lb (9525 kg)
MAX T/O: 34,832 lb (15,800 kg)

PERFORMANCE:
MAX SPEED: 864 mph (1390 kmh)
RANGE: 1500 miles (2415 km)
POWERPLANT: Pratt & Whitney J57-PW-39
OUTPUT: 16,950 lb st (75 kN)

FIRST FLIGHT DATE:
May 25, 1953

ARMAMENT:
Four M-39E 20-mm cannon in nose; maximum bomb/rocket/missile load of 7500 lb (3402 kg) on six underwing stores pylons

FEATURES:
Low-mounted swept-wing layout; tricycle landing gear; engine air intake in nose; swept tail; fighter type bubble canopy; low-mounted tailplane

North American T-28 Trojan/Nomad

two-seat, single-engined trainer/close-support aircraft

The T-28 was designed to answer a USAAF request for an aircraft to replace the T-6 Texan. The resulting aircraft featured a tricycle undercarriage, frameless canopy, and a Wright R-1300 radial engine, which gave the Trojan (as it was named) a top speed of 280+ mph. Some 1194 T-28As were procured by the Air Force starting in 1950, and two years later the type was also bought by the Navy following a decision to standardize training techniques and equipment between the two services. Navy T-28s were re-engined with 1425-hp R-1820-86 Cyclones, which drove a three-bladed propeller, as opposed the T-28A's "two-blader." Designated the T-28B, 489 were acquired, followed by 299 carrier-capable C-models fitted with arrestor hooks—the Navy used its Trojans until 1984. In 1960 the USAF acquired an armed variant for use in the close-support role, and 393 T-28As were so modified by North American into T-28D Nomads. These aircraft featured the R-1820 engine and six under-wing hardpoints, and were used extensively as FAC platforms in South Vietnam until 1968.

SPECIFICATION (T-28A):

ACCOMMODATION:
Two pilots in tandem

DIMENSIONS:
LENGTH: 32 ft 0 in (9.75 m)
WINGSPAN: 40 ft 1 in (12.22 m)
HEIGHT: 12 ft 8 in (8.36 m)

WEIGHTS:
EMPTY: 5111 lb (2318 kg)
MAX T/O: 6365 lb (2887 kg)

PERFORMANCE:
MAX SPEED: 283 mph (453 kmh)
RANGE: 1000 miles (1600 km)
POWERPLANT: Wright R-1300-1 Cyclone
OUTPUT: 800 hp (597 kW)

FIRST FLIGHT DATE:
September 26, 1949

ARMAMENT:
Up to 4000 lb (1814 kg) of bombs/rockets/gun pods on six underwing stores pylons (T-28D Nomad only)

FEATURES:
Low-mounted straight-wing; large canopy; tricycle landing gear; close-cowled radial engine

North American L-17/U-18 Navion

four-seat, single-engined liaison and light utility aircraft

With massive contracts for military aircraft like the P-51 and B-25 canceled soon after VJ-Day, North American was forced to broaden its manufacturing base by breaking into the civilian market. Its first attempt was the NA-145 Navion four-seater, which enjoyed great success in 1946-47—1100+ were built almost exclusively for the domestic market. The USAAF also showed an interest in the Navion, and a prototype was flown in April 1946. Later that year the first of 83 L-17AS (as the type was designated in USAAF service) was delivered, the aircraft being employed as liaison "hacks," personnel/cargo carriers, and trainers within the USAAF's university Reserve Officers' Training Corps program. In 1947 Ryan Aeronautical Company acquired the design and manufacturing rights for the Navion, selling a further 158 improved L-17BS to the newly created USAF. The first of these was delivered in November 1948, and five more were bought in 1949. Surviving L-17S became U-18s following the 1962 overhaul of all US military aircraft designations.

SPECIFICATION (L-17B):

ACCOMMODATION:
Pilot and three passengers seated side by side in two rows

DIMENSIONS:
LENGTH: 27 ft 6 in (8.38 m)
WINGSPAN: 33 ft 5 in (10.19 m)
HEIGHT: 8 ft 7 in (2.65 m)

WEIGHTS:
EMPTY: 1945 lb (882 kg)
MAX T/O: 2950 lb (1338 kg)

PERFORMANCE:
MAX SPEED: 163 mph (260 kmh)
RANGE: 700 miles (1120 km)
POWERPLANT: Continental O-470-7
OUTPUT: 185 hp (140 kW)

FIRST FLIGHT DATE:
April 1946

FEATURES:
Low-mounted straight-wing; large canopy; rectractable tricycle undercarriage; close-cowled engine

North American A-5/RA-5 Vigilante

two-seat, twin-engined bomber/reconnaissance aircraft

One of the most advanced aircraft of its time, the Vigilante introduced a wealth of new technologies when it entered service in 1961. Designed as a carrier-based attack jet, the A-5 featured auto-matically scheduled engine inlets and nozzles, a single-surface vertical tail, differential slab tailplanes, a comprehensive radar-inertial navigation system, and a linear bomb bay between the engines. Flap and leading edge blowing was also introduced to make the weighty aircraft carrier deck-capable. Just 59 A-5A/B bombers had been built when Navy carriers gave up the strategic nuclear role, leaving the Vigilantes to become photographic intelligence gathering platforms. Aside from those bombers modified through the fitment of cameras and electronic surveillance equipment, a further 63 RA-5CS were built in 1962-66, followed by 46 Phase II jets in 1969-71. The first frontline RA-5C unit undertook its maiden cruise in 1964. The Navy's premier reconnaissance asset during the Vietnam War, the Vigilante remained in fleet service until finally retired in 1979.

SPECIFICATION (RA-5C):

ACCOMMODATION:
Pilot and observer/radar operator

DIMENSIONS:
LENGTH: 75 ft 10 in (23.11 m)
WINGSPAN: 53 ft 0 in (16.15 m)
HEIGHT: 19 ft 5 in (5.92 m)

WEIGHTS:
EMPTY: 38,000 lb (17,240 kg)
MAX T/O: 80,000 lb (36,285 kg)

PERFORMANCE:
MAX SPEED: 1385 mph (2230 kmh)
RANGE: 3200 miles (5150 km)
POWERPLANT: two General Electric
J79-GE-10S
OUTPUT: 35,720 lb st (159 kN)

FIRST FLIGHT DATE:
August 31, 1958

ARMAMENT:
One nuclear weapon in linear bomb bay and 6000 lb (2722 kg) of bombs on four underwing stores pylons (A-5A/B only)

FEATURES:
Shoulder-mounted swept wing; tricycle landing gear; engine air intakes behind cockpit; swept tail; low-mounted tailplane; arrestor hook

North American (Rockwell) T-2 Buckeye

two-seat, single/twin-engined trainer

Built as a result of a Navy study into pilot training, which identified the need for an aircraft capable of taking a student that had graduated from the *ab initio* phase through to the point of initial carrier qualification, the T-2A Buckeye incorporated many features seen on previous North American designs, such as the T-28C's flight control system and the wing of the FJ-1 Fury, for example. The Buckeye featured robust landing gear, powered flight controls, large trailing edge flaps, and airbrakes on either side of the rear fuselage. The single-engined T-2A entered service in July 1959, and 201 were eventually delivered. The original Buckeye was underpowered, so North American commenced work on a twin-engined version soon after the first A-models had been delivered. The T-2B was powered by two J60-P-6s, and 97 were built. Another engine change saw J85-GE-4s fitted in pairs into the T-2C, of which 231 were procured by the Navy in 1969-75. The C-model is the only variant still in service today, and the last examples will be retired in 2007.

SPECIFICATION (T-2C):

ACCOMMODATION:
Two pilots in tandem

DIMENSIONS:
LENGTH: 38 ft 3.50 in (11.67 m)
WINGSPAN: 38 ft 1.50 in (11.62 m)
HEIGHT: 14 ft 9.50 in (4.51 m)

WEIGHTS:
EMPTY: 8115 lb (3680 kg)
MAX T/O: 13,180 lb (5979 kg)

PERFORMANCE:
MAX SPEED: 540 mph (840 kmh)
RANGE: 1047 miles (1685 km)
POWERPLANT: two General Electric J85-GE-4s
OUTPUT: 5900 lb st (26 kN)

FIRST FLIGHT DATE:
January 31, 1958

FEATURES:
Midmounted tapered wings; bubble canopy; tricycle landing gear; fuselage chin engine air intakes; wingtip tanks; arrestor hook

North American (Rockwell) OV-10 Bronco

two-seat, twin-engined forward air control/close-air support aircraft

The OV-10 Bronco was a purpose-built close-air support aircraft derived from Department of Defense studies carried out between 1959-65. North American's NA-300 had been one of several aircraft put forward by US manufacturers to meet the Marine Corps' LARA (Light Armed Recon Aircraft) specification, the Bronco being chosen as the winner in August 1965. An initial batch of 271 OV-10AS was delivered in 1967-68, of which 157 were supplied to the USAF for use in the forward air control (FAC) role in place of O-1/2s. Surviving OV-10CS soldiered on with both the USAF and Marine Corps into the early 1990s, with the latter service developing a specialized night FAC variant that drew on experience gained by the USAF in Vietnam. Designated the OV-10D, and featuring a modified nose housing sensor equipment, a 20-mm cannon turret, and uprated engines, 17 OV-10AS were converted in 1979-80—these aircraft subsequently saw action in Operation Desert Storm. Surviving USAF Broncos retired in 1992, followed two years later by the last Marine Corps Reserve OV-10DS.

SPECIFICATION (OV-10A):

ACCOMMODATION:
Pilot and observer

DIMENSIONS:
LENGTH: 41 ft 7 in (12.67 m)
WINGSPAN: 40 ft 0 in (12.19 m)
HEIGHT: 15 ft 2 in (4.62 m)

WEIGHTS:
EMPTY: 6969 lb (3161 kg)
MAX T/O: 14,444 lb (6552 kg)

PERFORMANCE:
MAX SPEED: 281 mph (452 kmh)
RANGE: 1428 miles (2298 km)
POWERPLANT: two Garrett T76-G-416s
OUTPUT: 1430 shp (1066 kW)

FIRST FLIGHT DATE:
July 16, 1965

ARMAMENT:
Four M60C 7.62-mm machine guns in sponsons, or one 20-mm cannon in ventral turret (OV-10D only); up to 3600 lb (1632 kg) of bombs/rockets/flares/missiles on four under-sponson, two underwing, and one under-fuselage stores pylons

FEATURES:
Shoulder-mounted straight wing; twin booms containing turboprop engines; podded fuselage; large blown canopy

Northrop YC-125 Raider

36-seat, three-engined transportation/rescue aircraft

The YC-125 was a militarized version of the Northrop's N-23 Pioneer commercial cargo aircraft, the Raider winning a USAF contest aimed at finding an aircraft capable of ferrying troops and equipment into small clearings in forward combat areas. Its short-field performance also made the Raider suitable for the specialist Arctic rescue mission. Twenty-three YC-125AS were ordered by the USAF in March 1948, and the first of these completed its maiden flight on August 1, 1949. The Air Force accepted its first YC-125A in early 1950, and 13 were delivered. The remaining ten Raiders were built as YC-125B Arctic rescue aircraft. Air Force trials soon found the aircraft to be significantly underpowered for its intended missions. It was also realized that the latest generation of military helicopters were a better solution for moving troops into forward areas, and for performing rescue missions in remote locations. As a result, all 23 YC-125s were quickly sent to Sheppard AFB, Texas, where they were used as ground maintenance trainers until declared surplus in 1955.

SPECIFICATION:

ACCOMMODATION:
Pilot and observer

DIMENSIONS:
LENGTH: 67 ft 1 in (20.45 m)
WINGSPAN: 86 ft 6 in (26.39 m)
HEIGHT: 23 ft 1 in (7.04 m)

WEIGHTS:
EMPTY: 25,000 lb (11,340 kg)
MAX T/O: 41,900 lb (19,005 kg)

PERFORMANCE:
MAX SPEED: 207 mph (331 kmh)
RANGE: 1856 miles (2970 km)
POWERPLANT: three Wright
R-1820-99s
OUTPUT: 3600 hp (895 kW)

FIRST FLIGHT DATE:
August 1, 1949

FEATURES:
Shoulder-mounted straight wing;
fixed undercarriage; three close-
cowled radial engines

Northrop F-89 Scorpion

two-seat, twin-engined fighter

The USAF's first two-seat all-weather interceptor, the F-89 Scorpion was designed specifically for the newly formed Air Defense Command (ADC). Two prototypes were ordered in December 1946, and the first of these made its maiden flight on August 16, 1948. The delivery of 18 production-standard F-89As began in June 1950, although a further year would pass before ADC got its hands on the Scorpion. Once in service, these aircraft were charged with the responsibility of protecting North America from attack by Soviet bombers. A further 30 improved F-89Bs followed, before production of 164 F-89Cs. The variant produced most often was the F-89D, which featured wingtip-mounted rockets—682 were built, and this version equipped most of ADC units from 1954. The final new-build Scorpion variant was the F-89H, which featured wingtip-mounted Falcon missiles. Some D-models were rebuilt as F-89Js, fitted with Genie and Falcon missiles. Early-build F-89s were relegated to ANG duty from 1954, and 16 units eventually received ex-ADC jets. The last of these were retired in 1969.

SPECIFICATION (F-89D):

ACCOMMODATION:
Pilot and radar observer in tandem

DIMENSIONS:
LENGTH: 53 ft 10 in (16.41 m)
WINGSPAN: 59 ft 8 in (18.19 m)
HEIGHT: 17 ft 7 in (5.36 m)

WEIGHTS:
EMPTY: 25,194 lb (11,428 kg)
MAX T/O: 42,241 lb (19,160 kg)

PERFORMANCE:
MAX SPEED: 636 mph (1023 kmh)
RANGE: 2600 miles (4184 km)
POWERPLANT: two Allison J35-A-41s
OUTPUT: 14,400 lb st (63 kN)

FIRST FLIGHT DATE:
August 16, 1948

ARMAMENT:
52 2.75-in Mighty Mouse air-to-air rocket projectiles in wingtip pods and four air-to-air missiles on four underwing stores pylons

FEATURES:
Midmounted straight wing; retractable landing gear; wingtip rocket pods/fuel tanks; low lateral engine intakes; bubble canopy; high-mounted tailplane

Northrop T-38 Talon

two-seat, twin-engined advanced trainer

As the first supersonic aircraft designed from scratch as a trainer, the T-38 has enjoyed a long career with the USAF. Developed by Northrop as the N-156T, the Talon was a spinoff product from the company's N-156C lightweight fighter program that spawned the F-5 Freedom Fighter. As with its forebear, work on the N-156T proceeded for two years as a private venture before the USAF announced a requirement for a supersonic advanced trainer. The first contract issued in May 1956 was for six YT-38 pre-production aircraft, while the premier production example completed its first flight in May 1960 and entered USAF service in March of the following year. By the time the final Talon had been delivered in January 1972, 1189 had been constructed. In the 1970s 130+ Talons were given gun-pod capability to provide fighter lead-in training—these aircraft were redesignated AT-38Bs. Recently, the 300 T/AT-38s that remain in frontline service as part of the USAF's Undergraduate Pilot Training program have been upgraded to T-38C standard to prolong their service lives to at least 2010.

SPECIFICATION (T-38A):

ACCOMMODATION:
Two pilots in tandem

DIMENSIONS:
LENGTH: 46 ft 4.50 in (14.14 m)
WINGSPAN: 25 ft 3 in (7.70 m)
HEIGHT: 12 ft 10.50 in (3.92 m)

WEIGHTS:
EMPTY: 7174 lb (3254 kg)
MAX T/O: 12,050 lb (5465 kg)

PERFORMANCE:
MAX SPEED: 858 mph (1381 kmh)
RANGE: 1094 miles (1761 km)
POWERPLANT: two General Electric J85-GE-5s
OUTPUT: 7700 lb st (34 kN)

FIRST FLIGHT DATE:
April 10, 1959

ARMAMENT:
One 7.62-mm SUU-11 gun pod on fuselage centerline (AT-38B)

FEATURES:
Low-mounted swept wing; retractable landing gear; fuselage air intakes below cockpit; bubble canopy; low-mounted tailplane

Northrop B-2 Spirit

two-seat, four-engined strategic bomber

The world's most expensive military aircraft, with a price tag of $2.2 billion per jet, the 21-strong fleet of B-2 bombers fielded by Air Combat Command is a critical component in the USAF's conventional and nuclear warfighting strategy. Designed from the outset by Northrop to be virtually invisible to radar, the B-2 can trace its history back to development work carried out in the late 1970s following the launch of the Advanced Technology Bomber program. A Northrop (with Boeing as the principal subcontractor) design was selected ahead of a rival concept from Lockheed/Rockwell in June 1981, the former receiving a $7.3 billion contract to produce a replacement for the B-1B Lancer.

The resulting B-2 drew heavily on work carried out by Northrop in the late 1940s into the flying-wing concept, as well as studies into remotely piloted vehicles. Possessing an inherently low radar cross-section, the flying wing was brought up to date through the B-2 being primarily constructed of graphite/epoxy, which formed a honeycomb radar-absorbent structure. Work progressed in secret until November 1988, when the B-2 was unveiled to the world. The aircraft made its first flight on July 17, 1989 from Air Force Plant 42 in Palmdale, California.

The Air Force had originally hoped to buy 132 B-2s, but the collapse of the Soviet Union and escalating development costs resulted in the production order being slashed to just 15 examples. Eventually the USAF managed to secure funds to enable 21 B-2s to be built, and the first of these was delivered to the 509th Bomb Wing at Whiteman AFB, Missouri, on December 17, 1993. It was not until 1997 that the Spirit fleet finally became operational with limited combat capability, and during subsequent Block upgrades, the jets' weapons compatibility has broadened dramatically.

The B-2 made its combat debut over the Balkans during Operation Allied Force in March 1999, hitting targets during 35-hour nonstop missions from Whiteman. The aircraft saw further combat over Afghanistan in 2001 and Iraq in 2003, flying missions from both Whiteman and Diego Garcia, in the Indian Ocean.

SPECIFICATION:

ACCOMMODATION:
Two pilots

DIMENSIONS:
LENGTH: 69 ft 0 in (21.03 m)
WINGSPAN: 172 ft 0 in (52.43 m)
HEIGHT: 17 ft 0 in (5.18 m)

WEIGHTS:
EMPTY: 125,000 lb (56,699 kg)
MAX T/O: 371,300 lb (168,422 kg)

PERFORMANCE:
MAX SPEED: 607 mph (972 kmh)
RANGE: 7292 miles (11,668 km)
POWERPLANT: four General Electric F118-GE-110S
OUTPUT: 76,000 lb st (338 kN)

FIRST FLIGHT DATE:
July 17, 1989

ARMAMENT:
Up to 40,000 lb (18,144 kg) of bombs/missiles on two rotary launcher assemblies in two internal weapons bays

FEATURES:
Flying wing with blended fuselage; serrated wing trailing edge

Northrop F-5A/B Freedom Fighter

single/two-seat, twin-engined fighter-bomber

In May 1958 the Department of Defense (DOD) released funds to Northrop to allow it to build prototypes of its privately developed N-156F lightweight, low-cost fighter, which had been created alongside the company's two-seat N-156T trainer. First flown in July 1959, the aircraft was subsequently selected by the DOD as its "Freedom Fighter," and it was to be supplied to approved foreign air arms through its Military Assistance Program (MAP). Pre-production YF-5As and two-seat F-5Bs were built in 1963-64, followed by production-standard F-5As. Although the aircraft was intended for MAP, the first of the 1100+ Freedom Fighters built were delivered to the USAF's 4441st Combat Crew Training Squadron, which had been established to train foreign pilots destined to fly F-5A/Bs. In October 1965, 12 F-5As were leased to the USAF from MAP for the Skoshi Tiger combat evaluation in South Vietnam. Redesignated F-5Cs, and fitted with inflight refueling probes and tip tanks instead of missile rails, these jets flew more than 3500 combat sorties through to June 1967, when the surviving ten aircraft were handed over to the Vietnamese Nationalist Air Force.

SPECIFICATION (F-5A):

ACCOMMODATION:
Pilot, or two pilots in tandem (F-5B)

DIMENSIONS:
LENGTH: 47 ft 2 in (14.38 m)
WINGSPAN: 25 ft 10 in (7.87 m)
HEIGHT: 13 ft 2 in (4.01 m)

WEIGHTS:
EMPTY: 8085 lb (3667 kg)
MAX T/O: 20,677 lb (9379 kg)

PERFORMANCE:
MAX SPEED: 924 mph (1487 kmh)
RANGE: 1612 miles (2594 km)
POWERPLANT: two General Electric J85-GE-13S
OUTPUT: 8160 lb st (36 kN)

FIRST FLIGHT DATE:
July 30, 1959 (N-156F)

ARMAMENT:
Two M39A2 20-mm cannon in nose; up to 4400 lb (1994 kg) of bombs/rockets/missiles on four underwing, one under fuselage and two wingtip (missiles only) stores pylons

FEATURES:
Low-mounted swept wing; retractable landing gear; wingtip tanks; fuselage air intakes below cockpit; bubble canopy; low-mounted tailplane

Northrop F-5E Tiger II

single/two-seat, twin-engined adversary aircraft

Developed by Northrop as an improved version of its highly successful F-5A Freedom Fighter, the F-5E Tiger II featured more powerful engines, enlarged wing leading edge extensions, permanent wingtip missile rails, and better avionics. Elements of the Tiger II were tested in a converted F-5A in March 1969, soon after which the design was submitted for the US Government's International Fighter Competition (IFC), managed by the USAF. Beating off the F-8, F-104, and F-4, the F-5E was officially selected for supply to approved foreign countries by MAP in November 1970. The first production single-seat Tiger II took to the skies on August 11, 1972, followed by the F-5F two-seater two years later. Like the F-5A, the F-5E/F proved very popular, with Northrop building 1300 between 1972 and 1986. The USAF and Navy/Marine Corps acquired more than 100 for use as aggressor/adversary trainers, the Air Force being the first operator to receive jets in early 1973—it retired its Tiger IIs in the late 1980s. The Navy/Marine Corps still have more than 50 F-5E/Fs on strength, however.

SPECIFICATION (F-5E):

ACCOMMODATION:
Pilot, or two pilots in tandem (F-5F)

DIMENSIONS:
LENGTH: 47 ft 4.75 in (14.45 m)
WINGSPAN: 27 ft 11 in (8.53 m)
HEIGHT: 13 ft 4.50 in (4.08 m)

WEIGHTS:
EMPTY: 9558 lb (4350 kg)
MAX T/O: 24,664 lb (11,187 kg)

PERFORMANCE:
MAX SPEED: 1056 mph (1700 kmh)
RANGE: 2314 miles (3720 km)
POWERPLANT: two General Electric J85-GE-21BS
OUTPUT: 10,000 lb st (49 kN)

FIRST FLIGHT DATE:
August 11, 1972

ARMAMENT:
Two M39A2 20-mm cannon in nose; up to 7000 lb (3195 kg) of bombs/rockets/missiles on four underwing, one under fuselage, and two wingtip (missiles only) stores pylons

FEATURES:
Low-mounted swept wing; retractable landing gear; wingtip missile rails; fuselage air intakes below cockpit; bubble canopy; low-mounted tailplane

Piper UO/U-11

four-seat, twin-engined communications aircraft

Derived from the PA-23 Apache family of twin-engined four-seaters developed by Piper from a Stinson design in the early 1950s, the Aztec was an enlarged and more powerful aircraft produced starting in 1960 through to 1982. During this time 4929 Aztecs were built, including 20 for the Navy and Marine Corps. In fact, the latter aircraft were among the first Aztec AS built by Piper, these "off-the-shelf" machines being purchased to perform the role of utility transports. They differed from civilian models in having propeller anti-icing gear installed, as well as an oxygen supply and an additional military radio. Delivered to the Navy as UO-1s, these aircraft were redesignated U-11As in 1962. Serving primarily within the continental USA as communication "hacks" at Naval Air Stations North Island, Roosevelt Roads, Alameda, and Mayport, to name but four, the aircraft were eventually replaced in service by Beech UC-12s in the early 1980s. Surviving U-11As were subsequently sold off into civilian ownership.

SPECIFICATION (U-3A):

ACCOMMODATION:
One pilot and three passengers

DIMENSIONS:
LENGTH: 27 ft 7 in (8.44 m)
WINGSPAN: 37 ft 0 in (11.27 m)
HEIGHT: 10 ft 1 in (3.07 m)

WEIGHTS:
EMPTY: 3310 lb (1507 kg)
MAX T/O: 4800 lb (2177 kg)

PERFORMANCE:
MAX SPEED: 215 mph (344 kmh)
RANGE: 1325 miles (2120 km)
POWERPLANT: two Lycoming O-540-A1A5
OUTPUT: 500 hp (373 kW)

FIRST FLIGHT DATE:
Early 1960 (PA-23 Aztec)

FEATURES:
Straight-wing layout; rectractable tricycle landing gear; twin, close-cowled engines

Raytheon Beech T-6A Texan II

two-seat, single-engined advanced trainer

In 1991 the Air Force and Navy established the Joint Primary Aircraft Training System program in order to find a replacement for the T-37 and T-34C. By choosing a common airframe "off-the-shelf," it was hoped that pilot training costs could be substantially reduced. Following four years of evaluation, the Beech-modified Pilatus-built PC-9 Mk II was named the winner in June 1995. Officially designated the T-6 Texan II in June 1997, by which time construction of the first production example was underway, the Beech (now part of Raytheon) trainer featured many improvements when compared with the original PC-9. Indeed, 90 percent of its structure was redesigned and strengthened, a more powerful PT6A-68 engine fitted, and zero-zero ejection seats installed. The USAF ordered 372 T-6As and the Navy 339, and the former commenced Joint Primary Pilot Training with the aircraft in October 2001. The Air Force is expected to have replaced all of its T-37s with T-6As by 2008. The Navy accepted its first Texan IIs in 2003, and the type is steadily taking over from the T-34C.

SPECIFICATION:

ACCOMMODATION:
Two pilots in tandem

DIMENSIONS:
LENGTH: 33 ft 4.75 in (10.17 m)
WINGSPAN: 33 ft 2.50 in (10.12 m)
HEIGHT: 10 ft 8 in (3.29 m)

WEIGHTS:
EMPTY: 4707 lb (2135 kg)
MAX T/O: 6500 lb (2948 kg)

PERFORMANCE:
MAX SPEED: 358 mph (573 kmh)
RANGE: 1020 miles (1642 km)
POWERPLANT: Pratt & Whitney Canada PT6A-68
OUTPUT: 1708 shp (1274 kW)

FIRST FLIGHT DATE:
July 15, 1995

FEATURES:
Low-mounted tapered wing; tandem seating; turboprop engine; extensive cockpit glazing; rectractable tricycle landing gear; enlarged dorsal fin

Republic F-84 Thunderjet

single-seat, single-engined fighter-bomber

Initially planned as nothing more than a jet-powered P-47, Republic's XP-84 Thunderjet ended up being a wholly new design powered by the then unfashionable Allison TG-180 (J35) axial flow jet engine. The aircraft's contemporaries all used centrifugal-flow turbine turbojets. The prototype XP-84 flew for the first time on February 28, 1946, and following the construction of 16 YP-84AS, the first of 226 P-84BS entered frontline service in November 1947. Redesignated the F-84 in June 1948, the Thunderjet was not easy to fly, but nevertheless proved popular with USAF pilots. A further 191 F-84CS were built in 1948-49, followed by 154 F-84DS. This variant became the first to deploy overseas, when the 27th Fighter Escort Group moved to Korea in 1950. The stretched F-84E proved to be the USAF's definitive Thunderjet model, 743 being built —the E-model was also the Air Force's principal fighter bomber in Korea. The final straight wing F-84 was the G-model, 1119 of the 3025 constructed being supplied to the USAF. The ANG was the last Thunderjet operator, retiring its F-84s in 1958.

SPECIFICATION (F-84E):

ACCOMMODATION:
Pilot

DIMENSIONS:
LENGTH: 38 ft 6 in (11.73 m)
WINGSPAN: 36 ft 5 in (11.10 m)
HEIGHT: 12 ft 7 in (3.84 m)

WEIGHTS:
EMPTY: 10,205 lb (4629 kg)
MAX T/O: 22,463 lb (10,189 kg)

PERFORMANCE:
MAX SPEED: 613 mph (986 kmh)
RANGE: 1485 miles (2390 km)
POWERPLANT: Allison J35-A-17
OUTPUT: 4900 lb st (21 kN)

FIRST FLIGHT DATE:
February 28, 1946

ARMAMENT:
Four Browning 0.50-in machine guns in nose and two in wing roots; maximum bomb/rocket load of 4000 lb (1814 kg) on four underwing stores pylons

FEATURES:
Centrally mounted straight wings; tricycle landing gear; engine air intake in nose; fighter-type bubble canopy; wingtip tanks

Republic F/RF-84F Thunderstreak

single-seat, single-engined reconnaissance/fighter-bomber

Essentially a brand new aircraft, the Thunderstreak shared its F-84 designation with its Thunderjet predecessor. Originally designated the YF-96A, the prototype flew for the first time on June 3, 1950. Featuring sweptback wing and tail surfaces and a Wright J65 turbojet, the Thunderstreak bore little resemblance to the Thunderjet. The first YF-84F flew on February 14, 1951, and problems with high-g stall pitchup soon occurred. The fitment of a powered "slab" surface horizontal tailplane partially solved the problem, but the F-84F was hampered by maneuverability restrictions throughout its career. With no other fighters available, the F-84F entered service with SAC as an escort for its long-range bombers in January 1954. A total of 2348 F-84FS were built, of which 1412 were supplied to USAF units. A dedicated photoreconnaissance variant was also built as the RF-84F, the aircraft boasting wing root engine intakes and six cameras in its nose, as well as four machine guns—329 entered USAF service. The ANG was an early recipient of the F/RF-84F in 1954, operating them until 1972.

SPECIFICATION (F-84F):

ACCOMMODATION:
Pilot

DIMENSIONS:
LENGTH: 43 ft 4.75 in (13.23 m)
WINGSPAN: 33 ft 7.25 in (10.24 m)
HEIGHT: 14 ft 4.75 in (4.39 m)

WEIGHTS:
EMPTY: 13,645 lb (6189 kg)
MAX T/O: 28,000 lb (12,700 kg)

PERFORMANCE:
MAX SPEED: 695 mph (1118 kmh)
RANGE: 1620 miles (2605 km)
POWERPLANT: Wright J65-W-3
OUTPUT: 7220 lb st (32 kN)

FIRST FLIGHT DATE:
June 3, 1950

ARMAMENT:
Four Browning 0.50-in machine guns in nose and two in wing roots; maximum bomb/rocket load of 6000 lb (2721 kg) on four underwing stores pylons

FEATURES:
Centrally mounted swept wings and tailplane; tricycle landing gear; engine air intake in nose (F-84F); fighter-type bubble canopy; swept tail

Republic F-105 Thunderchief

single/two-seat, single-engined fighter-bomber

Conceived by Republic in 1951 as the private venture model AP-63 nuclear strike fighter-bomber that carried its deadly load in a capacious internal bomb bay, the F-105 Thunderchief, which actually entered service seven years later, would win fame as a conventional tactical bomber that dropped iron bombs from pylons hung beneath its wings. Flight testing began with two YF-105AS in October 1955, and following technical delays, the first of 75 B-models entered service with the 4th TFW in May 1958. Boasting an all-up weight of at least 45,000 lb, which made it the biggest single-seat, single-engined combat aircraft in history, the F-105 required the most powerful engine then available. This was the Pratt & Whitney J75 two-shaft afterburning turbojet, which was fitted in all production-standard Thunderchiefs.

Aside from being a big aircraft, the F-105 was also immensely complex, and it took the 4th TFW two years to work up with the jet due to further production problems. In fact, it was not until the advent of the F-105D in 1960 that the jet's fortunes began to improve. This version boasted the General Electric FC-5 fully integrated automatic flight and fire control system, which featured a toss bomb computer, Doppler navigator, missile launch computer, autopilot, and search-and-range radar. Flown by USAF units both at home and in Europe and Japan, a total of 610 D-models were built by Republic up to 1965.

These aircraft would ultimately bear the brunt of the USAF bombing campaign in Vietnam from 1965 through to 1970, undertaking more strikes "up north" than any other US aircraft. The F-105 units paid a high price in the process, losing 397 jets in combat.

Joining the D-models in South-East Asia were two-seat F-105FS, 143 of which had originally been built as trainers in 1963-64. Featuring a lengthened fuselage and taller fin, 61 F-models were modified in 1965-69 to locate, classify, and attack enemy ground-based radar sites as electronic warfare F-105G "Wild Weasels." Surviving Thunderchiefs were issued to the Reserve and ANG during the 1960s, and these soldiered on until finally retired in 1984.

SPECIFICATION (F-105D):

ACCOMMODATION:
Pilot, and pilot and weapon systems officer in tandem (F-105F/G)

DIMENSIONS:
LENGTH: 64 ft 3 in (19.58 m)
WINGSPAN: 34 ft 11.25 in (10.65 m)
HEIGHT: 19 ft 8 in (5.99 m)

WEIGHTS:
EMPTY: 27,500 lb (12,474 kg)
MAX T/O: 52,546 lb (23,834 kg)

PERFORMANCE:
MAX SPEED: 1390 mph (2237 kmh)
RANGE: 2390 miles (3846 km)
POWERPLANT: Pratt & Whitney J75-P-19W
OUTPUT: 24,500 lb st (99 kN)

FIRST FLIGHT DATE:
October 22, 1955

ARMAMENT:
One M61A1 20-mm cannon; maximum bomb/rocket/missile load of 20,000 lb (9072 kg) on four underwing and two underfuselage stores pylons

FEATURES:
Midmounted swept wings; low-mounted swept tailplane; wing root engine air intakes; fighter-type bubble canopy; swept tail; ventral fin

Rockwell B-1B Lancer

four-seat, four-engined strategic bomber

Initially conceived by Rockwell for the low-altitude penetration nuclear-bomber role and developed for the USAF in response to the latter's Advanced Manned Strategic Aircraft requirement, issued in 1965, the B-1 was selected as a replacement for the B-52 in 1970 after it had seen off rival designs from Boeing and General Dynamics. The first of four B-1A prototypes performed its maiden flight on December 23, 1974, but in June 1977 the project was canceled by the newly elected Carter administration. The bomber was resurrected four years later, as part of President Reagan's rearming program, and 100 improved B-1BS were duly ordered—SAC had originally hoped to acquire 320.

The B-model featured improved avionics and systems, low observable features, such as radar absorbent material coatings to the outer fuselage skinning, strengthened undercarriage, fixed air inlets, and the all-important APG-164 radar for navigation and terrain following. The core of the aircraft's defensive systems was the troublesome Eaton ALQ-161 ECM suite, which proved unreliable once in service. The prototype completed its first flight on October 18, 1984, and production examples began reaching the 96th BW in July of the following year.

All 100 B-1BS had been delivered by May 1988, just as its primary nuclear strike mission against the USSR disappeared following the collapse of communism in eastern Europe. The USAF initially struggled to find a mission for its hugely expensive fleet of B-1s, but in the mid-1990s it commenced the Conventional Mission Upgrade Program, which saw the bomber modified so that it could carry guided and unguided ordnance. Although retaining its nuclear strike capability, the B-1 Lancer (so named in 1990) can now also employ GPS-guided J-weapons and conventional iron bombs.

The jet made its combat debut over Iraq during Operation Desert Fox in December 1998, and since then has also seen action over the Balkans in 1999 and during the ongoing Global War on Terror in Afghanistan and Iraq. Some 67 B-1s currently remain in the frontline inventory.

SPECIFICATION:

ACCOMMODATION:
Pilot, copilot, and offensive and defensive systems officers

DIMENSIONS:
LENGTH: 147 ft 0 in (44.81 m)
WINGSPAN: 136 ft 8.50 in (41.67 m)
HEIGHT: 34 ft 10 in (10.62 m)

WEIGHTS:
EMPTY: 192,000 lb (87,090 kg)
MAX T/O: 477,000 lb (216,360 kg)

PERFORMANCE:
MAX SPEED: 828 mph (1324 kmh)
RANGE: 7495 miles (11,992 km)
POWERPLANT: four General Electric F101-GE-102S
OUTPUT: 123,120 lb st (548 kN)

FIRST FLIGHT DATE:
December 23, 1974 (B-1A)

ARMAMENT:
Up to 75,000 lb (34,020 kg) of bombs/missiles in three internal weapons bays

FEATURES:
Variable-geometry wing blended into fuselage; engines in underfuselage pods; two small canards beneath forward fuselage

Ryan FR Fireball

single-seat, twin-engined fighter

The unique piston- and jet-engined Fireball gave the Navy its first experience of jet aircraft operations in the immediate postwar years. The Navy was forced to go down this mixed powerplant route because early jet aircraft required long takeoff and landing runs, and had short endurance. These characteristics were unacceptable to the Navy, which operated its aircraft from short carrier decks over vast expanses of ocean. Therefore, in late 1942 it issued a proposal requesting submissions for a composite aircraft. Nine manufacturers responded, with Ryan's XFR-1 being chosen as the most promising design. Despite having never previously built a combat aircraft, the company proceeded with great speed, and the prototype made its first flight in June 1944. Of conventional layout, the fighter featured a Wright R-1820 piston engine "up front" and a General Electric J31 turbojet in the rear fuselage. The Navy ordered 700 FR-1 Fireballs, but only 66 were eventually built in the wake of VJ-Day. Production aircraft saw brief sea time in 1945-47, after which the FR-1s were withdrawn.

SPECIFICATION:

ACCOMMODATION:
Pilot

DIMENSIONS:
LENGTH: 32 ft 4 in (9.85 m)
WINGSPAN: 40 ft 0 in (12.19 m)
HEIGHT: 13 ft 11 in (4.24 m)

WEIGHTS:
EMPTY: 7915 lb (3590 kg)
MAX T/O: 11,652 lb (5285 kg)

PERFORMANCE:
MAX SPEED: 426 mph (686 kmh)
RANGE: 1030 miles (1660 km)
POWERPLANT: Wright Cyclone R-1820-72W and General Electric J31-2
OUTPUT: 1425 hp (1063 kW) and 1600 lb st (7 kN)

FIRST FLIGHT DATE:
June 25, 1944

ARMAMENT:
Four Browning 0.50-in machine guns in wings; provision for up to 1000 lb (454 kg) of bombs/rockets on two underwing stores pylons

FEATURES:
Straight-wing layout; close-cowled radial engine; turbojet engine in rear fuselage; retractable tricycle undercarriage; bubble canopy; arrestor hook

Vought F6U Pirate

single-seat, single-engined fighter

In September 1944 the Navy issued a request for a single-seat shipboard fighter powered by the Navy-sponsored Westinghouse J34 turbojet. Vought submitted its V-340, which was selected by the Navy and redesignated the XF6U. The aircraft was of conventional straight-winged layout, with Metalite skinning (aluminum sheeting sandwiching balsa wood) covering the fuselage and wings, and the intakes and vertical tail clad in Fabrilite (fiberglass/balsa "sandwich"). Christened the Pirate, the jet was difficult to master in flight. In fact, Vought enlarged its vertical tail and made numerous other modifications in an attempt to improve its handling. The aircraft was also underpowered, so it was fitted with a Solar A-103A afterburner—the first Navy fighter with this form of power boost. Despite these problems, 30 F6U-1s were ordered in February 1947, and the first production aircraft was issued to development squadron VX-3 in March 1949. However, it soon became obvious that the Pirate was unsuited to frontline use, and all were relegated to ground-based trials work.

SPECIFICATION:

ACCOMMODATION:
Pilot

DIMENSIONS:
LENGTH: 37 ft 8 in (11.48 m)
WINGSPAN: 32 ft 10 in (10 m)
HEIGHT: 12 ft 11 in (3.93 m)

WEIGHTS:
EMPTY: 7320 lb (3320 kg)
MAX T/O: 12,900 lb (5851 kg)

PERFORMANCE:
MAX SPEED: 596 mph (959 kmh)
RANGE: 1170 miles (1880 km)
POWERPLANT: Westinghouse
J34-WE-22
OUTPUT: 3000 lb st (15 kN)

FIRST FLIGHT DATE:
October 2, 1946

ARMAMENT:
Four 20-mm cannon in nose

FEATURES:
Low-mounted straight wing;
tricycle landing gear; engine air
intake in wing roots; fighter-type
bubble canopy; wingtip-mounted
tanks

Vought F8U/F-8 Crusader

single-seat, single-engined fighter-bomber/reconnaissance

The Navy's first supersonic day interceptor and its last single-engined, single-seat fighter, the Crusader was built in response to a 1952 naval requirement for an aircraft with high-speed performance, but a 115-mph landing speed. It achieved the latter through the employment of a unique high-mounted variable incidence wing, which angled up to increase drag—it was also employed during takeoff, because it greatly increased lift. One of eight designs submitted to the Navy, Vought's XF8U-1 prototype made its maiden flight on March 25, 1955 and service deliveries commenced in March 1957. A total of 318 "Dash Ones" (redesignated F-8AS in 1962) were built, and these equipped both Navy and Marine Corps fighter units. These were followed in 1958 by 130 F8U-1ES (F-8BS), which featured limited all-weather interception capabilities thanks to the fitment of an AN/APS-67 radar.

By then the first of 144 F8U-1PS (RF-8AS) had reached the fleet, these aircraft swapping their cannon for five cameras in the forward fuselage. An important reconnaissance asset for the Navy over the next 25 years, 73 surviving RF-8AS were converted into RF-8GS in 1965-66—these aircraft had bigger engines, strengthened airframes, and improved cameras. The RF-8 saw action over Cuba in 1961 and Vietnam for the duration of the campaign.

The F8U-2 (F-8C) entered service in 1959-60, 187 examples featuring bigger engines and avionics upgrades, after which production shifted to the F8U-2N (F-8D). This aircraft had more armament, a larger engine, more fuel, and a better radar—152 were built in 1960-62. The last all-new Navy variant was the

F-8E, 286 of which were delivered starting in 1961. This aircraft had improved search and fire-control radar and provision for up to 5000 lb of external stores under the wings.

In 1966 Vought commenced a remanufacturing program which saw 373 Crusaders upgraded.

The jet proved its ability as a fighter in Vietnam with 18 confirmed MiG kills, and served as a bomber with the Marine Corps. Although the fighter variant disappeared from Navy ranks in the mid-1970s, the RF-8 soldiered on until 1987.

SPECIFICATION (F-8D):

ACCOMMODATION:
Pilot

DIMENSIONS:
LENGTH: 54 ft 3 in (16.53 m)
WINGSPAN: 35 ft 8 in (10.87 m)
HEIGHT: 15 ft 9 in (4.80 m)

WEIGHTS:
EMPTY: 17,541 lb (7957 kg)
MAX T/O: 29,000 lb (13,154 kg)

PERFORMANCE:
MAX SPEED: 1228 mph (1976 kmh)
RANGE: 1737 miles (2795 km)
POWERPLANT: Pratt & Whitney J57-PW-20
OUTPUT: 18,000 lb st (80 kN)

FIRST FLIGHT DATE:
March 25, 1955

ARMAMENT:
Four Colt 20-mm cannon in fuselage; maximum bomb/rocket/missile load of 5000 lb (2268 kg) on two underwing and four fuselage side stores pylons

FEATURES:
High-mounted swept wing, with variable incidence; engine air intake below nose; fighter-style canopy; ventral fins; all-moving tailplanes

Vought A-7 Corsair II

single/two-seat, single-engined attack aircraft

The A-7 Corsair II was the winner of the Navy's 1963 Light Attack Aircraft Competition, which sought to find a replacement for the A-4 Skyhawk. By restricting its performance to high subsonic speed, the A-7 was ideally suited to the role of carrier-based "bomb truck," because it could carry nearly twice as much nonnuclear ordnance as the A-4 over vast distances. In an effort to keep costs down, Vought based its design on the F-8 Crusader, which greatly appealed to the Navy. Having won the contract in February 1964, the company took just 18 months to progress to the flight-testing phase—the prototype Corsair II completed its maiden flight on September 27, 1965.

The first of 199 A-7A Corsair IIs reached the frontline in September 1966, and in December 1967 the aircraft made its combat debut over Vietnam. By then, in a rare example of cross-service unity, the USAF had also selected the Corsair II to fulfill a requirement for a tactical attack aircraft.

Having been impressed by the jet's load-carrying capacity and bombing accuracy, the Air Force bought 457 A-7Ds and 42 two-seat A-7Ks. The USAF jets introduced the definitive Allison TF41 (license-built Rolls-Royce Spey) turbofan in place of the Pratt & Whitney TF30, and saw combat in Vietnam in 1972-73. The Navy, however, chose to stick with the underpowered TF30 for its follow-on A-7B (196 built in 1968-69), as well as the first 67 A-7Es procured in 1970—the later were redesignated A-7Cs when the TF41s that were planned for these aircraft were delayed due to manufacturing problems. The Navy eventually received 535 re-engined A-7Es between 1969 and 1983, this definitive Corsair II variant featuring new and improved avionics, an M61A1 cannon, better hydraulics, and uprated antiskid brakes.

The backbone of the Navy's light strike force, the A-7E equipped up to 22 frontline units until its progressive replacement by the F/A-18 from the mid-1980s onward—two squadrons saw combat in Operation Desert Storm in 1991 during the type's final cruise. The ANG retired its last A-7D/KS in 1993.

SPECIFICATION (A-7E):

ACCOMMODATION:
Pilot, or two pilots in tandem (TA-7/A-7K)

DIMENSIONS:
LENGTH: 46 ft 1.50 in (14.06 m)
WINGSPAN: 38 ft 9 in (11.08 m)
HEIGHT: 16 ft 0.75 in (4.90 m)

WEIGHTS:
EMPTY: 19,490 lb (8841 kg)
MAX T/O: 42,000 lb (19,050 kg)

PERFORMANCE:
MAX SPEED: 693 mph (1109 kmh)
RANGE: 2300 miles (3680 km)
POWERPLANT: Allison TF41-A-2
OUTPUT: 14,250 lb st (66 kN)

FIRST FLIGHT DATE:
September 27, 1965

ARMAMENT:
One M61A1 Vulcan 20-mm cannon in fuselage; maximum bomb/rocket/missile load of 20,000 lb (9072 kg) on six underwing and two fuselage side stores pylons

FEATURES:
High-mounted wing; engine air intake below nose; fighter-style canopy; all-moving tailplanes

Vought F7U Cutlass

single-seat, twin-engined fighter-bomber

Its layout strongly influenced by experimental tailless designs built by Arado in World War II, the Cutlass appeared to offer the Navy an ideal solution to its unique requirements for carrier-based fighters. Theoretically boasting a high rate of climb and impressive top speed, all in a comparatively small package, three XF7U-1 prototypes were ordered in June 1946. These were to be powered by two Westinghouse J34 engines. The first example flew on September 29, 1948, and it was followed by 14 F7U-1s in 1950-51. Severe problems with the J34 resulted in the engine's cancelation, and an overall redesign of the Cutlass in light of poor handling characteristics saw the F7U-3 produced from late 1951. This aircraft featured a new nose shape and redesigned fins and, eventually, Westinghouse J46 engines. Some 180 were built, and these equipped four fleet squadrons. The final production variant was the missile-armed F7U-3M, 98 of which were constructed up to December 1955. Difficult to fly, and a maintenance nightmare, all surviving Cutlasses had been replaced by the F-8 by 1959.

SPECIFICATION (F7U-3):

ACCOMMODATION:
Pilot

DIMENSIONS:
LENGTH: 43 ft 1 in (13.13 m)
WINGSPAN: 39 ft 8 in (12.09 m)
HEIGHT: 14 ft 4 in (4.36 m)

WEIGHTS:
EMPTY: 18,262 lb (8284 kg)
MAX T/O: 31,642 lb (14,353 kg)

PERFORMANCE:
MAX SPEED: 696 mph (1120 kmh)
RANGE: 696 miles (1120 km)
POWERPLANT: two Westinghouse J46-W-8As
OUTPUT: 12,200 lb st (54 kN)

FIRST FLIGHT DATE:
September 29, 1948

ARMAMENT:
Four M-24 20-mm cannon in fuselage; maximum bomb/rocket/missile load of 5500 lb (2495 kg) on four underwing stores pylons

FEATURES:
Midmounted swept wing; tricycle landing gear, with extended nose gear leg; lateral engine air intakes behind cockpit; tailless fuselage (no horizontal tailplanes)

Un-
manned
Aerial
Vehicles

Boeing X-45A/C

Unmanned Combat Aerial Vehicle

Boeing's Joint Unmanned Combat Air System X-45 is an Unmanned Combat Aerial Vehicle (UCAV) being developed under a Defense Advanced Research Projects Agency (DARPA)/Air Force program to evaluate technologies and concepts for eventual frontline use in UCAVs that will operate as strike platforms for Suppression of Enemy Air Defense, electronic warfare, and other specialist mission profiles. Boeing was initially awarded a demonstration phase contract by DARPA/USAF for two X-45A subscale technology demonstrators in 1999, and the first of these flew in May 2002. Featuring a flying-wing configuration, the X-45A has stealth-design characteristics and a retractable under-carriage. Following cancelation of the follow-on X-45B in 2003, Boeing is concentrating its efforts on the larger, improved X-45C. The latter is contesting the Joint Unmanned Combat Air System (J-UCAS) program requirement with Northrop Grumman's X-47 Pegasus. Both UCAVs were being developed as common platforms for the USAF and Navy, but the former pulled out of the X-45 project in March 2006.

SPECIFICATION (X-45A):

ACCOMMODATION:
Unmanned

DIMENSIONS:
LENGTH: 27 ft 0 in (8.20 m)
WINGSPAN: 34 ft 4 in (10.30 m)
HEIGHT: 7 ft 0 in (2.10 m)

WEIGHTS:
EMPTY: 8000 lb (3628 kg)
MAX T/O: 15,000 lb (6804 kg)

PERFORMANCE:
MAX SPEED: 575 mph (920 kmh)
RANGE: endurance of three hours
POWERPLANT: Honeywell
F124-GA-100
OUTPUT: 6300 lb st (28 kN)

FIRST FLIGHT DATE:
May 22, 2002

FEATURES:
Swept flying-wing configuration; blended center fuselage; retractable undercarriage

General Atomics Gnat-750

Unmanned Aerial Vehicle

Initially developed by Unmanned Aerial Vehicle (UAV) pioneer manufacturer, Leading Systems, as a follow-on to its successful range of DARPA *Project Amber* UAVs, which were built in secrecy in the 1980s, the Gnat-750 was primarily derived from the company's Gnat-400 design. Development of the UAV was underway when Leading Systems was bought by General Atomics in 1990, the prototype Gnat-750 having made its first flight in mid-1989. Funding for production of the UAV for American use came from the Central Intelligence Agency's Directorate of Science and Technology under a program named *Lofty View*. A number of Gnat-750s were acquired, along with ground control stations and a Schweizer RG-8A Condor communications relay aircraft. In February 1994 two of the CIA's Gnat-750s became the first US endurance UAVs to be used operationally in almost 20 years when they were deployed to Albania. From here, they reconnoitered fighting in southern Yugoslavia, before shifting base to Hungary in March-April to conduct similar missions—monitoring air bases, troop entrenchments and movements, supply caches, and vehicle/tank convoys—over Serbia. CIA Gnat-750s saw further action in the Balkans in 1995.

SPECIFICATION:

ACCOMMODATION:
Unmanned

DIMENSIONS:
LENGTH: 16 ft 5 in (5 m)
WINGSPAN: 35 ft 4 in (10.77 m)
HEIGHT: 2 ft 4.50 in (0.75 m)

WEIGHTS:
EMPTY: unknown
MAX T/O: 1140 lb (517 kg)

PERFORMANCE:
MAX SPEED: 120 mph (192 kmh)
RANGE: endurance of 48 hours
POWERPLANT: Rotax 582
OUTPUT: 65 hp (48 kW)

FIRST FLIGHT DATE:
mid-1989

FEATURES:
Low-mounted straight wings;
inverted-vee tail; retractable
undercarriage; pusher propeller

General Atomics i-Gnat-ER

Unmanned Aerial Vehicle

General Atomics' i-Gnat-ER system is an improved, larger version of the company's Gnat-750 that offers the combination of long endurance, increased payload capacity, ease of use, and low maintenance. Originally designed to perform tactical surveillance at altitudes up to 25,000 ft, the i-Gnat-ER has been fitted with the extended wings of the Predator UAV and a more powerful, turbocharged, Rotax 914 four-stroke piston engine that allows it to operate up to altitudes to 30,500 ft. A wider variety of payloads can also be carried by the bigger i-Gnat-ER—up to 200 lb internally and 300 lb externally. Datalink antennas can also be mounted above and below the fuselage, while a synthetic-aperture radar can be housed in a bulged lower forward fuselage. The i-Gnat-ER's numerous roles include reconnaissance, surveillance, targeting, acquisition/designation, communication relay, electronic warfare, and signals intelligence, its impressive 40-hour flight endurance making it well suited to all these mission taskings. The Army recently acquired three i-Gnat-ERs and has employed them in Iraq on reconnaissance duties since March 2004.

SPECIFICATION:

ACCOMMODATION:
Unmanned

DIMENSIONS:
LENGTH: 18 ft 11 in (5.76 m)
WINGSPAN: 48 ft 8.50 in (14.85 m)
HEIGHT: 2 ft 1.50 in (0.65 m)

WEIGHTS:
EMPTY: unknown
MAX T/O: 1650 lb (748 kg)

PERFORMANCE:
MAX SPEED: 210 mph (336 kmh)
RANGE: endurance of 40 hours
POWERPLANT: Rotax 914
OUTPUT: 100 hp (75 kW)

FIRST FLIGHT DATE:
Unknown

FEATURES:
Low-mounted straight wings; inverted-vee tail; retractable undercarriage; pusher propeller

General Atomics RQ/MQ-1 Predator A

Unmanned Aerial Vehicle

In January 1994 General Atomics was awarded an Advanced Concept Technology Demonstration contract by the Defense Airborne Reconnaissance Office to produce ten RQ-1 Predator UAVs. This design was based on scaled-up elements of its Gnat-750, although it initially used the same engine. The first vehicle flew in July 1994, and examples entered service with the USAF early the following year. In July 1995 the Air Force sent three to Albania to replace CIA Gnat-750s in operations over Yugoslavia. A second Predator deployment took place in March 1996, when aircraft overflew Bosnia from Hungary. By then Predators had also started testing with the Navy, operating with carrier battle groups and submarines. The UAV made its Persian Gulf debut in 1999, flying missions over Iraq and Iran as part of Operation Southern Watch. In 2001 the Predator was cleared to fly with Hellfire and Stinger missiles, the UAV's designation when armed being changed to MQ-1L. USAF and CIA Predators have successfully deployed weapons in Iraq, Yemen, and Afghanistan.

SPECIFICATION:

ACCOMMODATION:
Unmanned

DIMENSIONS:
LENGTH: 26 ft 8 in (8.13 m)
WINGSPAN: 48 ft 8.50 in (14.85 m)
HEIGHT: 6 ft 11 in (2.11 m)

WEIGHTS:
EMPTY: 1130 lb (512 kg)
MAX T/O: 2250 lb (1020 kg)

PERFORMANCE:
MAX SPEED: 138 mph (222 kmh)
RANGE: endurance of 40 hours
POWERPLANT: Rotax 914
OUTPUT: 100 hp (75 kW)

FIRST FLIGHT DATE:
July 1994

ARMAMENT:
Single AGM-114 Hellfire or
FIM-92E Stinger missiles on
single underwing stores pylons

FEATURES:
Low-mounted straight wings;
inverted-vee tail; retractable
undercarriage; pusher propeller;
sensor turret under nose;
bulbous forward upper fuselage

General Atomics RQ/MQ-9 Predator B

Unmanned Aerial Vehicle

Having delivered 55 Predator As to the USAF by late 2000, and with a further 70 on order for the Air Force, Navy, and the CIA, General Atomics commenced work on the Predator B following demands by the military for a UAV that could carry larger payloads higher, farther, and faster. Sharing very few components with its predecessor, but capable of using its ground-control systems, the RQ-9 was designed from the outset for long endurance high-altitude surveillance. The prototype made its first flight on February 2, 2001, the UAV being powered by the Honeywell TPE331-10T turboprop engine. The first pre-production aircraft were delivered to the USAF in late 2003, and at least one of these was sent to the Middle East for evaluation the following year. Like the Predator A, the B-model can also be armed with Hellfire and Stinger missiles (and 500-lb GBU-38 JDAM), changing its designation to MQ-9. The Air Force plans to have the first of 60 MQ-9s in service by 2008, while the Navy also ordered the UAV in December 2005.

SPECIFICATION:

ACCOMMODATION:
Unmanned

DIMENSIONS:
LENGTH: 36 ft 0 in (10.97 m)
WINGSPAN: 66 ft 0 in (20.12 m)
HEIGHT: unknown

WEIGHTS:
EMPTY: 6000 lb (2722 kg)
MAX T/O: 10,000 lb (4536 kg)

PERFORMANCE:
MAX SPEED: 250 mph (400 kmh)
RANGE: endurance of 30+ hours
POWERPLANT: Honeywell TPE331-10T
OUTPUT: 950 shp (708 kW)

FIRST FLIGHT DATE:
February 2, 2001

ARMAMENT:
Single AGM-114 Hellfire or FIM-92E Stinger missiles, or GBU-38 JDAM, on single underwing stores pylons

FEATURES:
Low-mounted straight wings; upright-vee tail, with central ventral fin; retractable undercarriage; pusher propeller; sensor turret under nose; bulbous forward upper fuselage

Lockheed Martin/Boeing RQ-3 DarkStar

Unmanned Aerial Vehicle

Produced by the same team at Lockheed's "Skunk Works" that designed the F-117, the RQ-3 DarkStar was built for stealth employment, hence its distinctive shape. Described as a "flying saucer mated to a pair of sailplane wings" by one aviation journalist, the UAV's short, broad fuselage housed the engine, two avionics bays, and landing gear. Designed to meet a USAF requirement for a high-altitude UAV that could take off, fly to its target, operate its sensors, transmit information, and then return and land without human intervention, the RQ-3 only needed operator input should its flight plan and sensor orientation change while in flight—these alterations could be made through radio or satellite relay. Fitted with either an optical sensor or radar, the UAV could send digital information to a satellite while still in flight. The prototype made its first flight on March 29, 1996, but was destroyed trying to make its second on April 22. Struggling for aerodynamic stability, and failing to meet cost and performance objectives, DarkStar was terminated in January 1999.

SPECIFICATION:

ACCOMMODATION:
Unmanned

DIMENSIONS:
LENGTH: 15 ft 0 in (4.57 m)
WINGSPAN: 69 ft 0 in (21.03 m)
HEIGHT: 3 ft 6 in (1.10 m)

WEIGHTS:
EMPTY: unknown
MAX T/O: 8600 lb (3901 kg)

PERFORMANCE:
MAX SPEED: 288 mph (464 kmh)
RANGE: 575 miles (925 km)
POWERPLANT: Williams FJ44-1A
OUTPUT: 950 lb st (4 kN)

FIRST FLIGHT DATE:
March 29, 1996

FEATURES:
Straight wings; no tail; retractable undercarriage; circular, near-flat fuselage, with flush engine inlet on top; retractable undercarriage

Northrop Grumman/Teledyne Ryan RQ-4 Global Hawk

Unmanned Aerial Vehicle

Designed by Teledyne Ryan Aeronautical to fulfill an early 1990s DARO requirement for a multi-sensor UAV that could perform long-range surveillance missions for the USAF, the RQ-4 proposal was selected as the winner from a field of 14 entrants. Larger and more powerful than its rivals, but also very conservative in its layout, the Global Hawk made its first flight on February 28, 1998. Capable of flying higher than any other UAV currently in service, the RQ-4A is fitted with electro-optical sensors and synthetic aperture radar. Despite the second prototype being lost in a crash in March 1999, the Global Hawk proved its ability in a series of test flights both at home and abroad. In October 2001, two Global Hawks saw action over Afghanistan, flying missions lasting nearly 30 hours. The UAV also participated in Operation Iraqi Freedom in March 2003, and both theaters are regularly serviced by RQ-4As today. The first of 51 production-standard Global Hawks for the USAF was delivered in August 2003, and the Navy has ordered two for evaluation.

SPECIFICATION:

ACCOMMODATION:
Unmanned

DIMENSIONS:
LENGTH: 44 ft 0 in (13.41 m)
WINGSPAN: 116 ft 3 in (35.43 m)
HEIGHT: 15 ft 3 in (4.63 m)

WEIGHTS:
EMPTY: 9200 lb (4173 kg)
MAX T/O: 25,600 lb (11,612 kg)

PERFORMANCE:
MAX SPEED: 400 mph (644 kmh)
RANGE: 15,525 miles (24,985 km)
POWERPLANT: Allison/Rolls-Royce AE3007H
OUTPUT: 7050 lb st (31 kN)

FIRST FLIGHT DATE:
February 28, 1998

FEATURES:
Swept wings; no tail; upright vee-tail; retractable under-carriage; podded turbofan engine atop rear fuselage; bulbous forward upper fuselage

Northrop Grumman RQ-8 Fire Scout

Tactical Unmanned Aerial Vehicle

In February 2000 the Navy awarded Northrop Grumman a contract to develop its RQ-8 Fire Scout Tactical Unmanned Aerial Vehicle (TUAV) for service use. Based on the commercial Schweizer 330 series helicopter fitted with an Israeli-developed sensor payload, the Fire Scout beat rival designs from Bell and Sikorsky. The Navy hoped to use the RQ-8 to replace its elderly, Israeli-designed, Pioneer RQ-2 UAVs both ashore and at sea. Its primary roles would be intelligence/surveillance/reconnaissance, targeting using infrared/optical sensors and laser target designation. In May 2002 the prototype RQ-8 commenced flight testing, although several months later the program was terminated by the Navy due to a "change in tactical requirements." However, the Fire Scout was resurrected in 2003 because of the urgent need for a TUAV to operate from the Navy's future fleet of Littoral Control Ships (in service starting in 2008). It has committed to an initial purchase of 69 RQ-8s, 33 of which will be supplied to the Marine Corps—the first of these will enter service in 2007.

SPECIFICATION:

ACCOMMODATION:
Unmanned

DIMENSIONS:
LENGTH: 22 ft 10 in (6.97 m)
ROTOR DIAMETER: 27 ft 6 in (8.38 m)
HEIGHT: 9 ft 5 in (2.87 m)

WEIGHTS:
EMPTY: 1457 lb (661 kg)
MAX T/O: 2650 lb (1157 kg)

PERFORMANCE:
MAX SPEED: 144 mph (213 kmh)
RANGE: endurance of three hours
POWERPLANT: Allison/Rolls-Royce 250-C20W
OUTPUT: 420 shp (313 kW)

FIRST FLIGHT DATE:
May 19, 2002

FEATURES:
Pod and boom fuselage; faired-in engine above pod; skid undercarriage

Northrop Grumman x-47a/b Pegasus

Unmanned Combat Aerial Vehicle

Northrop Grumman's x-47 Pegasus Unmanned Combat Aerial Vehicle-Naval (UCAV-N) was a rival to Boeing's x-45 for the Joint Unmanned Combat Air System, although the "joint" nature of this competition ended in March 2006 when the Air Force chose not to proceed with the x-45—the latter is still being evaluated by the Navy, however. As with the x-45a, Northrop Grumman (or more accurately Scale Composites) has built the sub-scale x-47a Pegasus a as a demonstrator for its much larger, long-range and carrier-capable x-47b. The a-model is a near diamond-shape flying wing that has been designed with stealth attributes built in. Making its first flight on February 23, 2003, the x-47a's primary role is to demonstrate the UCAV-N's suitability for carrier operations – it has been fitted with an all-important arrestor hook for this phase of its flight testing. If selected for production, the x-47b will feature a "cranked kite" wing configuration, as well as two weapon bays. The Navy's hopes to fully integrate UCAV-Ns into its carrier air wings.

SPECIFICATION (x-47a):

ACCOMMODATION:
Unmanned

DIMENSIONS:
LENGTH: 27 ft 11 in (8.51 m)
WINGSPAN: 27 ft 0 in (8.23 m)
HEIGHT: 6 ft 1 in (1.86 m)

WEIGHTS:
EMPTY: 3835 lb (8455 kg)
MAX T/O: 5500 lb (2495 kg)

PERFORMANCE:
MAX SPEED: unknown
RANGE: endurance of more than one hour
POWERPLANT: Pratt & Whitney JT15D-5C-TF
OUTPUT: 3190 lb st (14 kN)

FIRST FLIGHT DATE:
February 23, 2003 (x-47a)

FEATURES:
Diamond-shape flying-wing configuration; blended center fuselage; retractable undercarriage

Helicopters
and
Rotorcraft

Bell HTL/HUL/H-13 Sioux

three-seat, single-engined light utility helicopter

The highly successsful and diminutive Bell Model 47 can trace its lineage back to the innovative Model 30 of 1943, which featured the elegant simplicity of a teetering rotor system. In 1946, it was the first helicopter to be certificated by the American Civil Aeronautics Administration (CAA). An order followed in 1946 for 28 Model 47Bs for evaluation by the USAAF, which designated the helicopters YR-13s—ten were transferred to the Navy and given the designation HTL-1.

Having been tested in hot and cold conditions, the Bell helicopter was the subject of a follow-on order in 1948 when the Army purchased 65 H-13Bs. These machines had bigger engines than the YR-13s and could be easily disassembled for transport on a Fairchild C-82. The Navy followed suit in 1949 when it ordered 12 near-identical HTL-2s. The Army's follow-on H-13D (87 built) and E (490 built) featured a skid undercarriage, stripped rear fuselage, and external stretcher carriers. The former, in particular, were put to very good use during the Korean War when the H-13 saw widespread use in the medevac role, having replaced fixed-wing Grasshoppers in this critical mission.

The Army continued to buy the Sioux in large numbers through to the mid-1960s, with each new variant usually featuring a more powerful engine and detailed refinements, which improved the long-lived design's performance. The H-13G model of 1953 was built to the tune of 265 airframes, followed by 470 H-13Hs (some of which went to the USAF) starting in 1956. In 1962 all Army H-13s became OH-13s, and during the following year the first of

265 s-models was delivered. The final Army variant was the TH-13T basic instrument trainer, 411 of which entered service beginning in 1965. The Navy HTLS (HULS from 1955) were significantly different from their Army brethren, and were bought in much smaller quantities—209 were acquired, spread over four models, in the 1950s. The last H-13S were retired from US military service in the early 1980s.

SPECIFICATION (H-13H):

ACCOMMODATION:
Pilot and two passengers

DIMENSIONS:
LENGTH: 27 ft 4 in (7.43 m)
ROTOR DIAMETER: 35 ft 1 in (10.69 m)
HEIGHT: 9 ft 6 in (2.92 m)

WEIGHTS:
EMPTY: 1564 lb (709 kg)
MAX T/O: 2450 lb (1111 kg)

PERFORMANCE:
MAX SPEED: 100 mph (160 kmh)
RANGE: 238 miles (381 km)
POWERPLANT: Lycoming VO-435
OUTPUT: 200 hp (149 kW)

FIRST FLIGHT DATE:
December 8, 1945 (Model 47)

FEATURES:
Blown-bubble canopy; lattice-frame tail boom; skid undercarriage; exposed engine

Bell UH-1 Iroquois

up to 16-seat, single/twin-engined utility/battlefield helicopter

Developed from the XH-40 prototype, which had been built by Bell in response to an Army requirement issued in June 1955 for a general utility and medevac helicopter, the first production HU-1A (Bell Model 204), as it was then designated, entered service in the late 1950s. In 1959 Bell started work on the larger HU-1B, which could seat eight, instead of four, passengers. With the first examples reaching the Army in March 1961, the HU-1B (which became the UH-1B in 1962 following the adoption of the triservice designation system) was deployed to Vietnam in large numbers, where it performed utility and armed-escort missions. A total of 1014 B-models were built for the Army in 1961-65.

Just as the UH-1B commenced production, Bell had begun flight testing the Model 205, which boasted an even longer fuselage and more powerful engine. Designated the UH-1D, this variant would be used primarily as a troop carrier (it could accommodate 12 soldiers) in Vietnam—2008 were bought by the Army. Built concurrently with the D-model, the smaller UH-1C (767 built starting in 1965) was similar in size to the earlier B-model, but featured an improved rotor and greater fuel capacity. In 1967 the D-model was replaced in production by the definitive UH-1H, this version being similar to its predecessor except for its bigger engine. Remaining in production until 1976, 5435 H-models were built for the Army.

Although more than 2500 UH-1s were lost in Vietnam, the Iroquois served on as the Army's standard transportation helicopter until largely replaced by the UH-60 Blackhawk in the 1980s. As of 2000, hundreds of UH-1H/VS equipped

Army National Guard and specialist test units. The USAF also procured more than 100 UH-1s for specialist missions. The Navy/Marine Corps bought substantially more, 212 UH/TH-1Es being acquired in the late 1960s, followed by 115 HH-1 rescue and TH-1 trainers. The twin-engined UH-1N has proven the longest lived, however, with survivors of the 204 received in the early 1970s still seeing frontline service (including combat in Iraq) today.

SPECIFICATION
(UH-1H):

ACCOMMODATION:
Pilot, copilot, and up to 14 passengers (UH-1H)

DIMENSIONS:
LENGTH: 41 ft 6 in (12.65 m)
ROTOR DIAMETER: 48 ft 0 in (14.63 m)
HEIGHT: 14 ft 6 in (4.41 m)

WEIGHTS:
EMPTY: 5210 lb (2363 kg)
MAX T/O: 9500 lb (4310 kg)

PERFORMANCE:
MAX SPEED: 127 mph (205 kmh)
RANGE: 262 miles (420 km)
POWERPLANT: Textron Lycoming T53-L-13
OUTPUT: 1400 shp (1045 kW)

FIRST FLIGHT DATE:
October 22, 1956 (XH-40)

ARMAMENT:
Pintle-mounted Browning 0.50-in machine gun in doorway and 7.62-mm miniguns/grenade launchers/rockets on fuselage-mounted weapon racks

FEATURES:
Squat fuselage; skid undercarriage; enclosed engine; two-bladed rotor

Bell HSL

four-seat, single-engined ASW helicopter

When the Navy realized that its early helicopters were too small to undertake the ASW mission, it launched a competition in June 1950 for a purpose-built ASW machine. Bell's Model 61 was the winner, and Bell received a contract to construct three XHSL-1S. For the first, and only, time in Bell's history, they adopted a tandem-rotor layout. The fore and aft rotors were interconnected, and could be folded for carrier operations. Fitted with an autopilot and equipped with sonar for submarine detection, the HSL-1 was the biggest naval helicopter to be ordered into production in the USA when Bell received a contract to build 78 examples in 1953. The helicopter suffered numerous teething problems, however. Carrier trials finally took place in March 1955, when its large size, awkward deck stowage process and high cabin noise when hovering revealed the HSL-1's unsuitability for the ASW mission at sea. The production order was cut to 50, and HSLs began reaching HU-1 in January 1957; none were used operationally. All had been retired by the early 1960s.

SPECIFICATION:

ACCOMMODATION:
Pilot, copilot, and two sonar operators

DIMENSIONS:
LENGTH: 39 ft 11 in (12.17 m)
ROTOR DIAMETER: 51 ft 5 in (15.70 m)
HEIGHT: 14 ft 5 in (4.40 m)

WEIGHTS:
EMPTY: 13,073 lb (5930 kg)
MAX T/O: 17,000 lb (7711 kg)

PERFORMANCE:
MAX SPEED: 116 mph (185 kmh)
RANGE: 352 miles (185 km)
POWERPLANT: Pratt & Whitney R-2800-50
OUTPUT: 2400 hp (1790 kW)

FIRST FLIGHT DATE:
March 4, 1953

FEATURES:
Twin-rotor configuration; fixed undercarriage; exposed engine in rear fuselage; stabilizing fins at rear

Bell UH-1Y and AH-1Z

up to 12-seat, twin-engined utility and battlefield helicopter

In 1996, the Marine Corps explored modernizing the UH-1N and AH-1W airframes simultaneously while improving their commonality. Both helicopters had originally used many of the same components, but two separate and complicated logistics trains emerged as each aircraft became more specialized. The H-1 program will bring them to an 84% commonality thus reducing procurement costs, parts inventories and training cycles. Common components included a new 4-bladed hingeless composite rotor with greatly reduced vibration and improved low-G maneuvering capability as well as common tailbooms, "glass cockpit" avionics suite and a substantially enhanced twin T700 engine package. The UH-1Y will double the range and payload of the UH-1N while the AH-1Z will improve on the AH-1W with tripled range and doubled weapons load-out while also carrying two AIM-9L Sidewinders for self-defense. By 2006, the H-1 program order stood at 180 AH-1ZS and 100 UH-1YS with the bulk being "new-builds" rather than remanufactured airframes.

SPECIFICATION (UH-1Y):

ACCOMMODATION:
Pilot, copilot, and up to ten passengers

DIMENSIONS:
LENGTH: 44 ft 4 in (13.51 m)
ROTOR DIAMETER: 48 ft 0 in (14.63 m)
HEIGHT: 13 ft 10.50 in (4.23 m)

WEIGHTS:
EMPTY: 11,400 lb (5171 kg)
MAX T/O: 18,500 lb (8392 kg)

PERFORMANCE:
MAX SPEED: 127 mph (184 kmh)
RANGE: 404 miles (646 km)
POWERPLANT: two General Electric T700-GE-401S
OUTPUT: 3446 shp (2570 kW)

FIRST FLIGHT DATE:
December 20, 2001

ARMAMENT:
Pintle-mounted 7.62-mm minigun or 0.50-in machine gun in doorway and rockets on fuselage-mounted weapon racks

FEATURES:
Squat fuselage; skid undercarriage; enclosed twin engines; four-bladed rotor

Bell OH-58 Kiowa and TH-57 Sea Ranger/Creek

up to five-seat, single-engined scout/training helicopter

Bell's Model 206 (initially given the military designation HO-4) was one of three finalists in the Army's 1960 four-seat Light Observation Helicopter (LOH) competition, which was eventually won by the Hughes OH-6 Cayuse. The redesignated OH-4A had flown in prototype form in December 1962, and although rejected by the Army, Bell developed the machine into the Model 206A for the civil market. Christened the JetRanger, the aircraft entered production in 1966, and has since become the world's most successful light turbine helicopter. In 1967 the Army reopened the LOH competition because of rising costs and the late delivery of the OH-6, and this time Bell received orders for the 206A in OH-58A Kiowa form. The Army duly bought 2200 helicopters over five years, with deliveries commencing in May 1969. The Kiowa reached Vietnam several months later, where examples saw widespread use in the visual observation and target acquisition roles through to 1973.

In 1976 the Army contracted Bell to improve the Kiowa through the fitment of a more powerful engine, flat glass canopy, and infrared suppression equipment. Designated the OH-58C, Bell upgraded 435 A-models between 1976-85. In September 1981, the Kiowa was selected for the Army Helicopter Improvement Program (AHIP), which would see the machine developed into an armed scout helicopter. Designated the OH-58D Kiowa Warrior, the AHIP machine featured a four-bladed main rotor, more powerful engine, and extensively revised avionics, including a mast-mounted sight for 24-hour combat aerial reconnaissance. The OH-58D could also employ Hellfire air-to-ground and Stinger air-to-air missiles, as well as gun and rocket pods. Bell reworked 585 OH-58A/CS into OH-68DS between 1985-91.

The Kiowa is still in widespread use with both frontline Army and National Guard units, and has seen much combat in Iraq since 2003. The Navy has also used the Model 206A since 1969, having acquired 180 TH-57 Sea Rangers to fulfill its requirement for a light turbine primary training helicopter. Belatedly following the Navy's lead, the Army bought 137 Model 206BS in 1993 to serve as its New Training Helicopter, these machines being designated TH-67A Creeks.

SPECIFICATION (OH-58C):

ACCOMMODATION:
Pilot and up to four passengers

DIMENSIONS:
LENGTH: 34 ft 4.50 in (10.48 m)
ROTOR DIAMETER: 35 ft 4 in (10.77 m)
HEIGHT: 9 ft 5 in (2.87 m)

WEIGHTS:
EMPTY: 1600 lb (726 kg)
MAX T/O: 3200 lb (1452 kg)

PERFORMANCE:
MAX SPEED: 141 mph (226 kmh)
RANGE: 358 miles (572 km)
POWERPLANT: Allison T63-A-720
OUTPUT: 420 shp (313 kW)

FIRST FLIGHT DATE:
December 8, 1962 (OH-4A)

ARMAMENT:
7.62-mm minigun or 0.50-in machine gun; rocket/grenade launchers and missiles on fuselage-mounted weapon racks (OH-58D only)

FEATURES:
"Tadpole" fuselage; skid undercarriage; enclosed engine; large glazed cockpit area; mast-mounted sight (OH-58D only)

Bell AH-1 HueyCobra

two-seat, single/twin-engined attack helicopter

The AH-1, the world's first dedicated attack helicopter, began as an in-house project at Bell known as the Model 209. It mated the powerplant, transmission and rotor of the UH-1B/C with a new fuselage, tandem cockpit, chin turret and stub wings for additional ordnance. In 1965, the Army selected the AH-56 Cheyenne as its primary armed helicopter, but escalating operations in Vietnam required an interim armed escort. Bell's foresight had put it far ahead of any potential contenders, easily winning it a production contract that would run to 1,126 AH-1Gs, including 38 for the Marines. The troubled AH-56 never came to be and the AH-1 remained in Army service from its combat introduction in 1967 until its final retirement from the National Guard in 2002. The last year of Vietnam combat demonstrated a need for an anti-armor role and post-war, the "G" models evolved through "Q", "S", "P", "E" and "F" variants featuring TOW missile capability. In 1996, some Vietnam-era Cobras were still in combat in Somalia.

SPECIFICATION (AH-1F):

ACCOMMODATION:
Pilot and gunner in tandem

DIMENSIONS:
LENGTH: 44 ft 7 in (13.59 m)
ROTOR DIAMETER: 44 ft 0 in (13.41 m)
HEIGHT: 13 ft 6 in (4.11 m)

WEIGHTS:
EMPTY: 6479 lb (2939 kg)
MAX T/O: 10,000 lb (4536 kg)

PERFORMANCE:
MAX SPEED: 173 mph (276 kmh)
RANGE: 359 miles (574 km)
POWERPLANT: Textron Lycoming T53-L-703
OUTPUT: 1800 shp (1342 kW)

FIRST FLIGHT DATE:
September 7, 1965 (Model 209)

ARMAMENT:
M197 20-mm cannon in nose turret; grenade launchers/ rockets/antiarmor missiles on fuselage-mounted stub wings

FEATURES:
Lateral engine intakes behind tandem cockpit; slim fuselage; skid undercarriage; enclosed engine/s; gun turret beneath nose

Bell AH-1J/T SeaCobra and AH-1W SuperCobra

two-seat, twin-engined attack helicopter

During Vietnam War trials with the AH-1G, the Marine Corps determined that the extended over-water exposure of amphibious operations required a twin-engine capability. The PT6 "Twin Pac"-powered AH-1J SeaCobra resulted. Up-armed with a turret-mounted 20-mm cannon, the first of 69 AH-1Js began limited combat service in Vietnam during 1971. Beginning in 1976, AH-1Js were rebuilt to AH-1T standard with a new rotor system and Pratt & Whitney T400 engines with an additional 700 shp. An anti-armor TOW missile capability was also added. By March 1986, the greatly enhanced AH-1W SuperCobra began entering service with nearly double the shaft horsepower, advanced avionics and better armament, including the laser-guided Hellfire. Forty-three of the 57 AH-1Ts were rebuilt to AH-1W standard while the Marine Corps acquired another 179 "new-builds". The "Whiskey" Cobra has seen extensive combat, primarily in Iraq (Operations Desert Storm and Iraqi Freedom) and Afghanistan, where it has proven highly effective.

SPECIFICATION (AH-1W):

ACCOMMODATION:
Pilot and gunner in tandem

DIMENSIONS:
LENGTH: 45 ft 0 in (13.72 m)
ROTOR DIAMETER: 48 ft 0 in (14.63 m)
HEIGHT: 14 ft 7 in (4.44 m)

WEIGHTS:
EMPTY: 10,215 lb (4635 kg)
MAX T/O: 14,750 lb (6690 kg)

PERFORMANCE:
MAX SPEED: 176 mph (282 kmh)
RANGE: 367 miles (587 km)
POWERPLANT: two General Electric T700-GE-401S
OUTPUT: 3446 shp (2570 kW)

FIRST FLIGHT DATE:
April 1980 (AH-1T+)

ARMAMENT:
M197 20-mm cannon in nose turret; grenade launchers /rockets/antiarmor and anti-aircraft missiles/bombs on fuselage-mounted stub wings

FEATURES:
Lateral engine intakes behind tandem cockpit; slim fuselage; skid undercarriage; enclosed twin engines; gun turret beneath nose; bulged cheek fairings

Bell/Boeing V-22 Osprey

27-seat, twin-engined tilt-rotor transport

The V-22 Osprey evolved from a joint services program launched in the early 1980s aimed at developing a transport based on the Bell/NASA XV-15 demonstrator. In 1983 the Navy contracted Bell/ Boeing to develop their V-22, and the prototype made its maiden flight in March 1989. Since then, the Osprey has endured a protracted development phase due to fatal crashes and budget blowouts. It has survived cancelation because its combat radius allows it to support the amphibious doctrine of "vertical envelopment" in a manner previous assault helicopters could not. Powered by two Allison T400 turboprops mounted in tilted nacelles, the Osprey can perform all the missions of a helicopter, yet cruise at twice the speed carrying nearly twice the payload of the CH-46. Full-scale production was authorized in September 2005, and the Marine Corps has commenced converting its first frontline unit onto the MV-22B. The Marine Corps have a requirement for 360 MV-22BS, the Navy 48 HV-22BS for Combat Search and Rescue and the Air Force 50 CV-22BS for use with Special Forces.

SPECIFICATION (MV-22B):

ACCOMMODATION:
Pilot, copilot, crew chief, and 24 troops

DIMENSIONS:
LENGTH: 57 ft 4 in (17.48 m)
ROTOR DIAMETER: 38 ft 0 in (11.58 m)
HEIGHT: 21 ft 9 in (6.63 m)

WEIGHTS:
EMPTY: 33,140 lb (15,032 kg)
MAX T/O: 57,000 lb (25,855 kg)

PERFORMANCE:
MAX SPEED: 318 mph (509 kmh)
RANGE: 2431 miles (3890 km)
POWERPLANT: two Rolls-Royce/Allison T406-AD-400S
OUTPUT: 12,300 shp (9172 kW)

FIRST FLIGHT DATE:
March 19, 1989

ARMAMENT:
Pintle-mounted Browning 0.50-in machine gun in rear loading ramp

FEATURES:
Engines in rotating nacelles at wingtips; twin fins; rear-loading ramp; retractable, wheeled undercarriage

Boeing H-46 Sea Knight

28-seat, twin-engined multirole utility helicopter

Tried and tested in combat, the H-46 has been the Marine Corps' primary assault troop transport since 1964. Developed as a private venture by Vertol (later acquired by Boeing), the H-46 evolved from the Model 107, which flew in prototype form on April 22, 1958. Vertol adopted the tandem main rotor layout so as to avoid the need for an antitorque tail rotor, thus creating a helicopter with an unobstructed main cabin and rear loading freight ramp. The Army initially looked into buying the 107, but chose the larger CH-47 Chinook instead. However, the Marine Corps selected the CH-46 as a replacement for its UH-34s, and the first of 160 A-models entered service in June 1964. A further 266 CH-46Ds and 174 CH-46Fs were also bought, and the survivors were all upgraded to CH-46E standard from 1977 onward. The Navy acquired 14 UH-46As and ten UH-46Ds in 1964-65, and these were retired in 2004 following the delivery of MH-60Ss. Marine Corps H-46s have continued to see widespread frontline service (especially in Iraq), although they will gradually be replaced by MV-22Bs.

SPECIFICATION (CH-46E):

ACCOMMODATION:
Pilot, copilot, crew chief, and up to 25 passengers

DIMENSIONS:
LENGTH: 44 ft 10 in (13.67 m)
ROTOR DIAMETER: 50 ft 0 in (15.24 m)
HEIGHT: 16 ft 9 in (5.09 m)

WEIGHTS:
EMPTY: 11,585 lb (5255 kg)
MAX T/O: 24,300 lb (11,022 kg)

PERFORMANCE:
MAX SPEED: 166 mph (267 kmh)
RANGE: 694 miles (1110 km)
POWERPLANT: two General Electric T58-GE-16s
OUTPUT: 3740 shp (2790 kW)

FIRST FLIGHT DATE:
April 22, 1958 (Model 107)

FEATURES:
Twin rotor configuration; fixed tricycle undercarriage; enclosed engines; rear fuselage sponsons

Boeing H-47 Chinook

47-seat, twin-engined multirole utility helicopter

The Chinook was selected by the Army as its standard vertical takeoff and landing battlefield mobility transport in March 1959. The Army had initially been interested in purchasing the smaller Model 107, but instead selected the much larger Model 114, which featured the former design's tandem-rotor and rear-loading ramp layout. The Chinook was capable of carrying 40 troops with full equipment, and it could also lift underslung loads up to a weight of 20,000 lb. The prototype YHC-1B (the Chinook was redesignated the CH-47 in 1962) made its first flight on September 21, 1961, and production A-models reached frontline units starting in August of the following year. A total of 354 CH-47As would be built for the Army up to 1967, and these saw widespread service in Vietnam hauling troops, ammunition, weaponry, food supplies, and aircraft parts, among other things.

The improved B-model went into production in 1967, 108 examples being built. The considerably more powerful, and longer-ranged, CH-47C started to reach Vietnam in September 1968, this version being able to lift its full payload in hot or high conditions. Aside from the 270 newly built C-models delivered to the Army, Boeing also upgraded numerous CH-47A/BS to this specification. In the late 1970s Boeing Vertol developed the updated CH-47D, which boasted bigger engines, composite rotor blades, vastly improved avionics, and a triple cargo-hook arrangement. The prototype YCH-47D flew for the first time on May 11, 1979, and the Army duly had 328 CH-47CS rebuilt as D-models. Just over 100 brand new machines were also acquired.

In 1987 the Army bought 50 armed MH-47ES for use by Special Operations Forces, these helicopters having still bigger engines with digital avionics, greater fuel capacity, aerial refueling capability, and improved avionics. Like the D-models, the MH-47ES have seen widespread use in Iraq and Afghanistan. On June 25, 2001, the first remanufactured CH-47F—fitted with the bigger MH-47E engines and a "glass" cockpit—commenced flight testing as the Army's Improved Cargo Helicopter, and the first of 302 F-models (rebuilt CH-47DS) should enter Army service in 2007.

SPECIFICATION (CH-47D):

ACCOMMODATION:
Pilot, copilot, crew chief, and up to 44 passengers

DIMENSIONS:
LENGTH: 51 ft 0 in (15.54 m)
ROTOR DIAMETER: 60 ft 0 in (18.29 m)
HEIGHT: 18 ft 11.50 in (5.78 m)

WEIGHTS:
EMPTY: 23,401 lb (10,615 kg)
MAX T/O: 53,500 lb (24,267 kg)

PERFORMANCE:
MAX SPEED: 186 mph (298 kmh)
RANGE: 350 miles (560 km)
POWERPLANT: two Allied Signal (Lycoming) T55-L-712S
OUTPUT: 9000 shp (6712 kW)

FIRST FLIGHT DATE:
September 21, 1961 (YHC-1B)

ARMAMENT:
Door- and ramp-mounted 7.62-mm or 0.50-in machine guns

FEATURES:
Twin rotor configuration; fixed-wheeled undercarriage; podded engines; rear-loading ramp

Boeing (McDonnell Douglas) AH-64 Apache

two-seat, twin-engined attack helicopter

The Army's only dedicated attack helicopter since the retirement of the AH-1, the AH-64 Apache can trace its lineage back to the 1972 Advanced Attack Helicopter competition. The winning design was the Hughes Model 97/YAH-64, which was selected for development over Bell's Model 409/YAH-63 in December 1976. Having flown for the first time in prototype form on September 30, 1975, the Hughes design had to wait until 1982 before it received production approval. In 1984 Hughes Helicopters was acquired by McDonnell Douglas, and that same year production-standard AH-64As started reaching the Army. Built to replace the AH-1F Cobra, the Apache boasted the nose-mounted Lockheed Martin AAQ-11 Target Acquisition and Designation Sight and Pilot Night Vision Sensor—this equipment set the AH-64 apart from all other attack helicopters that had preceded it. The Apache was also equipped with a specially developed M230 30-mm chain gun, as well as four stub-wing hardpoints for Hellfire air-to-ground and unguided rocket pods.

A total of 827 A-models were built for the Army, with production ending in 1997—McDonnell Douglas had been acquired by Boeing 12 months earlier. By then the Apache had seen combat in Panama in 1989 and in Operation Desert Storm in 1991. Surviving A-models commenced an upgrade program in 1996 that has seen them rebuilt as AH-64Ds, this Apache variant featuring improved avionics in enlarged cheek fairings. Of the 530 scheduled to be upgraded, 227 will be AH-64D Longbow Apaches. This variant has a distinctive Westinghouse mast-mounted millimeter-wave fire control radar, which is used to guide radio frequency-seeking Hellfire missiles launched by radarless AH-64A/DS.

Although enjoying great success as a tank hunter in Desert Storm, the Apache has not fared so well in the Global War on Terror in Iraq and Afghanistan. In fact, a number of AH-64s have been destroyed by small arms fire and shoulder-launched missiles in highly dangerous urban environments such as Baghdad. Despite these mounting losses, the AH-64 remains a potent weapon in regular Army, National Guard, and Reserve service.

SPECIFICATION (AH-64D):

ACCOMMODATION:
Pilot and copilot/gunner in tandem

DIMENSIONS:
LENGTH: 58 ft 2 in (17.73 m)
ROTOR DIAMETER: 48 ft 0 in (14.63 m)
HEIGHT: 16 ft 3 in (4.95 m)

WEIGHTS:
EMPTY: 11,800 lb (5352 kg)
MAX T/O: 23,000 lb (10,433 kg)

PERFORMANCE:
MAX SPEED: 166 mph (265 kmh)
RANGE: 300 miles (480 km)
POWERPLANT: two General Electric T700-GE-701CS
OUTPUT: 3880 shp (2894 kW)

FIRST FLIGHT DATE:
September 30, 1975 (YAH-64)

ARMAMENT:
M230 30-mm chain cannon in nose; rockets/antiarmor and anti-aircraft missiles on fuselage-mounted stub wings

FEATURES:
Shoulder-mounted engines behind tandem cockpit; enlarged cheek fairings; nose-mounted sensor turret; stub wings; wheeled undercarriage; mast-mounted sight (AH-64D Longbow Apache)

Hiller HTE/H-23 Raven

two/three-seat, single-engined light observation/training helicopter

Adopted as the standard Army observation helicopter in 1950, the H-23 was the end product of pioneering helicopter development carried out by Stanley Hiller Jr. in 1944. The first 100 built for the Army were acquired with optional dual controls and associated equipment for carrying two stretcher casualties in external panniers. The Navy also bought 16 examples to act as helicopter trainers in 1950, designating them HTE-1s. An additional 35 HTE-2s, with either quad landing gear or skids, were purchased in 1951. The Army re-ordered again with the advent of the H-23B, buying 273 fitted with skids rather than the A-model's tricycle gear. The three-seater, one-piece canopy H-23C followed (145 built), again for the Army, while in 1957 the first D-models (348 built) were introduced into service at the Primary Helicopter School. This variant featured greater reliability, a more powerful engine, and a new transmission and rotor system. Redesignated the OH-23 in 1962, the final variant to enter Army service was the three-seat dual-control OH-23G, 793 of which were delivered up to 1967.

SPECIFICATION (H-23D):

ACCOMMODATION:
Pilot, and two passengers

DIMENSIONS:
LENGTH: 27 ft 9.5 in (8.45 m)
ROTOR DIAMETER: 24 ft 5 in (7.46 m)
HEIGHT: 9 ft 9.50 in (2.98 m)

WEIGHTS:
EMPTY: 1816 lb (824 kg)
MAX T/O: 2700 lb (1225 kg)

PERFORMANCE:
MAX SPEED: 95 mph (153 kmh)
RANGE: 197 miles (315 km)
POWERPLANT: Lycoming VO-450-23B
OUTPUT: 250 shp (186 kW)

FIRST FLIGHT DATE:
November 1947 (Hillier 360X)

FEATURES:
Bubble canopy; thin, sloped tail boom; skid undercarriage; exposed engine

Hughes TH-55 Osage

two-seat, single-engined training helicopter

The Army's standard helicopter primary trainer from the mid-1960s through to the mid-1980s, the TH-55 Osage was the military derivative of the Hughes Model 269. First flown in October 1956, the Model 269 evoked Army interest in 1958 when five aircraft were acquired for evaluation at Fort Rucker. Designated YHO-2HUS, the modest two-seaters were tested in the scout and observation roles, although it was as a primary trainer that the type was finally selected for Army service in 1964. Acquired to replace the OH-23 Raven, the TH-55A Osage was issued to the Primary Helicopter School at Fort Wolter, Texas, from 1965. A total of 792 TH-55AS were delivered, and more than 60,000 Army pilots learned to fly helicopters in them during three decades of service. Close to 100 TH-55s were placed in storage at Davis-Monthan AFB, Arizona in 1971-74, but the remainder served on until 1988, when they were finally replaced by the TH-57A Creek.

SPECIFICATION:

ACCOMMODATION:
Instructor and student

DIMENSIONS:
LENGTH: 22 ft 4 in (6.81 m)
ROTOR DIAMETER: 26 ft 10 in (8.18 m)
HEIGHT: 8 ft 2.70 in (2.50 m)

WEIGHTS:
EMPTY: 1008 lb (457 kg)
MAX T/O: 1850 lb (839 kg)

PERFORMANCE:
MAX SPEED: 75 mph (120 kmh)
RANGE: 204 miles (328 km)
POWERPLANT: Lycoming HIO-360-A1A
OUTPUT: 180 shp (134 kW)

FIRST FLIGHT DATE:
October 1956 (Model 269)

FEATURES:
Bubble canopy; thin tail boom with v-shaped bracing strut; skid undercarriage; exposed engine

Hughes OH-6 Cayuse and McDonnell Douglas AH/MH-6 Little Bird

up to five-seat, single-engined scout/special operations helicopter

In 1960 the Army drew up a specification calling for the production of a four-seat light observation helicopter to replace its aging Bell and Hiller types. The new aircraft had to have high performance, turboshaft power, easy maintenance, and a low purchase cost. All the major manufacturers submitted proposals, and the Hughes OH-6A Cayuse (based on the Model 369) was declared the winner in May 1965. The helicopter entered Army service four months later, and 1415 were eventually acquired. Of this number, 658 were lost in combat in Vietnam and a further 297 written off in accidents. The survivors were handed over to the Army Reserve and National Guard following the selection of the OH-58 to replace the OH-6 from 1967—the last examples were retired in 1997.

Small numbers of Cayuse were modified into EH/MH6-BS and AH-6CS for use with Special Forces, the helicopters being chosen for special operations work in the wake of the failed US Embassy hostage rescue attempt in Iran in 1980. The Army's Task Force 158 was formed to develop covert procedures and tactics involving military helicopters, and among those tested was the OH-6. Both fast and maneuverable, the helicopter had been given an offensive capability by manufacturer Hughes in the early 1980s through the fitment of stub-mounted Gatling gun pods and rockets.

The Army was impressed with the armed OH-6, its small size, quiet noise signature, and larger-than-expected payload seeing newly built helicopters adopted for the special operations-oriented Task Force 160, now known as the 160th Special Operations Aviation Regiment (SOAR). Based on the T-tailed Hughes 500D and MD500 Defender, these machines were designated EH/MH-6E and AH-6F. The EH variant (four built) was configured for Elint/Sigint/command-post duties, the MH (16 built) for stealthy insertion/extraction, and the AH (ten built) for attack. In the early 1990s all surviving H-6s were reconfigured either as AH-6G attack or MH-6H troopship variants. A number of newly built MH-6HS (16) and AH-6GS (five) were also delivered. The Army is presently in the process of upgrading all of its H-6s (36 airframes) to a common AH/MH-6J specification.

SPECIFICATION (OH-6A):

ACCOMMODATION:
Pilot and four passengers

DIMENSIONS:
LENGTH: 23 ft 0 in (7.01 m)
ROTOR DIAMETER: 26 ft 4 in (8.03 m)
HEIGHT: 8 ft 1.40 in (2.48 m)

WEIGHTS:
EMPTY: 1229 lb (557 kg)
MAX T/O: 2700 lb (1225 kg)

PERFORMANCE:
MAX SPEED: 150 mph (241 kmh)
RANGE: 1560 miles (2510 km)
POWERPLANT: Allison T63-A-5A
OUTPUT: 317 shp (236 kW)

FIRST FLIGHT DATE:
February 27, 1963 (Model 369)

ARMAMENT:
XM27E1 7.62-mm or 0.50-in machine-gun pods, XM75 40-mm grenade launcher or 70-mm rocket pods on stub wings (MH-6 only)

FEATURES:
Egg-shaped cabin; thin tail boom; skid undercarriage; enclosed engine; T-tail on AH/MH-6

Kaman HOK/HTK/HUK/H-43 Huskie

four/eight-seat, single-engined light utility/search and rescue helicopter

Kaman's first successful helicopter design, the H-43 Huskie gained fame for its combat search-and-rescue missions during the Vietnam War. The turbine-powered HH-43B Huskie of the Air Force had its roots in the rudimentary piston-powered open-cockpit Kaman K-225, first tested by the Navy in 1950. Featuring Kaman's distinctive contrarotating and intermeshing twin-rotor system, 29 three-seat HTKs were bought for training purposes in the early 1950s. The Navy followed this up with an order for 24 larger HUK-1s and 81 HOK-1s for the Marine Corps—these were delivered between 1956-58. The USAF ordered 18 as H-43As in 1957 for crash rescue and fire suppression. The H-43B turbine variant quickly followed, with Kaman ultimately delivering 202, along with 37 further improved HH-43Fs. By mounting the powerplant above the cabin rather than behind it, Air Force Huskies were considerably more roomy and boasted rear clamshell doors. The HH-43 became the standard Local Base (LBR) platform at USAF bases worldwide throughout the 1960s. All Huskies had been retired by the mid-1970s.

SPECIFICATION (HH-43B):

ACCOMMODATION:
Pilot, aircrewman, and two/four passengers

DIMENSIONS:
LENGTH: 25 ft 2 in (7.68 m)
ROTOR DIAMETER: 47 ft 0 in (14.33 m)
HEIGHT: 12 ft 7 in (3.84 m)

WEIGHTS:
EMPTY: 4469 lb (2027 kg)
MAX T/O: 5969 lb (2708 kg)

PERFORMANCE:
MAX SPEED: 120 mph (192 kmh)
RANGE: 277 miles (445 km)
POWERPLANT: Lycoming T53-L-1B
OUTPUT: 860 shp (641 kW)

FIRST FLIGHT DATE:
Early 1951 (XHOK)

FEATURES:
Rounded glazed nose; twin contrarotating intermeshing rotor blades; twin tail booms; wheeled undercarriage; engine partially exposed to rear of cabin

Kaman H-2 Seasprite

up to twelve-seat, twin-engined utility/ASW helicopter

The Seasprite was built to fulfill a 1956 Navy requirement for a long-range, all-weather multirole utility helicopter. Kaman's K-20 design was chosen for development, and the prototype completed its maiden flight on July 2, 1959. A total of 190 UH-2A/BS were built in the early 1960s, helicopters reaching the fleet in December 1962. Capable of carrying up to 11 passengers, these machines were used as fleet utility transports, performing search-and-rescue and vertical replenishment missions. In October 1970 the UH-2 was chosen as the basis for the ASW Light Airborne Multi-Purpose System (LAMPS) helicopter, and 20 were converted into SH-2DS through the fitment of search radar and ASW equipment. In May 1973 Kaman converted 88 UH-2/SH-2DS into LAMPS 2 SH-2FS, with bigger engines and improved ASW avionics. A further 52 newly built helicopters were delivered from 1981, followed by six re-engined SH-2GS and 18 converted SH-2FS in 1991. Replaced by the SH-60B in the mid-1980s onward, the last SH-2s were retired by the Navy Reserve in 2001.

SPECIFICATION (SH-2F):

ACCOMMODATION:
Pilot, copilot, and sensor operator

DIMENSIONS:
LENGTH: 36 ft 7 in (11.15 m)
ROTOR DIAMETER: 44 ft 0 in (13.41 m)
HEIGHT: 15 ft 6 in (4.75 m)

WEIGHTS:
EMPTY: 8652 lb (3925 kg)
MAX T/O: 13,500 lb (6125 kg)

PERFORMANCE:
MAX SPEED: 153 mph (245 kmh)
RANGE: 410 miles (656 km)
POWERPLANT: two General Electric T58-GE-8FS
OUTPUT: 2700 shp (2013 kW)

FIRST FLIGHT DATE:
July 2, 1959 (YHU2K-1)

ARMAMENT:
7.62-mm machine gun on pintle mounting in each cabin doorway; two Mk 46/50 torpedoes on external stores pylons

FEATURES:
Rectractable wheeled undercarriage; podded engines; four-bladed main rotor; radome under nose

Kellett YG-1

two-seat, single-engined artillery-spotting Autogiro

Forerunner to the helicopter, the Kellett family of Autogiros could trace their lineage back to 1929 when brothers Rod and Wallace Kellett commenced experimentation with the K-1X. By 1933, the company had sold nearly 20 K-2/-3 winged Autogiros commercially. In 1934, the USAAC ordered two wingless Autogiros for evaluation in liaison and artillery spotting roles – a Kellett YG-1 and a Pitcairn YG-2. After delivery, the YG-2 crashed and an order for a further YG-1A ensued, the Kellett design being seen as more reliable. Field trials followed and by 1937, seven YG-1Bs were on order to meet the demands by the field artillery, coast artillery, cavalry and infantry boards. In 1938, the German Fieseler Storch demonstrated that a light airplane could match most of the performance advantages of the Autogiro, but with great improvements in useful load and maintenance issues. After testing, USAAC pilots reported that the YG-1B offered no great advantage over fixed-wing aircraft at the time, and several YG-1Bs were passed on to the US Border Patrol in Texas.

SPECIFICATION (YG-1B):

ACCOMMODATION:
Pilot and observer in tandem

DIMENSIONS:
LENGTH: 19 ft 4 in (5.89 m)
ROTOR DIAMETER: 40 ft 0 in (12.19 m)
HEIGHT: 10 ft 3 in (3.13 m)

WEIGHTS:
EMPTY: 1596 lb (724 kg)
MAX T/O: 2244 lb (1018 kg)

PERFORMANCE:
MAX SPEED: 120 mph (192 kmh)
RANGE: 200 miles (320)
POWERPLANT: Jacobs R-755-3
OUTPUT: 225 hp (167 kW)

FIRST FLIGHT DATE:
December 1935 (YG-1)

FEATURES:
Aircraft-style fuselage; fixed taildragger undercarriage; fully exposed radial engine; open cockpits

Piasecki HRP

ten-seat, single-engined utility/rescue helicopter

Frank N. Piasecki made a breakthrough with the development of the first successful tandem rotor helicopter, which overcame the center-of-gravity limitations then present in Sikorsky's single rotor helicopters and allowed for substantial increases in internal capacity and payload. The Navy contracted Piasecki on January 1, 1944 to build the XHRP-X as a prototype shore-based rescue platform for the Coast Guard. Dubbed the "Flying Banana" due to its shape, the metal-framed fabric-covered fuselage seated a crew of two and eight passengers, or six litter casualties or cargo. When operating in the rescue role, it could pick up eight rescuees at a radius of 300 miles. The prototype XHRP-1, as it was designated by the Navy, made its first flight in March 1945. From August 1947, the Navy took delivery of 20 HRP-1s, most of which served with the Marine Corps' HMX-1, pioneering air assault doctrine, though the Coast Guard and Navy also evaluated the type in the land-based air-sea rescue and ASW roles.

SPECIFICATION:

ACCOMMODATION:
Pilot, copilot, and eight passengers

DIMENSIONS:
LENGTH: 47 ft 2 in (14.38 m)
ROTOR DIAMETER: 41 ft 0 in (12.50 m)
HEIGHT: 12 ft 6 in (3.81 m)

WEIGHTS:
EMPTY: 5150 lb (2336 kg)
MAX T/O: 8000 lb (3629 kg)

PERFORMANCE:
MAX SPEED: 105 mph (170 kmh)
RANGE: 300 miles (482 km)
POWERPLANT: Pratt & Whitney Wasp R-1340-AN-1
OUTPUT: 600 hp (447 kW)

FIRST FLIGHT DATE:
March 7, 1945 (XHRP-X)

FEATURES:
Twin rotor configuration; distinctive "banana" shape fuselage; fixed tricycle under-carriage, with single wheel at front; enclosed engine in tail; twin tailfins

Piasecki HUP Retriever and H-25 Mule

seven-seat, twin-engined utility/rescue helicopter

Piasecki's response to a Navy requirement issued in 1945 for a helicopter designed for seaborne operations, the HUP was both compact enough to fit aboard a variety of ships, yet capable of performing vertical replenishment, casevac, rescue, and plane-guard duties. Following the success of its pioneering HRP tandem-rotor helicopter, Piasecki duly adopted such a layout for the HUP, which was placed into series production in 1948 following receipt of an order for 32 HUP-1 Retrievers. With space for five passengers or three stretchers, the HUP-1s made their fleet debut in early 1949. Continued development work by Piasecki resulted in the Sperry autopilot-equipped HUP-2, of which 165 were delivered (some of which were fitted with ASW equipment). Army interest in the helicopter saw the company produce the H-25A Mule, which had boosted flight controls and a strengthened cargo floor—70 were built in 1952-53, 50 of which went to the Navy as HUP-3s. Surviving HUP-2/3s were redesignated UH-25B/CS in 1962, though they were retired soon after.

SPECIFICATION (HUP-1):

ACCOMMODATION:
Pilot, copilot, and five passengers

DIMENSIONS:
LENGTH: 31 ft 10 in (9.70 m)
ROTOR DIAMETER: 35 ft 0 in (10.67 m)
HEIGHT: 13 ft 2 in (4.01 m)

WEIGHTS:
EMPTY: 3928 lb (1782 kg)
MAX T/O: 6100 lb (2767 kg)

PERFORMANCE:
MAX SPEED: 108 mph (174 kmh)
RANGE: 340 miles (547 km)
POWERPLANT: Continental R-975-34
OUTPUT: 525 hp (391 kW)

FIRST FLIGHT DATE:
March 12, 1948 (XHJP-1)

FEATURES:
Twin-rotor configuration; fixed undercarriage, with single wheel at rear; enclosed engine in tail

Piasecki (Vertol) H-21 Workhorse/Shawnee

22-seat, twin-engined transport/assault/rescue helicopter

In 1949, the Coast Guard received an order for five HRP-2s – a refined version of the Rescuer, but with a larger all-metal skin in place of the HRP-1's fabric. Unfortunately, the HRP-2 was grossly underpowered, but it became an important lesson for Piasecki, then working on a competition for an USAF arctic rescue and support helicopter. With a far more powerful engine, the resulting H-21 won out over Sikorsky's H-19 for the contract. The USAF aquired 18 YH-21s, 38 H-21A Workhorses and 163 H-21BS (with more powerful engine) and the Army followed with a large purchase of 334 H-21C Shawnees for its newly established transportation companies. The Air Force used a number of its H-21s in the utility role in Alaska, supporting various bases and radar sites being built in the area, while the Army sent 33 H-21Cs to South Vietnam as early as December 1961, making the Shawnee one of the first US military aircraft to arrive in-theater. They would see service transporting troops, supplies and wounded in South Vietnam until their replacement in 1963. 1969 marked their retirement from the Army.

SPECIFICATION (H-21C):

ACCOMMODATION:
Pilot, copilot, and 20 passengers

DIMENSIONS:
LENGTH: 52 ft 4 in (15.98 m)
ROTOR DIAMETER: 44 ft 6 in (13.56 m)
HEIGHT: 15 ft 1 in (4.60 m)

WEIGHTS:
EMPTY: 8700 lb (3946 kg)
MAX T/O: 13,500 lb (6124 kg)

PERFORMANCE:
MAX SPEED: 130 mph (209 kmh)
RANGE: 300 miles (482 km)
POWERPLANT: Wright Cyclone R-1820-103
OUTPUT: 1425 hp (1062 kW)

FIRST FLIGHT DATE:
April 11, 1952 (YH-21)

FEATURES:
Banana-shaped fuselage; twin-rotor configuration; fixed undercarriage, with single wheel at front; enclosed engine in tail; prominent twin tailfins

Sikorsky R-4/HNS

two-seat, single-engined light utility helicopter

The world's first operational helicopter, the R-4 evolved from Sikorsky's VS-300, which made its first tethered flight on September 14, 1939. In 1940, the USAAC had selected the Platt-LePage XR-1 as its first helicopter over a Sikorsky design. However, by 1941, the Air Corps was finding the XR-1 unsatisfactory and gave Sikorsky a "back-door" contract for an entirely new design, which was designated the XR-4. First flown on January 14, 1942, the prototype ushered in the age of the American military helicopter. Twenty-nine YR-4A/BS were ordered, and these soon proved the versatility of the helicopter by carrying out shipboard landings and rescues under combat conditions in Burma. A further 100 R-4BS were ordered for the USAAF, Great Britain and the Navy/Coast Guard, these being designated in the latter's service as HNS-1. Though ostensibly intended as trainers, the USAAF deployed approximately two-dozen of the underpowered R-4BS to the Pacific in the last year of the war as an expedient due to delays in follow-on models.

SPECIFICATION (R-4B):

ACCOMMODATION:
Pilot and passenger

DIMENSIONS:
LENGTH: 35 ft 5 in (10.80 m)
ROTOR DIAMETER: 38 ft 0 in (11.58 m)
HEIGHT: 12 ft 5 in (3.78 m)

WEIGHTS:
EMPTY: 2020 lb (916 kg)
MAX T/O: 2535 lb (1150 kg)

PERFORMANCE:
MAX SPEED: 75 mph (121 kmh)
RANGE: 130 miles (209 km)
POWERPLANT: Warner R-550-1
OUTPUT: 180 hp (134 kW)

FIRST FLIGHT DATE:
January 14, 1942 (XR-4)

FEATURES:
Fabric-covered, lattice-frame fuselage; fixed undercarriage, with single wheel at rear; heavily glazed cockpit

Sikorsky R/H-5 and HO3S

four-seat, single-engined light utility helicopter

Having proven the viability of the helicopter with the R-4, Sikorsky set out to develop a machine better suited to the requirements of the USAAF and Royal Navy. This was the vs-327, designated the R-5 by the USAAF. The prototype made its first flight on August 18, 1943, and the USAAF acquired 65 for evaluation and service use. Unlike the under-powered R-4, the more refined R-5 featured a more capable engine and larger rotor system, making it the first true American utility helicopter, though too late for wartime service. A number of R-5s were issued to the USAAF's Air Rescue Service. The USAAF quickly became dissatisfied with the tandem seat R-5A and shifted production to the 4-seat R-5D with a widened cabin. The H-5 served as the primary Air Rescue helicopter for the first year of the Korean War. A further 88 were procured by the Navy as HO3S-1s, several of which were the first helicopters into combat in Korea with the Marine's vmo-6. Others would serve with HU-1 aboard ship. Air Force H-5s would see extensive combat with the 3rd Air Rescue Squadron.

SPECIFICATION (R-5A):

ACCOMMODATION:
Pilot and observer in tandem

DIMENSIONS:
LENGTH: 41 ft 2 in (12.55 m)
ROTOR DIAMETER: 48 ft 0 in (14.63 m)
HEIGHT: 12 ft 11 in (3.69 m)

WEIGHTS:
EMPTY: 3770 lb (1710 kg)
MAX T/O: 5000 lb (2268 kg)

PERFORMANCE:
MAX SPEED: 90 mph (144 kmh)
RANGE: 300 miles (480 km)
POWERPLANT: Pratt & Whitney R-985-4B Wasp Junior
OUTPUT: 450 hp (336 kW)

FIRST FLIGHT DATE:
August 18, 1943 (XR-5)

FEATURES:
All-metal fuselage; fixed tricycle undercarriage; heavily glazed cockpit

Sikorsky R-6/HOS

two-seat, single-engined liaison helicopter

Sikorsky developed the R-6 at the same time as it was working on the more successful R-5, the former being little more than a refined R-4. Refinements included a vertically mounted engine, improved rotor and a lighter semi-monocoque fuselage. The R-6A's engine, which was designed for horizontal installation in airplanes, caused extensive maintenance and reliability issues because of its vertical installation. Nash-Kelvinator was contracted to build 900 R-6As (including 26 YR-6As) though only 219 were delivered due to end-of-war cancelations. The Navy, procuring largely for the Coast Guard, also committed to the helicopter, receiving three XR-6As (redesignated XHOS-1s). A further 36 HOS-1s were acquired, some of which were used postwar by the Navy's first rotary-winged unit, helicopter experimental squadron, VX-3. The R-6 could also be fitted with pontoons, and was employed on a variety of duties including air-sea rescue, casualty evacuation, and observation. Frequently beset by engine difficulties, the R-6 was soon replaced by the more reliable R-5.

SPECIFICATION:

ACCOMMODATION:
Pilot and passenger

DIMENSIONS:
LENGTH: 33 ft 11 in (10.34 m)
ROTOR DIAMETER: 38 ft 0 in (11.58 m)
HEIGHT: 10 ft 5 in (3.20 m)

WEIGHTS:
EMPTY: 2035 lb (923 kg)
MAX T/O: 2590 lb (1175 kg)

PERFORMANCE:
MAX SPEED: 96 mph (154 kmh)
RANGE: 116 miles (185 km)
POWERPLANT: Franklin 0-405-9
OUTPUT: 240 hp (179 kW)

FIRST FLIGHT DATE:
October 15, 1943

FEATURES:
Metal-skinned fuselage; fixed tricycle undercarriage, with single wheel at rear; heavily glazed cockpit

Sikorsky HO5S

four-seat, single-engined light utility helicopter

Derived from the Sikorsky's S-52, which was the first US helicopter to feature metal rotor blades and offset flapping hinges, the HO5S was procured by the Navy in order to replace the HO3S in service with the Marine Corps. The S-52 had been built as a two-seater, powered by a 178-hp Franklin engine, and following Navy interest in the helicopter, Sikorsky doubled its seating capacity and fitted a 245-hp Franklin O-245-1 engine instead. The S-52 prototype had initially flown in February 1947, and the four-seat variant was produced several years later. The first HO5S helicopters reached the Marine Corps in March 1952 and soon proved invaluable in the evacuation of wounded from the frontlines in Korea. The nose opened to allow stretchers to be loaded internally, thus preventing further injuries due to exposure. Though almost exclusively a Marine Corps aircraft, eight of the 79 HO5S-1S went on to the US Coast Guard as HO5S-1GS from September 1952. Finally, the USAF and Army evaluated the S-52 under the designation YH-18. The Marine Corps retired its surviving HO5SS in 1958.

SPECIFICATION:

ACCOMMODATION:
Pilot and three passengers

DIMENSIONS:
LENGTH: 27 ft 5 in (8.38 m)
ROTOR DIAMETER: 33 ft 0 in (10.05 m)
HEIGHT: 10 ft 4 in (3.16 m)

WEIGHTS:
EMPTY: 2000 lb (907 kg)
MAX T/O: 2770 lb (1256 kg)

PERFORMANCE:
MAX SPEED: 105 mph (168 kmh)
RANGE: 190 miles (304 km)
POWERPLANT: Franklin O-425-1
OUTPUT: 245 hp (182 kW)

FIRST FLIGHT DATE:
February 12, 1947 (S-52)

FEATURES:
All-metal pod- and boom-fuselage; fixed undercarriage; heavily glazed cockpit

Sikorsky HO4S/HRS/H-19 Chickasaw

12-seat, single-engined utility helicopter

Few designs advanced the cause of rotary-winged flight as much as Sikorsky's S-55. The S-55 had a novel engine arrangement that saw the helicopter's powerplant located in the nose, allowing the passenger cabin to coincide with its center-of-gravity. This configuration, combined with offset flapping hinges on the rotor and hydraulically-boosted controls allowed the single-rotor transport helicopter to become a reality. Sikorsky built the S-55 to meet Air Force requirements for an arctic rescue helicopter, but lost to the Piasecki H-21. However, the USAF recognized its potential for the Air Rescue service. By 1951, the first of 319 Air Force H-19A/BS were operating in Korea. The Marine Corps followed with 250 HRS-1/2/3S, some of which would implement the "vertical envelopment" concept of air mobility. The H-19/HRS would be the only transport helicopter to see combat in Korea. Sikorsky also constructed 89 HO4S-1/3 Navy and 30 HO4S-3G Coast Guard models. In 1952, the Army began acquiring 373 H-19C/D Chickasaws, some of which saw limited service in the Korean War.

SPECIFICATION (H-19B):

ACCOMMODATION:
Pilot, copilot, and ten passengers

DIMENSIONS:
LENGTH: 42 ft 3 in (12.88 m)
ROTOR DIAMETER: 53 ft 0 in (16.16 m)
HEIGHT: 13 ft 4 in (4.07 m)

WEIGHTS:
EMPTY: 5250 lb (2381 kg)
MAX T/O: 7900 lb (3583 kg)

PERFORMANCE:
MAX SPEED: 112 mph (180 kmh)
RANGE: 360 miles (578 km)
POWERPLANT: Wright R-1300-3 Cyclone
OUTPUT: 800 hp (596 kW)

FIRST FLIGHT DATE:
November 10, 1949 (YH-19A)

FEATURES:
Pod-and-boom fuselage, with ventral fairing joining pod with boom; fixed four-wheel undercarriage; engine in nose; raised cockpit above cabin

Sikorsky HR2S/H-37 Mojave

28-seat, twin-engined transportation helicopter

The first in a series of large Sikorsky transportation helicopters built for the Marine Corps, the HR2S was created following the issuing of a requirement for just such a machine in 1950. For more than a decade after its first flight, on December 18, 1953, the Mojave was the world's largest non-Soviet helicopter. Both the Army and Marine Corps wanted a rotary-winged aircraft that could carry up to 26 troops or soft-skinned vehicles and other military equipment. Although featuring a standard Sikorsky single-rotor layout, a helicopter of this size needed two engines. In order to keep the fuselage clear for cargo, the engines were located in nacelles on stub wings, into which the main legs of the landing gear retracted. Clamshell doors in the nose aided the straight-in loading of freight. Initially designated the HR2S-1 by the Marine Corps, the first of 55 production aircraft was delivered in July 1956. The Army also received 94 Mojaves up to 1960, which saw employment in Vietnam alongside their Marine counterparts. All were redesignated CH-37s in 1962.

SPECIFICATION:

ACCOMMODATION:
Pilot, copilot, and 26 passengers

DIMENSIONS:
LENGTH: 82 ft 10 in (25.25 m)
ROTOR DIAMETER: 72 ft 0 in (21.95 m)
HEIGHT: 22 ft 0 in (6.07 m)

WEIGHTS:
EMPTY: 20,831 lb (9449 kg)
MAX T/O: 31,000 lb (14,061 kg)

PERFORMANCE:
MAX SPEED: 121 mph (195 kmh)
RANGE: 335 miles (540 km)
POWERPLANT: two Pratt & Whitney R2800-PW-54s
OUTPUT: 3800 hp (2834 kW)

FIRST FLIGHT DATE:
December 18, 1953

FEATURES:
Twin engines, mounted in nacelles on stub wings; retractable undercarriage; clamshell doors in nose; fixed tailwheel

Sikorsky HSS-1 Seabat, HUS Seahorse, and H-34 Choctaw

18-seat, single-engined utility helicopter

The first effective helicopter ASW platform, the HSS-1 (redesignated H-34 in 1962) was created by Sikorsky in response to delays with the troubled HSL-1. The prototype XHSS-1 retained many of the features seen in the highly successful H-19, including the nose-mounted engine, but the fuselage design was completely new. The latter, combined with a new transmission system, bigger engine, and four-bladed main and tail rotors, gave the helicopter an impressive lift capability for its size. And being destined for Navy service at sea, the helicopter's main rotor blades could be folded aft and its entire rear fuselage and tail folded forward in an effort to ease shipboard storage.

Flown in prototype form on March 8, 1954, the HSS-1 had already been ordered into production "off the drawing board" by the Navy, which was feeling the pressure being exerted by an ever-growing Soviet submarine force. The first of 306 HSS-1 Seabats reached fleet units in August 1955, aircraft being operated in pairs as submarine hunter/killers—one helicopter would be equipped with dipping sonar to detect the submarine and the second machine would be equipped with torpedoes to attack it.

In October 1954 the Marine Corps also chose a derivative of the HSS-1 as its new troop-transportation helicopter, no fewer than 515 examples of the HUS-1 (christened the Seahorse) being delivered starting in February 1957. Seabats began to be replaced by the HSS-2 Sea King in 1961, and the surplus helicopters (redesignated UH-34s in 1962) were stripped of their ASW gear and turned into utility helicopters.

Like the Marine Corps, the Army also operated the helicopter in the assault-transportation role. Designated the H-34 Choctaw, the Army received its first examples just a month after the Seabat had entered service with the Navy. Several hundred H-34A/B/CS would eventually be acquired, though none saw combat. The Air Force Reserve also operated a small number of ex-Navy UH-34DS in the utility role in the 1960s.

SPECIFICATION (UH-34D):

ACCOMMODATION:
Pilot, copilot, and 16 passengers

DIMENSIONS:
LENGTH: 46 ft 9 in (14.25 m)
ROTOR DIAMETER: 56 ft 0 in (17.07 m)
HEIGHT: 15 ft 11 in (4.60 m)

WEIGHTS:
EMPTY: 7900 lb (3583 kg)
MAX T/O: 14,000 lb (6350 kg)

PERFORMANCE:
MAX SPEED: 123 mph (197 kmh)
RANGE: 247 miles (400 km)
POWERPLANT: Wright R-1820-84
OUTPUT: 1525 hp (1137 kW)

FIRST FLIGHT DATE:
March 8, 1954 (XHSS-1)

ARMAMENT:
Two homing torpedoes, bombs, or depth charges on fuselage pylons (HSS-1)

FEATURES:
Engine in nose; raised cockpit above cabin; four-bladed rotor; fixed undercarriage, with single wheel at rear; engine mounted in nose

Sikorsky HSS-2/H-3 Sea King

up to 19-seat, twin-engined ASW/utility/search-and-rescue helicopter

The Sea King was the end result of a Navy requirement for a single helicopter that could both hunt and kill enemy submarines following its experience with the Seabat in the ASW role. The new helicopter needed to be able to carry search equipment in the form of a dipping sonor and sonobuoys, 840 lb of ASW weaponry (torpedoes and depth bombs), and instrumentation to allow the crew to perform this vital mission 24 hours a day in any weather. In order to fit all this equipment in, Sikorsky designed a helicopter considerably larger than the HSS-1. Powered by two podded turboshaft engines above the cabin, which left the latter free for ASW gear, dunking sonar and radar, the helicopter also featured a watertight boat hull for amphibious operations.

Sikorsky had received a contract to develop the helicopter in 1957, and the YHSS-2 prototype made its first flight on March 11, 1959. Fleet deliveries began in September 1961, with aircraft being simultaneously issued to squadrons on both the Pacific and Atlantic coasts. Exactly 12 months later the unified triservice system of aircraft designation came into effect, and all HSS-2s became SH-3As. Sikorsky built a total of 245 A-models up to 1966, when the advent of more powerful engines saw the designation change to SH-3D—a further 73 were acquired through to 1970.

Sikorsky then commenced a rebuild programme that saw 105 SH-3A/DS upgraded to SH-3G standard, these machines featuring fuel-related improvements that had first been introduced with the 12 HH-3A built to perform the Navy's combat search-and-rescue mission in Vietnam. Other small-run production versions of the Sea King acquired by the Navy included nine SH-3AS converted into mine-sweeping RH-3AS and 19 VH-3A/DS produced for the Executive Flight Detachment (HMX-1) that serves key personnel in Washington, D.C. The Navy's final ASW variant was the SH-3H, 145 of which were created through the upgrading of existing airframes. Replaced as ASW helicopters in the early 1990s, surviving UH-3s conducted the utility mission with the Navy until retired in 2005.

SPECIFICATION (SH-3H):

ACCOMMODATION:
Pilot, copilot, and two sensor operators

DIMENSIONS:
LENGTH: 44 ft 7 in (13.59 m)
ROTOR DIAMETER: 62 ft 0 in (18.90 m)
HEIGHT: 16 ft 10 in (5.13 m)

WEIGHTS:
EMPTY: 13,465 lb (6108 kg)
MAX T/O: 18,897 lb (8572 kg)

PERFORMANCE:
MAX SPEED: 166 mph (266 kmh)
RANGE: 628 miles (1005 km)
POWERPLANT: two General Electric T58-GR-10S
OUTPUT: 3000 shp (2237 kW)

FIRST FLIGHT DATE:
March 11, 1959 (YHSS-2)

ARMAMENT:
Two homing torpedoes or depth charges on fuselage pylons up to weight of 840 lb (380 kg)

FEATURES:
Twin engines above cockpit; retractable main undercarriage, with single wheel at rear; boat-like hull; flotation gear in undercarriage sponsons

Sikorsky HH-52 Sea Guardian

up to 14-seat, single-engined search-and-rescue helicopter

In 1962 the US Coast Guard selected a version of the commercial Sikorsky S-62 to replace its small fleet of HH-34F search-and-rescue helicopters. The prototype S-62 had first flown on May 24, 1958, and it had the distinction of being the first amphibious helicopter produced by Sikorsky. Utilizing the dynamic components of the S-55 married to a single turbine of the type used on the HSS-2/SH-3, the S-62's unique features were its watertight fuselage and two outrigger floats, which housed retractable landing gear. On January 9, 1963 the US Coast Guard received the first of 99 S-62s, which were given the designation HH-52A and christened Sea Guardians. Thanks to its ability to land on water, along with its unique folding rescue platform and overhead winch, the HH-52A has the honor of having rescued more people at sea than any other helicopter in the world. Aside from being based at locations along the vast US seaboard, a number of HH-52As also flew from US Coast Guard cutters and ice breakers. Sea Guardians were replaced by HH-65A Dolphins in the 1980s.

SPECIFICATION:

ACCOMMODATION:
Pilot, copilot, and up to 12 passengers

DIMENSIONS:
LENGTH: 44 ft 7 in (13.62 m)
ROTOR DIAMETER: 53 ft 0 in (18.44 m)
HEIGHT: 16 ft 0 in (4.88 m)

WEIGHTS:
EMPTY: 5083 lb (2305 kg)
MAX T/O: 8100 lb (3674 kg)

PERFORMANCE:
MAX SPEED: 109 mph (174 kmh)
RANGE: 474 miles (758 km)
POWERPLANT: General Electric T58-GE-8B
OUTPUT: 1250 shp (932 kW)

FIRST FLIGHT DATE:
May 24, 1958 (S-62)

FEATURES:
Single engine above cockpit; fixed undercarriage, with single wheel at rear; boatlike hull; flotation gear in undercarriage sponsons

Sikorsky CH-54 Tarhe

five-seat, twin-engined heavy crane helicopter

Built specifically as a crane helicopter, the CH-54 Tarhe had its fuselage replaced by a slim beam, which was left as unobstructed as possible so as to allow bulky loads to be slung centrally from it. The helicopter was operated by a three-person crew, one of whom faced aft at all times watching the load and manipulating the hooks and winches. Sikorsky built six YCH-54A preproduction helicopters in 1962-63, five of which were issued to the Army for evaluation. An order for 54 A-models was soon received, and the first of these entered service in 1964. A further 37 CH-54Bs were subsequently delivered, these featuring uprated engines and twin-wheel landing gear. A series of purpose-built Universal Military Pods were also acquired, these being configured either for the carriage of 46 troops or 24 stretchers. Others were kitted out as mobile command posts or surgical hospitals. The Tarhe saw considerable use in Vietnam, lifting M114 howitzers, armored vehicles, bulldozers, troops, and 380 damaged aircraft. The helicopter was retired from Army National Guard service in the early 1990s.

SPECIFICATION:

ACCOMMODATION:
Pilot, copilot, loadmaster, and jump seats for two loader/technicians

DIMENSIONS:
LENGTH: 70 ft 3 in (21.41 m)
ROTOR DIAMETER: 72 ft 0 in (21.95 m)
HEIGHT: 25 ft 5 in (7.75 m)

WEIGHTS:
EMPTY: 19,234 lb (8724 kg)
MAX T/O: 42,000 lb (19,050 kg)

PERFORMANCE:
MAX SPEED: 126 mph (203 kmh)
RANGE: 230 miles (370 km)
POWERPLANT: two Pratt & Whitney T73-1s
OUTPUT: 9000 shp (6711 kW)

FIRST FLIGHT DATE:
May 9, 1962

FEATURES:
Cockpit pod and beam-type fuselage; twin (exposed) engines above cockpit; fixed under-carriage, with single wheel at front; starboard stabilizer on top of tail unit

Sikorsky H-53 Sea Stallion/Super Jolly

58-seat, twin-engined medium/heavylift and search-and-rescue helicopter

The H-53 was developed by Sikorsky in response to a 1960 requirement issued by the Marine Corps for a replacement for its CH-37 Mojave. Using the CH-54 as a basis, the company combined the Tarhe's proven dynamic systems with an all-new watertight fuselage that featured a rear-loading freight ramp. Capable of carrying (underslung) a 1½-ton truck and trailer, 105-mm howitzer, Hawk missile system, or 38 troops, the first of two prototypes flew on October 14, 1964—it was the world's largest helicopter at the time. Production deliveries of the CH-53A Sea Stallion commenced in mid-1966, and the Marine Corps deployed its first examples to Vietnam 12 months later.

Following the production of 130 A-models, Sikorsky switched to the construction of the more powerful CH-53D, which could carry 55 troops. This version also had main and tail rotors that folded automatically for stowage aboard aircraft carriers. A further 174 CH-53Ds were delivered to the Marine Corps between March 1969 and January 1972. The USAF was also an early recipient of the H-53, procuring eight HH-53B Super Jollies to fulfill its requirement for a new combat aircrew rescue aircraft in 1967. These machines were equipped with 1200 lb of armor plating, three 7.62-mm miniguns, a retractable flight-refueling probe, external fuel tanks, bigger engines, and ejection seats for the pilots. The helicopters were rushed to Vietnam in September 1967. A further 44 improved HH-53Cs followed beginning in August 1968, and the USAF also purchased 30 CH-53Ds as standard utility helicopters without the specialized rescue equipment.

In 1975 eight HH-53s were upgraded to HH-53H Pave Low standard through the fitment of night vision avionics and terrain-following radar. Used by Special Operations Forces, these machines were redesignated MH-53Hs in 1979, and a further 31 HH-53B/CS were modified into MH-53J/M Pave Lows to perform this mission in 1987-90. The Navy was also a specialist H-53 operator for a number of years, acquiring 30 RH-53DS in 1973-74 for mine countermeasures. These machines were passed on to the Marine Corps as standard utility helicopters in the mid-1980s.

SPECIFICATION (CH-53D):

ACCOMMODATION:
Pilot, copilot, aircrewman, and 55 passengers

DIMENSIONS:
LENGTH: 67 ft 2 in (20.47 m)
ROTOR DIAMETER: 72 ft 3 in (22.02 m)
HEIGHT: 24 ft 11 in (7.34 m)

WEIGHTS:
EMPTY: 23,485 lb (10,653 kg)
MAX T/O: 42,000 lb (19,050 kg)

PERFORMANCE:
MAX SPEED: 196 mph (315 kmh)
RANGE: 1026 miles (1641 km)
POWERPLANT: two General Electric T64-GE-413s
OUTPUT: 7850 shp (5860 kW)

FIRST FLIGHT DATE:
October 14, 1964 (YCH-53A)

ARMAMENT:
Single 12.7-mm machine gun and 7.62-mm minigun on pintle mounts on fuselage ramp or in doorways

FEATURES:
Long cabin with tail ramp; twin podded engines on upper fuselage sides; retractable undercarriage; starboard stabilizer on top of tail unit; center fuselage sponsons

Sikorsky H-3 Jolly Green Giant

up to 28-seat, twin-engined utility/search-and-rescue helicopter

The Air Force first showed an interest in the H-3 Sea King in April 1962, when it borrowed three HSS-2s to fly resupply missions to its radar outposts in the Atlantic. Impressed with the basic design, it contracted Sikorsky to modify the airframe by building a loading ramp into a reconfigured rear fuselage. The resulting CH-3C won the competition for the Air Force's long-range rotary-wing support system in July 1963. Seventy-five CH-3Cs were acquired, followed by 45 re-engined CH-3Es in 1966—41 CH-3Cs were also upgraded to this specification. A similar version, designated the HH-3E, was bought for the USAF's Aerospace and Recovery Service, eight being acquired new and 50 CH-3Es being modified to this standard through the fitment of armor protection, self-sealing tanks, an in-flight refueling probe, defensive armament, and external tanks. Christened Jolly Green Giants, these helicopters saw action in Vietnam. Also serving with the ANG, the last HH-3Es were retired in 1992. Finally, the US Coast Guard operated 40 HH-3Fs (installed with radar) until 1995.

SPECIFICATION (HH-3F):

ACCOMMODATION:
Pilot, copilot, aircrewman, and up to 25 passengers

DIMENSIONS:
LENGTH: 57 ft 3 in (17.45 m)
ROTOR DIAMETER: 62 ft 0 in (18.90 m)
HEIGHT: 18 ft 1 in (5.51 m)

WEIGHTS:
EMPTY: 12,423 lb (5635 kg)
MAX T/O: 22,050 lb (10,002 kg)

PERFORMANCE:
MAX SPEED: 164 mph (262 kmh)
RANGE: 480 miles (768 km)
POWERPLANT: two General Electric T58-GE-5s
OUTPUT: 3000 shp (2237 kW)

FIRST FLIGHT DATE:
June 17, 1963 (CH-3C)

ARMAMENT:
Pintle-mounted Browning 0.50-in machine guns firing through windows (HH-3E)

FEATURES:
Twin engines above cockpit; rear fuselage sponsons for retractable undercarriage; boat-like hull; rear-loading ramp

Sikorsky H-53E Super Stallion/Sea Dragon

58-seat, three-engined heavylift and mine countermeasures helicopter

The largest helicopter operated by the US military, the H-53E was developed by Sikorsky to meet a Navy and Marine Corps requirement for a heavy-duty multipurpose machine with greater capability than the CH-53D. The prototype YCH-53E featured a lengthened fuselage, a third engine, new seven-bladed main rotor, and uprated avionics. Christened the Super Stallion, production examples of the CH-53E began reaching the Marine Corps in June 1981, and 175 were eventually built through to the end of the 1990s. A small number of these were supplied to the Navy for use as utility helicopters in support of the fleet. The Navy also acquired a more specialized airborne mine countermeasures variant to replace its RH-53Ds. Featuring enlarged sponsons for the carriage of extra fuel, as well as specialized anti-mine gear, the first of 32 MH-53E Sea Dragons entered service in April 1987. Like the Marine Corps' CH-53Es, these machines saw action in Operations Desert Storm and Iraqi Freedom. The Sea Dragons are often stripped out and used as utility helicopters.

SPECIFICATION (CH-53E):

ACCOMMODATION:
Pilot, copilot, aircrewman, and 55 passengers

DIMENSIONS:
LENGTH: 73 ft 4 in (22.35 m)
ROTOR DIAMETER: 79 ft 0 in (24.07 m)
HEIGHT: 29 ft 5 in (8.99 m)

WEIGHTS:
EMPTY: 33,228 lb (15,072 kg)
MAX T/O: 69,750 lb (31,639 kg)

PERFORMANCE:
MAX SPEED: 196 mph (315 kmh)
RANGE: 1290 miles (2064 km)
POWERPLANT: three General Electric T64-GE-416s
OUTPUT: 13,140 shp (9798 kW)

FIRST FLIGHT DATE:
March 1, 1974

ARMAMENT:
Browning 0.50-in machine guns on pintle mounts on fuselage ramp or in doorways

FEATURES:
Long cabin with tail ramp; twin podded engines on upper fuselage sides; retractable undercarriage; starboard stabilizer on top of tail unit; center fuselage sponsons

Sikorksy UH-60 Black Hawk, HH/MH-60 Pave Hawk, and MH-60S Knighthawk

up to 17-seat, twin-engined utility and battlefield helicopter

Developed by Sikorsky as a replacement for the Army's UH-1H Iroquois, the YUH-60A duly beat the Boeing Vertol YUH-61A in a flyoff as part of the 1972 Utility Tactical Transportation Aircraft System competition. First flown on October 17, 1974, production UH-60AS attained frontline status with Army units in 1979. Featuring twin General Electric T700 turboshaft engines, which give the helicopter excellent performance in most conditions, the Black Hawk is designed to carry an 11-man infantry squad in a crash-survivable environment. Almost 1000 A-models were built up until production switched to the improved UH-60L in 1989. A number of specialist variants were constructed during the helicopter's first decade in service, including EH-60A Quick Fix command and control aircraft and the MH-60K/L for Special Operations employment. An MH-60L modification, the Direct Action Penetrator (DAP), serves as an armed escort for special operations missions with 7.62 mm minigun, 30 mm chain gun and unguided rocket pod combinations.

The USAF also bought 100+ MH/HH-60G Pave Hawks to perform the combat rescue and Special Operations missions, these machines being equipped with improved avionics (including radar), refueling probes, extra armament, and hardpoints for external fuel tank carriage. The Army's UH-60s first saw combat in Grenada in 1983, and then experienced considerably more action in Operation Desert Storm in 1991, where the USAF's MH-60s also earned their battle spurs. The UH-60L featured more powerful engines that allowed the helicopter to operate at higher gross weights. This version also introduced the Hover Infrared Suppression System into frontline service. The UH-60A/L is the Army's primary rotary-winged transportation platform, being used by general support, assault, command, and medical battalions assigned to division, corps, and theater aviation brigades. Among the newest versions to enter Army service is the UH-60Q dedicated ambulance variant, which is being delivered to medical companies.

The Army is hoping to reconfigure up to 357 UH-60AS as UH-60QS. EH-60AS are also being rebuilt as EH-60LS, this variant boasting improved avionics and sensors. In 2001 the Army was given permission to procure the follow-on UH-60M version of the Black Hawk, this model featuring many improvements including upgrades to the airframe and a digital cockpit. The Army intends to rebuild all 900+ of its UH-60AS as M-models, as well as procuring 1200+ new machines starting in 2007 onward. In 2002, the Navy began replacing its UH-46 fleet support helicopters with the MH-60S Knighthawk—a navalised UH-60L— featuring the dynamic components of the SH-60 with folding tail and blades.

SPECIFICATION (UH-60L):

ACCOMMODATION:
Pilot, copilot, crew chief, and up to 14 passengers

DIMENSIONS:
LENGTH: 50 ft 1 in (15.26 m)
ROTOR DIAMETER: 53 ft 8 in (16.36 m)
HEIGHT: 12 ft 4 in (3.76 m)

WEIGHTS:
EMPTY: 11,500 lb (5216 kg)
MAX T/O: 17,000 lb (7711 kg)

PERFORMANCE:
MAX SPEED: 185 mph (296 kmh)
RANGE: 1152 miles (1843 km)
POWERPLANT: two General Electric T700-GE-701CS
OUTPUT: 3880 shp (2894 kW)

FIRST FLIGHT DATE:
October 17, 1974 (YUH-60A)

ARMAMENT:
Two pintle-mounted 7.62-mm miniguns in doorways

FEATURES:
Side-by-side cockpit; wheeled undercarriage, with single tailwheel; enclosed twin engines; four-bladed rotor; full tailplane at base of fin

Sikorksy SH/HH-60 and MH-60R Seahawk and HH-60J Jayhawk

up to 17-seat, twin-engined ASW, utility, and search-and-rescue helicopter

Using its UH-60 as a base, Sikorsky developed the SH-60B to meet the Navy's Light Airborne Multipurpose System (LAMPS) Mk III program requirement for an ASW/utility helicopter. Featuring navalized T700 engines, a repositioned tailwheel, and specialized ASW avionics and weaponry, the Seahawk reached fleet units in 1983. Two years later, the SH-60F variant was chosen by the Navy as its next "CV-Helo" to perform the inner-zone ASW mission for carrier air wings. The F-model was fitted with a dipping sonar and additional weapons stations. The Navy bought 81 SH-60FS (as well as 260 B-models), and these entered service in June 1989. Just two months later the first of 45 HH-60HS was also delivered, these machines being designed for combat search and rescue. The MH-60R, first flown in 2001, will replace the SH-60B/F and features significantly improved avionics and detection gear, along with a Hellfire missile capability. Finally, the US Coast Guard has flown 42 HH-60J Jayhawks in the medium-range recovery mission since 1991.

SPECIFICATION (SH-60B):

ACCOMMODATION:
Pilot, airborne tactical officer, and sensor operator

DIMENSIONS:
LENGTH: 52 ft 1 in (15.87 m)
ROTOR DIAMETER: 53 ft 8 in (16.36 m)
HEIGHT: 12 ft 6 in (3.79 m)

WEIGHTS:
EMPTY: 13,648 lb (6190 kg)
MAX T/O: 21,884 lb (9925 kg)

PERFORMANCE:
MAX SPEED: 146 mph (233 kmh)
RANGE: 170 miles (272 km)
POWERPLANT: two General Electric T700-GE-401S
OUTPUT: 3800 shp (2830 kW)

FIRST FLIGHT DATE:
December 12, 1979

ARMAMENT:
Pintle-mounted 7.62-mm minigun or Browning 0.50-in machine gun in doorway; Mk 46/50 torpedoes or AGM-114 Hellfire/AGM-119 Penguin missiles on stub pylons

FEATURES:
Side-by-side cockpit; wheeled undercarriage, with single tailwheel mounted below mid-fuselage; enclosed twin engines

Photo Credits

Photo Credits

Mark Avino, National Air and Space Museum, Smithsonian Institution
331

Ted Carlson   428

Ross Chapple, National Air and Space Museum, Smithsonian Institution
135

Courtesy of F-35 Joint Strike Fighter Program
334

Doug Glover   357

Via Tony Holmes   40, 41, 154, 173, 235, 239, 241, 244, 247, 248, 250, 252,
54, 261, 288, 289, 302, 303, 305, 307, 308, 322, 324, 326,
328, 330, 333, 336, 345, 352, 354, 355, 356, 358, 360, 375,
377, 380, 381, 382, 385, 388, 390, 391, 397, 400, 401,
402, 403, 404, 405, 406, 407, 408, 415, 416, 417, 419,
420, 422, 424, 427, 444, 445, 448, 449, 451, 452, 453

Jamie Hunter   349

via Philip Jarrett   20, 29, 33, 34, 35, 36, 37, 38, 39, 44, 45, 48, 50, 57, 59,
60, 62, 64, 68, 71, 73, 75, 76(x 2), 81, 84, 90, 92 (x 2),
101, 103, 105, 106, 109, 112, 115, 117, 123, 130, 134,
137, 138, 152, 155, 156, 161, 162, 163, 164, 165, 166,
169, 171, 172, 176, 181, 182, 184, 186, 191, 192, 196, 198,
200, 201, 202, 204, 205, 210, 212, 214, 216, 220, 222,
224, 225, 228, 231, 232, 242, 243, 245, 246, 249, 255, 257,
258, 259, 260, 262, 263, 264, 265, 266, 267, 268, 269,
270, 271, 274, 275, 276, 278, 280, 283, 284, 286, 287, 296,
301, 304, 306, 309, 312, 315, 317, 323, 325, 328, 329, 340,
341, 347, 351, 359, 362, 365, 366, 369, 372, 374, 376, 378,
386, 387, 389, 392, 393, 395, 410, 411, 413, 414, 423, 425,
426, 429, 431, 433, 435, 436, 437, 441, 443, 446, 447, 454

LightSpeed Media, LLC, copyright Smithsonian Institution, National Air and
Space Museum   124